Cambridge Studies in Oral and Literate Culture   14

MEDIEVAL POPULAR CULTURE

Cambridge Studies in Oral and Literate Culture

Edited by PETER BURKE and RUTH FINNEGAN

This series is designed to address the question of the significance of literacy in human societies: it will assess its importance for political, economic, social and cultural development, and examine how what we take to be the common functions of writing are carried out in oral cultures.

The series will be interdisciplinary, but with particular emphasis on social anthropology and social history, and will encourage cross-fertilisation between these disciplines: it will also be of interest to readers in allied fields, such as sociology, folklore and literature. Although it will include some monographs, the focus of the series will be on theoretical and comparative aspects rather than detailed description, and the books will be presented in a form accessible to non-specialist readers interested in the general subject of literacy and orality.

Books in the series

This book is published as part of the joint publishing agreement established in 1977 between the Fondation de la Maison des Sciences de l'Homme and the Press Syndicate of the University of Cambridge. Titles published under this arrangement may appear in any European language, or, in the case of volumes of collected essays, in several languages.

New books will appear either as individual titles or in one of the series which the Maison des Sciences de l'Homme and the Cambridge University Press have jointly agreed to publish. All books published jointly by the Maison des Sciences de l'Homme and the Cambridge University Press will be distributed by the Press throughout the world.

Cet ouvrage est publié dans le cadre de l'accord de co-édition passé en 1977 entre la Fondation de la Maison des Sciences de l'Homme et le Press Syndicate of the University of Cambridge. Toutes les langues européennes sont admises pour les titres couverts par cet accord, et les ouvrages collectifs peuvent paraître en plusieurs langues.

Les ouvrages paraissent soit isolément, soit dans l'une des séries que la Maison des Sciences de l'Homme et Cambridge University Press ont convenu de publier ensemble. La distribution dans le monde entier des titres ainsi publiés conjointement par les deux établissements est assurée par Cambridge University Press.

MEDIEVAL POPULAR CULTURE: PROBLEMS OF BELIEF AND PERCEPTION

ARON GUREVICH

translated by
JÁNOS M. BAK AND PAUL A. HOLLINGSWORTH

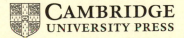 CAMBRIDGE
UNIVERSITY PRESS

EDITIONS DE LA MAISON DES SCIENCES DE L'HOMME

Published by the Press Syndicate of the University of Cambridge
The Pitt Building, Trumpington Street, Cambridge CB2 1RP
40 West 20th Street, New York, NY 10011–4211, USA
10 Stamford Road, Oakleigh, Victoria 3166, Australia
and Editions de la Maison des Sciences de l'Homme
54 Boulevard Raspail, 75270 Paris Cedex 06

First published 1988
Reprinted 1988, 1990
First paperback edition 1990
Reprinted 1992

Printed in Great Britain at the University Press, Cambridge

British Library Cataloguing in Publication Data

Gurevich, A. Aĩ
Medieval popular culture: problems of belief and perception.—
(Cambridge studies in oral and literate culture; 14). 1. Civilization,
Medieval
I. Title II. Problemi Srednevekovoy narodnoy Kulturi. *English*
940.1   CB351

Library of Congress Cataloguing in Publication Data

Gurevich, Aron Aĩkovlevich.
Medieval popular culture.
(Cambridge studies in oral and literate culture; 14) Translation of:
Problemy srednevekovoĭ narodnoĭ
kultury.
Bibliography
Includes index.
1. Civilization, Medieval. 2. Europe–Popular
culture. I. Title. II. Series. CB353.G8713 1987   940.1   87-9318

ISBN 0 521 30369 9 hardback
ISBN 0 521 38658 6 paperback
ISBN 2 7351 0206 8 hardback (France only)
ISBN 2 7351 0346 3 paperback (France only)

CONTENTS

The translation of the Foreword and Chapter 1 was prepared with the cooperation of Jack McIntosh.

EDITORIAL PREFACE

Now in his early sixties, Aron Iakovlevich Gurevich, Professor at the Institute of General History, Academy of Sciences, Moscow, is one of the most gifted historians at work in the U.S.S.R. and one of the most original medievalists anywhere in the world. He began by studying the peasantry of Anglo-Saxon England and medieval Scandinavia (more especially Norway). One of the topics which particularly interested him was the world-view of this culture, especially its conception of space and time. Another was the importance of gift exchange, the rituals accompanying the gift, the setting (usually a feast), the kinds of object bestowed (swords, rings, etc.), the obligation to reciprocate, and so on.[1]

With interests like these he could already have been described in the 1960s as a historical anthropologist, and he did indeed draw inspiration from anthropology, most obviously from the economic anthropology of Bronislaw Malinowski and Marcel Mauss, who had begun his famous essay on the gift with a quotation from a medieval Scandinavian poem, the *Edda*.[2] Gurevich might also have been described as a historian of mentalities, in the manner of French medievalists such as Marc Bloch, Jacques Le Goff (who had published an article on 'Church Time and Merchants' Time'), and Georges Duby (who was turning his attention to the functions of gift exchange in the medieval economy).[3] However, his view of France and its place in medieval Europe is rather different from theirs, as became apparent in a book he published in 1970 on the problem of the genesis of the feudal system, in which he worked from Scandinavia outwards to discuss concepts of property and the individual person in the whole of Western Europe.[4] Two years later he published a still more ambitious study of the basic categories of medieval culture.

Categories of Medieval Culture is divided into three parts. The third chapter carries on from his previous book and discusses conceptions of property, pointing out, for example, how anachronistic it is to project the modern idea of 'economic man' on to the early Middle Ages, when gold and silver had a sacred or magical rather than an economic value. The first part, on conceptions of space and time, is a development and a generalization from his earlier work on the medieval Scandinavian world-view and emphasizes the lack of abstractions in medieval thought, the concreteness of its categories. The central section is mainly concerned with the equally central idea of law, before and after the spread of

vii

Christianity, and with the links between the conception of law and the conception of the individual.[5] What the author has done, in sum, is to present what might be called a 'model' (in the sense of a deliberately simplified picture), of medieval culture, pointing out connections between different parts and emphasizing the extent to which it formed a system.

By now something of Gurevich's originality and his strategy should be apparent. Historians of medieval culture in general and of feudalism in particular have often taken France as the paradigm and discussed other regions in terms of divergence from this pattern. Gurevich has entered the Middle Ages by the back door and this has led him to notice and to stress features of the culture which other scholars have tended to neglect. Another advantage of starting with Scandinavia is that it was on the periphery of the Christian world, into which it was incorporated late. In Iceland, for example, Christianity was officially accepted only in A.D. 1000. The sources for the reconstruction of the pagan world-view are therefore particularly rich in this region.

Historical studies of world-views are nothing new; what makes Gurevich's approach particularly interesting – and close to anthropology – is his use of some of the concepts of the semioticians. He looks at medieval culture as a system of signs. His early work on gift exchange referred to Lévi-Strauss, but his main inspiration has been from the so-called 'Tartu school' in the Soviet Union – notably from Jurij Lotman, who has made important contributions to the cultural history of medieval Russia, together with Boris Uspenskij and Dmitri Likhachëv. In the work of all these scholars, Gurevich included, it is not difficult to detect the inspiration of the brilliant and many-sided Mikhail Bakhtin (1895-1975), who was a literary critic, a philosopher and a cultural historian rolled into one, concerned himself with the changing forms of laughter, language and popular culture, and moved with ease from the poetics of Dostoevsky to the world of Rabelais or Dante.[6] The sources with which Gurevich has worked most closely have been literary texts, from the Icelandic sagas to Dante's *Divine Comedy*. Not the least of his assets has been his awareness of literary forms and genres, an awareness relatively uncommon among historians of law, property and economic behaviour.

There are two obvious criticisms to make of *Categories of Medieval Culture*. Although it was central to the medieval world-view, religion is virtually absent from the book, despite the author's passing reference to theology as the 'universal semiotic system' of the period. In the second place, the stress on 'system' made it difficult for the author to say much in this book about either cultural variation (regional variation, for example) or cultural conflict – the tension between official and unofficial beliefs, Christianity and paganism, learned culture and popular culture.

His new book, published in Russian in 1981, reads like an answer to these criticisms. Since 1972 Gurevich has been working on medieval visions of the Other World, as a series of articles attests.[7] Drawing on these and other sources, he has brought religion to the centre of the stage. The book is essentially concerned with the relationship between clerical and popular religion. Although Gurevich continues to emphasize what he calls the 'relative homogeneity' of the medieval world-view, his new book is organized around the problem of the relationship between learned culture and popular culture in the Middle Ages. Its six chapters deal with different literary genres – sermons, penitentials, visions, lives of the saints, and so on; Gurevich continues to stress the close links between content and literary form. However, all the chapters grapple with the problem of discovering the attitudes of the lay majority in a period when the sources were produced by a clerical élite, and of excavating oral culture, vernacular culture, from literary texts in Latin. Not that the author believes that popular attitudes can be found in any 'pure' state; the stress on the interaction and interpenetration of the two cultures is one of his central themes and marks him off from some of the predecessors he most admires, from Bakhtin to Le Goff.

One of the most striking examples of Gurvevich's method and conclusions is his interpretation (below, ch. 4), of the Latin, clerical version of the vision of Thurkill, a thirteenth-century Essex peasant. Thurkill's attitudes are drawn out of this composite text by a process of close reading – or reading between the lines – with special reference (as so often in Gurevich's work) to the expression of perceptions of space and time. From texts like these he concludes, unlike Jacques Le Goff in his recent book, that the scholastic theologians 'did not invent purgatory'. What they did was to impose their own 'conceptual structure' on popular ideas, such as Thurkill's, which were already in existence.[8] More generally, clerical culture did not so much replace as restructure popular culture, just as the transition from paganism to Christianity involved a reorganization of existing beliefs rather than a clean sweep. 'Parish Christianity' was in this sense a kind of syncretism.

Gurevich has much in common with the leading French historians of *mentalités*, but he maintains his independence. He criticizes French colleagues such as Duby and Le Goff for their unfamiliarity with Soviet semiotics, their overemphasis on empiricism and their neglect of what he calls the 'really long-term' factors in cultural history, thinking here not of Braudel but of Bakhtin.[9] On the other hand, he is not afraid to fault Bakhtin (as below, ch. 6) for treating the official culture of the Middle Ages as completely serious, or even gloomy, and for failing to see how gravity and levity interacted with each other, how they were combined or synthesized.

Aron Gurevich's books have been translated into a number of

languages, including French, German, Italian, Norwegian, Swedish, Czech, Polish and Hungarian. A translated text is a new text, and a book which is republished in another culture is not the same book. What the importance of Gurevich's work may be for Russian readers is hard for an Englishman to see or say. Its significance is unlikely to be quite the same in Scandinavia, France and the English-speaking world, particularly among professional medievalists, who may be irritated or puzzled by the author's failure to cite some recent studies, inaccessible to him, or think obvious a few of the conclusions he stresses most. On the other hand, *Problems* has compensating merits. Like some other works in the Russian tradition (Karsavin, Bakhtin, Lotman), it stands out for its sense of system and its author's ability to see medieval culture as a whole.[10]

PETER BURKE

ABBREVIATIONS

CCSL	Corpus Christianorum, Series Latina, Turnholt, 1965–
Dial.	Grégoire le Grand, *Dialogues*, ed. A. de Vogue, Sources chrétiennes 251, 260, 265 (Paris, 1978–80)
DM	*Caesarii Heisterbacensis monachi Dialogus miraculorum*, ed. Josef Stange, 2 vols (Cologne–Bonn, 1851). (English translation: *Caesarius of Heisterbach: The Dialogue of Miracles*, trans. H. von E. Scott and C. C. Swinton Bland, with an introd. by G. G. Coulton (New York, 1929))
E	Yves Lefèvre, *L'Elucidarium et les lucidaires*, Bibliothèque des écoles françaises d'Athènes et Rome, 180 (Paris, 1954)
HE	*Historia ecclesiastica gentis Anglorum: Bede's Ecclesiastical History of the English People*, ed. B. Colgrave and R. A. B. Mynors (Oxford, 1969)
Hist. Fr.	*Gregorii episcopi Turonensis Historiarum libri decem*, ed. Bruno Krusch and Rudolph Buchner, 2 vols. Ausgewählte Quellen zur deutschen Geschichte des Mittelalters. Freiherr vom Stein–Gedächtnisausgabe 3, 1–2 (Darmstadt, 1970–2). English translation: *The History of the Franks by Gregory of Tours*, trans. O. M. Dalton, vol. II (Oxford, 1927)
MGH	Monumenta Germaniae Historica (Hanover, etc., 1823–)
Conc.	Legum sectio II: Concilia
Const.	Legum sectio III: Constitutiones
Epp. Kar.	Epistolae Karolini aevi
Epp. sel.	Epistolae selectae
Ldl	Libelli de lite
LL	Leges
Poet. lat.	Poetae latinae
SS	Scriptores
SS rer. Mer.	Scriptores rerum Merowingicarum
SS rer. Germ.	Scriptores rerum Germanicarum in usum scholarum separatim editi

xi

PL   Patrologiae latinae cursus completus, Series Latina ed.
                      J. -P. Migne, (Paris, 1841–64)
Schmitz   Herm. Jos. Schmitz, *Die Bussbücher und Bussdisziplin
                      der Kirche. Nach handschriftlichen Quellen dargestellt*,
                      2 vols. (Mainz 1882; repr. Graz, 1958). (Partial English
                      translation: *Medieval Handbooks of Penance. A trans-
                      lation of the principal 'libri poenitentiales' and selections
                      from related documents*, trans. John T. McNeill and
                      Helena M. Gamer (New York 1938; repr. 1965)
Scott–Bland   *see above* under DM (English translation)
Wasserschleben   F. W. H. Wasserschleben, *Die Bussordnungen der
                      abendländischen Kirche* (Halle, 1851; repr. Graz, 1958).
                      (Partial English translation as above, McNeill 1938)

FOREWORD

Problems of Medieval Popular Culture is a continuation of my earlier work *Categories of Medieval Culture* (Moscow: Iskusstvo, 1972, 2nd edn 1984); English translation by G. L. Campbell (London: Routledge, 1984). The present monograph is likewise devoted to analysing the culture of the Middle Ages and the conceptions of medieval man about the world and himself. However, it is not merely a continuation of the previous study, but develops the inquiry along somewhat different lines. In *Categories* I attempted to reconstruct the cognitive frame of the medieval *Weltanschauung* and grouped the material around a few basic elements: time and space, law, work, property and wealth. These, along with some others, had defined the historically determined outline of medieval human personality. In analysing these elements, I examined them separately from the general fabric of medieval culture. Once this had been done, it seemed useful to take a second look at the medieval vision of the world, this time, however, not in separate categories, but in the complex unity of its various aspects. In other words, I now wish to move from the 'anatomy' of culture to its 'physiology'. For this project it was necessary to shift the level of abstraction, to select a new set of sources and to adopt new modes of analysis. Whereas in *Categories* evidence for each of the elements was taken from heterogeneous sources, it is now more appropriate to examine definite genres which are relatively homogeneous. We shall study writings belonging to a distinct layer of medieval culture, drawing conclusions from the content and form of the texts as well as from their socio-cultural function. Deeper penetration into the fabric of the sources will have to be paid for by narrowing the scope of the material studied.

In my previous book I was guided by the assumption that the notion 'medieval man' is a valid abstraction for scholarly inquiry. While this may suffice for a certain level of abstraction, this time I should like to differentiate between the culture of the élite and that of illiterate commoners. The sources on which the present study is based were created by the intellectual élite which had monopolized literacy and education. However, I intend to concentrate on that aspect of their writings which would express not so much their own world-view as such elements of their thought as were not defined by their education and privileged status. As a rule, the medieval image of the world, as reconstructed by modern scholars, is inevitably biassed in favour of the vision of the élite. I should like to avoid this and try to see the medieval world not only through the eyes of the 'intellectuals', but also from the vantage-point of the ordinary people. But how, if at all, are we able to perceive the popular culture of the Middle Ages? The ideologues of feudal society not only succeeded in barring the common people from the means of recording their thoughts and moods, but by the same token they also deprived future researchers of the opportunity to reconstruct the main features of the mental world of the non-literate folk. The common people are often referred to as the 'great mute', the 'great absent one', 'people without archives or faces', for direct access to written record was denied them. In consequence, an aristocratic, élitist view of medieval culture, based only on the thoughts of 'high-brows' – theologians, philosophers, poets and historians – became firmly established and has dominated scholarship. Until recently the legend of the 'Christian Middle Ages' or the 'Age of Faith', as an epoch under the absolute and complete dominance of Catholic ideology, was unshaken. The millennium between the end of Antiquity and the Renaissance was characterized merely on the basis of theological *summae*, canons of councils, annals, chronicles and religious literature. It used to be axiomatic to ascribe to all members of feudal society the same type of religiosity which was typical of priests, monks and mystics. Opposition to the ruling ideology was to be found only among heretics; but heresy in fact remains within the same religious framework, as the converse of orthodoxy. This picture of an unlimited domination by church and dogma was supplemented by references to a budding secular culture arising from the development of cities and their burghers. But the great majority of the population in feudal Europe, the peasantry, has been ignored by cultural historians just the same. It has been denied 'its right to a history' (Geremek 1978: 6).[1]

Medieval popular culture is a relatively new topic, still virtually undeveloped in scholarship. Usually when it is referred to, the conspicuous remnants of ancient myth, epic and survivals of paganism are cited. Scholars who have written on the 'unofficial' culture of the masses have focussed on scattered fragments embedded, apparently, in official religiosity. It has been recognized that the peasants assimilated church doctrine poorly and with difficulty, simplified it and shrouded it with all sorts of superstitions and prejudices. However, the issue usually remains that of quantitative rather than of qualitative differences: popular religiosity is conceived of as a vulgarized version of Christianity. When modern specialists treat medieval popular religion, they tend to use terms such as 'naive', 'primitive', 'crude', 'superficial', 'prelogical', and 'infantile' to describe religion replete with superstition and orientated towards the fabulous and fantastic (Delaruelle 1975). Clearly, they are borrowing their standards from the 'high' religion of the educated élite. The task is, however, to analyse the consciousness and emotional life of the common people 'from within', in accordance with its own logic (Schmitt 1976: 941ff.; Davis 1974: 308ff., against Delaruelle). In recent years the intrinsic discussion of medieval popular culture has been placed on the agenda,[2] and, although not much has been done so far, there is no longer any doubt about the urgent need to address the problem (Manselli 1975; Le Goff 1986; Schmitt 1976; Isambert 1977).

My present venture aims at concentrating on that 'low' layer of medieval culture which was barely if at all influenced by schools of classical or patristic tradition but which had preserved vital links with the mythopoetic and folkloric–magic consciousness. That world-perception which emerges from the complex and contradictory interaction of the reservoir of traditional folklore and Christianity I shall call 'medieval popular culture'.

Students of popular culture are faced with a dearth of studies on both problems and sources. To search the latter out and select one's topic in this field is in itself a pioneering, interesting and challenging task. A few very penetrating studies on medieval culture have been published recently; however, they mostly concentrate on the end of the Middle Ages and the early modern period (Bakhtin 1965; Mandrou 1964; Davis 1974, 1975; Thomas 1971; Toussaert 1960; Le Roy Ladurie 1978; Soriano 1968; Geremek 1978; Ginzburg 1980; Burke 1978). From those centuries survive incomparably richer sources, which allow us to approach the mentality of the masses. These sources are qualitatively different from the ones that come down to us from the earlier Middle Ages. The main difference is that in the fifteenth to seventeenth centuries popular culture acquired a definition: it was the culture of the lower social strata in the process of secularization that also found its expression in written and printed form (Davis 1975: 190ff.). It was based on a comparatively developed self-awareness among common men and women. On the other hand, the very concept 'popular culture' as applied to the high Middle Ages remains to a great extent undefined. Was it only the culture of the lower, oppressed classes of society? Or was it the culture of all *illiterati*, as opposed to that of educated people? (It should be remembered that in the Middle Ages the uneducated were by no means identical with the lower orders of society, as the great majority of lords were also illiterate.) Or, more broadly, should that layer of medieval culture be styled 'popular' which in one way or another belonged to all people but which among the élite was usually concealed by official theology, book learning and classical traditions, whereas among the commoners, untouched by Latin education, it came out to the surface? Or should one, following the Romantics, see popular culture as the creation of the people, as their collective artistry? Finally, one might define this culture as one created not *by* but rather *for* the people by other layers of society, with the purpose of popularization or 'lowering' cultural treasures to the populace. While nobody seems to deny the existence of something called 'popular culture of the feudal epoch', nobody has as yet provided a clear and unambiguous definition of it (Lacroix, Boglioni 1972: 53ff.; Schmitt 1976: 941ff.; Isambert 1977: 161–84). Jacques Le Goff speaks of two cultures in medieval society: the culture of the clergy or 'learned' culture, and popular or 'folkloric culture' (1977: 223ff., 236ff.). He emphasizes that the relations between the two cultures were highly diverse. There was an antagonistic attempt to 'block out' folkloric culture by the civilization of the 'learned'. Folkloric elements were suppressed by the church or distorted or partially adapted to the demands of official ideology. And there was also incomprehension by the clergy of the popular culture, since the latter, dualistically ambivalent, stood in opposition to the 'rationalism' of clerical culture which divided the world neatly into good and evil. The dominant civilization proved unable to eliminate the folkloric element and hence partially absorbed it. This interaction of cultures was facilitated by the fact that in both cultures earthly and supernatural, material and spiritual planes merged. Cultural adaptation to the common people was necessary for the clergy to achieve its mission: ecclesiastical culture had to be absorbed into folkloric culture. In Le Goff's argument the idea of 'internal acculturation' (that is, mutual adaptation of cultures) is central.

These propositions of Le Goff and his pupils (Schmitt 1979) shift the centre of gravity from popular religiosity to the deeper and more complex notion 'folkloric culture'. The religion of the common people is only one epiphenomenon of this culture. This reformulation of the problem is very important and helpful. Although religious ideas and practices comprised an extremely important aspect of the spiritual life of medieval men and women, the content of popular culture, however immersed it was in a sacred atmosphere, comprised more than beliefs and rituals. Moreover, popular interpretation of Christian truths bore exceedingly diverse fruits which can be assessed properly only in the wider context of 'folkloric culture'.

I do not hasten to formulate my understanding of medieval popular culture at this point: I hope it will emerge in the course of the study. Still, we need some frame of reference for the gathering of material and its analysis. I shall concentrate on medieval man's *Weltanschauung* (the means by which he perceived the world), his mental make-up and the collective psychological setting. What was the 'mental equipment' of these people? What were their 'spiritual tools'? (Duby 1961; Dupront

1961; Bloch 1961; Le Goff 1974.) I am less concerned with clearly stated ideas and doctrines, not typical of this low stratum of culture, than with implicit models of consciousness and behaviour. The period of my investigation, the sixth to thirteenth centuries, has been a 'dark age' in the history of popular culture. Not that there would be a true dearth of sources; we merely have to make the proper choices for the study of our subject. We have to find the sources among literary monuments well known to specialists but not usually cited for the purpose of our project. Once we 'discover' these sources they may prove to exist in sufficient quantity. It will not even be possible to include all of them in our analysis – nor, as a matter of fact, will it be necessary. The problem lies elsewhere: these sources are not very diverse. One cannot change the angle of inquiry as often as one might like. As a result, my observations and conclusions are, willy-nilly, fragmentary and one-sided. I have to agree with J.-C. Schmitt that 'the lack is not so much of sources as of cognitive tools for decoding them' (1979: 234).

In contrast to the authors of those works on medieval culture and religion of which I am aware, I do not intend to pose the problem in a general form or attempt to discuss all aspects of it. My selection of sources allows me to choose one specific aspect worthy of attention, the phenomenon which may be called the paradox of medieval culture. It lies in the fact, documented in the intersection of popular culture and the culture of educated people, that Latin writings of scholars and teachers contain substantial elements of the non-literate folklore tradition almost against their authors' will. How can these levels combine and penetrate each other within a single mind? What transformations do they suffer in this confluence? In trying to answer these questions, I may be able to contribute to the understanding not only of popular consciousness, but also of some essential features of the medieval mind in general. It seems to me that this investigation may also shed light on certain features of medieval aesthetics. By aesthetics I do not mean, of course, a theory of art, but a system of implicit norms, such as the early Byzantine 'poetics' analysed by S. S. Averintsev (1977: 3ff.).

I feel I should explain why I excluded a great number of sources that had been studied extensively in my *Categories of Medieval Culture*. There I had discussed much Germanic and Scandinavian material from a culture that typologically preceded the Latin Middle Ages. Ancient Scandinavian literature is rich in information about popular conceptions of the world. It even relates more directly to the consciousness of the uneducated mass than do the Latin sources studied in this book. However, in a book on popular culture it would be difficult to combine the analysis of Scandinavian epic and poetry with the study of Latin sources. The mythopoetic tradition in Nordic culture was a highly productive organic whole combining archaism with refinement (Gurevich 1979). In the context of medieval Latin literature this tradition had an entirely different place. The culture common to all people in a pre-class society becomes the culture of the 'common people' in a class society, counterposed to the 'official' clerical culture; it becomes a persecuted culture driven back to the periphery of spiritual life. Paganism, which has permeated myth and epic, degenerates into 'superstition'. The traditional vision of the world is broken into fragments under the blows of ecclesiastical ideology and is only partially absorbed by the new world-view. The triumph of the new culture does not imply the total defeat of the archaic. In many respects popular culture retains its 'pre-medieval' features. We cannot understand the spiritual life of medieval society adequately without the mythopoetic and folkloric tradition, the heritage of the common people, which was only partially absorbed by the 'official' culture. But these remnants are very different from Scandinavian culture *in floribus* and we cannot well include the latter in our analysis of medieval popular culture.

The formulation of the problem has determined the character of this study. It is not a philosophy or a history of culture, nor is it a medieval aesthetics. Rather it is an attempt at discussing an unexplored layer of medieval culture in terms that are perhaps closest to social anthropology. Hence writings from the sixth to the thirteenth centuries will be interpreted 'synchronically', so to speak in order to explore a particular cultural layer. In other words, I am not now interested in the development of a culture over several centuries, but in its internal system, which remained fairly immobile and reproduced its basic features over and over again. I believe that such an approach is rare, and for that reason alone it seems justified. It may be that this particular point of view will provide new insights into the culture as a whole as well.

The vagueness of the concept 'medieval popular culture' requires some additional comments. In the first place, popular culture should not be regarded solely as a single entity distinct from official or 'learned' culture: popular culture itself was composed of widely divergent components and tendencies. The cultures of peasants, knights and townspeople, with their own contents and traditions, can be distinguished from ecclesiastical tradition. Although my book concentrates primarily on peasant culture, any discussion of medieval culture must bear in mind the entire range of its constituent parts. Georges Duby, in the foreword to the French translation of my earlier book (*Catégories de la culture médiéval*, Paris 1983: xii), correctly notes that there is a danger of simplification in drawing the contrast 'learned culture–popular culture'. But in the period covered in this book, when the overwhelming majority of the population were peasants and their style of thinking necessarily affected the totality of social consciousness, such a contrast is entirely meaningful.

Secondly, the way the notion 'culture' is used in this book needs more precise definition. I have not focussed on the concrete cultural products usually studied by historians of literature, art and philosophy; I have attempted instead to 'dig down' to the intellectual, ideational, affective and socio-psychological soil in which culture arose and by which it was sustained. Perhaps it would be more precise to speak not about culture, but about that layer of consciousness in which its elements originated and were defined, namely the more amorphous, unstructured sphere of images, notions, beliefs and stereotypes hovering in social consciousness. To this end, I have sought that level of consciousness situated 'lower' than the level of ideas and artistic works.

As a result, the task is to elucidate those mental constructs and customary orientations of consciousness, the 'psychological equipment' and 'spiritual rigging' of medieval people which were not clearly formulated, explicitly expressed or completely recognized. In studying a culture's mental substratum, the historian looks behind the direct indications of the texts to discover those aspects of their world-view which their creators could only 'utter' unwittingly. Beyond the 'plane of expression' he seeks the 'plane of content', looking to discover about his subjects and their consciousness what they themselves probably were unaware of, and to penetrate into the mechanism of that consciousness and understand how it functioned and which of its layers were the most active. Hence my preference for the unintentional evidence of the sources over the conscious, well-considered expressions of medieval authors.

Such indeed has been the trend of recent scholarship: historians have considered medieval society not only 'from above', from the viewpoint of the intellectual élite, but also, 'from below', from the position of the 'unlettered *simplices*' (see Gurevich 1981). Scholars have sought approaches to sources that permit catching the voices of common people and drawing near to their world-view. In modern scholarship this level of social consciousness is called 'mentality', a term just as indefinite as the phenomenon it designates. Yet this approach is not some sort of 'romantic populism', it opens new avenues in understanding medieval culture and social structure. It has gradually become clear that mentalities form a particular sphere, with specific normalities and rhythm, connected with the world of ideas but by no means reduced to it. The history of ideas 'in a pure form' (studied by historians of religion and philosophy) on the one hand, and the 'social history of ideas' (the study of the preparations and preconditions of their formation in the socio-psychological sphere) on the other are two different, frequently divergent orders, and knowledge of the latter is essential for understanding the history of culture and the historical process as a whole.

Finally, let me stress that my subject is not medieval popular culture itself, but its 'meeting' with official culture and the mutual influence of both traditions of consciousness. In examining medieval Latin sources, I have aimed at discovering the 'junction' of these two traditions and the border of their contacts; these can be seen only in their interlacing, in a complex and contradictory synthesis which I call a 'dialogue–conflict' of the two forms of consciousness. I have not tried to isolate popular culture by removing its Christian overlays, for such a 'pure form' did not and could not exist in the Middle Ages. Both traditions must be understood in their dialectic and in their historical mutual influence, for they existed as the inseparably linked poles of a single cultural universe. Only in the force-field created by both poles – the consciousness of the élite and the consciousness of the *idiotae* – did medieval culture, with all its alogisms, 'oddities' and paradoxes, acquire its social meaning.

Some chapters of the present work were previously published in journals. However, bringing them together into a book has involved restructuring and at times fundamental changes. A number of conclusions and statements expressed in previous published versions have been revised or clarified. A few comments on the literature that has appeared since the Russian edition are contained in the notes to each chapter. At various stages in the preparation of this book I have discussed its contents with colleagues and friends; I take this opportunity to thank them all for their valuable advice and assistance. I should also like to express my appreciation for the work of the English translators.[3] Their expert rendering of my thoughts and their collegial advice on several points enhanced the value of my original.

1

POPULAR CULTURE AND MEDIEVAL LATIN LITERATURE FROM CAESARIUS OF ARLES TO CAESARIUS OF HEISTERBACH

The subject of this book is the popular culture of the Middle Ages as reflected in Latin literary monuments. My project is to find evidence on the world-view of the common people who did not know Latin, in works written in a language foreign to them. *Prima facie*, this attempt may appear rather odd. However, no other approach seemed possible, because for many centuries the vernacular languages and popular dialects of Western Europe were used chiefly for verbal communication and could not take hold of the world of writing. Letters remained entirely under the domination of Latin, a language inherited from an earlier epoch, which served as the official and professional language of the only group in society that had monopolized education: the clergy. Latin enjoyed absolute primacy in the hierarchy of languages. For a long time it was the only written language, but even when its monopoly had been broken and literary vernaculars developed alongside it, Latin maintained a privileged position. It was seen as the sacred language guaranteeing unity of faith. Laymen did not know Latin; to be literate, one had to know Latin. Accordingly, the division of people into *litterati* and *illitterati*, a notion of late Antiquity, remained decisive. The former were the educated, those who knew Latin; the latter were the illiterate, the *idiotae*. *Idiota* was understood as a person knowing merely his crude native tongue, given him in childhood, while Latin could be acquired only by persistent, extensive study (Grundmann 1958).[1] Thus, the opposites Latin–vernacular and *litteratus–illitteratus* correspond to the dichotomy of school *vs* life or culture *vs* nature (Mohrman 1955: 53). Christian truth had to be expounded primarily in Latin, and it was specifically in that language that one was to address God. Western Europeans forgot that the Vulgate was a translation of Hebrew, Aramaic and Greek Scriptures, and were convinced that Latin was the very language in which the teachings of the Lord were given to mankind (Ullmann 1963: 185). Thus, works written in Latin indisputably enjoyed an elevated position and higher authority than anything in the vernaculars. 'The Latin Middle Ages', a term coined by literary historians, describes this state of affairs very succinctly.

The historian who intends to study the popular culture of the Middle Ages cannot help using Latin authors, for we have hardly any other literary works from the period. However, the problem is whether these

1

works, informed as they were by official doctrine, permit us to discover the thinking of the broad strata of the lay population. Would a researcher not risk mistaking the outlook of the clergy for that of the masses?

Of course, if we hoped to find an immediate expression of mass consciousness in the texts of leading theologians or philosophers, or if we attempted to draw conclusions from these on the frame of mind of the 'average person', we would fall into the most profound error. The thoughts of these 'theoretical experts' were entirely removed from the thinking of the common people in both form and content. In order to become 'prevailing ideas', the ideas of the élite had to be translated into a language comprehensible to all. For the most part, this was done by preachers who were in direct contact with their flock. Parish priests, monks and missionaries had the task of rendering intelligible to the people the fundamental propositions of theology, inculcating principles of Christian behaviour and rooting out alien ways of thought. Special genres were created which set out Christian doctrine in a popular style, giving the flock models to follow. Parts of this literature were intended for the priests' use in day-to-day activities: for example, the penitentials. These aids for the confessional were not addressed to the parishioners; they contain questions to be asked in confession and measures of penance to be imposed for various sins and transgressions. Other works were addressed to the flock, such as sermons, admonitions, stories of miracles and of visions, lives of saints, and catechisms. These and many more genres, intended for a wide audience, were designed to be comprehensible even to *idiotae*. In these types of literature, the reader will not find sophisticated theology, comparable to the treatises of John the Scot, Anselm of Canterbury, Abelard or Thomas Aquinas, but a general, simplified or extremely condensed version of it. 'It is difficult to exaggerate this simplicity' (Richter 1976: 57). We find here an impressive attempt to transform Christian doctrine from the learned heritage of the ecclesiastical élite into the world-view of the broadest strata of the population.[2] It was through these sermons and tales about devils, demons and saints that Christianity, developed in monasteries and hermitages, found its way into the consciousness of the people, who had their own cultural tradition in myth, epic, pagan ritual and magic. In the struggle waged by the church for the minds and souls of the common people, these genres played a crucial part. They were the most important channels of communication between clergy and masses, as it was through them that churchmen gained control of the spiritual life of the lay people.

For this very reason, these works could not help but reflect certain significant aspects of folk religiosity and the popular world-view. Preachers, who strove to penetrate the mind of each listener, could achieve this only by adapting to their audiences. They did so by speaking in a comprehensible and simple language, resorting to familiar images, confining themselves to subjects within the mental horizon of the flock, referring to folklore and even making use of the stylistic features of tale and song.

It is important to remember that, in a society where the vast majority remained illiterate, the written word was not the most important means of communication. Thus, we who are forced to study this society mainly through preserved texts (discounting the rather limited material remains), are faced with a deceptive representation. The image of medieval culture thus reconstructed is one inevitably 'shifted' towards a fixation on the literary aspects. However, in the Middle Ages, the majority of spiritual treasures circulated without being recorded on parchment or paper, and substantial segments of medieval society were not in touch with written language.[3] These features have to be kept in mind when discussing medieval literature and culture as a whole.

Moreover, one should not forget that literacy was a privilege, and a definite social advantage, in the Middle Ages. The antagonisms of medieval society were augmented and complicated by the highly important dichotomy between the literate (educated and ordained) and the ignorant (illiterate and unordained). *Docti* had access to the depositories of knowledge; *idiotae* had none, and had to be content with those morsels of truth that the *litterati* were prepared to hand out to them. Thus to their feudal, political and economic dependency was added a spiritual one, due to the élite's monopoly on the written word. As an anonymous treatise of the thirteenth century, 'On the Clergy', states: 'He who is educated [i.e. knows Latin] is a natural lord over the ignorant' (Richter 1976: 79). It was a function of the owners of knowledge to distribute it, in limited doses and with appropriate interpretation, to those who were deprived of direct access to books.

Many literary works were created for circulation exclusively among the ordained. The Scriptures, as well as certain devotional books and theological treatises, were forbidden to laymen. Their translation into the vernacular was prohibited.[4] Other works, although written in Latin, were intended for a wider public and were to be expounded to that audience by the clergy. Writing was intended much less for individual silent reading than for reading aloud to a community.[5] Since not every text was to be read to any audience, the guardians of sacred knowledge also had the task of creating texts for the instruction of the unordained. It is obvious that texts designed to be the exclusive property of the intellectual élite and those meant as popularizations were constructed along different lines. The former followed established tradition and were subject to the laws of genre, in particular of *imitatio* (extensive citation, direct or implicit, of religious authorities) and the use of rhetorical *topoi* which remained unchanged for centuries. The texts intended for *simplices* were to a greater or lesser extent adapted to the level of understanding of their audience and had to make allowance for its tastes and spiritual orientation.

One treatise of the late eleventh century points out that the preacher should take into consideration the personalities of those to whom he is addressing his sermon: in an imperial palace one should not speak in the same manner as in a poor man's hut. The preacher should use the language of the people to whom he is preaching.[6] Frequently sermons were preached separately to clergy and laymen, for it was assumed that priests and monks would understand them in Latin while others needed to hear them in their native tongue. Moreover, the content of the sermons for clergy and for laity was hardly identical. For example, in 1095 in Bury St Edmunds, the bishop was reading a sermon to the clergy in the choir while a priest preached another to the flock assembled in the nave of the church. The content of the bishop's sermon is not recorded, but we are told that the priest spoke to the laymen about the holy martyrs 'who serve as intercessors for all people before the Lord' and 'call forth abundant rainfall when we have long awaited it'. That was the level on which sainthood was presented to the people (Richter 1976: 58).

Writings 'for everyone' took their themes not so much from the genres of high, literary culture as from those of folklore. Actually, the motifs of saints' lives, legends, visions of the Other World and miracle stories were frequently borrowed from folklore. The fact is that in the Middle Ages the written word was a small island in a sea of oral literature,[7] and this left its mark on most writings. The interdependence of oral and written cultures is convincingly demonstrated by Brian Stock (1983). It is a signal feature of the creative process in folklore that it is subject to a kind of 'preliminary censorship' by its collective listeners: the community chooses acceptable productions and rejects others; hence only that survives which was approved or accepted by the audience and suited its taste (Jakobson 1966: 116–18). In literature, there may be a discrepancy between contemporary taste and a particular work, so that even if it is rejected by the public it still continues to exist and may in the future receive a new lease of life. In folklore, 'preliminary censorship' is unconditional: products of individual creativity which the collective refuses to incorporate socially are doomed to perish.

Yet, in the Middle Ages, the boundary between folklore and literature may not have been that clear. It was with reference precisely to the literature of that epoch that Jakobson and Bogatyrev introduced the concept of a 'boundary zone' between individual and collective creation, between literature and folklore. They had in mind such 'creations' as that of copyists of literary works who unintentionally made changes to the texts. Of course, the matter cannot be reduced to merely the 'licence' of copyists. Medieval literature contains numerous works in which the very same subject is developed in different forms. Surely, this was due to the fact that interest in the topic emerged again and again, and triggered a re-working of subjects which lived on in oral tradition and enjoyed wide popularity. This is true not only of the epic, but also of legends of saints or miracle-stories, so popular throughout the Middle Ages. The hand of the 'author', the monk or priest who wrote down the edifying narrative, gave it the form in which it became a literary work. But the genesis of this very narrative could have been within the sphere of folklore, as stories about healings and other miracles of popular saints or tales of wanderings in the afterworld arose everywhere spontaneously among the common people.[8] Being re-worked and written down, the oral legend became part of literature, then subsequent readings of the text to the faithful led to its renewed spread in oral form, in which it again became subject to transformations following the laws of folklore. 'This oral, unrecorded layer of culture is to some extent the key to written texts, making it possible to decipher their core content' (Lotman, Uspenskii 1977: 150). It is as if several layers of the genres of medieval literature overlapped and were in constant interaction, permeating each other (Levinton 1975: 78ff.). The pages of popularizing medieval texts contain an ongoing hidden dialogue between official doctrine and folkloric consciousness, leading to their convergence but not to their fusion. Here is an ecclesiastical literature which, because it is directed to the illiterate mass of simple people, and therefore orientated towards their minds, is in turn strongly influenced by them. Intentionally or not, these texts are 'infected' by folklore. As a matter of fact, the efficacy of this type of literature depended on the degree to which the authors were able to enter into the thought-structure of their audience. In the twelfth century Bishop Albero of Trier was reproached that his sermons were not achieving their aim, not so much because his native tongue was French and he spoke German poorly, as because he 'discussed subjects that were too complex'.[9]

One should not conceive of the influence of official ideology on the popular world-view as a one-way process of planting new ideas and beliefs into virgin soil. There was an interaction between church ideology and pre-Christian (or more accurately, non-Christian) popular culture. The result of this multifarious and conflicting mutual influence was a cultural–ideological complex which might be called 'popular Christianity' or 'parish Catholicism'.

The assumption that it is possible to find evidence of popular attitudes in these literary genres is based on the fact that the clergy, who preached the sermons to the congregation and made use of the penitentials came from the same milieu as their parishioners. Friedrich Engels characterized the 'plebeian part of the clergy' in fifteenth- and early sixteenth-century Germany as standing 'close enough to the life of the masses' owing to their origin and to their 'plebeian... sympathies' (1956: 34). This holds true for the preceding centuries of the Middle Ages as well. Of course, even the simple monks and parish priests were different from the common people: their tonsure or ordination, their education, however meagre, and the functions they performed all irrevocably placed them in a distinct group.[10] While this social position could not but leave its mark on the preacher's consciousness, the mental baggage and spiritual make-up of rank and file priests and monks were not very different from those of their parishioners. Even if there were well-read poets and patristic scholars among the clergy, illiterate clerics were far from exceptional.[11]

The authors of the many kinds of pastoral literature were often highly educated people, famous theologians and writers, preachers and members of the ecclesiastical hierarchy. Yet, when they composed sermons or saints' lives, formulated questions for the penitentials or described visions of the elect, they had in mind that audience to which the parish priests and monks were to read or paraphrase their work. They were almost unconsciously compelled to adapt the language and content of their writings to the familiar mental horizon of the rank and file preachers who in turn expounded, interpreted and translated them, awakening a particular set of ideas and concepts in the minds of their flock.

That the popularizing genres of medieval Latin literature were widely appreciated and copied from century to century with little alteration is the best evidence of their effectiveness in the eyes of churchmen. This kind of literature was not some sort of peripheral or secondary branch of medieval culture, but its most important and active channel of communication. Directly linked as it was to the spoken word, this lowest layer of culture served as the 'base' for the more original, highly celebrated artistic creations. While theological treatises were the property of a small group of schoolmen, and verses and songs of the *vagantes* remained confined to the milieu of wandering scholars, there could have been no one who was unaffected by preaching, or by the stories of demons, devils and wanderings around heaven and hell. Everybody attended confession and had to answer questions taken by the priest from the penitentials. What we have here is a truly mass literature which in one form or another reached absolutely everybody. It not only was adapted to its audience but also received strong influence from it. Hence, popular beliefs and ideas, at times most remote from the orthodox picture of the world, or even directly at odds with official dogma, 'break through' into these writings despite the authors' intentions. It is precisely in this kind of literary monument that we may expect medieval authors to 'blurt out' things which they probably did not intend to say at all, and what is more, could not consciously have disclosed.

The higher genres of church literature came into contact with folklore not directly, but through the medium of 'low-brow' popularizing literature. As a rule, this 'low-brow' layer of Latin literature escapes the eyes of historians of medieval culture. Hence, discussions of the nature of Christianity in the Middle Ages, of popular piety and related subjects seem to be, so to speak, suspended in mid-air. But surely it was just this diffuse 'parish literature' that nourished the thinking of the *simplices*, which in turn fed that literature with subjects and themes, informing it with a special 'democratic' tone.

It is easy to find examples of ancient popular traditions co-existing in people's minds with Christian orthodoxy. Alcuin condemned in a letter the monks of an English monastery because during their common meals they listened 'not to a reader, but to a harpist, and not to sermons of church fathers, but to pagan songs'. 'What do Christ and Ingeld [a Germanic hero] have in common?' Alcuin asked indignantly.[12] One might put down this denunciation as a symptom of a not yet overcome pagan heritage or an imperfect Christianization, if one did not encounter the same phenomenon centuries later. Meinhard, the schoolmaster of Bamberg, complained about his bishop, Gunther (1057–75), that 'he never thinks of Augustine or Gregory, but always of Etzel, Amalung and such like' (von See 1971: 150). Etzel is Attila and Amalung refers to Dietrich von Bern, the epic persona of Theodoric the Great. These names of German epic heroes take us back to the epoch of the *Völkerwanderung*, the memory of which lived on so tenaciously in the minds of medieval people. There is an interesting anecdote in the thirteenth-century *Dialogue on Miracles*, by the German Cistercian Caesarius of Heisterbach. The negligent monks were dozing off at prayer, some were even snoring gently, when the abbot exclaimed: 'Listen, brothers, do listen, I am going to tell you a remarkable new story: once upon a time there was a king called Arthur...' Here he stopped and continued the tale no further, but drew the lesson: 'You see, brothers, how unfortunate it is that when I speak to you about God, you sleep, but if I just begin on something trifling, you wake up at once and are all ears!'[13] This story, like many others in medieval Latin literature, turns out to be a paraphrase on an ancient theme: 'Demades was giving a speech at an assembly, but the people were not listening. Then he began to tell a story: "Demeter, a swallow, and an eel were travelling together; they came to a river, and the swallow flew across and the eel plunged into the water." Here he stopped; they began to ask: "But what about Demeter?" "Demeter is angry with you", replied Demades, "because you are not thinking about matters of state, but are amusing yourselves with Aesop's fables"' (Gasparov 1971: 19). The similarity is obvious. Nevertheless, the choice of this motif and its use by Caesarius is significant.

Over many centuries the clergy maintained a vivid interest in epic literature, heroic poetry and tales of chivalry. Many examples could be cited, but suffice it to recall that a number of medieval epics came from the pens of the clergy. If the heroes of pagan poetry, far-removed from Christian piety and orthodoxy, captivated the minds of monks and priests, this must have been all the more true of laymen. This is one more aspect of that interaction of different layers of culture, from archaic beliefs to Christian ecclesiastical culture, which characterized medieval men, from peasant to bishop.

Considering all this, I proceed on the assumption that in the above-mentioned categories of medieval Latin literary sources, that aspect of medieval consciousness which cannot be disclosed by other, more direct, means will to some extent break through to the surface. The best way to test this hypothesis is to study these sources in depth. If it is verified – that is, if we can prove that the pressure of the audience on the authors of these works was strong enough to make their writings valid sources for popular culture – then entirely new perspectives will open up for the study of the inner life of the 'silent majority' of feudal society. We may be able to a certain extent to penetrate the minds of the anonymous masses, even if they could not find direct expression in the literature of the epoch.

I selected the two Caesarii whose names appear in the title of this chapter because they may stand as major milestones in the development of didactic literature in the West. Caesarius of Arles, eminent churchman, organizer of monasteries, archbishop and pastor in Provence, died in A. D. 542. Caesarius of Heisterbach, a Cistercian monk from the German Rhineland, author of the popular *Dialogue on Miracles*, died around A. D. 1240. They are separated by seven centuries which span almost the entire Middle Ages. Caesarius of Arles is almost as remote in time from his namesake as the latter is from us.

In the centuries separating the two writers European culture went through radical changes. This statement is indisputable if by culture we mean philosophy, education, art and poetry. There is no need to recall the impressive heights European culture had reached by the thirteenth century. But medieval culture contains not only the unique works of Chrétien de Troyes and William of St Thierry, of troubadours and

Minnesänger, of Otto of Freising and Snorri Sturluson, Romanesque basilicas and Gothic cathedrals. It also had its own 'subsoil' consisting of a particular medieval vision of the world, a specific understanding of time and space, the soul and the relation between this and the Other World. It had a peculiar regard for the forces governing life and death and a distinct attitude to human personality, both to its individuality on the one hand and to its subsumption in the community on the other. These habits of thought are not obvious at every step but they had all the more strength through a certain 'automatism', and by virtue of this and their traditional character were all the more pervasive (Gurevich 1984: 13ff.).

It seems to me easier to detect such stereotypes in 'average' authors who deviate least from the accepted norm than in the work of outstanding creative thinkers (Karsavin 1914: 10ff., 1915: 8ff.). The name of neither Caesarius is particularly connected to masterpieces of medieval culture. Neither the sermons of Caesarius of Arles nor the *Dialogue on Miracles* of Caesarius of Heisterbach marks a high point in medieval Latin literature. They do not contain either refined philosophy or sublime theological thought, nor do they display particular stylistic beauty. But for an understanding of 'the fonds of general culture' (in L. P. Karsavin's words) and the general consciousness of the epoch, these writings are, together with ones that are similar in spirit, content and purpose, of signal value.

The study of these authors presents us with an amazing fact. We should expect that the sermons of Caesarius of Arles and the dialogues of Caesarius of Heisterbach, separated as they are by an immense epoch – in terms of both duration and historical development – would be vastly different. In the time of Caesarius of Arles the settlement of Roman provinces by barbarians was barely completed, their Christianization was under way, monastic orders were just being founded. The confrontation and interaction of barbarian and Roman social and cultural institutions was preparing the way for the future emergence of feudalism. In a word: the Middle Ages had only just begun. In the time of Caesarius of Heisterbach, however, the Middle Ages – if we take this arbitrary term to mean the epoch of the development of feudalism, of the dominance of the church and of the heyday of theocratic power – had reached its highest point or had even passed it. The long-established seigneurial system was undergoing profound transformations, the feudal castle was challenged by a new centre of economic and societal activity – the city. The crusades were coming to an end, the church had lost its monopoly on education and learning, literatures in the new vernacular languages were developing, and waves of heretical movements were sweeping through Europe. While Caesarius of Arles's time marked the end of the patristic age, that of Caesarius of Heisterbach marked the transition to late scholasticism. I mention all these generally known phenomena only to emphasize the profundity of the changes which had filled the centuries separating the first Caesarius from the second.

However, reading the sermons, dialogues, catechisms, lives of saints, *exempla* and other popularizing works, one finds that didactic literature had hardly developed at all. The characteristic features of these genres are, in principle, the same in the sixth and the thirteenth centuries.

Nothing could be easier than to explain this immobility in terms of the proverbial traditionalism of medieval literature in general, and of ecclesiastical writings in particular. In contrast to the literature of modern Europe, medieval letters were subject to a strict code and to clichés that were passed on from century to century. Medieval authors were proud to use plenty of *loci communes* and habitual, familiar *topoi*. Reliance on authority and tradition engendered an enormous 'redundancy' of information. Of course, it is only from the modern point of view, which places the highest value on originality and seeks always new information, that medieval works appear 'uninformative'. Medieval authors and their readers found satisfaction in the repetition of familiar verities and formulas, in the overabundance of overt and covert citation and in endless variations on themes that had been set once and for all.

Yet, outstanding minds of the epoch were not satisfied with repetition. Each of them introduced something new, not necessarily rejecting previous tradition, but including himself within it. It is at times difficult to separate the new or original, for it is engulfed in a sea of 'commonplaces' and long-established verities. But obviously in their time the most minute nuances, even seemingly insignificant shifts of accent, were recognized much more acutely than today. True, medieval literature, art and philosophy were subject to ecclesiastical control and, since truth was seen as one and as revealed once forever, orthodox authors were expected merely to add new illustrations to it. Nevertheless, literature and art did not stand still.

I doubt, therefore, that the stagnation of didactic literature can be explained exclusively in terms of the traditionalism which was indeed typical of the Middle Ages. Other branches of literary creation are not characterized by such a degree of immobility. I am, rather, convinced that the uniformity of edifying works is primarily due to the distinctive features of the audience for which they were written. The overwhelming majority of the population was rural; its way of life was defined by routine and its horizon extremely limited. Conservatism was an indefeasible characteristic of that milieu. Anything novel was received in a guarded, suspicious way and with mistrust. For all novelty was pregnant with violation of the equilibrium regarded as the ideal state in all spheres, the spiritual included.[14] The preservation of the *status quo* concerned everybody. Hence rank and file listeners to sermons and legends did not expect new thoughts from their pastors. They were not even capable of appreciating originality. Their mental appetite, unwhetted as it was by reading, received intellectual satisfaction precisely from hearing things that were familiar. Cognition for most medieval minds consisted of integrating new data with old: in a word, of recognition.

The increasing complexity in the parishioners' social composition, the growing number of burghers, merchants, tradesmen and knights, did not immediately lead to significant changes in these deeply rooted mental habits. They were shared by all strata of society, not just its lowest levels. One should not forget that in all parts of medieval society vital information spread almost exclusively by direct personal contact. Its chief source was oral narrative. This means of communication is characterized more than any other by uncritical acceptance of information, 'taking one's word' for things,[15] and it is liable to distortion on account of many and varied factors. As it was not exactingly and unambiguously recorded, incoming information was readily reshaped by the mechanism of collective perception in accordance with the laws of folkloric consciousness. It was brought into line with previous ideas and made to fit the usual clichés. Medieval imprecision with all quantitative data – numbers, dates, times, spaces and measures of weight, area and length – is well known. It is a typical manifestation of the approximate character of ordinary perception in those centuries. Willingness to accept any kind of fantastic news, inclination to believe in the supernatural, organization of received information in accordance with canons of story and legend, were characteristic of the collective consciousness not only in the age of saints and thaumaturges. It is in just such times that mythopoetic thought is especially prevalent.

Another feature of the consciousness which interests us here is its disinclination for abstract concepts. General and abstract notions are comprehended exclusively in their concrete and tangible forms. The most spiritual beings are transformed into demonstrably material things, are personified and embodied. An educated man, priest or monk, may have perceived, for example, personifications of sins and virtues as metaphors or allegories, but his listeners most certainly added flesh and blood to the metaphor and believed in its real existence.

As already discussed, the intellectual level and education of most of the clergy, especially in the parishes, was not too different from that of the common people. Furthermore, the father confessor could only be effective if he was well understood by his parishioners. On whose intellectual territory, so to speak, would they find a common language? To what degree could a priest raise his flock to a level necessary for instilling in them a minimum of undistorted religious ideas? Or did he, rather, stoop to the mental level of his listeners in order to popularize the doctrine for them?[16] Precisely in what mental context did this encounter take place? What did the teachers have to sacrifice in order to be at least partially understood?

Answers to these questions, which are of crucial importance for understanding the collective consciousness of the Middle Ages, can be sought in the works of such authors as Caesarius of Arles, Caesarius of Heisterbach, Pope Gregory the Great, of such historians as Gregory of Tours and the Venerable Bede and of the often anonymous writers of saints' lives and similar texts.

These men were centuries apart and there are considerable differences among them, owing to their individual characteristics and to the contexts in which they lived and wrote. The prime task of Christian preachers in the early Middle Ages was the conversion of pagans to the new faith and the eradication of the remnants of old cults. Priests of later epochs had to contend with entirely different problems, especially with widespread heresy. But, since their writings interest us now for the inverse effect of their audience on them, these differences, however significant they may have been, become hardly relevant. As noted already, the basic features of ecclesiastical literature written for the laity did not change; hence, it may be regarded as a uniform corpus from Caesarius of Arles all the way to Caesarius of Heisterbach. This being so, in order to characterize this enormous material, one does not have to study all the works it comprises, a task far beyond the capacity of any historian. A random sampling of these writings can convince anybody of the relative homogeneity across the centuries of the vision of the world and its perception. I propose, therefore, to concentrate on a few works representing various genres: the sermons of Caesarius of Arles, the *Dialogues* of Gregory I, the narratives of Gregory of Tours on saints and miracles, Merovingian and Carolingian saints' lives, visions of the Other World, *exempla*, writings of popularizing theology, penitentials, Caesarius of Heisterbach's *Dialogue on Miracles* and the *Memorable Histories* of Rudolph of Schlettstadt.[17]

Yet this selection includes works of widely known medieval authors. This seems to contradict my earlier proposition that monuments lacking in originality are more 'representative' for the study of mass consciousness. Pope Gregory the Great was one of the most important, constantly cited authorities; Gregory of Tours was an eminent Frankish bishop–historian, and the Venerable Bede was no less renowned. Nevertheless we can draw upon their works for our purposes – mainly, however, upon writings of certain genres.[18] From the works of Caesarius of Arles the sermons are of particular interest to us, from Pope Gregory's the *Dialogues*. As to Gregory of Tours and Bede, we shall focus our attention not so much on their historical works as on their contributions to hagiography.

Both Caesarius of Arles and Gregory I were among the most highly educated men in the West in the sixth century. Nevertheless, in contrast to Boethius or Cassiodorus, they cannot be regarded as continuators of classical education. They were 'founders of the Middle Ages'; with them began a new stage in the history of culture. Recall the angry reproaches of Gregory I directed at Desiderius, bishop of Vienne, who, dispirited by widespread ignorance, began to teach people Latin grammar using some literary works of Antiquity. Gregory I forbade such lessons: 'the same lips cannot pronounce "Jupiter" and "Christ" in the same breath!'. For a bishop to quote what a layman should not even read was 'unheard of and quite out of place'.[19] The pope was not, of course, coming out against the teaching of grammar in general, which was necessary even to understand Holy Writ, but was condemning lessons in worldly literature as an end in itself. Here we see the centre of attention shifting from the beauty and refinement of the literary form to the proper interpretation of the theological text, where barbarisms and solecisms are no problem (Riché 1962: 196ff.). In just the same way, when Caesarius of Arles apologized to his readers for his 'simple, popular sermon' (literally, 'pedestrian ravings'), he was in essence laying down the postulate for a new style. Rhetorical eloquence was no longer necessary. The simplicity and lack of sophistication advocated by church authors of the early Middle Ages were not regarded by them as a shortcoming. The *pedester sermo* or *rusticitas* was the form most suited for expressing the new content.[20]

In the prefaces to their works, medieval Latin authors frequently confess their inability to express themselves in an elegant style; a plea for indulgence towards crudeness of expression is a commonplace. These declarations have often been seen as symptoms of the decline in erudition after the end of Antiquity. Other scholars interpret them as mere humility *topoi*, a tradition that was established by early Christian authors: it was to express that humans are unable to give worthy expression to the Word of God. Roman rhetoric, permeated as it was by a pagan spirit, was seen as inadequate for that purpose.[21] There is some truth in both interpretations. But this approach to medieval Latin literature is too narrow. The attachment of medieval authors to traditional literary topics, as demonstrated by E. R. Curtius (1963), can hardly be rightly understood as meaning that their thoughts were invariably derivative and banal. Recent research has shown how differentiated in fact their use of *loci communes* was. These were not simply passed on as an inheritance of ancient times from one work to another; when they were included in a new context, they acquired a different sense and could be filled with a novel meaning. Consequently, it is important that citations of classical and early Christian authorities be considered within the actual context (Beumann 1959: 497–511; Veit 1963: 120–63). In particular, one should not be misled by the topics of affected modesty and humility of style so often used by medieval authors (Curtius 1963: 83–5, 411; Hagendahl 1959: 184–93).

In point of fact Caesarius of Arles, Gregory of Tours and other writers deliberately chose this form of discourse. As Auerbach pointed out (1965: 68, 77, 191ff.), the old reading public, which in its time had been able to understand and appreciate the grammatical and stylistic refinement of the literature of Antiquity, had vanished. Moreover, the contents of their popularizing writings called for a simple style. The phenomena and spiritual conditions which they wanted to describe could not be expressed in the literary forms of high classical tradition; from that standpoint, they would have appeared too low. The writings of our authors were directed at an audience which was illiterate or nearly so, which did not read as much as it listened to the words of its pastors and hence had entirely different expectations. Ecclesiastical authors loved to repeat Augustine's rhetorical question: 'who needs a language beyond reproach if the listeners cannot grasp the meaning?'.[22] The Lord does not care about grammar. He listens to the heart, not the words. Not only was illiteracy not seen as a barrier to the salvation of the soul; it was, on the contrary, an advantage. '...I know no letters, and thus I shall enter the Kingdom of Heaven,' said Parzifal the 'holy idiot' (Eggers 1963).

Bewailing their lack of literary polish was a specific new form of self-affirmation for authors. This is illustrated with exceptional clarity in Gregory of Tours. In the foreword to his *Of the Virtues of the Blessed Martin*, Gregory confesses that he set out to write with much trepidation and only after long hesitation, as he felt himself to be 'inops litteris, stultus et idiota'. But then his mother appeared to him in a vision and convinced him that 'the way you speak' is preferable to any literary refinement because it is understood by the people, hence he would be delinquent were he to remain silent and not complete this pious enterprise.[23] Distressed at his own ignorance Gregory then consoled himself with the thought that the Lord 'chose not orators, but fishermen, not philosophers, but peasants to cast down the vanity of worldly wisdom'.[24] In this juxtaposition of earthly and divine wisdom, philosophy and Holy Writ, the bishop of Tours recognized truth on one side alone. Rejecting the 'fables' about Saturn, Juno, Jupiter, Neptune, Cupid, Achilles, Laocoon and other pagan personages, Gregory of Tours turns to the story of the miracles performed by the elect of God, the saints.[25] But in order to tell of the glory of the martyrs one need not know grammatical genders, cases and other subtleties. Gregory admitted, possibly partly in jest, that being a 'bumpkin and an ignoramus', he sometimes mistakes masculine gender for feminine, takes feminine to be neuter, or uses masculine instead of neuter....[26] For 'few understand a philosophizing rhetorician, but many understand when a peasant speaks'.[27] In the concluding chapters of the *History of the Franks* Gregory lists his works, and, while mentioning again the 'roughness' of his own style, he nevertheless adjures his successors in the episcopal see of Tours not to change anything he has written, but to preserve his works unaltered in their entirety.[28] Can there be a more eloquent testimony to the author's high self-esteem?[29] The roots of this new self-consciousness in early medieval authors lie in their understanding of the importance of the writer's function in society. They knew that now, when the small, educated public had vanished, a wide audience was open to listen to their unsophisticated and crudely constructed but generally understood sermons and legends (Riché 1962: 130–1, 318–19, 536–7).

In order to be understood by the common people, wrote Jerome, a priest may even violate the rules of grammar, not out of ignorance, but because 'there is a great multitude of simple, uneducated people in church' (quoted by Strunk 1970: 18), and it is precisely to them that the writings of ecclesiastical authors should be addressed. Words to the effect that the Saviour selected his disciples from among fishermen and shepherds, not rhetoricians or philosophers, were passed on from one work to another. However, that is not only a *locus communis* (such as the juxtaposition of the 'crudeness' and 'lack of polish' of *rusticitas* with the 'refinement' or 'learning' of the *urbanitas*), but also a *topos* expressing an important position of Latin authors throughout a long epoch in European culture. They consciously turned towards a wide audience consisting mainly of illiterate and uneducated people, sought direct contact with them and strove as much as possible to reduce the distance that separated them.

Thus, what we have here is a literature with new tasks and a new position, expressing the requirements of the society in which it developed and flourished. The spoken word which breaks through in the pages of Gregory of Tours and others is a symptom of a radical turnabout not only in literary style, but also in the relation of author and public.

As discussed above, ecclesiastical authors wrote two kinds of works – popularizing ones and strictly theological ones – and clearly recognized the distinctions between them. Gregory the Great, whose *Commentary on the Book of Job* was not meant to be an *opus populare*, as it could scarcely have been to the taste of 'coarse listeners',[30] addressed his

Dialogues on the Lives and Miracles of the Holy Fathers of Italy to the widest audience. The importance which the pope attached to religious enlightenment and education emerges clearly in his letter to Bishop Serenus of Marseilles. Gregory I forbade him to destroy images of saints: as long as they do not become objects of idolatry, they are of exceptional importance for the unlettered, as important as the written word is for the literate.[31] The preface to the *Lives of St Remi* by Hincmar of Reims (to which we shall return) contains the key, as it were, to the structure of all such writings: Hincmar speaks of two layers in the *Lives* – one intended for study by educated men, another for public reading to illiterate listeners – and he consistently upholds this principle throughout the text.

The orientation of hagiographical and edifying literature towards the common people is indisputable. This is exceptionally clear in the sermons of Caesarius of Arles. His listeners were rural inhabitants of southern Gaul. As he interpreted religious subjects, Caesarius eagerly resorted to comparisons from everyday village life. He wrote a whole sermon on the theme that 'we have to be as concerned for the soul as we are for the tilling of our fields'.[32] He concluded another sermon with these words: 'I should be glad to say a bit more about Joseph, but since the poor people are in a hurry to get back to work, we had better leave it for tomorrow'.[33] It is not difficult to guess to whom he directed his many admonitions about the wiliness of the devil and the need to reject pagan practices, particularly agrarian cults. Just as obvious is the target of another sermon, in which he quotes the words of some peasants: that they were coarse, illiterate people, overworked in the fields and so, supposedly, able neither to read nor to listen to the Word of God; yet, Caesarius adds, they eagerly sing 'filthy and shameful devilish and love songs'. They can easily learn those and remember what the devil teaches them. Why then, asks he, can they not understand what Christ teaches? There are two kinds of fields, continues Caesarius, the field of the Lord, which is the human soul, and the field of man, which is his *villa*: how can one till one and neglect the other? This parallel, based on rural life, is then developed in great detail.[34]

The *Vita* of Caesarius also notes the distinctive qualities of his teaching: he did not discourse on general themes, but always cited graphic examples from everyday life.[35] Indeed, Caesarius himself spoke of this: 'When I expound Scripture as the holy Fathers did, this food nourishes only a few learned men, while the mass of the people remains hungry. Therefore', he continued, addressing the literate members of his audience, 'I most humbly beg you: let your learned ears mercifully tolerate my rustic speech so that the Lord's entire flock might receive spiritual food in its simple, and, so to say, vulgar idiom...'.[36] The language and thought of Caesarius were in fact very clear and simple. As a final example, let me refer to a sermon in which he exhorts his parishioners to restrain their sexual instincts. He explains that marriage is permissible solely for the purpose of procreation, and immoderate sexual intercourse, even with one's own wife, is impermissible. To make this clear to his listeners, Caesarius resorts to a rather rude comparison. He reminds them that surely no peasant would plough and seed the same field several times a year and expect several harvests.[37]

The sermons, lessons, miracle-stories and saints' lives were manifestly intended for the rank and file ignorant listener, whence the distinctive features of their style and language. The thoughts expressed in them were devoid of abstractions and generalizations but were expressed in simple similes and vivid images. The authors looked at the world with different eyes from their classical predecessors. Auerbach (1953: 90; 1965: 109) speaks about the 'taste for the concrete' as an important feature of the expressive talent of Gregory of Tours, but this was a characteristic feature of all writers working in these genres. In all likelihood the Latin sermons known to us in writing are the result of the literary re-working of sermons originally delivered in the vernacular; or conversely, they served as the basis for oral presentation in the vernacular (Riché 1962: 537). However, translation from the local tongue into Latin meant a transition from one system of ideas and modes of expression into a substantially different one, because the vernaculars differed from Latin in their lack of abstractions, greater concreteness and fluidity of form (Gurevich 1975).

This taste for the concrete and graphic, that which would be easily grasped and remembered, is characteristic of all the writings of Gregory of Tours. Nevertheless, the distinction between history and hagiography in form and content can be recognized in his work as well. Gregory is usually praised for his *History*, in which he combined the history of the Frankish kingdom and its rulers with the history of the church and the Christianization of Gaul, including both in his view of Biblical universal history. It also contains many hagiographic passages, but they do not play an independent role here, being introduced incidentally, as it were, in order to resolve problems of history writing.[38] His *History* differs decisively from his saints' lives in purpose and structure and the possibilities inherent in the two genres (Bernoulli 1900: 88–9; Delehaye 1930: 218–19; Walter 1966: 292–3).

To begin with, the historian subordinates his account to chronology and ties the events he describes to particular segments of time. The hagiographer, on the other hand, is indifferent to these requirements: in the lives or legends we almost never find indication of the year or month of the birth or death of a saint, although the day of the week or even the hour, and the church holiday with which his blessed passing coincided, or the age at which he concluded his earthly existence, is often given. Incidentally, the age of a saint did not have the same significance as that of a simple mortal, for the saint usually possessed, already in childhood, 'the heart of an old man' – that is, wisdom and spiritual insight – regardless of his earthly experience. Hence the expression *puer senex* is common in hagiography (Curtius 1963: 108–9, 113). The hagiographer is usually just as little concerned about other dates. His indifference to placing the life of his saint within a historical context is a matter of principle: a saint abides outside of time; he belongs to the world of eternal truth and virtue. Therefore he can only be correlated, strictly speaking, with the time of the liturgical cycle. For him, the earthly, historical world is nothing more than a place of transitional and burdensome sojourn, 'captivity', 'pilgrimage in a foreign land'. It is precisely in that 'foreign land', however, that he accomplishes his feats of sainthood.

Another noteworthy feature distinguishing the hagiographic from the historical genre was its different attitude to causality. Unlike the authors of saints' lives, medieval historians were mostly not satisfied with noting continual divine providence; they also needed to refer to rational causes of events. The chronological sequence in itself implied such an explanation. However, in stories about saints and the miracles they performed, each exploit was seen as significant in itself, not as a link in a chain of causes. A miracle is in principle acausal, a violation of earthly causality. A saint acts in accordance with the will of God, with the *causae primae* being moved immediately by him, so that human *causae secundae* are merely obstacles for him to overcome (von der Steinen 1967: 17). For the saint is the embodiment of a type that is atemporal, unbound by human or more generally, by earthly conditions. The ideal type of behaviour which he represents is the opposite of the real behaviour of people who experience actual history and participate in it. It was first and foremost this aspect that made legends and saints' lives so valuable for the church.

Like many other ecclesiastical authors, Gregory of Tours recognized the didactic function of legends of saints and laboured much in the field of hagiography. For the most part these writings are short, concise, and simply written and centre on the miracles performed by saints and confessors. These features of Gregory's hagiographic writings are interrelated: a brief narrative of a miraculous or exemplary deed of a saint was exactly right for being read or recounted during the service, usually on the given saint's day. A lengthy biography would not have filled this purpose.

Gregory of Tours followed the same principles of morally edifying preaching as had Caesarius of Arles. A comparison of Gregory's accounts of the same topic in two different genres is very telling. There are several passages in the *History* about theological disputes between Catholics and Arian heretics or Jews.[39] Gregory himself participated in some of these debates. The theological arguments are described in great detail in the *History*, with citations from the Old and New Testaments by both sides. While striving to assert and glorify Catholic orthodoxy, Gregory does not conceal that these polemics did not always lead to the triumph of the Catholics and to the conversion or humiliation of unbelievers. Such descriptions, just like the *History* in general, were clearly not intended to be understood by 'ignorant *simplices*'. The same disputes between Catholic and Arian clerics are also described in Gregory's *Books of Miracles*. There, no theological arguments or appeals to authorities are adduced. Rather, a miracle occurs in the form of an ordeal by hot water from which the Catholic emerged unscathed while the Arian was proved wrong by being scalded to the bone.[40]

The uneducated, ignorant common people were not capable of analysing the utterances of religious authorities. For them, an unpretentious tale about the miracles of a local saint was far more effective. Hence the great popularity of hagiography, the continuous reproduction of motifs, and the prolific output of such hagiographers as Gregory of Tours, with his *Books of Miracles, Book on the Glory of the Blessed Confessors, Four Books on the Miracles of Saint Martin*, and *Lives of the Fathers*.

As we have seen, the narrative form most suitable for sermons was found rather early – the short novella. Caesarius of Arles wrote sermons lasting at most a half-hour, adjusted to the attention span of his listeners. The subject-matter of such a story was as simple as possible, with usually one or two characters. The narrative leads the reader without digression to the pious denouement – the moral for which it was written. I almost said 'invented', but the authors invariably emphasize that they have neither made up anything nor added to the true story which either they themselves, their acquaintances, or other reliable persons have witnessed.

The longer saints' lives also consist of short self-sufficient fragments which could be used on their own. The whole was represented in every fragment, for each described some exploit of a hero of the faith, a miracle which demonstrated the supernatural connection between the saint and higher powers. Such descriptions simply follow one after another: D. S. Likhachev called this the 'agglutinative principle' in hagiography. In the biography of the holy man there is no development of character; his saintliness is revealed from the very beginning, often in childhood, and in some cases is even foretold before his birth. The sequence of his deeds is not interrupted by his death; on the contrary, after his 'birth' as a saint miracles increase, especially healings. Hence the value of possessing his relics.

Hagiography, which became widespread in the Merovingian period, enjoyed exceptional popularity throughout the Middle Ages. In the thirteenth century, Jacopo da Voragine collected many of them into his *Golden Legend*. The lives display an impressive array of variations on a single set of themes. They contain much of popular fantasy, with its familiar motifs and images. Delehaye (1906: 28) called hagiography 'the obedient echo of popular tradition'.[41] At the same time, the lives reflect the editorial activity of the clerical author, who altered the character and structure of the legend by reinforcing its ecclesiastical-ideological tendency. The modern reader may be amazed and fatigued by the tenacious uniformity of these stories. However, this was not the reaction of medieval readers and listeners. They found intellectual satisfaction precisely in the repetition of the already known, be it the life of a saint, a story of a visit to the Other World, a popular tale or an epic.

No less well known than the lives were the stories of visions and wanderings in the Other World. Tales of people who, either in their sleep or after death, found themselves in the world beyond the grave, and then returned to life to tell what they had seen and experienced in heaven and hell were of singular interest to the medieval man. We find here that same thematic monotony and extreme traditionalism in the genre. A comparison of the travels to the Other World, from the *Dialogues* of Gregory the Great, through Bede and Hincmar of Reims to the twelfth and thirteenth centuries, and right down to the immediate forerunners of Dante, yields by and large the same images and motifs.[42] Over time the narratives became more verbose and more coherent (for example, the *Vision of Tnugdal*), and scholars have seen in some the 'rough drafts', as it were, of the *Divine Comedy*. All in all, in spite of some development of the genre, the stories from the sixth to the thirteenth centuries are essentially products of one and the same mode of thought.

The authors of visions addressed a most diverse audience; pictures of heaven and hell cast a spell over everyone from *simplex* to monarch. So-called 'political visions', which told of the fate of a ruler in the Other World, were especially addressed to those in power, telling them that their fate depended much on their attitude to the clergy. In the hands of the prelates, these 'political visions', especially popular in the Carolingian period, served as a means of direct pressure on the bearers of state authority (Levison 1948).

Thus, it would be incorrect to see in the Latin literature of the early Middle Ages merely indications of the decline of classical education. The social context in which the authors were writing had changed; in place of the select and comparatively narrow reading group of the ancients, their audience came from the broadest strata of *simplices* – peasants, city-dwellers, soldiers – almost all illiterate. Literature had changed correspondingly. Along with Latin poetry intended for a small circle of devotees living on classical tradition, the most prominent place was occupied by hagiography, visions, sermons and the short morally edifying novella, the *exempla*. They were not so much read individually as listened to from the lips of the priest. The kind of interpersonal relations characteristic of the Middle Ages is manifest in the method of passing on information: the book does not stand between the author – or his representative, the priest – and the addressee; direct oral delivery dominates, with all of its emotional components, its inherent suggestiveness, and its close connection to the personality expounding the word (Manselli 1975: 32–3).

The visions, saints' lives and sermons deeply moved all medieval men and women, regardless of their social position or education. It would be quite rash to assume that these literary genres were intended primarily for the privileged or educated, while ordinary people were expected to be content with folklore. As Likhachev (1967: 63) so correctly put it: 'however different folklore and literature were in the Middle Ages, they had many more points of contact than in modern times. Folklore was part of the culture not only of the labouring class, but of the ruling class as well.'[43] Even though this was written about Old Russian literature, it applies equally well to Western Europe.

A comparison of the *Dialogues* of Gregory the Great or of Merovingian saints' lives with the *Dialogue on Miracles* by Caesarius of Heisterbach makes it clear how stable the genre of hagiographic and edificatory literature had been. An unsuspecting reader may not even be able to tell apart the stories from the sixth to eighth centuries and those of the Cistercian monk of the thirteenth. This type of literature had virtually not developed over the centuries: once formulated, it remained the same. The *Index Exemplorum* (Tubach 1969) lists 5,400 subjects from relevant medieval works. They are amenable to many kinds of classification, but it is obvious that a chronological one would not make sense.

Caesarius of Heisterbach's *Dialogue on Miracles* is a voluminous compendium of tales for moral edification.[44] As the author indicates in the Prologue, he has gathered stories on miraculous events which occurred in the Cistercian order for the spiritual benefit of the reader. Following an old formal tradition, the material is presented as a pseudo-dialogue between a monk and a novice; essentially it is the monk who does all the talking, only rarely does his pupil interrupt him with short questions. Caesarius' compendium contains no fewer than 750 short novellas illustrating church doctrine by examples taken from the most diverse areas of life. They are grouped in twelve sections: 'On Conversion', 'On Contrition', 'On Confession', 'On Temptation', 'On Devils', 'On Simplicity', 'On Holy Mary', 'On Visions', 'On the Sacrament of the Body and Blood of Christ', 'On Miracles', 'On Dying' and 'On Retribution in the Hereafter'. The sequence of the sections is governed by, apart from conceptual connections, numerical symbology. Thus, the section on temptations is placed in the fourth position because the number four stands for stability, and only by being steadfast can one resist the temptations of the Evil One. Number seven is 'the number for virginity'; hence, the seventh section is devoted to the Virgin Mary. The eleventh hour of the day is the time of sunset, writes Caesarius, a symbol of growing old and approaching death; therefore the eleventh section discusses dying.[45]

The actors in the little scenes sketched by Caesarius of Heisterbach are almost always monks or priests. Cistercians, of course, enjoy a particularly favoured position among them.[46] But his horizon was by no means limited by the walls of the monastery. The most diverse figures come to life in the *Dialogue*: kings and knights, crusaders and parish priests, popes and bishops, burghers, usurers, artisans and peasants, women and children, pagans and heretics. Most of the novellas are placed in western Germany, but some take place in France, Italy or the East. Caesarius' attitude towards different layers of society is definitely not even-handed. In the relatively few instances where he speaks of peasants, he does not conceal his contempt: they are described as rude, ignorant and violent; they strive to get rich at the expense of others and lead an iniquitous life.[47] In this respect Caesarius differs from his predecessors, possibly because the *Dialogue* is addressed primarily to monks and burghers. By the thirteenth century the urban and knightly audience had to be taken quite seriously (see Geremek 1978: 53–4, on the development of the *exemplum* genre).

The diversity of social and personal situations in his stories distinguishes Caesarius of Heisterbach from earlier authors in this genre. However, the style and tone of the narrative, its mental level, the conception of miracles – all the basic elements of edifying Christian literature – remain just the same as they were in the times of Gregory the Great and Gregory of Tours. In the thirteenth century, just as in centuries before, the flock wanted to hear entertaining examples from life, and only through them were the common people able to grasp moral lessons and religious instruction; abstract considerations had no effect on their minds.[48] It was also in accordance with time-hallowed tradition when Caesarius used examples from recent events, which could be confirmed by eyewitnesses or first-hand reports.[49] The author himself could have been present at these occurrences and witnessed them.[50] Caesarius insists that all his stories are true, and he believes them without reservation. There is nothing implausible in a miracle, although it is a violation of the natural order of things: when this created world comes into contact with the other, eternal world, the most unexpected and unusual things can happen. Caesarius and his contemporaries were convinced that such things take place all the time. Reading the *Dialogue* one gets the impression that miracles are an inseparable part of reality. Hundreds of people see devils; many are being tormented by them. Quite a few people have been allowed to see Christ, the Mother of God, angels or saints face to face, and Caesarius himself knows some of these elect. Caesarius of Heisterbach's demonology is particularly rich and diverse. His close familiarity with the Evil One and all his tricks and designs not only matched, but probably surpassed, that of his venerable predecessors, such as Pope Gregory I. The *Dialogue* is a most valuable evidence for the popular beliefs of his time (Kaufmann 1974).

However, the wondrous things which Caesarius relates have to do not only with the intrusion of otherworldly forces into human life. From time to time purely fairy-tale motifs find their way into his stories. There is, for example, the story of the wolf who carried off a little girl from a village into the forest so that she would pull from the throat of another wolf a piece of bone that was choking him, whereupon the girl was safely delivered to her parents.[51]

What has been said above about the *Dialogue on Miracles* applies just as well to the *Memorable Histories* written by a countryman of Caesarius, the Dominican prior Rudolph of Schlettstadt: the same subjects, themes and methods of treatment, aimed at the same audience, the same lack of erudition, perhaps even a bit more barbarous Latin. However, Rudolph wrote not in the beginning of the thirteenth century, but almost a hundred years later. His *Memorable Histories* differs from Caesarius' *Dialogue* mainly in its lack of organization: Rudolph recounts miracle stories without any system, apparently in the order he remembered them. One does not sense the scholastic training which in spite of everything comes through in the *Dialogue*. Another difference between them is the even greater degree to which Rudolph creates a feeling of actuality. All his stories are supposed to have happened very recently. He often gives a precise date or links his narrative to well-known events in the contemporary history of the upper Rhineland or Franconia. When writing about the perfidy of the Jews, he refers explicitly to the anti-Jewish riots in Würzburg.

The editor of the *Memorable Histories* noted the closeness of the author's language to the colloquial speech of the common people and suggested that the mode of narration was also dictated by the composition and level of the public to which these writings were addressed.[52] Curiously, in contrast to Caesarius of Heisterbach, this Dominican prior never refers to the Bible or to the Fathers. The stories of Rudolph of Schlettstadt are simple to the point of crudity and presuppose listeners and readers totally unfamiliar with theological literature. Thus, this work offers an insight into the interests of both the clerical and lay – urban and petty noble – populations of late thirteenth-century Germany. Clearly, the author used current oral stories, and after they were written down, they spread further and obtained, so to speak, a second life. Intrusion into daily life by the devil, women giving birth to monsters after falling under the power of demons, soothsaying, ritual murders and defilement of the Eucharist by Jews, divine punishment inevitably overtaking inveterate sinners and unbelievers all were topics which exercised the minds of this audience.[53] Rudolph also has stories resembling tales or fables: for example, the one about a maid who overheard a conversation between roosters.[54] No less entertaining is the *verissima historia* of a certain villager who found a tree with many hats hanging on it. When he put one of them on, he immediately rose into the air and flew like a bird. Flying into the cellar of some rich man, he got drunk and, being flushed with the wine, took off the hat, whereupon he lost the power to get out of the cellar. The master discovered the thief and took him to a magistrate, who sentenced him to death, and only by chance was the victim of misfortune saved: someone put the hat back on his head, whereupon he at once disappeared.[55]

People at the turn of the thirteenth to the fourteenth century still lived in a world where a miracle could happen at any moment. They were, as before, predisposed to believe in wonders and find in them confirmation of the traditional image of 'both-worldly' reality.

Sermons, saints' lives and stories of visions do not exhaust the arsenal of churchmen in their efforts to influence their flock. Confession and penance also occupy a special place. Christians were required to submit their personal behaviour to examination by the clergy and to receive a rating based on a scale of incentives and prohibitions. The confessional was designed as a place of self-analysis, under the guidance of the priest. Penance began with the admission of sins committed in thought or deed, whereupon penance was imposed by the father-confessor and once it was completed, absolution was granted. In the early church, confession was public; the transition from open to secret confession was a gradual one during the Middle Ages. As late as the thirteenth century, public chastisement of sinners was practised, along with auricular confession.[56] The replacement of confession in the presence of the community by private conversations between priest and parishioner was closely connected with the transformation of the ethical status of the individual.

In the early Middle Ages, ecclesiastically formulated norms of behaviour were not yet entrenched among the baptized. A father-confessor could not rely on his parishioners' knowledge of religious morality. In order to compel them to confess, he had to quiz them as to whether they had trespassed against Christ's teachings and the code of behaviour befitting a believer. Apparently not even all priests had a sufficiently clear idea about the boundaries dividing permissible from sinful behaviour or knew what penance is appropriate to which transgression. Hence, eminent churchmen felt called upon to develop guidelines for confessors.

Thus arose the penitentials, containing lists of sins and the penance due for them. Some of these books take the form of more or less detailed lists naming sins and the appropriate sanctions: fasting, prayer, temporary expulsion from the community, and so on. Other penitentials are compiled in the form of questionnaires for the father-confessor: what to ask his parishioners to establish the nature and gravity of the transgressions and thus decide the commensurate penance. This type of ecclesiastical literature seems to have appeared first in the fifth and sixth centuries in Ireland, whence it travelled with Celtic monks to the Frankish realm (in the late sixth century), to England (in the seventh century) and finally to all other countries of the Catholic world. At one time, church councils condemned 'confession books, the errors of which are obvious, the authors, unknown' and prescribed that bishops withdraw these 'codicilli qui contra canonicam auctoritatem scripti sunt' from use and commit them to the flames 'so that ignorant confessors no longer can use them to deceive people'.[57]

Thus, this genre of medieval Latin literature did not originate in ecclesiastical doctrine itself, but was rather a response to the demands of parish practice. The needs of local priests thrust upon the church the necessity of using penitentials despite the opposition of higher clergy. Prohibition and persecution could not stop the spread of penitentials: the need of the clergy to educate and restrain their flock was stronger than proscriptions.

Scores of penitentials have come down to us from the seventh century to the early thirteenth. The earliest ones are anonymous or have been ascribed *post factum* to outstanding church authorities such as Archbishops Theodore of Tarsus and Egbert of York, or the Venerable Bede. Later ones were written by well-known churchmen: for example, the *Corrector*, compiled in the early eleventh century by Burchard, bishop of Worms, as the nineteenth volume of his *Decretum*, a compendium of canons.

All these works were written in vulgar Latin, a language that was rather simple, if not primitive, so that their content would be clear to any confessor. Parish priests were supposed to read from the penitential to their parishioners, translating the questions and injunctions into the spoken language. A written translation of one of the Anglo-Saxon compilations survives as the Penitential of Egbert. The reason for the translation is said to have been 'so that the uneducated might understand it more easily'.[58] The need for a detailed listing of all possible sins in the form of a wide range of questions is justified by such counsel as this: 'Seeing that he [the parishioner at confession] is ashamed, the priest should say these words to him: "Beloved, since you may not recall all your deeds, I shall ask you questions, so that you will not, at the devil's prompting, hide anything." Then he should ask him these questions.'[59]

Other treatises warn that they may be used only by priests who have the right to hear confession. Laymen should not know the contents of a penitential, as the devil might lead them into temptation through the list of sins and prompt iniquitous thoughts and deeds.[60] But even when observing this caveat the priest resorted to interrogation of the parishioner, albeit in a condensed form. After a preliminary talk with the confessant and some prayers, the priest addressed him: 'My son, be not ashamed to be open about your transgressions, for there is no one without sin, except God alone. It is most fitting for you to consider your own sins and repent of them'; and he went on cursorily to list possible transgressions. The penitential, with its detailed explication of all sins and the appropriate penalties, served the priest as a guide in determining the character and extent of penance required.[61]

The 'penitentials' represent a massive body of source-material with very wide application; everybody was directly affected by them. However, a study of the morals of the Middle Ages through the penitentials is fraught with great difficulties. Not only the list of sins in general, but even the very words in these books, were repeated over the centuries. The tradition of confession was rooted in the early Middle Ages. Authors of penitentials borrowed questions and formulas extensively from their earliest predecessors. Even more than in other genres of medieval literature, the confessional treatises display an immense dependence on authorities which they tend to follow to the letter. Strictly speaking, the penitentials are sources not only for the study of popular mentality, but at least as much for the frame of mind of the priests who created and used them. The authors of these books assumed that conflict between the sinful and uncivilized *homo naturalis* and the *homo Christianus* – man as he should be according to Christian teaching – was inevitable. They saw this conflict as an expression of the dichotomy between the heavenly and the earthly, a contradiction which would be resolved only with the end of human history. Therefore, it would be rash to aver that the penitentials directly and fully reflect the state of religiosity and morality of the time in which they were written (Oakley 1940: 215–16). The list of sins became, to a large extent, petrified. Moved by the same intentions as the authors of medieval encyclopaedias and *summae*, who strove to encompass the whole of life's diversity, the writers of penitentials attempted to provide guidance in the event of all possible sins, regardless of the actual state of affairs.

On the other hand, *libri poenitentiales* were compiled for practical purposes in the confessional. The questionnaires of the confessional codices could not and did not become rigidly fixed in torpid clichés copied by their authors from their predecessors. Precisely because of their practical use, much new appears in them, both in formulation and in substance. For example, the author of the 'Merseburg Penitential' explicitly mentions that his work is based partly on 'the tradition of the elders' and partly on 'our own knowledge and reasoning'.[62] The most detailed and representative compendium, the *Decretum* of Burchard of Worms, contains much from earlier works (Fournier 1911), but the author treated these models rather freely. Burchard refers explicitly to the pitiable conditions in his own diocese which impose upon him the duty of upholding church discipline (Vogel 1974: 751–60).[63] Thus, actual behaviour of their parishioners exerted a strong influence on the authors of the penitentials, who were mostly active churchmen. The breath of life can be felt in the pages of these treatises on sins and punishments.

The penitentials permit the cultural historian in a way to eavesdrop on the private conversations of medieval people. Moreover, these conversations – which even in their own times were secret – took place face to face.[64] They had to be conducted with complete frankness: reticence or slyness at confession was a very grave sin. Fearing divine punishment, the parishioner would reveal to the priest his most secret thoughts and deeds, things he would certainly not have confessed to anybody else. Medieval literary works written in the form of confession or autobiography are incomparably less revealing than the confessions implied in the questions of the penitentials. To be sure, we can overhear only one half of these secret conversations, and that only partially: the voice of the father-confessor reaches us, but not that of the person making confession. Nevertheless, the questions asked by the priest shed light on many aspects of the society and its mores.

The nature of the penitentials invites comparison with the records of law in the early Middle Ages. Both the guides for confessors and barbarian law-codes contain lists of offences and indicate punishments for them. The law-codes frequently mention that, in addition to secular punishment, the guilty person must also do penance (Oakley 1923: 136–7). It has been argued that the casuistry and the detailed lists of transgressions in the penitentials were influenced by secular legislation which displays very similar features (Hildebrand 1851: 2–3). We do not need, however, to postulate immediate influences to explain the extreme concreteness of the penitentials. They, and the barbarian law-codes, were both engendered by one and the same type of thinking, focussed on a concrete and graphic perception of reality and devoid of generalizations and abstract concepts. Although the penitentials were written by clergy, some even by eminent ecclesiastical authors well versed in abstract logical operations, their content and form connect them to popular consciousness. They were created for the widest strata of the population and were not devoted to the theology of sin and redemption in itself, but exclusively to its practical application. Penitentials were consciously adapted to the ordinary mind of an uneducated and ignorant person. Even if we do not hear the answers of the confessant, the priest's questions themselves are posed in the language of the commoner.

The penitentials and barbarian law-codes, even if similar in intellectual 'background', are profoundly different in other respects. First and foremost, there is the concept of crime. Secular law was not concerned with the motives of the criminal; what mattered was the fact of an unlawful deed. Punishment was stipulated regardless of the mental state and intentions of the offender. In the laws of the early Middle Ages, people figure only as objectively guilty or innocent, and even this is established by certain ritual procedures, not by the admission of guilt by the accused. By contrast, sin represents an interiorized offence, that is, a crime involving the inner state of an individual. Sin remained sin if the intention only was there and no action followed, even though penance in such cases may have been lighter.[65] Confession presupposed something not required in the law: acknowledgment of sin by the guilty person and repentance. Of course, the penalties imposed according to the penitentials were in many respects different from those of the barbarian law-codes. Thus, codes of law and aids for confessors offer pictures of two quite distinct aspects of social reality and reflect in the last resort two different systems of values.

Having emphasized the difference between them, let us not mistake them for opposites. Early medieval lists of sins and penances 'had in mind more the sin than the sinner' (Le Goff 1977: 169–70), demanding of him not so much contrition of heart and repentance of sin as the performance of penance rituals. The best evidence for this attitude is when a sinner was permitted to hire a man to fast in his place (such a substitute was called a *justus*). The church was not at all quick or definite in condemning such practices, which foreshadowed the later trade in indulgences.[66] According to the penitential of Bishop Halitgar of Cambrai (*circa* A.D. 830), persons incapable of fasting and having the means to pay for it were allowed to commute penance – rich people at the rate of twenty shillings for seven weeks; less fortunate ones at ten shillings, and the poor at three shillings.[67] In England, the rule was that a magnate condemned to seven years' penance could absolve himself if on his behalf twelve persons first fasted for three days, and then seven times 120 persons for three days each on bread, water and greens; otherwise, the fast would have had to continue for as many days as there are in seven years.[68] Both legal punishment and church penance concentrate on deed and retribution, while the human personality recedes into the background behind the all-important rituals and procedures.

It was stipulated, for example, that the murderer of a relative or a lord had to fast, abstaining from meat and wine, not bathing, not taking up arms (except in a war against pagans), not conversing with other Christians, going at all times on foot, not riding a horse or in a vehicle.[69] Beyond prayers, fasting and vigils, penitents were also ordered to sleep in water, on nettles, on nut-shells on the floor, in a cold church, or even in a tomb next to a corpse. Some penances were as good as torture: the 'cross', which meant to stand with outstretched arms reciting verses of the Bible, the *palmatae* (i.e. beating one's palms on the floor), or *disciplina* (i.e. flagellation and self-flagellation). Some punishments dictated by the penitentials were essentially the same as those prescribed by the barbarian law-codes. The price of a female slave was demanded for an injury inflicted on a bishop or prince if the scar remained visible after three years. If hair was pulled from a bishop's head, twelve hairs were to be pulled from the offender's head for every hair of the bishop's. The penitentials bear the distinct stamp of the society whose sins they were to correct; it was a society in which cruelty and physical violence were not considered unusual or inhumane.

The penitentials intended that the soul of the sinner be influenced by means of the suffering inflicted on his body. Is this not what the phraseology of the penitentials implies? In them – and in fact in all church literature – the understanding of penance as a remedy for the soul predominates. Medicinal analogies abound in these treatises. Burchard of Worms's *Corrector* also bears the title *Medicus*. The principle of classical medicine that 'opposite cures opposite' ('contraria contrariis sanantur') is consistently applied to the sinner: the proud man should be broken by humiliation; greed should be cured by having to bestow charity; idleness by diligent labour; loquacity by a vow of silence; adultery by abstinence; and gluttony or drunkenness by fasting. Sin is understood here as a sickness, as something that has 'befallen' the human soul from without. But the healing of sins, the sickness of soul, was a more difficult matter than treating physical ailments, 'for wounds of the spirit are more hidden than wounds of the body, and administering for souls is the art of all arts'.[70]

Yet we leave the picture incomplete if we note only that individuality has been pushed aside, as it were, by concern about an impersonal balance between sins and penances. A number of the penitentials expressed the notion that punishments should not be merely equivalent to the corresponding transgressions, but also appropriate to the personality of the sinner. 'All are one in sin, but not everyone should be measured by the same measure.' It was necessary to differentiate on the basis of sex, age, status and spiritual condition. Rich and poor, monk, priest and layman, educated and ignorant, infant, child, adolescent, young and old, healthy and sick, freeman and slave[71] do not need the same spiritual healing, and the confessor must take into account the individual characteristics of his 'patient' in exactly the same way as a doctor does.[72] To be sure, one cannot help noticing that it is social and age categories, not personal characteristics, that are encompassed by such differentiation, but in that epoch individuality was, by and large, defined by a person's status. Besides, in individual cases it is emphasized that it is incumbent upon the confessor to consider how long the offender has abode in indecent conduct, with what kind of passion he has been seized, whether he has resisted or given in easily, and so on.[73]

In sum, the penitentials, which came out of clerical circles, were in both form and spirit adapted to a significant degree to the general milieu of their age. Just as civil law largely amounted to setting penalties for crimes in the form of fines defined for distinct situations, the aids for confessors interpreted the moral life of laymen and clergy through concepts of equivalency of transgression and penance conceived of with the same measure of explicitness and concreteness. A person should have it explained to him that for a given act he will incur such and such a punishment. In this respect the construction of many of the penitentials is instructive. First, a general discussion of sin is given, followed by an enumeration of the deadly sins usually according to the scheme worked out in the fifth century by John Cassian and revised in the sixth by Gregory the Great.

Cassian's scheme is (giving the sins in ascending order of gravity): gluttony, adultery, avarice, anger, sloth, vanity, and pride. Gregory I, retaining *superbia* in the first position, placed next *luxuria*, interpreted as lust or intemperance. Thus, rebellion of the spirit against God and rebellion of the flesh against the spirit are chief among deadly sins. The rest, derivatives of the deadly sins, were regarded as less serious.[74] From this general classification, the penitentials proceed to a most detailed analysis of distinct forms of transgression, and the seven or eight classes are no longer followed. Material for the discussion comes not from books, but from life.

It is, therefore, easy to establish which violations of morality threatencd the church above all, and which were the enemies against which she had to fight. Such paramount fiends were idolatory, adultery, and gluttony. According to the penitentials, these deadly sins infected not only laymen, but also the clergy. The struggle against them is reflected in all the penitentials without exception, from the very earliest right up to the treatises of the high Middle Ages. Repetition of the same sins and penances with the addition of new details is scarcely just a tribute to literary tradition. The 'questionnaires' shed light on the spiritual world of the people to whom they were addressed, their behaviour, and their religious practice – not as it should have been according to church doctrine, but as it actually was. They also suggest the stability and vitality of certain features of popular life. The conflict between the Christian ideal of the righteous man and real life was permanently unresolvable.

The emphasis in the penitentials was naturally on iniquitous, sinful behaviour and it would be just as mistaken to judge the moral life of medieval centuries on the basis of these documents as it would be to assess criminality from the criminal code. However, law-codes do not assume that every member of society is guilty, though for the authors of the penitentials there existed a blatant presumption of guilt. Their questions about transgressions could be asked of any parishioner even before he had admitted to committing misdemeanours. Not everyone commits capital offences, but everyone is guilty before the Lord, and the penitential demanded of the believer analysis of his own moral life.

The penitentials, which I shall discuss in detail in chapter 3, interest me less as proofs of the sinfulness of medieval men and women, or of the tireless efforts of the church to instil in them Christian behaviour (Manselli 1975: 181–2), than as a means by which it may be possible to reconstruct one aspect of the parishioners' view of the world.

In his search for sources for the study of the *Weltanschauung* of the simple people in the medieval period, the historian cannot ignore the popular texts on theology intended for the rank and file clergy. These works, unlike treatises and *summae* by outstanding theologians, do not contain independent ideas or give any original interpretations of Catholic principles. Their purpose is something else – to tutor priests and monks in the cardinal teachings of theology and to elucidate in intelligible form the most important tenets of Holy Writ and its interpretation by church Fathers and other authorities, so that the priests and monks in turn could tell their flock the essentials of this doctrine.

In these books, the thoughts of leading theologians are served up in simplified and dogmatic form. As a rule, they contain no comparison of

points of view, no presentation of arguments, no dialectics and in general
no mental exercises. They are textbooks, designed for persons of little
education untrained in scholastic wisdom. Hence, these works of popular
edificatory literature are not usually included in surveys of medieval
philosophy and theology. Their authors tend to disappear in the shadow
of the great schoolmen upon the crumbs of whose scholarship they lived.
However, in the eyes of the historian of medieval popular culture, these
fruits of vulgar theology have a unique and indisputable advantage over
the elevated philosophical–theological literature. Their circulation was
many times broader and the circles for whom they were intended were
the wide ones of the lower clergy and laymen.

Aside from his prayerbooks, the parish priest was equipped with a
penitential and a catechism. He used both directly in his daily pastoral
duties in the parish. Catechisms[75] had a long and wide popularity; they
were many times repeated and finally translated from Latin into the
vernaculars. In this process they were inevitably further simplified,
adapted even more to the needs of the people who were reading them
or to whom they were being read. It is reasonable to see in them not
only the vulgarized thought of doctors of the church, but also a reflection
of the spiritual needs of broad strata of society, for the public for these
texts must have exerted, albeit indirectly, a perceptible influence on their
contents.

By studying 'popularizing theology' we may find answers to certain
questions: What religious and moral problems concerned the laymen
and in what form were these answered? Which elements of Catholic
doctrine were assimilated by the ordinary Christian in the first instance?
We may become somewhat more closely acquainted with the general
religious background of those thousand years of ideological domination
by the church. The penitentials enable us to see the 'negative' side, as it
were, of 'popular Catholicism', while works of popularizing theology
offer a glimpse of its 'positive' aspect.

Prominent among these works is the much-read twelfth-century *Elucidarium* and its derivates. The author's name is not given in the text, and
in the prologue he expresses his desire to remain anonymous 'so as not
to arouse envy'. It has been ascribed to Honorius of Autun,[76] that
enigmatic author about whose life we know next to nothing.[77] Although
he left about forty theological and historical treatises, Honorius was not
among the prominent thinkers of his time and he made no noteworthy
contribution to the development of theology. The *Elucidarium* is regarded
as his earliest work, written around 1200 probably under the direct
influence of Anselm of Canterbury, whose pupil he may have been. The
text of the *Elucidarium* also contains evidence as to Augustinian and

patristic influence which Honorius may have received through the writings of Anselm.[78]

Neither Honorius' scholastic contemporaries nor later schoolmen refer to his works; undoubtedly, they had a not-unfounded low opinion of his learning. All the more striking is the exceptional fate of the *Elucidarium*. It was copied, paraphrased and reissued several times up to the fifteenth century and was translated into almost all the languages of Western Europe. We know of Old French, Provençal, Italian, Welsh, English, Low and High German, Old Icelandic and Old Swedish versions, and also of metrical translations into French and Dutch (Schorbach 1894; Kelle 1901; Endres 1906; Grabmann 1946; Sanford 1948). The *Elucidarium* is known to have been in numerous monastic libraries; many priests and laymen had copies. This 'catechism' circulated in simple manuscripts, easily accessible to readers. In France alone, over eighty copies have survived, and, as its recent editor has pointed out, these represent only a fraction of the number of texts in circulation in the Middle Ages.[79]

Surely it was not the scholastic theologians who promoted this youthful work of Honorius, which at best reflected only certain trends of early scholasticism which became irrevocably obsolete in the following centuries. The tremendous success of the *Elucidarium* was due to the fact that it set out the fundamentals of dogma and the main points of sacred history, from the Creation to the Second Coming, in the easily understandable form of answers to an imaginary pupil's questions. This form (the set of questions), the simplicity of presentation and the picturesque examples made it easy to understand and memorize the catechism. Honorius' work reached an extremely wide audience and, as Jacques de Ghellinck (1948: 20) put it, 'long nourished the religious life of the multitude'.

A detailed survey of the genres and titles to be considered in the following chapters seemed useful because these works are not generally known even to students of medieval history. They are usually considered from literary points of view, such as the genesis and development of genre, the fate of classical and early Christian traditions and the transition from medieval to Renaissance literature. The function of these genres in medieval culture, and their interaction with their audience, are rarely if ever investigated. Such a study is the object of this book, which should bring us closer to an understanding of medieval popular culture. I hope to demonstrate that the study of this culture indeed requires a new angle and a new kind of inquiry.

To be sure, the project has severe limitations. The approach must be

an indirect one, since all our information on popular culture is filtered through the consciousness of the clergy. But then, we have no direct way of investigating the deep cultural layer.[80]

In undertaking this study, it is necessary to take into account the non-equivalency in terms of cognitive possibilities of the various levels of 'low' literature of the Latin Middle Ages. In the penitentials, the positions of father-confessor and parishioner are sharply separated and counterposed; the interrogator critically assesses the behaviour of the penitent. This 'adversary' situation is also characteristic of preaching: the priest intends to dissuade his listeners from sin; he is privy to the truth, which he instils in his flock. In these constellations, the popular mind stands before the author like a target. The position is reminiscent of the Christian missionary's among pagan savages.

The situation is different in hagiography, in stories about the Other World, and in the *exempla*. To be sure, even in these genres authors are most conscious of their moral–edificatory and didactic tasks. Nevertheless, not only do they attempt purposefully to find a common language with the audience, but it is also clear that this 'common language' is predetermined. They share with their audience ideas about the world, the supernatural and its miracles, the soul, time and space, and the unity of corporeal and ideal. In contrast to the preacher and the father-confessor, who confronts the magical practices of his parishioners, the reciter of stories about saints, miracles, heaven and hell affirms the set of ideas and beliefs present in the minds of his audience. In these works one often encounters invective against 'sceptics' who have dared to express doubt as to the veracity of miracles, who have not believed in the supernatural powers of the saints, or who have not wished to bow to relics. About half the stories about the miracles of St Benedict, for example, mention punishments meted out to those who mocked the saint, failed to observe his feast, or encroached on the land of his monastery. A man who expressed disrespect to St Emmeram had his tongue stuck to his palate, and a woman who, 'hoisting her skirt, showed the saint her posterior' was covered with terrible boils (Sumption 1976: 41).[81]

Apparently, even authors of the stature of Gregory the Great, Gregory of Tours or Bede held the same views as their popular audience as to miracles and the power of divine intervention. This was true not only at the beginning of the Middle Ages, but right to their very end. Jean Gerson, fifteenth-century chancellor of the University of Paris and a famous critic of vulgarized Christianity, indignant upon seeing a statuette of the Virgin Mary which opened up to reveal in her womb the Holy Trinity, was bothered by the dogmatic issue of representing all three hypostases of the Godhead, but did not even note the rather rude graphic and literal presentation of the sacred mysteries of Christianity (Sumption 1976: 45). For all their erudition, the authors of Latin edifying works to a large extent shared a common understanding of religion with their audience.

Let us test the hypothesis about the representative character of these works of edificatory medieval Latin literature by a 'thought experiment'. Soon after the conversion of the Icelandic people, translations began to be made from Latin into Old Norse. What were the titles selected by the clergy for this project? They were the *Dialogues* of Gregory the Great, several other lives of saints, the *Elucidarium* of Honorius of Autun and the *Vision of Tnugdal*. Priests engaged in the true conversion of the Scandinavians, who persisted in paganism after being baptized, were keen to acquire exactly that type of writings we have been studying. I believe we can trust the 'expertise' of the clergy in recognizing that these works expressed Christian doctrine in the form most accessible to the populace.

Returning, in conclusion, to the methodology for source analysis adopted in this study, I should emphasize the cardinal importance of the connection between author and audience. 'The event of the life of a text, that is, its authentic essence, always develops on the boundary of two consciousnesses'; it is a dialogue between addresser and addressee, and this relationship is reflected 'in the structure of the utterance itself' (Bakhtin 1976: 127, 145). This invisible presence of the listener, or the reader, in medieval Latin literature may indeed permit us to approach the *Weltanschauung* of the flock being addressed through works written by ecclesiastical authors.

> Every utterance [continues Bakhtin (1976: 149 – 50)] has an addressee (different in character, degree of proximity, concreteness, degree of realization, and so on), and the author of an oral work seeks and respects in advance its reciprocal understanding. But, in addition to this addressee (the second party), the author of an utterance more or less consciously presupposes a higher third person, a "superaddressee". An absolutely correct reciprocal understanding by that superaddressee, either in the metaphysical distance or in a remote historical time, is presupposed. Every dialogue takes place against the background of a reciprocal understanding with an invisibly present "third person" who stands above both participants in the dialogue.

In our documents the constant attention of a 'court of highest instance' as it were, is definitely implied; all utterances are orientated towards him. While the 'second person', the audience of believers, demanded a conscious adaptation – simplicity, graphic illustration, concreteness, and so on – the 'highest instance of reciprocal understanding' required that the authors follow the path of absolute truth and avoid any conscious fabrication. The 'poetic licence' of these ecclesiastical authors does not cover the contents: they see themselves as mouthpieces of collective consciousness and transmitters of information which has to be beyond any doubt authentic. The knowledge of the presence of a 'third Person' in and above the dialogue between pastor and flock constituted a strong bond between addresser and addressee.

The distinct style, content, purpose and function of our sources prescribe that they be studied separately. Each genre had its own features, which have to be taken into consideration.[82] The penitentials, catechisms, lives of saints, *exempla*, or otherworldly wanderings reflect in their specific ways separate segments of the spiritual life of the Middle Ages. Yet the following chapters are not meant to be isolated essays, but successive stages of a single movement of thought bringing us closer to a solution of the paradox of medieval culture I have spoken of before. By gradually rotating the investigative prism, we may succeed, if not in solving this problem, then at least in formulating it in a new way.

This chapter's treatment of the immobility of medieval Latin didactic literature is in contrast to the completely different interpretation given by D. Harmening (1979), who draws textual connections between medieval texts, particularly the penitentials, and their predecessors, especially the works of Caesarius of Arles. Moreover, he asserts that later authors simply copied Caesarius' sermons, irrespective of the social reality surrounding them. Therefore, writes Harmening, the greater part of medieval sources concerning superstitions have a purely traditional–literary character and in no way reflect reality.

I have serious doubts about such categorical assertions. If one accepts them, how is one to explain medieval theologians and writers expending so much time and energy on copying texts without any correspondence to their own experience? Harmening includes among these detached copyists such an active ecclesiastical and political figure as Burchard of Worms, as if he too were completely dependent on Caesarius of Arles. But how can this be the case with the many sections of his penitential which offer entire ethnographic sketches of contemporary popular superstitions and not a monotonous repetition of ancient texts? The composition of his penitential was an integral part of Burchard's general attempts at reorganizing the Worms diocese; it pursued practical goals.

The traditionalism of medieval ecclesiastical literature is well known, but one must be prepared to see, beyond the stereotypes and citations, the expression of the actual needs which dictated appealing to ancient authorities. That Halilgar of Cambrai, for example, merely compiled 'his' penitential does not reduce its value, for the choice of traditional passages is significant in itself (Kottje 1980: 253f). The authors of penitentials were actively concerned with eradicating superstitions and non-Christian customs among their parishioners; their works were practical guides and not exercises of abstract learning devoid of any connection with the time when they were composed. Repetitions in them should rather be regarded as evidence of the stability of the vital phenomena which they interpret. Furthermore, Harmening does not take into account that other works, in which such textual links are not established, also speak about specific particularities of popular religiosity. If he had examined the fourteenth and fifteenth centuries, he would have found in the most diverse sources indications of the ineradicable vitality of precisely those customs and magical practices met in the earlier medieval period. Therefore, we are not dealing with the simple copying of texts, but with the preservation in peasant culture of traditional mentality.

To study the relationship of medieval oral and literate cultures I draw upon two reports of otherworldly visions which can be qualified as 'peasant'. One belongs to the Holstein peasant Gottschalk and is dated to 1189, and the other to the peasant Thurkill of Essex, who had his vision in 1206. There is no doubt of the influence of folklore in the first vision. In the Other World Gottschalk saw a tree on whose branches grew boots for the souls of the departed, since they must cross a field strewn with terrible thorns. Then he came to a stream in which sharp weapons were floating, and only those souls who climbed on to rafts could escape mutilation. Finally, he came to a crossroads with three paths to which an angel was directing souls. After reanimation Gottschalk's preoccupation with earthly matters and relations with his neighbours became clear; this even prevented him from paying sufficient attention to his vision, for which he was reproached by the priest who wrote down his narrative. All those whom Gottschalk met in the Other World were acquaintances from Holstein; they were placed 'there' owing to their belonging to the parish 'here' (Lammers 1982).

Thurkill's story sheds light on how the spontaneous vision was fixed and formed. At first, Thurkill could speak of the vision only 'in fragments, recalling this or that episode and omitting and passing over much in silence'. Then, after talking with the parish priest, who probably gave him the necessary directions, Thurkill's story acquired coherence and fullness. It was this finished, 'redacted' form that Thurkill repeated to his fellow-parishioners and lord, and in the monasteries to which he was invited; it was this version that was written down. In this way, the vision passed through a sort of ecclesiastical censorship and was brought into accord with received tradition. Thus, the vision as a fact of popular culture could not be fixed; it had to be included within ecclesiastical tradition. Only in a certain symbiosis with learned tradition could medieval popular tradition exist (Gurevich 1984a).

2

PEASANTS AND SAINTS

When St Martin was close to death the inhabitants of Poitiers and Tours gathered at Candes to be present at his blessed demise. Immediately after his death a 'great altercation' broke out between them, the inhabitants of Poitiers saying to the men of Tours: 'This monk is ours; among us was he made an abbot. We demand his return. It is sufficient for you that, while he was a bishop in this world, you heard his discourses, you dined with him, you were strengthened by his blessings, and above all you were filled with joy by his miracles. Be satisfied with all this, and let us receive his dead body.' The men of Tours retorted: 'You say that his miracles are sufficient for us, but know this: he worked more of them for you than he did here. For, leaving a good deal by the side, recall that among you he raised two dead men, but only one for us. And as he himself said on more than one occasion, his miraculous power was greater before he became bishop than it was afterward. This means that what he did not accomplish for us while alive he should effect posthumously. God took him from you and gave him to us...'

They quarrelled thus until nightfall. Then they locked the church in which Martin's body lay and both groups set a guard. The inhabitants of Poitiers could have taken the body by force in the morning, but 'almighty God would not permit Tours to be deprived of its patron'. At midnight the men of Poitiers were overcome by sleep, and the men of Tours took Martin's mortal remains out through a window, placed them on a boat, and rowed off towards Tours. The men of Poitiers were awakened by the hymns and psalms of their departing rivals, and in great embarrassment they returned home, 'without acquiring the treasure which they were guarding'.[1]

Gregory of Tours's story hardly requires comment, for it presents an understanding of the saint as a miracle-worker, whose deeds are totted up along with 'missing' miracles, with exceptional directness and clarity. It is perhaps worth mentioning again that Gregory both here and in other places of the *History*, as well as in his remaining works, does not distance himself from such a naively 'consumers' ' attitude towards the saint: namely, that the saint is the property of the inhabitants of the particular locality where his relics repose. Gregory's sympathies lie on the side of Tours, since Martin was after all the patron of the diocese of which Gregory was now the head, and he shares the opinion of his fellow-citizens that the saint is obliged to work miracles, and in full.

Another such story is preserved in Gregory's works. In the *Lives of the Fathers* he narrates the death of St Lupicinus. But this time the competition for the saint's relics flared up between the inhabitants of the locality where he died and a matron from another neighbourhood. To substantiate her claims the woman recalled that she had repeatedly provided the saint with wheat and barley for him to eat and give to others. Her opponents responded: 'This man belongs to our people. He drew water from our river, and our land transferred him to heaven.' After these wranglings the local inhabitants buried the saint, but as soon as they were gone the matron abducted the body and ordered it carried to her property on a litter. Only then did her adversaries repent that they had opposed her demand. Recognizing God's will in her actions, they requested permission to take part in the saint's burial. However, Gregory adds, Lupicinus subsequently worked many miracles in both places.[2]

The fact that while alive the saint received gifts was itself already a reason for requiring miracles from him in return. The principle of 'a gift ought to be rewarded' was one of the basic principles of social relations in barbarian and early feudal society, and it also extended to relations between laymen and saints. Therefore, offerings were gladly brought to the churches and monasteries of saints who worked miracles. If no healings and other miracles took place, no gifts were brought.

Another basis of claims for his miracle-working relics was the saint's contact with the faithful while alive. Living and performing his feats in a given locality, the saint accordingly belonged to its inhabitants and could not part with them after death. The faithful and the saint formed a single association within the limits of which blessings, prayers, miracles and gifts circulated. This association was considered indissoluble, and neither the saint's worshippers nor the saint himself had the right to break off contact unilaterally. As a result, it is not surprising that the Frankish king Chilperic ordered that a letter be placed on St Martin's grave requesting a written answer on whether Chilperic could remove his enemy from a church dedicated to Martin. The deacon who delivered the king's letter to the saint's tomb placed a blank piece of parchment on it and waited three days for an answer in vain.[3]

In order to ensure a saint's 'services' for themselves people acquired his relics, and a lively traffic of these 'popular goods' throve in medieval Europe (Guiraud 1892). Both relics and objects connected with saints – shrouds, dust from their tombs, etc. – became objects of veneration. The traffic in relics was also accompanied by their theft: after the Crusaders sacked Constantinople in 1204 a flood of relics poured into Europe. It was believed that the theft of relics could only be successful with the saint's permission.

There were extreme instances when believers did not even stop at killing a saint in order to obtain his relics. Peter Damian tells how the mountain-dwellers of Umbria learned of St Romuald's intention to abandon them and move to another place. 'They were extremely alarmed and took counsel about how to prevent his intention', but found nothing better than to send murderers to him: '...if they could not keep him while he was alive, they would receive his lifeless body as the patron of their land'. The educated author of Romuald's life condemned this plan as 'impious piety' and 'mad stupidity'.[4] But piety of this sort, which seemed savage to the clergy, was obviously perceived by the common people as something natural and as expressing the essence of the ideal relations between the saint and his parishioners. The fact that the saint's body was reposing in their land served in the eyes of the local inhabitants as a guarantee of prosperity. From Damian's point of view there may not have been much piety in this, but it completely accorded with the popular interpretation of sanctity. One need only recall the legend of the glorious Scandinavian king whose body was posthumously cut into pieces and buried in different regions, so that the 'luck' and 'fortune' contained in them would remain their property. In a similar way St Romuald would have served as their patron forever if his worshippers had succeeded in carrying out their bloodthirsty, pious plan.

Parishioners considered the saint their own property. They boasted of his miracles and compared them favourably with the feats of 'foreign' saints. The ninth-century life of Bishop Rigobert of Reims tells how a woman suffering from fever tested saints: she decided to ask three saints for help, and to that end she lit three wax candles of equal length, one for St Theodoric, one for St Rigobert and one for St Theodulf, reckoning that the comparative power of the saints would be revealed by how long the candles burned. With the help of such an 'experiment' she wanted to learn, 'as this was the custom among the common people', to which of the saints she should offer her vow. The candle of the city's patron – St Rigobert – burned longer than the others, and so the woman prayed to him and received the desired result.[5]

The relations between the saint and the faithful were thought of in customary medieval categories of mutual fidelity and aid. The population was ready to venerate and preserve a saint in response to his patronage and healings. When men of the archbishop of Orleans came to St Martin's tomb in order to seize a fugitive who had sought refuge there, the local peasants armed themselves and came to their patron's defence: '...they would not bear their saint to be dishonoured' (Fichtenau 1949: 179).

The particularism of social life found full analogy in religious particularism, in the cult of local saints. One can speak of a 'force-field' within the bounds of which the sanctity of a saint was active. One anchorite was possessed by a demon and was delivered from torment only after he was brought to Tours, where the power of St Martin overwhelmed the demon. However, Martin's healing power was effective only so long as the monk remained in Tours. When he returned to his former abode he was possessed again.[6] Of course, the saint could also act beneficially away from his home, but it was precisely there that his miracle-working capabilities were most effective. The cult of local saints sometimes successfully competed with the cult of the Apostles themselves. An old woman living near Tours was cured of blindness, and although relics of Peter and Paul were preserved in the city, she asserted that her sight had been returned by the local patron, St Martin.[7] A man who had become deaf and dumb was on his way to Rome to implore the saints there for healing. But on the way, in Nice, he was healed by St Hospicius, and the deacon accompanying him exclaimed: 'I was seeking Peter, I was seeking Paul and Lawrence, and the other saints who glorified Rome with their blood. And here (i.e. in Nice) have I found them all, here have I seen them all!'[8]

Veneration of a saint often covered a definite area, and saints had regions of primary influence (Zender 1959). In the later medieval period the tendency towards the 'specialization' of saints intensified: to each of them a particular function was attributed (patronage of a certain trade, the ability to heal a particular illness). However, 'pluralization' was also admitted into this relationship. For example, St Gertrude, although the guide of the deceased's soul immediately after death, also protected against mice. At the same time, believers attempted to enlist the aid of as many heavenly defenders as possible by gathering them all into the altar of a single church or into one city. Cologne was distinguished by having a cult with 11,000 virgins, 6,666 soldiers of the Theban legion, and 10,000 knights – in all the inhabitants of Cologne could count on 27,666 intercessors before God!

Just as a locality was under the patronage of a definite saint, so also the individual saw a patron in the saint whose name he had been given in baptism. A name was not a neutral designation; in a mysterious way it affected a man's essence, and a definite connection was established between the heavenly eponym and his mortal namesake. A Bonn canon's disrespect towards John the Baptist had the most lamentable consequences, and in telling of them Caesarius of Heisterbach indicates directly that the saint was particularly angered by the fact that his namesake dared to offend him.[9]

The cult of the saints was an integral part of medieval religious life.

The saints' role was all the greater in that the notion of a miracle-working patron, to whom one could turn for aid and whose relics were located nearby in a church or cathedral, found a much easier path to the consciousness of the common people than did the idea of a distant, invisible, and awe-inspiring God. Attitudes towards God lacked that 'intimacy' and 'sincerity' which united the faithful with the local saint.

The saint's image was a result of the interaction of different tendencies. In him the ideals of Christian humility preached by the church were embodied. Devotion to Christ, renunciation of earthly pleasures, mortification of the flesh, complete concentration on saving the soul and serving God – these motifs were the commonplaces of hagiography. Their ubiquitous presence in hagiography aids the scholar in judging the direction of the audience's interests, for it was precisely in such commonplaces and in the constant repetition of the same motifs that certain fundamental social values were confirmed. Even if the ideal of a holy life was unattainable by the overwhelming majority of believers, the presence of this ideal in the context of the culture was in itself an important fact of religious education. The saint was the most popular hero of medieval society; his feat was the highest feat that could be accomplished on earth. That this feat was manifested in rejecting this world and serving the other bears witness to the depth of the reorientation of social consciousness in the Middle Ages, as compared with the barbarian age with its heroes and the ancient age with its cult of the body and civic virtues.

At the same time saints were supposed to respond to the universal and compelling need for miracles. The saint, always and invariably, was a miracle-worker and healer capable of delivering his worshippers from natural and social misfortunes. Various members of the clergy (for example Agobard of Lyons, Claudius of Turin) from time to time spoke out against what they considered to be the excessive spread of the cult of saints and the veneration of relics, seeing in them a rebirth of pagan idolatry, but these appeals had no serious effect. Despite repeated declarations that the age of miracles was long past, the masses required miracles, demanded them, and were convinced that they composed an essential side of life. After the death of the bishop Illidius many people muttered: 'He is not a saint, since after all he only worked a single miracle.' But, Gregory of Tours adds, immediately new miracles followed.[10] Gregory himself kept strict account of the miracles he described, clearly attempting to collect as much evidence as possible about St Martin's sanctity.[11]

However much the clergy reiterated that the main thing in a saint was his rejection of the world, his contact with higher powers, his asceticism, his moral perfection and purity and his 'imitation of Christ', their parishioners required miracles. The sanctity of John the Baptist himself, whom the church placed first among all the saints, was doubted by the common people, since nothing was known of any miracles performed by him. Not only the saint's relics, whole or in pieces, were supposed to possess magical power, but also his personal effects, tears, saliva, even dust from his tomb – everything that had any connection with him whatsoever. The saint's speech also had enormous power. It was authoritative over people and demons;[12] animals and inanimate material also obeyed him. In hagiography there are many episodes in which birds and wild animals repent before saints of having committed some offence. One saint compelled a bear that had devoured his donkey to carry out the work of his victim, and, submitting to the saint's will, the bear went into the harness himself.[13] St Goar asked an illegitimate three-day-old infant for the name of his father, and the baby named the bishop Rusticus. Rusticus confessed and was removed from his position, and Goar became Trier's bishop.[14] We will see further that the dead were also obedient to the saint's authority.

In fact, the cult of the saints had much in common with paganism. How strong was the conviction that the saint could defend even an unrighteous and heinous sinner is visible from the Irish *Life of St Mochemock*. Count Engussa committed a murder, and the abbot Mochemock was on the verge of cursing him, when the count answered that he had no fear of damnation, since he had been blessed by St Cumin. The count evidently interpreted the saint's blessing as a sort of defensive incantation or amulet acting irrespective of the internal state of the possessor. Nevertheless, the abbot uttered his damnation and killed the count's daughter and war-horse. Only after this did the terrified count agree to repent, and Mochemock returned his daughter and horse to life (Hertling 1931: 283–4). It has been pointed out that themes from folk-tale and themes from hagiography were unconsciously mixed, and pagan motifs were assimilated into Irish saints' lives, forming an odd fusion (Bieler 1975: 14ff.). But this was not an Irish speciality.

The contemporaries of Gregory of Tours often did not distinguish between pagan auguries and witchcraft on the one hand and the veneration of saints on the other. A Frankish count sent by the king to murder a disgraced courtier availed himself of auguries, 'as is customary among the barbarians', to learn whether he would be successful in the undertaking. But, since it lay before him to use deceptive promises to extract the courtier from the church in which he had sought refuge (the king had ordered that the church should not be defiled), he also attempted to find out whether St Martin's miraculous power had recently manifested itself against perjurers[15] Auguries could also be made with sacred texts, and these were considered true by Gregory of Tours, in contrast to the forecasts of soothsayers.[16] The use of saints' relics sometimes calls to mind the use of pagan talismans. One Syrian merchant retained in his household a relic of St Sergius: a finger that had formerly helped an Eastern ruler put an enemy army to flight when worn on his arm. Naturally, King Gundovald wanted to acquire this relic, which had already saved the merchant's home in Bordeaux from a fire. The patrician Mummolus went to the Syrian, found a small box with the saint's finger, and cut it into several pieces. 'I do not think', notes Gregory of Tours, 'that the holy martyr was pleased by their treatment of him.' Mummolus and the Syrian divided the relics, and the patrician carried away a part of the saint's finger, but, adds Gregory, 'without the martyr's blessing'.[17]

The cult of relics was born in the East, but with the beginning of the Middle Ages it acquired enormous popularity in the West. Even though some clerical authors disapproved of the veneration of relics and considered it idolatry, in practice the church encouraged it. On the one hand, the church did not have the power to oppose its quiet dissemination, and, on the other, it used it in its own ideological and material interests (Hermann-Mascard 1975). According to one modern historian, the cult of the saints was imposed on the church by common believers, and popular influence determined the clergy's attitude towards miracles (Sumption 1976: 43, 53ff.).

Thus, the society depicted in hagiography consisted of people and saints. The people were in close contact and mutual interaction with the saints, and the saints actively participated in and influenced human life and guarded their own interests. Delivery from storms, fires and drought, healing of the sick and exorcism of the possessed, safety for those in shipwrecks, the prevention of enemy attacks, the exposure of liars, etc. – this was the routine practice of the saint, the people's protector and defender. Saints offer help in laborious tasks; this miraculous capability was a sort of compensation for the poor state of technology in early-medieval society. When, for example, a church of St Lawrence was being repaired, one beam turned out to be shorter than necessary. The priest prayed to the saint for help, and immediately everybody saw the beam grow out to the required length.[18] Some monks occupied with clearing waste land could not move a rock in their way, even with the aid of half a dozen oxen. But through the power of a prayer of blessed Nonnos the rock was removed.[19] Saints gladly chased out annoying flies and exterminated serpents and other unclean beasts. Repeating the miracles of the Gospels, they filled up stocks of wine, bread and other provisions – these motifs passed from one biography to another.

Worshippers did not only pray to their saint and bring him gifts; they also considered that these acts gave them the right to make demands on him in those instances when he himself apparently had not surmised the sort of help they were expecting. A pious poor man came to the church of St Julian on the saint's feast-day, leaving his horse nearby. The horse disappeared and could not be found. Returning to the church, the man reproached the saint: he had done nothing wrong to him and had brought him gifts. 'But why, I ask you, have I lost my property? I implore you to return what is lost and restore what I need.' With these words and in tears the man went outside and there saw his horse.[20]

Believers would pray to the saint for aid, but in certain situations they resorted to violence. In the tenth and eleventh centuries a particular ritual was practised, 'the humiliation of saints'. Suffering oppression from a powerful neighbour and unable to secure protection from secular authorities, monks would gather in the church, bring out the saint's relics from the altar, and set them on the floor; there they would place a crucifix; the saint's grave would be sprinkled with thorns; the monks themselves would lie prostrate during the liturgy, which was conducted 'in an undertone' and was accompanied by ritual damnations of peace-breakers. This ceremony, inverting the normal course of the liturgy and visually 'lowering' the saint, was supposed to demonstrate the abuse which the saint's monastery was suffering at the hands of an unrighteous layman.

But there was also another element present in this ritual: the relics of saints who seemed lax in their monasteries' protection were consciously subjected to humiliation in order to rouse them to action. While the saint's humiliation by the monks was mainly symbolic, laymen did not shrink from violence. They would attack the altar holding the relics and appeal loudly to the saint for protection, accusing him of negligence: 'Why are you not defending us, holy lord? Have you forgotten about us and sleep? When will you deliver your servants from our enemy?' (*Miracles of St Calais*). The *Miracles of St Benedict of Fleury* mention a story of peasants working on monastery land who cried out while beating the saint's altar: 'What have you done, Benedict, are you some kind of lazybones? Do you sleep all the time? How could you permit this to happen to your servant?' The ritual of the 'humiliation of the saint' clearly suggests two systems of culture, learned and popular, each of which had its own symbolism and traditions (Little 1979: 54–8; Geary 1979: 34–9).

Saints, for their part, demanded attention and veneration. Numerous hagiographical accounts record that saints whose graves were unknown revealed their location and actively assisted in the discovery and translation of their relics into the church they had selected.[21] Saints were quick to take offence and were frequently vindictive.[22] A knight whose broken arm was healed by St James forgot to visit the saint in Reading, whereupon the saint punished him by breaking his other arm (Sumption 1976: 140). A peasant avoided a liturgy in honour of St Avitus and continued to till his vineyard with the excuse that the saint himself had been a toiler. Immediately his neck was broken, and only after earnest prayers did he merit the angry saint's forgiveness and healing.[23] Gregory of Tours tells of the ruin of a peasant by a fire provoked by his doubt in the sanctity of the anchorite Marianus.[24] St Leutfred punished an impious steward for disrespect of his name. When the abbot, admonishing this steward and asking him to be more gentle with the servants, mentioned the name of Leutfred, the steward exclaimed, 'You called on Leutfred? Who is this Leutfred? My father had a swine-herd who was also named Leutfred' Soon thereafter he received a blow from a monk who appeared to him in a dream.[25] I shall have more to say later on the vengefulness and cruelty of saints in medieval Latin literature.[26]

Saints did not put up with unpleasant neighbours. The coffin of a criminal who had desired to be buried in the church of St Vincent was one night tossed out of the window by force. The man's relatives did not comprehend the miracle's meaning and re-installed his coffin in the church, but once again it was turned out.[27] This story was told in the sixth century. Now a story written at the turn of the fourteenth century tells how an impious and spendthrift bishop of Lubeck was buried next to his pious predecessor. One night the latter abandoned his grave and three times knocked on his neighbour's tomb. He called him out, and the impious bishop quickly appeared in all his vestments and with his crozier. The good bishop ordered him to leave the church and picked up and hurled a huge candlestick after him so that it stuck in the door. The canons found the candlestick there, which was seen by Rudolph of Schlettstadt as proof of the veracity of this miraculous and frightful occurrence.[28]

The saint zealously saw to the inviolability of his own property, namely the property of the church possessing his relics and dedicated to his name. King Pepin encroached on the possessions of Rheims, and in a dream St Remi appeared to him and said: 'What are you doing? By what right have you intruded into a villa that was given to me?' The saint beat the king soundly, so that bruises were visible on his body, and Pepin was forced to withdraw. St Remi was in general distinguished for touchiness and vindictiveness. When the inhabitants of a villa bestowed by the king on the saint refused to submit to him, Remi foretold eternal labour and poverty for them, and 'to this day his words remain in force'.[29]

One could continue with such examples at length. Despite their variations they exploit the same theme: saints know and guard their rights. Humility, self-denial and forgiveness were the basic Christian values constantly preached by the clergy and demonstrated in hagiography, but in some strange fashion they were not considered as contradicting the saints' anxieties about their possessions and about maintaining their prestige and authority. This contradictory blend of heaven and earth in the person of the saint will have to be explored through sources other than hagiography.

The folkloric roots of many of these scenes are obvious. In another episode connected with St Remi an argument flared up between him and a proprietor over a mill: the bishop claimed that they both should own it. Since his demands were not met, the 'mill's wheel immediately began to turn in the opposite direction'. This miracle produced the necessary impression, and the mill's owner yielded. But Remi angrily retorted: 'Neither mine, nor yours', whereupon a ditch opened up on the spot and the mill vanished.[30] The fact that the wheel turned in the opposite direction is especially striking, since inversions of every sort in medieval literature (movement against the sun's course, reading prayers backwards, kissing the anus, etc.) were invariably seen as the interference of evil. This was the way sorcerers, witches, heretics and even Satan himself behaved! Here, however, this inversion was evoked by a saint. The motif was almost certainly borrowed from folklore, but what is significant is its context, where it stands out by its discrepancy with the image of the saint. We cannot know, however, whether it was perceived as alien by the author himself and the medieval audience.

The theme of punishment for encroaching on a saint's property was subject to endless variation in hagiography for understandable reasons. One pagan tried to plunder the grave of the blessed Ilius of Lyons, but when he got into it, the saint seized him with his arms and would not let him go: thus people found him in the saint's embrace. He was about to be arrested and handed over for judgment, but the saint continued to hold him fast until they understood his will: the saint wanted the thief's life preserved. 'O holy vengeance mixed with mercy!' concludes Gregory of Tours.[31] King Childebert's encroachment on 'possessions' of the anchorite Metrius evoked the saint's vengeance: the king fell ill, grew bald (long hair was the distinguishing feature of the Merovingians), lost his beard, and came to look like a disinterred corpse. He finally repented, returned the villa to the saint, and placed a good sum of money on his grave.[32] Gregory writes about the martyr Vincent: '...he was a cruel avenger to those who encroached on his possessions'.[33] A deacon seized some sheep belonging to the church, although the shepherd told him that those animals were the property of the holy martyr Julian. The deacon replied: 'You don't think that Julian eats mutton, do you?' 'The wretch did not understand', notes Gregory, 'that those who take property from the homes of saints cause injustice to the saints themselves...' The deacon was taken ill; the saint burned him, so that when he was sprinkled with water smoke rose from his body as from an oven; he became blackened from the heat consuming him and emitted an unbearable stench, finally dying.[34] The tortures of the sick deacon were meant to indicate that although his visible body remained on earth, in fact he was already burning in hellfire.

Saints in need of proving the legality of their rights thought nothing of producing witnesses even from the other world. So it happened during a suit between the abbot St Fridolinus and a landowner who disputed his rights to a property given to the monastery by his (the landowner's) late brother. Seeing that he would not be vindicated in court, Fridolinus ordered the grave of the former owner opened and invited him to come forth. Appearing at the landgrave's court, the dead man said to his brother: 'Why, brother, are you ruining my soul by taking away the property which belonged to me?' The terrified defendant hastened to return to the saint all the land, including his own part, and the dead man returned to the grave.[35] Having told of the punishment suffered by King Charibert for encroaching on church properties, Gregory of Tours exclaims: 'Know about this, all you who possess authority; recompense thus, so that you do not plunder others; round off your own riches thus, so that you do not cause injury to churches. The Lord is a cruel avenger of his servants.'[36] Of course, in all these stories the hand of the monk or cleric representing the interests of his monastery or church is obvious. Gifts were made to the church to obtain the salvation of the donor's soul or of that of a kinsman. A saint's life served as, among other things, a legal document certifying the property rights of his or her church. Reading the life in the presence of the faithful had very practical significance. Gregory of Tours writes: 'It is the custom of peasants to venerate more zealously those of God's saints whose feats are read to them'. Thus only one small chapel was dedicated to the martyr Patroclus, and the local inhabitants expressed little veneration toward him, since they were uninformed about his sufferings; but after the text of his life was found, the cult of Patroclus became more popular and a new church was built in his memory.[37]

The saint himself was clearly modelled on a human image and likeness, endowed with human emotions, passions, interests and reactions – nothing human was foreign to him. Yet his attractiveness for the mass of parishioners was based above all on the fusion in him of sanctity and thaumaturgy. These people venerated power – supernatural power capable of defending its own interests and protecting its clients. Besides biblical and patristic traditions one can also trace popular fantasy and folk-tale motifs in the formation of the *vitae*. Their structure, the selection of the facts in them, and the suitable volume of information were subject to the laws of collective consciousness. Despite the fact that the hagiographer was invariably a cleric, the character of his work clearly betrays the features of a popular culture. Hagiographical texts embodied, according to one of their most knowledgeable students, 'the memory of the crowd' (Delehaye 1921: 438).

Collective memory selected few and simple facts, grouping them in conformity with the course of epic narrative and attributing all the historical events to one hero. It retained primarily those events which could engage people reared on myth, epos, folk-tale; it easily fused together different heroes, particularly bearers of the same name. The popular mind was careless in regard to chronology and topography, effortlessly transferring events from one age to another and from place to place. In these texts emotion dominated over reason. Lack of receptivity to abstraction, a tendency towards its visual materialization and love of the supernatural, perceived as miraculous – these were the characteristic features of popular culture as revealed in hagiography. The fact that the subjects, events and characters of the *vitae* were not fully identified bothered neither the author nor his audience. 'The legend of the saint', writes Delehaye, 'is property without an individual owner' (1906: 118). The image of the Christian saint was not directly connected with the image of a pagan god, as some scholars suggest (e.g. Saintyves 1907), but, in Delehaye's opinion, both were the result of an identical state of mind (1906: 189ff).

Hagiographers had to consider the fact that their listeners preserved a vital connection with ancient epic and heroic poetry saturated with ideals opposed to those guiding the clergy.[38] Even monks had an interest in pagan poetry. Earlier I mentioned Alcuin's letter on Ingeld and Christ. According to the *Quedlinburg Chronicle*, German peasants in the late tenth century sang songs about Dietrich von Bern, that is, heroic songs about Theodoric.[39] In the *Life of St Liudger* there is mention of a singer Bernlef, who was very popular among the Frisians owing to his songs about exploits and wars of kings.[40] *Vulgaria carmina* about Frankish kings were current in Charlemagne's time.[41]

The unusual vitality of old heroic ideals is also shown in works of Christian poetry in Germanic languages. In the ninth-century Saxon poem *Heliand*, which narrates Christ's life and passion, the meaning and style of the Gospel narrative are essentially reworked. Christ figures as a warlike king heading a retinue of Apostles. The struggle between the forces of good and evil appears not as a conflict of two principles, but as an armed battle. The 'Lamb of God' is transformed into a 'glorious chief', who dispenses not blessings, but lavish gifts. Belief in the Saviour is interpreted as fidelity of retainers. The Saviour does not save from evil (in the sacramental sense), but protects his followers against the devil, just as he delivers them from hunger. Satan in the poem is the incarnation of infidelity, and Judas is the transgressor of oaths. Christ's words addressed to the Apostles ('One of you will betray me') are thus 'translated' in the *Heliand*: 'One of you twelve will violate his fidelity to me and hand me over to his princes, proud lords'.

Such is a Saxon's reading of the Gospel. The *Heliand*'s author was evidently a cleric, and therefore a man who must have known the genuine contents of the Gospel. In any case, one would expect from a priest a conscientious attitude towards retelling the Bible, and it is difficult to suspect him of intentionally distorting the Saviour's story. The transformation of the Gospel into a Saxon epic signified a transition from one system of thought into another. Voluntarily or involuntarily, the translator adapted the text to the understanding of the people for whom he created it. As a result, the 'good news' lost its extreme spiritualization as it drew near in meaning to Germanic heroic songs.[42]

These are the ideals, ethical aims and aesthetic models that continued to live in the environment in which hagiographers worked. It is necessary to recall this in order to understand correctly the reception of hagiography by a wide popular audience in the early Middle Ages. Clerics wanted to oppose to the warlike king, the fearless hero and the faithful retainer the saint, who embodied other, directly opposite standards of conduct. They had a difficult task. On which aspects of sanctity should they focus their audience's attention?

Some help is given by one of the notable representatives of Frankish hagiography, by an important ecclesiastical and political figure of the Carolingian period: namely, the *Life of St Remi*, written in 878 by Hincmar of Rheims to replace the short description of Remi's feats by Gregory of Tours.[43] St Remi was regarded as the 'Apostle of the Franks', by virtue of having converted Clovis, and was one of the most venerated saints in the Western Frankish realm. Hincmar's work is tendentious; the information it contains on the political conditions in sixth-century Gaul is unreliable, and scholars have long rejected this life as a defective historical source. However, from the point of view of factual reliability very few hagiographical texts bear critical examination. But if we see in them monuments of culture reflecting the spiritual life of the environment which generated them and for which they were created, our assessment will be completely different.

Hincmar knew his audience very well indeed. In the preface to the life he recommends that it should be read to the people on the feast of St Remi and that different parts should be used for different audiences. The passages intended to be read to the *populus*, 'so that like candles they will illumine the ignorant', are marked off; 'but for those who by God's mercy are illuminated' other sections, omitted in reading to the *simplices*, are indicated. Actually in the manuscript each chapter was marked by signs which permit one to distinguish easily the lessons for *minus scientes* and those for *illuminati*.

These differences are very instructive. The common people were to hear about miracles, healings, assistance and other manifestations of saintliness. St Remi's unusual moral qualities are emphasized and extolled. The manner of exposition is simple, in places crude. For example, there is a story about the exorcism of a demon through vomiting evoked by Remi's intervention. The author – head of the diocese of St Remi – is concerned in these sections with the acquisition of villas and land-holdings by the church during Remigius' life and with enumerating the peasant's obligations, accompanying this information with exhortations about the necessity of labouring for the benefit of 'God's people'.

The chapters to be read to the 'educated' have a different character. Only in these parts of the work are there abstract discussions and references to the Bible; the author repeatedly compares characters in the life with biblical personages. In these sections he discusses the sacramental nature of sin, God's creation *ex nihilo*, free will, and other matters which were clearly considered inaccessible to common minds. Sometimes the same subject is differently treated in the two sets of chapters. Thus, where in the story of Clovis' baptism, a dove appears in the church, the chapter intended for the educated adds a symbolic interpretation and a commentary on spiritual and material baptism. In the same way the popular story about the saint's punishment of heretics and the recalcitrant is accompanied 'for the advanced in faith' by an analysis of the spiritual meaning of penitence. As is customary in hagiography, Hincmar describes in detail the miracles performed after the saint's death. In particular, he narrates the magical effect of dust taken from the church of Remi's burial, and then in the discussion for the educated there follows an interpretation of the higher meaning of these miracles.

Here we have two clearly separated versions of the same life. Recall my earlier comparison of Gregory of Tours's account of the theological disputes of Catholics and heretics in the *History* with the description in the *Books of Miracles* of a competition between Catholic and Arian priests settled by an ordeal of boiling water. In another instance Gregory resorts to more visual evidence of the supremacy of Catholicism over Arianism. Two priests, a Catholic and an Arian, were invited to a home; the Arian was determined to deride the Catholic, but immediately after having swallowed hot food, he died. Seeing this miracle, the host, a heretic, immediately converted to the true faith. Indeed, does one need weightier proof?[44]

In the 'popular' version of the Life of St Remi the accent is placed on two somewhat contradictory aspects of saintliness. First of all, the saint appears as an ideal Christian, the bearer of all moral virtues. (Ultimately the saint's life in one way or another was always an 'imitation of Christ'.) However, Remi has several other features, such as touchiness and vindictiveness. It remains unclear, however, whether the medieval audience realized this contradiction.

An even greater impression on the masses was to be produced by the visual and active manifestation of the saint's holiness: his ability to work miracles. In this regard the *Life of St Remi* is absolutely typical of the genre as a whole: saints invariably appeared as magicians and healers. Miracles, naturally, received a Christian colouring in hagiography: the saint was capable of healing and otherwise helping people with God's help. It is completely clear from the lives that in the person of the saint the people venerated a nimbus-crowned magician filled with goodness and compassion. Such a figure was all the more intelligible to the people; this belief completely responded to their own magical ideas and customs. In the *Ecclesiastical History* Bede reports that, during his first meeting with Augustine, King Ethelbert did not hide his fear that the monks might resort to harmful magic: the preachers of Christianity were taken for sorcerers.[45]

The enormous corpus of hagiography depicts every manner of miracle worked by saints. Such traditions and motifs were much older than Christianity itself (Loomis 1948), but when they were included in the hagiographic system they acquired new meaning. Pagan sorcerers and magicians worked miracles owing to their proximity to natural forces, spirits and idols. The powers behind the saint's miracle were different. In worshipping the saint, people were taught to revere those higher powers and essences, although their notion of the Trinity was fairly primitive. The image of the saint opposed the surrounding world of greed, violence and tyranny, and offered a moral counterbalance. The might of the saint, his authority surpassing the authority of any earthly power, his function as protector of the weak and unfortunate – all this commanded the common man's respect to the highest degree.

Hagiography offered a distinct pattern of interpretation according to a set model. The saint starts by isolating himself from his or her peer group and rejects its norms. However, when his exclusiveness, that is his saintliness, is fully revealed, it begins to exert influence on the social environment from which he has withdrawn, and this in turn is reformed, grouping around the saint. This reunification of the saint with the collective can be expressed in various forms: the saint interrupts his retreat in order to instruct his brethren; he is selected by the bishop or abbot to lead the group; or he returns after death in the form of valuable relics, morally and physically influencing the congregation. The saint's behaviour, originally appearing as an anomaly, becomes the group's new ideal norm. The exception is transformed into the rule, and the connection of the saint with the social surroundings is restored. Thus, the saint is depicted in hagiography not only as a contrast to laymen, but also as an embodiment of their hope for achieving equal sanctity (Altman 1975: 4–8): the saint displayed to the parishioners another world and gave access to it by relativizing all the earthly values at which they grasped.

The hagiographic interpretation of miracles leads sometimes to a grotesque ambivalence. Bede reports the miraculous liberation from captivity of a wounded retainer named Imma. His enemies chained him, but each time the fetters fell off. His captor expressed the fear that Imma was using magical incantations or runes. But the real reason was that his brother, an abbot, thinking that Imma had died in battle, buried a corpse he thought was his brother's and began to say masses for the repose of his soul. Each time that he would begin prayer, the chains would fall off Imma.[46] This is one of the numerous miracle stories Bede uses to demonstrate the omnipotence of the church. In this instance prayers are said over the corpse of an unknown man, whereas Imma, who is unexpectedly and effectively helped by them, is alive. This miracle seems far from appearing as a manifestation of God's mercy: the abbot prays for the salvation of a deceased Imma, but his prayer acts as a magical incantation that disintegrates the fetters. It is symptomatic that even such an educated man as Bede admits this proximity between pious prayer and sorcery. This is not surprising, for in the Christian miracle traditions of popular sorcery were preserved, and both shared the same understanding of causality and the role of the supernatural.

The miracle was too effective a means of socio-psychological influence on believers for the church to disregard them; hence, the clergy attempted to direct the social need for the miraculous into the proper channels. While among the pagans sorcerers, shamans and other holy men practised magic, in the Christian context the miracle became the monopoly of the ecclesiastically approved saint. The supernatural came under the clergy's control. Saints were the necessary intercessors before a distant and abstract God, who was too far and foreign to minds geared to the close, to the visual and to sensible perception. 'For as a consequence of a poor capacity for love man in his imperfection feels greater love towards some saint than towards God', wrote Jacopo da Varagine in the *Golden Legend*.[47]

The problem of faith in the miraculous and of the so-called credulity of medieval people cannot be reduced to assuming deception of ignorant layfolk by clever monks, or medieval man's readiness to believe in anything. Of course, in the pursuit of propagandistic aims falsification and trickery cannot be excluded. Already in the early Middle Ages doubts were expressed as to the authenticity of certain miracles. But in what instances? Gregory of Tours, for example, accused the Arians of deception, but these accusations were dictated by his hostility towards heretics, and not by a scepticism about miracles as such: he believed in orthodox miracles and condemned those who questioned them. He tells of a peasant who doubted the saintliness of Marianus, whose feast-day he refused to celebrate, and who was punished by having all his property burned up. 'What will you do now, you crude man? You were always muttering against God and his friends, and look at the damage you have suffered as a result!'[48]

It has been argued that Guibert of Nogent stands rather alone in expressing critical thoughts about relics and their authenticity in his tractate *On the Relics of Saints*. However, A. Lefranc's comparison of Guibert with Calvin, Rabelais and Voltaire is completely groundless, for Guibert had no doubts about the cult of saints as such; he distrusted only distinct instances of veneration of relics and of what he saw as 'unreasonable' enthusiasm on the part of the common folk for false saints. Guibert was no philosophical sceptic, but he attached greater meaning to true faith, to internal spirituality, than to external worship of sacred objects (Morris 1972: 55–60).

Medieval men did not believe in everything indiscriminately, and there is no basis for suspecting that they were completely lacking in critical attitudes towards certain information. But the border between the likely and the unlikely did not lie where it does today. Confidence in the possibility of the miraculous was exceptionally strong, since it responded to a deep need of the human mind. Idea and reality were in a particular relation to each other: events had to be related to higher values and to correspond to them. Accordingly, only that which demonstrated a common idea was considered a genuine fact. The famous forgeries by clergy are a case in point. What the clerics who forged them thought is less important than that contemporaries believed in their authenticity – authenticity not in the scholarly sense, but in that of conforming with the proper order of things. Faith did not oppose fact, but embraced a circle sufficiently wide to include facts. Reconciliation of faith and reason, which exercised and tormented theologians, did not arise on the level of consciousness we are studying here.

Medieval man was not an isolated individual, facing the world on his own; he was a member of a group in which the moods, sentiments and traditions of his consciousness were rooted. It was primarily from collective beliefs and notions that he drew his convictions, including criteria for truth and falsehood. Truth was what the collective believed, and he did not contrast his own 'personal convictions' with the truth of the community. Moreover, belonging to the collective created in the individual the need to affirm those truths which were vitally important for that collective (Meyer 1936; Silvestre 1960; Schreiner 1966, 1966a; Gaiffier 1968; Gurevich 1972: 160ff.). Truth was not absolute; it was a collective value, conditioned by the aims and traditions of the group, and found its basis only in them.

Such social psychology offered fertile soil for faith in saints, relics and miracles. It is here that one should seek the reasons for the exceptional popularity of hagiography. If for the modern mind the stability of the same motifs in hagiography serves as a sign of inauthenticity, for medieval men the 'literariness' of these reports, built as they were on the models of the epos with their repetitions, was actually proof of their truth. For while we conceive historical events as momentary and unique, they imagined the world as invariable, and saw events as mere temporal accidents in its eternal substance, not challenging its ahistoric monotony. Truth manifested itself in the contiguity of both worlds, and properly only in those instances when through the transient phenomena of this world the other world shone through and genuine truths were revealed to the believer's gaze.

In the miracles close to the common people the 'social miracle' had a special place. Amongst the topics of early medieval hagiography the motif of the saint's help to paupers, widows, orphans and the socially humble and destitute played an important role. A very popular story was the tale of Peter the Publican, who saved himself by giving charity to a poor man. Particularly frequent in Carolingian hagiography was the theme of the saint's liberating captives, slaves and people condemned to death or imprisonment. In lives of this sort, clearly dear to the 'common man', one can see a contrast of characters: the merciful saint and the cruel judge. The authority figure does not appear in them as an 'unrighteous judge'; the justice of the verdict is usually not cast in doubt; but disapproval is provoked by the inflexibility of its administrator, lacking the blessed spirit of forgiveness with which the saint is filled. Thus, we should speak not of a contrast between secular injustice and higher Christian justice, but of a conflict between *potestas* and *caritas*. It is the compassion of the saint's unearthly goodness, and not the innocence of the one liberated, that is the core of the story (Graus 1961: 82ff., 154ff.). In other words, the saint's miraculous liberation of some unfortunate is only the manifestation of his boundless love, which embraces sinners and criminals, and is no more than a correlate of socio-political activity.

Even if a protector of the destitute, the saint was not an opponent of secular authority and not a fighter against oppression. He was higher than that authority in the sense in which the church is more righteous than the state and the City of God truer than the earthly city. The saint was not depicted as an opponent of slavery and oppression; their alleviation through his miraculous intervention was no more than a private occurrence. In a similar way, when a vicious king or lord was chastised, it was invariably as a concrete person; a person could be evil, but not an institution or an estate. Such for example, was the intervention of St Leutfred in defence of the monastery's tenants against a cruel steward,[49] or of St Servatius on behalf of some oppressed serfs (Hügli 1929: 35ff.). But all this does not denote an ethical opposition between the lower and the higher orders. According to the lives, the ideal conduct of a lord was mildness and compassion for his subjects, but its occasional violation was to be corrected by the oppressor himself or by the intervention of the saint; the common people were supposed to endure their adversities patiently. Lack of freedom and equality was a natural condition of the society in which the saint acted. It is taken for granted that saints have slaves and servants. St Gamalbert pacified his slaves, who were quarrelling amongst themselves, giving them some clothing or other gift; he spared them from the hardest work, but only that.[50] Compassion for the oppressed and poor and almsgiving – these were sufficient proofs of saintliness.

Furthermore, it is essential to note that early medieval saints came as a rule from noble backgrounds and were of high social standing. Exceptions to this rule are extremely rare.[51] According to several scholars, hagiography emphasized the tight mutual connection of sanctity and nobility (Bosl 1965: 167ff. Keller 1968: 313ff.). František Graus (1974: 146, 172ff.), however, doubts the existence of a specific type of 'noble saint'. He suggests that hagiographers were interested in sanctity, not in noble origins; the saint was supposed to be close to the people and to respond to their expectations. Thus, nobility of descent was to a certain extent replaced by the noble character of the holy man. One of the most widespread *topoi* of early medieval hagiography was that a saint was noble by birth, but more noble by religiosity ('natalibus nobilis, religione nobilior', 'natalibus nobilis, sed nobilior mente').

The basic triad of the structure of early medieval life – people, king, saint – was supplemented by a new element: 'nobility', with the latter gradually pushing the monarch into the background or completely excluding him. Hagiography reflected the intensified feudalization of social life. Already in Merovingian hagiography a pair of opposing concepts, *fidelis–perfidus*, was applied now in the sense of 'believer–unbeliever', now in the sense of 'loyal–disloyal'. This displacement of meaning, the extension of purely religious concepts to social bonds, was an important symptom of the reorganization of social consciousness. In the Carolingian period the term *fidelis* became a technical term in hagiography (Graus 1965: 359ff.). The ideology of feudal loyalty became an organic part of church literature, exerting influence through hagiography on wide layers of the people.

Thus, hagiography, in the formation of which folklore and collective consciousness played such a large role, became, with the feudalization of society, enmeshed in that society's dominant structure. The outcome of the fantasy of the masses was returned to them by monks and clerics in a socially and religiously filtered version.

The lives also suggest that saints did not always have harmonious relations with the people; they were frequently rejected and persecuted by both the powerful and the commoners. The hagiographers explained these clashes by charging the saints' opponents with ignorance or by aligning them with the devil. In conformity with the medieval inclination to attribute events to a hero, these conflicts were depicted as the saint joined in single combat with an individual opponent embodying evil. But a fact remains: representatives of the church, especially during the Christianization of the barbarians, ran into manifold opposition.

There are several examples. The population of Cologne attempted to kill St Gall for encroaching upon a pagan shrine.[52] In the *Life of St Remi* there is a story of a conflict between the saint and the inhabitants of a village called Celtus, 'which was always rebellious and unruly'.[53] The missionary St Amand was repeatedly attacked by the people; they beat him and tried to drown him, but he worked a miracle that roused the pagans to convert to the true faith.[54] When St Walaric ordered the cutting down of a tree worshipped by pagans, they attacked him with weapons, but their arms were frozen in mid-air as they aimed their blows.[55] The bishop Rusticus was killed by local inhabitants during 'great agitations' that seized Cahors.[56] Peasants living near Nantes mocked the anchorite Friard and his righteous way of life. As they were attacked by a swarm of wasps, they derisively said to the saint, 'Let the blessed one come, let the pious one come, who never stops praying and putting a cross to his ears and mouth...' The jokers were disgraced: Friard chased the evil insects away with a prayer.[57]

In narrating the clashes between the holy preacher and the ignorant pagan fools, hagiographers stressed that these conflicts were usually resolved in the saint's favour.[58] His miracles convinced the people of the veracity of the faith, or, at worst, his martyr's death served as the impetus for the conversion of unbelievers.

The reason, however, for clashes between the saint and the common people was not necessarily antagonism between Christianity and paganism. Such clashes could also appear among the already converted. There were also other factors that occasionally generated tension between the mass of believers and those who claimed to teach and lead them. The saint was, in one way or another, a representative of the church organization, frequently an abbot or bishop. The conflicts between the people and the church, inevitable during the feudalization of the latter, created the conditions for the appearance of another type of saint: non-orthodox and officially unrecognized saints, who nevertheless enjoyed influence among the people. Self-styled saints and prophets of this sort originated from the masses and expressed their aspirations and sentiments more directly and fully than the 'canonical' saint, who was bound by the limits of orthodoxy and the official cult.

'False prophets' of the early Middle Ages are only sporadically mentioned in the sources, but this does not mean that they were a rare phenomenon, even if they did not lead wide mass movements and did not leave a noticeable trace in history. In modern scholarship non-orthodox saints and prophets are, as a rule, mentioned in connection with other subjects, usually in general essays on church history. 'False saints' have attracted attention from scholars of medieval heresy, who see them as forerunners of the developed and powerful heresies of the high Middle Ages (Hauck 1922: 515ff.; Laux 1935; Schieffer 1954; Russell 1965; Cohn 1970: 41ff.) Such an approach is completely legitimate, but information about 'self-styled saints' of the Frankish period can also be put in another context, in that of their own age and of opposition to the growing official cult of saints.

Church recognition was required to guarantee that the sanctity of a martyr or holy man was beyond doubt. In a later period, from the end of the tenth century, the church introduced the process of canonization, inquiring into the evidence as to authenticity of martyrdom and saintliness. Heresy was the inevitable and constant companion–antipode of orthodoxy, which necessarily both caused and persecuted it. The antitheses 'God–Satan' and 'paradise–hell', which lay at the foundation of the medieval world-view, assumed the presence in society of the devil's servants. The social contradictions of the age presented fertile soil for movements that deviated from orthodoxy. The development of the church as an institution instigated and deepened certain contradictions between the ideal and actual practice; these contradictions encouraged the rise of heresy. People who proclaimed themselves saints, Christ's messengers, and prophets equal to the Apostles appeared throughout the Middle Ages.

However, non-orthodox prophets and saints did not always present their own teachings in opposition to church orthodoxy, though what is invariably present in the behaviour of these 'saints' and their followers is a 'resistance to church authority'. Therefore, the characterization of early anti-clerical movements as 'heretical' may not be entirely accurate; it may be more precise to qualify them as anti-authoritarian. Popular saints of the early medieval period often came from the lower strata of society and shared the unstable sentiments, mixed and confused beliefs, and dim searches for truth and justice, of the environment that generated them. The sources in which they figure are scattered; they belong to different regions of the Frankish realm (Gaul, Germany); and they are very different as to the wealth of information contained in them. One need hardly mention that all these sources are tendentious.[59]

In the ninth book of his *History* Gregory of Tours mentions a certain Desiderius, who maintained that he was capable of working every sort of miracle, and who boasted that he was connected to the Apostles Peter and Paul by messengers. At a time when Gregory was not in Tours this impostor attracted a multitude of common people. The blind and the sick were brought to him, and he cured them, not by his own saintliness, stresses Gregory, but by black magic. Desiderius' servants would straighten and stretch the doubled-up limbs of paralytics and cripples, and those who were not healed died. This wretch, continues Gregory, went so far as to place himself above St Martin and equal with the Apostles. But Gregory notes that there is nothing surprising in his claim to be equal to Apostles, since the instigator of all evil, the devil, will declare himself Christ at the end of the world. The fact that Desiderius resorted to black magic is clear from his astonishing ability to hear at a distance, which was possible only owing to the demons who transmitted what was said to him. Desiderius wore a tunic and wool cloak and in public abstained from eating and drinking, while in private he gorged himself so much that his servant could not give him enough dishes. Gregory's people, however, unmasked him and expelled him from the city. As we can see, Gregory, clearly troubled by the popularity of this newly-appeared 'saint', attempts to blacken him in every possible way and to cast doubt on his virtues. The main means of discrediting the objectionable saint is by declaring him to be the devil's servant, and also depicting him as a sorcerer and trickster.

In connection with Desiderius Gregory recalls another impostor, who appeared in Tours seven years earlier and by his guile drew many into temptation. His name was unknown. He was dressed in a sleeveless cloak and carried a cross with small vessels hanging from it, full, he said, of holy oil. He said that he came from Spain and brought relics of the holy martyrs Vincent and Felix. Bursting into the church of St Martin, he summoned Gregory to receive the relics, but the bishop indicated the late hour and responded that it could wait a while. Then the impostor came to Gregory's cell and rebuked him for the inhospitable reception, threatening to complain to King Chilperic. 'His speech was awkward, his expressions shocking and indecent; not a single reasonable word issued from his mouth'.

Unsuccessful in Tours, the self-styled saint went off to Paris. His appearance during a church festival in unusual clothing (imitation of an Apostle?), with a cross in his hand and at the head of a crowd of prostitutes and common women composing his 'choir', apparently confused the bishop of Paris. The latter invited him to take part in the holiday, but received insults in response. Then the bishop understood that before him was a trickster and 'seducer of the people', and he ordered him locked up in a cell. They found a large bag on him that was full of roots of all sorts, moles' teeth, mouse bones and bear fat. It became clear that all this was sorcerer's equipment, and the bishop ordered them thrown into the river. They also took away the impostor's cross, but he fashioned himself a new one and returned to his old ways. Finally, he had to be chained and tossed into prison.

At that time Gregory himself was in Paris and he witnessed these events. This 'miscreant' escaped from his guard and, without even removing his shackles, fell asleep drunk in the church of St Julian, right on the spot where Gregory was accustomed to pray. When at midnight Gregory came to pray, he was kept out of the church by the impostor's frightful stench, which surpassed all the sewers, gutters and latrines in odour. A priest holding his nose attempted to wake him, but the impostor was so drunk that he got nowhere. Then four clerics at Gregory's command dragged the indifferent body into a corner, washed down the polluted spot with water and sprinkled fragrant herbs over it, after which Gregory could say his prayers. When the impostor was finally roused, Gregory handed him over to the bishop of Paris on the condition that 'no sort of harm would come to him'. Soon thereafter the bishops gathered in Paris, and he was brought before them. The bishop of *Beorretanae* (Upper Pyrenees?) recognized him as his runaway servant. 'There are many such people', Gregory concludes, 'who do not stop at leading the ignorant people into error and seducing them'.[60]

Both false prophets are depicted by Gregory as sorcerers and servants of the devil. The incredible stench coming from the impostor – as from the false Christ in Sulpicius Severus (see above, n. 59) – is apparently also a symptom of his complicity with the powers of hell. Gregory is openly hostile to these 'sorcerers' and 'necromancers', and these 'apostles' do not conceal their hostility towards the church and its servants. Their falsity becomes patent by their lack of restraint in eating and drinking, for asceticism is a key sign of a true saint. But, even given all of Gregory's tendentiousness, we can hardly attribute to his fantasy the report of the presence on the Paris impostor of a bag full of roots, bones, claws and fat. Magical actions with the help of such remedies were highly popular not only at the time, but also for centuries after: the penitentials prohibited, upon pain of punishment, the use of roots, herbs, fat, and potions containing a mouse.[61]

Were not the saint and the sorcerer sometimes fused in the mind of the common people? To the majority of the population the difference between amulets, which were strictly forbidden by the clergy, and holy relics was not too clear. Why was it considered sinful to use potions, but recommended to toll the bells against a storm? Priests condemned the remedies used by soothsayers and sorcerers for healing the sick but agreed that dust from the altar or a pouch of earth taken from a saint's grave possessed healing properties. Magic was admitted by the church into its practices and rituals; the border dividing Christian magic from what was condemned as *maleficium* was indefinite and surely unclear to the parishioners.

Not in all instances did the church favour the sudden elimination of the opposition of idolatry to the Christian cult. Thus, Pope Gregory I advised Archbishop Mellitus of Canterbury to baptise the Anglo-Saxons gradually and not to attempt at once to break all their ties with paganism, counselling him in particular not to demolish the old shrines, but to destroy only the idols, to sprinkle the temples with holy water and place in them altars and relics. After all, it would be easier to convert pagans to the new faith in those 'sacred' places known to them. These people, the pope writes, have the custom of sacrificing to demons a large quantity of cattle, and one should give them something festive instead, permitting them to gather for religious feasts on saints' days. Let them not offer animals in sacrifice to the devil, but let them kill them for their own subsistence in honour of the Lord and thank him for everything. 'Since some external joys are preserved for them, it will be easier for them to perceive internal delights'. There is no doubt, continues Gregory, that it is impossible fully to cleanse crude minds straightaway, and that is why one must act gradually, just as the Lord revealed himself to his chosen people. 'Thus also with the hearts of people being liable to change: they should refrain from one part of the sacrifice, having preserved another, and even if these be the same animals that they had customarily immolated, however inasmuch as they come to sacrifice them to God, and not to idols, the same sacrifice will no longer be as the former.'[62]

In recommending that the psychology of the former pagans be taken into account and that open conflict between the two religions be avoided as much as possible, Gregory displayed a wise understanding of the complicated situation created by the conversion of pagans. He recognized that their perception of Christianity could not help including the vast stock of their traditional beliefs and notions. He was not worried that these beliefs and notions had fused in the minds of the new converts with a superficial and partially distorted assimilation of Christianity. As a result, an ambivalent and grotesque world-view appeared that was essentially different from that preached by church doctrine.

False prophets were particularly frequent in difficult times, when hunger, devastation and anarchy prevailed. The Merovingian period, to judge from Gregory of Tours's works, was filled with every sort of calamity. Frequent bad harvests were accompanied by impoverishment and massive mortality; civil wars and devastating enemy raids brought in their wake plundering, fires, tribute payments and captivity; epidemics of infectious diseases frequently flared up in different parts of the country; cruel rulers used every means to oppress the common people and to eliminate dissenters; there was widespread amorality, undoubtedly connected with the political instability of the period after the fall of the Roman Empire and with the deep psychological crisis brought on by the conversion of the barbarians. This was fertile soil for discontent.

Gregory evidently saw a connection between these conditions and the people's readiness to believe in self-styled saints. As a preface to a story of one such pseudo-Christ he reports an epidemic in Provence and a famine in the regions of Angers, Nantes and Le Mans. ' "These are the beginning of sorrows", as the Lord said in the Gospel, "and there shall be famines, and pestilences, and earthquakes, in divers places"; "for false Christs and false prophets shall rise, and shall shew signs and wonders, to seduce, if it were possible, even the elect". And all this has come to pass in our time.'[63] After this discussion Gregory turns to a story about a self-styled saint, and the reader is supposed to get the impression that the people's reception of the new false saint was not simply prepared by natural disasters: it was foretold by Christ and is a symptom of the approaching end of the world.

An inhabitant of the region of Bourges, reports Gregory, went once into the forest to chop firewood and was attacked by a swarm of flies, so that he was mad for two years. It is clear to Gregory that 'all this was concocted by the devil'. Then the man wandered around neighbouring towns and came to Provence. Dressed in a bearskin, he preached 'as if he were a holy man'. The 'enemy' who had seduced him (that is, the devil) gave him the ability to prophesy. In the area of Poitiers he exalted himself and did not fear to set himself up as Christ and call the woman accompanying him Mary. It was not his brazenness that exasperated Gregory, but the fact that the common people, needing a miracleworker, believed him – their need also created him. For, as Gregory recognizes, the people thronged to him and brought their sick, whom he healed by his touch. The gold, silver and clothes brought to him he distributed to the poor, and he ordered the people to worship him. He foretold the future: to some illnesses, to others losses, but to a few imminent salvation. He did all this with the power of some unknown diabolical art and witchcraft. 'And in this way he succeeded in seducing a huge multitude of people, and not only the commoners, but even some clergy. More than three thousand people followed him.'

There was nothing unusual about the distribution of property to the poor, but in this story there appears a motif of violent actions: the pseudo-Christ, 'whom one should sooner call the Antichrist', resorted to robbery in order to give the plunder to the poor. He threatened bishops and townsmen with death, if they would not venerate him. This brought about his destruction in a clash with the bishop of *Vellavae*, who had him murdered. After his death 'Mary' was tortured and revealed all his tricks and sorceries. Nevertheless, the people seduced by his diabolical devices continued to believe in him as Christ and to consider 'Mary' a participant in his divinity. One scene is telling for elucidating the frame of mind and psychological state of his followers: he sent to the bishop heralds to announce his arrival; they danced and jumped around naked, rousing the bishop's indignation. The sources of both this and later periods repeatedly mention 'indecent dances': the clergy emphatically condemned and prohibited them, seeing in them paganism and the devil's inspiration.[64] Gregory's report concludes with an allusion to the prevalence of such impostors: 'But also throughout all Gaul such people appeared in great number; by means of sorcery they attracted women, who worshipped them in a frenzy as saints, and set themselves up as somebody great;[65] we ourselves knew many from their number whom we condemned and attempted to deliver from delusion'.[66]

Self-styled miracle-workers represented a danger for the church, since they gathered around themselves a large number of followers from the common people. The terms *rustici, rusticiores, rusticitas populi, populus rusticus*, used by Gregory in his stories about impostors, did not necessarily signify the rural population; Gregory wanted to emphasize the ignorance, spiritual darkness and blind credulity of the common people who followed these frauds and were led into temptation. The impostors were active in both towns and villages.

The 'seducers' of the people set themselves up as saints or even as Christ: their followers evidently felt a pressing need for a tangible, visual embodiment of the divine principle, with which they could enter into direct contact and from which they could expect and demand direct blessings *hic et nunc*, and not only in the other world. The official church-church-controlled cult of saints was not always able to satisfy the common people, who were troubled by observing bishops priding themselves on intimacy with saints and yet absorbed in earthly affairs such as taking part in wars and obtaining earthly riches. Gregory of Tours makes frequent mention of popular uprisings against bishops and of expulsions of bishops from their dioceses. He speaks of bishops who received their sees through bribes or gifts and the help of powerful patrons. He does not conceal the fact that in his own Tours there are corrupt and unworthy clergy.

As we saw, however, in addition to characteristics of Christian saints, the impostors were credited with features of pagan magicians, sorcerers, soothsayers and shamans, as being capable of bringing themselves and their followers to an ecstatic state. Gregory repeatedly speaks of the prophets and prophetesses who drew to themselves many ignorant 'simpletons'. There is no doubt that he himself believed that some people, other than saints, can predict the future, reveal what is hidden and produce supernatural actions: their ability is explained by contact with the forces of evil or possession by a demon.[67] Everyone at that time, from bishop to commoner, lived in an atmosphere of miracle, but 'authorized' miracles were worked only by church-approved saints, and not by every sort of impostor. Gregory tells how one young monk saved the monastery's harvest from a storm by prayer. The monks were confounded by this miracle, but the abbot, in order to turn the young novice from vainglory, beat him and put him in his cell to fast: 'It is more fitting for you, my son, to grow in fear and humility before God, and not to exalt yourself through signs and wonders.'[68]

Gregory's stories of false saints date from the last decades of the sixth century, whereupon a lengthy lacuna sets in and similar indications do not emerge again in the sources until the middle of the eighth century – that is, until the time of Boniface's missionary and reforming activity. The 'Apostle of Germany' clashed with a priest named Adelbert about whose activities he had serious misgivings. At the time when Boniface was making every effort to reorganize the Frankish church and turn it into a single disciplined and solid force capable of securing the final victory of Christianity within the realm, Adelbert created a sect to which he drew a large number of people from the lower strata of society. Adelbert ordered the erection of crosses in meadows, by springs, or wherever he fancied; he called people to pray to God not in the bishops' cathedrals, but in small chapels raised in open fields; moreover, he denied the necessity of confessing in church. Naturally, Boniface hastened to declare Adelbert a 'fraudulent priest', 'heretic', 'schismatic', 'servant of the devil', and 'forerunner of the Antichrist'. Adelbert was condemned originally at a meeting of Frankish bishops in 744,[69] and then again in 745 at a Roman synod presided over by Pope Zachariah.[70]

At the trial it turned out that Adelbert, 'by birth a Gaul', declared himself a holy miracle-worker and managed to persuade a multitude of women and peasants to believe in him, 'having penetrated into many homes', so that they all were convinced that he was a 'man of apostolic sanctity' and a worker of miracles. He seduced even ignorant bishops, who ordained him. As a result, he became so proud that he imagined himself equal to Christ's Apostles. As an extract from Adelbert's letter (introduced into the synod's protocol) testifies, he was of humble origins.

According to him, he was marked by God's grace even before he came into the world: when he was in his mother's womb he had a vision signifying the grace sent down upon him. Adelbert maintained that an angel had brought to him from the extreme limits of the earth miraculous relics, through the power of which he could ask God for whatever he wanted. He also possessed a letter of Christ himself, which had fallen from heaven in Jerusalem and had been found by the archangel Michael. Extracts from the text of this letter are cited in the acts of the Roman synod. The chapels which Adelbert had ordered erected were consecrated in his honour, and prayers were offered to him by throngs of people who disregarded other bishops and abandoned their former churches. People prayed to him, saying 'The services of St Adelbert will help us.' The veneration went as far as the distribution of Adelbert's nails and hair as holy objects, similar to the relics of St Peter. People prostrated themselves before him and were ready to repent of their sins, but he considered confession superfluous: 'I know all your sins, for your secrets are known to me. There is no need for confession, but your past sins are absolved. Return to your homes in tranquillity and peace.'[71]

The synod also heard the text of a prayer composed by Adelbert: along with a fervent address to God the Father and Christ he entreats the angels Uriel, Raguel, Tubuel, Michael, Adin, Tubuas, Sabaok and Simiel. When this prayer was read out before the synod, the bishops demanded that it be burned as sacrilegious, for the names to which Adelbert appealed were in fact, except for Michael, the names of demons. The church recognizes the names of only three angels: Michael, Gabriel and Raphael. This address to the forces of evil served as the main basis for condemning Adelbert. The pope and the bishops declared him a 'madman' and 'irresponsible'. He was defrocked, sentenced to severe penance and warned not to persist in his sins and delusions. If he continued to seduce the people, he would be anathematized.[72] The crosses he had erected were ordered burned.[73]

The same synod condemned also a priest named Clement. He had two sons 'born in fornication', denied the command of clerical celibacy and propagated 'Judaism', saying that a brother should take his brother's widow to wife. However, the main 'temptation' into which he led the common people was the following: 'despite the teaching of the holy fathers', he asserted that Christ, descending into hell after his resurrection, did not leave anyone there, but delivered them all, both believers and also unbelievers, both 'those who praised the Lord and those who worshipped idols'. Moreover, concerning Christ's predestination he taught 'much that was frightful', contradicting orthodoxy.[74] From these accusations one can conclude that Clement denied the orthodox doctrine of sin and redemption and, accordingly, doubted the role of the church. The names of Adelbert and Clement – 'blasphemers', 'obstinant men', 'pseudo-prophets' and 'pseudo-Christians' – are met in the correspondence between the pope and Boniface for several years, since they did not admit their guilt and attempted to continue their activity.[75] Then these notices break off.[76]

Echoes of this conflict can be heard in later periods. In Charlemagne's *Admonitio generalis* (789) there is a special enactment 'about spurious compositions' and 'false noxious letters' contradicting orthodoxy that in past years, according to 'some deluded men who led others into delusion', 'fell from heaven'. Such works were not to be read or believed, but were to be burned, lest they deceive people. It was only permitted to read canonical books and tractates and the sayings of holy authors.[77] This may very well be a reference to the 'letter of Jesus Christ' which Adelbert asserted had fallen from heaven. If that were the case, this letter, despite its having been condemned, would have to have been preserved for several decades and travelled from hand to hand, or at least memory of this miraculous letter would have to have been kept alive. However, letters of Christ, 'fallen from heaven', appeared in Europe throughout the Middle Ages, sustaining the naive beliefs and hopes of the people (Delehaye 1899: 171–213; Jones 1975: 164ff.).

The *Admonitio generalis* also prohibits repeating the names of 'unknown angels' – other, that is, than Michael, Gabriel and Raphael – and forbids venerating false martyrs and 'dubious saints'.[78] If Adelbert was not specifically meant here, the very tradition of numbering among the saints and martyrs officially unapproved and uncanonized people is significant. Apparently, the struggle of church and state against unauthorized religious activity was not completely effective. Just as ineffective were the repeatedly renewed attacks on itinerant priests and bishops in canons of councils and in capitularies. It is curious that it was also ordered 'to expel the itinerant bishop even if the flock desires to retain him' (Mikoletzky 1949: 85). Such *episcopi vagantes* sometimes enjoyed great popularity, which once again troubled the authorities.[79]

But let us return to Adelbert. In the years of the struggle against him and similar 'falsos sacerdotes et hypochritas',[80] Boniface wrote to the bishop of Winchester: 'What we have planted they do not water so that it might grow, but strive to destroy and ruin, forming new sects and drawing the people into every sort of delusion...'[81] The obstinacy of Adelbert and Clement in their 'delusions' even after their condemnation is difficult to explain, unless one assumes that their followers did not abandon them. For having Adelbert shut up in a monastery Boniface was attacked by others, as he himself admits. He complained to the pope that the teaching of the church was suffering losses, and that he was being persecuted and abused by many hostile to him who saw in Adelbert 'a most holy apostle', a 'patron and protector, a champion of justice and worker of miraculous signs'.[82]

As also in the episodes described by Gregory of Tours, in this instance we are dealing with a 'saint equal to the apostles', a man who while alive became the centre of a popular cult, the object of blind faith and worship. It is significant that Adelbert exerted influence in the first place on women, that is, on the most easily excited part of the population (Russell 1965: 238; Koch 1962; Manselli 1975: 188ff.). Does this not suggest that Adelbert's cult was based on the emotional excitability of its followers? Everything else that we know about it also supports such a conclusion: his hair and nails served as sacred relics; people prostrated themselves before him and believed that he read their souls and knew their sins without any confession; his prayer (in the extant extracts) was a selection of fervent exclamations and invocations.

We have noted similar features in Gregory of Tours's stories. A bishop's runaway servant sets himself up as a saint and marches around Paris at the head of a singing and dancing throng of women – Gregory uses the expression 'choir'. The self-styled 'Christ' announces his approach by sending ahead people who jump and dance and expose themselves. Gregory particularly stresses that he himself was a witness of how such miracle-workers drove gullible women into a frenzy. This does not mean, of course, that only women fell under the influence of such pseudo-saints; we know that men followed them as well, and even clerics, including 'ignorant bishops', who did not avoid temptation but recognized them as saints. The reason for such wide influence lies in the psychological predisposition of early medieval people to perceive a 'Messiah' or 'saint', in the need for a spiritual leader and in the craving for the miraculous.

This suggestion can be supported by another example of unofficial prophesying. This took place exactly one hundred years after the Adelbert affair, when a woman appeared as a prophet. As narrated by the Fulda annals under the year 847, in the region of Mainz a certain *pseudo-prophetissa* by the name of Thiota proclaimed herself.[83] She 'roused with her prophecies' much of the population of the villages through which she travelled, preaching that she had received a revelation from God and that she knew 'the Lord's secrets', in particular the exact time of the end of the world: earthly history would be completed that very year.

Her preachings and prophecies attracted a large number of people of both sexes; seized by fear, they brought her presents, entreating her to pray for them, 'as if she were a saint', The extent of her influence is shown by the fact that not only common people followed her, but, 'what is worse still' (and what invariably accompanied heretical movements), also some monks and priests, who abandoned their vows for her sake.

However, Thiota was not permitted to preach for long. She was taken under guard, brought to Mainz and led before the archbishop, Rabanus Maurus, and the clergy. At the interrogation she said that she only did what she had been ordered, but when asked who ordered her to wander through villages 'preaching nonsense', she had no better answer than a reference to 'some priest'. More likely, the frightened woman was simply searching for an excuse to alleviate her guilt. In contrast to the affair of Adelbert, which had terrorized the higher clergy to a great degree, Thiota's case did not appear particularly serious to the archbishop, and he merely forbade her to preach and ordered her to be whipped publicly. These measures were apparently sufficient for suppressing her prophecies, and her further fate is unknown.

The episode with Thiota deserves attention most of all because the eschatological motif is heard in it with greater clarity than in the previous appearances of popular saints. Both the pseudo-Christ mentioned by Gregory of Tours and Adelbert also probably predicted the approaching end of the world; the ecstasis and agitation evoked by their preaching remain unintelligible without it. But the sources do not speak directly about this.[84] The Mainz prophetess seems to have predicted an imminent Last Judgment. Prophecy of this sort was inevitably connected with appeals for repentance and for renunciation of earthly goods and joys. That this prophet was a woman implies that her preaching had a particularly emotional appeal.

Our sources do not permit a closer reconstruction of the spiritual aspect of popular saints. The information on them is too summary, and the clerical authors too tendentious and hostile, attempting to depict them as tricksters, gluttons, drunkards, madmen and sorcerers. As a result, one should withhold judgment on whether they were conscious hoaxers and impostors, self-deluded visionaries, or psychologically unstable, abnormal people; we cannot penetrate their psyche. It is another matter, however, to explain the functions that such a 'saint' was supposed to fulfil in order to be recognized.

The self-styled saint was above all a miracle-worker. It was miracles and signs that attracted people to him or her: without miracles and prophecies, there would have been no followers. With certain reservations Gregory of Tours recognizes Desiderius' ability to perform miracles. There are no refutations of Adelbert's miracles in the letters of Boniface and the pope or in the acts of the Roman synod. But the clergy explained the supernatural capabilities of the 'false saint' as the intervention of the forces of evil. As a result, in order to prove his own sanctity, a self-styled saint over-emphasized his direct connection with God, as, for example, in Thiota's declaration that God's secrets and his intentions about the end of the world were revealed to her; in the 'letter of Jesus

Christ' and also the relics entrusted to Adelbert by an angel; and in the exchange of messengers between Desiderius and Peter and Paul.

In comparing stories of church-recognized saints with the assertions of impostors about their contacts with God, angels or Apostles, one is struck by the loudness with which these 'Messiahs' declared their intimacy with the higher powers. Orthodox saints never boasted of their contact with God. In hagiographical accounts, saints invariably stressed that they were unworthy of the grace vouchsafed them, and they were cautious and apprehensive in discussing this with their followers. According to the rules of hagiography, the saint could not call himself the Lord's elect; it was the believers who recognized him as such. The saint's chief feature was humility, and the most terrible of sins was pride.[85]

Even allowing for the bias in the reports about 'popular saints', one must still suggest that these impostors, precisely because of their opposition to the church, had to emphasize their own participation in Christ's power. Behind the official saint stood the traditions and authority of the faith and all its institutions, whereas the impostor could rely on himself alone. Therefore, his first concern was with asserting himself and defending his right to lead his followers. Accordingly, pride featured among the main accusations against the false saint. Gregory of Tours speaks of Desiderius with a quotation from Acts about Simon Magus: '...qui se magnum quendam esse dicebat', and he applies these same words to all such impostors. Pope Zachariah also called Adelbert a 'new Simon'.

Very serious contradictions were concealed behind these accusations. The orthodox saint was the extreme instance of the elimination of human individuality and of the conscious rejection of everything 'accidental', that is, earthly. The saint received exceptional meaning in the eyes of believers because of his full submission to religious canon, to a sacred norm, and of the extreme fusion of his personality within the church. Precisely because of his rejection of the particular ego, he could become an ideal personality, a standard of Christian conduct. On the other hand, the basis of the personality of the heretical 'Messiah' was his exceptionality. Popular 'prophets', similar to Adelbert and Clement, insisted on the idea of individual direct inspiration from God unmediated by any religious institution or establishment. The church did not stand behind them; it opposed them. Therefore, the sanctity of self-styled saints, in contrast to the humility of church saints, was aggressive.

The opposition between church and false saints expressed two poles within one type of the human personality defined by the historical situation. For the personality of the non-orthodox saint was in its own way also determined by the religious canon. Like every saint, he was supposed to work miracles; he did not perform these miracles independently, but through contact with higher powers and their grace and approbation. The false saint was no more of an autonomous personality than the orthodox saint, and for their followers each appeared as God's instrument. The opposition of the two embodiments of sanctity was an opposition within the same cultural context.

Since the self-styled saint had to demonstrate his participation in the supernatural, he appealed to the emotions of the excited and miracle-craving mass of believers, and inevitably had to resort to remedies that the church had forbidden. Magic and sorcery will be discussed later at some length; it appears that both the sixth-century false saints mentioned by Gregory of Tours and Adelbert were involved in them. Besides distributing his hair and nails, which his followers obviously considered possessed healing power,[86] Adelbert invoked in his prayer the names of eight angels. Seven of these names belonged to demons in the church's view, but Adelbert may not have drawn a clear distinction between good and fallen angels. The denial of the irreconcilable opposition between Christians and pagans is apparent in the utterances of Clement about Christ having liberated from hell 'laudatores Dei simul et cultores idulorum'.[87]

An anti-clerical tendency is more distinctly visible in Adelbert's conduct. He was charged with having diverted people from visiting old churches and having ordered them to pray at crosses and in his chapels. The threat of losing some of the faithful triggered the condemnation of Adelbert for heresy and schism. Boniface complained that Adelbert's flock worshipped in fields and meadows and by springs; Zachariah denounced the practice of 'their false liturgy not in Catholic churches, but in forest places and in peasant huts, where their ignorant stupidity could be hidden from bishops'.[88]

The pope may have had grounds for assuming that in forests or peasant dwellings false priests and schismatics could evade the bishops' control, but Adelbert himself made no effort to hide from anybody and gathered his faithful in open places, precisely where local inhabitants had been accustomed to gather since times immemorial. Royal legislation, canons, sermons and penitentials invariably attacked these old holidays, sacrifices and pagan rituals, threatening violators with frightful punishments in this and the other world. The 'List of Superstitions and Pagan Rituals', by an eighth-century Anglo-Saxon missionary in Saxony, mentions sacrifices in forest sanctuaries and on stones among other forbidden rites.[89] The 'Sermon on Sacrileges', also apparently belonging to the eighth century, cautions the faithful against returning to pagan altars in groves, by trees, on rocks, and in other such places.[90] The cult of natural forces, harmonious with the specific world-view of the age, proved to be exceptionally vital even well after the process of conversion.

As Gregory of Tours narrates, many of the peasants settled in the area of Poitiers had the custom of sacrificing to a mountain lake, into which on certain days they threw linen and woollen fabrics, cheese, wax, bread and other products, 'each according to his income'. They also brought with them food, drink and animals to be sacrificed, and they feasted there for three days.[91] Pope Gregory I wrote with sadness about the veneration of trees and rocks, widespread from Corsica and Sardinia to England.[92] Caesarius of Arles cautioned against the danger of mixing religions: many Christians bring sacrifices, visit old cult-sites, and take part in diabolical feasts in groves, by springs and next to trees.[93] Hagiography is also full of references to this same cult. In the *Life of Willibrord* Alcuin mentions a sanctuary, *Fositesland*, on the border between Frisia and Denmark. This sanctuary was so revered by pagans that it was forbidden to touch anything there and to take water from the spring. Willibrord, however, baptized three men in the spring and destroyed the cattle dedicated to the idols.[94] Bishop Amand, who preached among the Basques, came up against the fact that they 'venerated trees as gods', telling fortunes from them and worshipping the demons contained in them.[95] In Brittany there existed the 'mad custom' of venerating forest animals; it was abolished by the efforts of St Lucius.[96] But in the same region we come across an interesting case of the syncretism of paganism and Christianity in the cult of trees. The holy abbot Martin drove his staff into the ground, and out of it grew a tree the branches of which had healing power. The local inhabitants, including the nobility, so venerated that tree that before going into church they approached it and worshipped Christ. Normans who attacked the locality wanted to fashion bows from the sacred tree but were cruelly punished for their impious endeavour.[97] The author of the life, writing in the ninth or early tenth century, saw nothing impious in worshipping Christ in front of a tree. What we have here is a highly durable custom that did not vanish after the Christianization of the pagans, despite all the efforts of the church.[98] Penitentials imposed punishments as late as the year 1000 for pagan sacrifices performed at springs or trees, on rocks, at crossroads or at highway crosses.[99]

Adelbert celebrated liturgy precisely in such places, forbidden by the church but consecrated by pagan tradition, and this undoubtedly added to his popularity among the peasants. While the church, concentrating the liturgy exclusively in the church building attempted to sever the tight bonds between the rural population and nature,[100] the 'folk saints', by raising crosses and chapels in fields and by mixing relics with witchcraft, reinforced this connection anew. The Christianity of heretical priests sometimes smacked greatly of paganism. In the above-mentioned letter Pope Zachariah repeats Boniface's invectives against 'sacrilegious priests': they 'immolate bulls and goats to pagan deities, partaking of the sacrifices in memory of the dead'.[101] These accusations may also have concerned Adelbert. In any case, they were not new, and several years previously Pope Gregory III had castigated German sorcerers and fortune-tellers pursuing magic in groves and by springs with similar expressions,[102] just as the late eighth-century 'List of Superstitions and Pagan Rituals' opens with a title on sacrileges done at graves.[103]

Self-styled saints also differed from official saints by standing outside the church and being persecuted as its enemies. Appearing at moments of intensified social tension, sensitive to the agitated mood of the common people, these 'Messiahs' were just as highly emotional as their followers.[104] We may safely dismiss the ecclesiastical view that the 'false saints' were cool, calculating tricksters. They believed in their divine mission and in their close connection to God. The 'folk saint', who stood at the head of an excited and miracle-craving throng[105] and found himself outside the law, was hardly an even-tempered person.[106]

Yet exactly these saints offered the people a grotesque fusion of Christian and pagan motifs that was apparently more to their liking than orthodoxy. The pope, exposing the 'deceivers of the people, itinerants, fornicators, murderers, committers of sacrilege, hypocrites, acting under the guise of priests and bishops', lamented that 'pseudo-priests are more numerous than Catholics'.[107] While this was hardly a reliable quantified analysis, it betrays the anxiety which non-orthodox saints aroused in the head of the Western church.

This survey of different aspects of the attitude of early medieval people towards saints permits a few conclusions.

First of all, although hagiographers wished to instil in believers a lofty ideal to which each Christian was to strive to attain, the most attractive thing about the saint was his ability to work miracles. The saint, connected with higher powers, employed his magical capabilities to help his worshippers, easing their lives, healing their illnesses, averting natural or social calamities, freeing the unfortunate and the powerless from oppression. In return, the saint required obedience, veneration, and gifts for the church foundation under his patronage. Negligence, or refusal by the parishioners to carry out these obligations provoked cruel punishments from the holy patron. As we have seen, the saint, although the model of humility and non-resistance, was at the same time a stern and pitiless chastiser and avenger.[108]

The cult of the saints grew in the Middle Ages to colossal proportions. The distant and incomprehensible deity was overshadowed by intimate and accessible saints, endowed with human features and active among the people. Each locality had its own saint, who was an integral member of society to whom people would resort whenever they required help beyond human power. Miracle-working characteristics impressed the people most; a saint who did not perform miracles did not enjoy popularity and veneration. In return for their gifts and prayers the parishoners wanted to receive swift and full recompense in the form of a miracle. Despite all its insistence that the main feature of a saint was his righteousness and election by God, the clergy found itself powerless to oppose the universal need for magical actions. Saints' lives were filled with stories of miracles; miracles were constantly happening at saints' graves and reliquaries. The universal faith in miracles yielded enormous riches to churches and monasteries.

The saints' supernatural actions were not easily distinguished from pagan magic, and the two were inseparably united in popular consciousness. The clergy had to elucidate, apparently without success, the border between a genuine miracle and sorcery or black magic. But, in fact, clerics themselves did not always distinguish *miracula* from *maleficia* as they were quite similar in appearance. The basic criterion of demarcation seems to have been the performer of the action: the true miracle was worked by the saint, while false miracles were performed by the devil or his agents – shamans, sorcerers and pseudo-saints. The church claimed a monopoly on the performance of miracles, excluding all other forms of magical practice.

If God was the embodiment of the sacred principle on the macrocosmic scale, the saint fulfilled this function within the limits of the microcosm, the local social world. But it was in such small communities that, essentially, all early medieval life was concentrated.

Nevertheless, orthodox saints did not always fully satisfy the needs of the people, precisely because they were placed in direct and indissoluble connection with the church hierarchy. Hence the inevitability of the appearance in the popular environment of prophets and Messiahs who opposed official, feudalized ecclesiastical institutions. 'Saints' outside the church and false Christs grounded their holiness in their own personal qualities, inspiring their followers and undoubtedly themselves with the thought that God's spirit dwelt in them. They were messengers called from heaven to save people from perdition at the approaching Last Judgment, despite the false church.

One need not see in the appearance of early medieval anti-authoritarian figures merely the anticipation of the more developed heresy of a later period. Prophecy and Messianism are not the exclusive domains of the 'world religions'. They are also prevalent in pre-class societies, especially in periods of breakdown of the traditional equilibrium and intensification of social or natural adversities. Under such conditions all sorts of saviours and saints appear, acting according to the model of cultural heroes and exploiting the eschatological expectations of their fellow-tribesmen, searching for supernatural salvation from the threat-ening social situation. The customary sign of these healers and prophets is magic and shamanism (Guariglia 1959; Mühlmann 1968).

Scholars note the increased frequency of prophecy and Messianism among so-called 'primitive peoples' during periods of acculturation, when an archaic culture clashes with a more developed civilization. In these terms, the meeting of the barbarian peoples of Europe with Christianity and classical civilization, when the traditional bases of their socio-political and religious-ideological system were broken down, can very well be called acculturation (Wachtel 1974: 143ff.; Le Goff 1986: 346; cf. Manselli 1975: 19ff.). As we saw, pseudo-Christs and false saints appeared among the Franks precisely in circumstances of social agitation intensified by natural disasters, when apprehensions arose about the approaching end of the world especially easily. At a time when the church was teaching that the Second Coming could be expected only upon the completion of earthly history, self-styled saints expressed the people's impatience, fears and expectations, proclaiming themselves Christs and saints equal to the Apostles. The gaps in the conversion of the barbarians permitted the rebirth of natural cults and popular magic. Eschatology merged with paganism, suggesting the superficial assimila-tion of Christian doctrine. While the later heresies demanded a return to primitive Christianity, early medieval pseudo-saints rather revived pre-Christian cults and their inherent magical practices, which had not yet been forgotten, despite all the activity of the church and the state to eradicate them.

New questions are posed by this material. Most of all, what moved hagiographers to present the saint invariably as a miracle-worker? How were different beliefs combined in a single consciousness and what did their unity represent? For simply stating that paganism was fused with Christianity or that Christianity was superficially assimilated hardly explains the character of early medieval popular culture. What was the nature of this combination of the seemingly incompatible? Was this evidence of the transition from paganism to Christianity, or was it a durable and essential feature of medieval popular culture? In order to draw closer to resolving these questions we must turn to works in other genres.

The popular interpretation of saints discussed above was not exclusive to the early Middle Ages; materials of the later period portray essentially the same picture. A. Vauchez's outstanding new work (1981) not only reveals a shift in the criteria of sanctity in the thirteenth and fourteenth centuries, but also demonstrates the lengthy prevalence, to the very end of the Middle Ages, of the stereotype of the saint found at the beginning of the period. The attitude of the church towards the cult of the saints was distinguished by a duality from the beginning: Vauchez emphasizes the divergence in the conception of sanctity between the educated clergy, which stressed the saint's piety and way of life, and the laymen and lower clergy, who judged a saint by his miracles. The initiative in creating a cult always belonged to the believers, which frequently disquieted the church and provoked its reaction. It was not without reason that the papal court did not canonize local saints to whom the people attributed thaumaturgic powers. Scholars estimate the number of local saints in thirteenth-century Catholic Europe in hundreds, but there were only seventy canonization inquiries in the period between 1185 and 1431, and only half of them ended in canonization. Important differences existed between the saints recognized by the church and the mass of local saints it did not 'approve'. Vauchez speaks about two levels of the cult.

Up to the twelfth century saints of the early church were venerated, but then the number of more recently deceased saints began to grow. After the Gregorian reform the perspective in which holiness was seen changed, and contemporaries placed their own time on a par with that of the church Fathers. Christianity, which developed in the thirteenth and fourteenth centuries, according to G. Duby (1981: 268), from the religion of the élite to be the religion of the masses, was adapted to the latter's spiritual needs and aspirations; the cult of the saints was 'brought to earth' and partially vulgarized. New saints, closer in space and time, seemed more effective patrons; seen while still living, they could be counted upon as compatriots for patronage and feelings of solidarity. Each town and village strove to possess its own saint; the cult of the saints, in Vauchez's words, was particularized. But particularism, as we have seen, was inherent in the cult of the saints from the early Middle Ages.

The cult of the saints always wore two faces: its popular sources were combined with the influence of the local clergy, who were supposed to approve and formulate veneration. Little evidence is available regarding popular saints, and those few pieces are only the tip of an iceberg hidden from the scholar's view. There are several instances in which veneration of a popular saint provoked ecclesiastical interdictions (which were rarely effective). The cult of St Werner was forbidden by Emperor Rudolph and the archbishop of Mainz in 1288 (the year after Werner's death), but soon thereafter several bishops acknowledged his sanctity; in the fourteenth century the cult was again forbidden, the ban being lifted only in 1426. Over time the cult was transformed: legend made Werner a martyr killed by Jews, but in the sixteenth century, the period of the cult's greatest popularity, he was venerated as the patron of vinegrowers.

For the most part, the cult of popular saints arose in a rural and undereducated environment indifferent to saints proposed by the church.

Exceptionally interesting are Vauchez's observations concerning the connection between paradigms of holiness in different regions of Europe (he indicates two 'models' – Mediterranean and North European) and the character of the social structure: the *popolani* type of Italian saint is distinguished from the more abstracted type of saint in France or Germany, where primarily nobles and bishops were canonized. Lord–vassal relations also were manifested in the attitude towards the saint: the believer entrusted himself to the saint and promised to be loyal to him, but on the condition that the saint render him aid, or else the contract would be severed. Belief in a saint's magical properties (expressed in venerating relics and expecting miracles from him) was characteristic of all medieval people, from commoner to pope – this was an integral part of medieval mentality (Lecouteux 1981: 273–90). Differences between the popular and official conceptions of saintliness emerged in an unequal interpretation of miracles, which served for the people as the decisive criterion of a saint's holiness and for the educated as a sign of his election.

Lionel Rothkrug (1979, 1980) has published interesting, although highly debatable studies on the cult of relics in Western Christianity and on the differences between the veneration of saints in France, where it set down deep roots, and in Germany, where there were almost no local saints. The veneration of relics was directly connected with pilgrimages. The late Victor Turner examined pilgrimages as a 'liminal' stage in the process of a man's change in condition or status, as a rite of passage. In the anthropological perspective the fetishistic nature of relics, which were used for magical purposes, is especially evident (Turner 1978). These recent works suggest the many aspects of this topic which still need detailed study.

3

POPULAR CULTURE IN THE MIRROR OF THE PENITENTIALS

In the preceding chapter on hagiography, we have seen how form and style of the saints' lives were adapted to the expectations of the congregation. Under the pressure of his audience, the hagiographer had to present the saints as miracle-workers and protectors of the poor and oppressed. The teachings of the church were embedded in a rich context of folkloric tradition, and this peculiar mixture, which could no longer be divided into its component parts, became incorporated into popular culture. Popularization of the fundamental tenets of Christianity was inevitably accompanied by its transformation. Still, in the sphere of hagiography the adjustment of the requirements of theology to the requirements of the masses remained under the church's control: the legend, the *vita* and the 'miracles', whatever their folkloric sources may have been, flowed out of the clergy's pen.

The church had to deal with popular traditions not only about saints, but also in a much wider circle comprising beliefs, perceptions and practices, in order to subordinate these to the demands of official religiosity. For this aspect of spiritual life in the Middle Ages, we have to study another genre: the penitentials, confession handbooks and guides for priests in casuistry.

First, these should be placed in the general context within which the priests acted. While historians have amply studied such units of medieval society as the family, the manor, the landed estate, the feudal principality and the kingdom, little attention has been paid to perhaps the most essential organizational form of social exchange, the parish.[1] It was precisely in the frame of this local 'molecule' of the church that most medieval people spent their lives. Established and supported by both secular and spiritual authorities, the parish tended to supplant all other human associations. The ideological and moral control of the population was accomplished within it; one belonged to one's parish from birth to death and even beyond. The infant received baptism here, thereby becoming a social-moral creature; the child and adult attended service here, listened to the sermon, confessed his or her sins, got married in the parish church and received the last sacrament from the parish priest. One remained bound to the parish even after death: no one was permitted to be buried outside the parish; bodies interred elsewhere were frequently exhumed and brought home.

Parish churches were more than religious centres. Civic life was to a great extent focussed on them; bargains were struck there, festivities held, grain stored; and often the parish church, the only stone building in the village, was the last refuge from bandits and invading armies. The churchyard was the place for games and sports; even such holidays as contained considerable pagan elements were celebrated here,[2] perhaps, as C. Erikson (1976: 76) suggests, without conscious element of sacrilege. If the priest kept a tavern, beer could also be had at church premises, and larger churches were the longest-lasting centres of markets and fairs.

Parishioners were kept under strict control by their parish priest. But there was also a collective social control in the community. D. Sumption (1976) registered that the notion that everybody's sin was a common concern of all parishioners was a tacitly accepted premise among medieval people. Of course, almost the whole life of every villager passed in front of the eyes of his fellow-parishioners, who kept a close watch on one another. Confession, although made in secret, was still a matter overseen by others. Many people left their parishes just to get away from the vigilant supervision of the priest and their fellows. It was easier to wash off one's sins outside the bounds of the home community, while not controlled by it at every step.[3]

Belonging to the local parish had, of course, deep spiritual roots. The ancestors had lived there, the majority of social and human ties bound a person to the parish where his or her body was going to rest after the end of this earthly existence. This microcosm determined the behaviour of the people who belonged to it and defined the structure of their thoughts and emotions. Bergson recorded an anecdote about a man who remained imperturbable among a church full of people crying over the sermon and, being asked why he alone did not shed tears, replied: 'I am from another parish'. One could hardly express any better the social and mental cohesion of the parishioners and the 'foreignness' of the outsider. The head of this community, the parish priest, had the task of directing the religious life of his flock. It would have been very difficult to control successfully their private and public behaviour without confession and that useful tool that helped to organize it, the penitential.[4]

Penitentials were written in and for communities which, for all practical purposes, were already converted to Christianity. But it is difficult to establish to what extent Christian teachings and norms managed to overcome and replace the pre-Christian religion and get a firm hold on the mind of the baptized. The penitentials offer valuable material regarding this question, significantly different information from that gained from hagiography. In the legends the conversion of the unbeliever is usually achieved by a miracle, a deed of a saint, a moving sermon.

But the saints' lives do not contain the whole story: the everyday task of conversion and of keeping the purity of faith. We have to find a path to real life and see what kinds of problems the clergy had to face in day-to-day reality; a road is offered through the penitentials.

Naturally, father-confessors did not deal with pagans: only Christians came to confession. Medieval parishioners seem to have been regular churchgoers; at least, no penalties feature in the penitentials for being absent from divine service. First the confessant affirmed his belief in the Trinity and its unity, then the priest began to question him or her about the sins committed. A medieval theologian who likened the confessional to a trial by ordeal in which the priest, the 'vicar of God', was the judge, defined the parishioner as both defendant and prosecutor.[5] It was expected that the confessants should be able and willing to analyse their actions by the standards of Christian tenets, to appraise them and to repent if they found themselves culpable of a trespass.

Of special interest for our inquiry are those passages in the penitentials in which the pagan beliefs of the parishioners are discussed. Of course, we have many references to heathen practices and popular superstitions in saints' lives, synodal canons, papal letters and royal legislation as well. But nowhere else does this aspect of the religious and cultural life of medieval people receive such concentrated attention as in the penitentials. In other sources the denounced practices appear as survivals of paganism being gradually but successfully extirpated by the church. Traditional beliefs and Christianity appear from these texts as two consecutive, even though overlapping, stages in the religiosity of the European peoples.

The study of penitentials, on the other hand, seems to open up another avenue of analysis. From them it appears rather that beliefs inherited from long-past centuries and Christianity were present simultaneously and in constant interaction and conflict. They seem to represent two synchronous aspects of medieval social consciousness. This specific unity may be termed 'popular Christianity'. The contents and structure of this set of beliefs have been neglected by historians for a long time – not surprisingly, since documents about religion in the Middle Ages either originate from orthodox theologians or reflect the ideas of heretics. There is no direct evidence as to what went on in the minds of simple parishioners unfamiliar with both abstract theology and the heterodox teachings of dissenters.

Students of early medieval culture have frequently tried to establish which of the pagan survivals denounced by the ecclesiastical authors go back to ancient Germanic beliefs and which derive from classical Greco-Roman religion (Boudriot 1928). They rarely succeed in finding a satisfactory answer to this question, because the beliefs and ideas proscribed in church writings (such as penitentials) do not fit either of these categories, but reflect rather a deeper, 'primary', layer of popular consciousness. First of all they are connected with magic, a specific mode of human behaviour which disregards natural causality and is based on the expectation of results from men's participation in the universe (Tokarev 1959). There is plenty of evidence in the sources on magical practices and healings, love magic and fertility magic of different sorts, all of which were much less vestiges or 'survivals' of pre-Christian practices than integral elements of daily life in agrarian society. Penitentials are especially rich in information about magic, and I do not intend to discuss all aspects of this impressive amount of evidence.

From the needs of peasants logically follows that many of the 'illicit' and 'pagan' rites prohibited in the confession books were aimed at a rich harvest. That demands above all the correct sequence of the cycles of nature. The flow of the seasons is not self-evident for the 'primitive' mind, which considers it necessary to exert magical influence over the elements, the sun, the moon and the stars, to secure their proper movement. To bring about the new moon after days of dark nights, people thought that they had to 'help the moon restore its radiance';[6] hence, meetings were called and magical ceremonies performed. During a lunar or solar eclipse the frightened people attempted to protect themselves by witchcraft.[7] The relationship of men and natural phenomena was conceived as one of interaction or even as mutual aid. The natural forces can help or harm man, who in turn is able to influence them in ways that are advantageous for him.

In the system of these archaic beliefs men think of themselves in the same categories as the rest of the world, not isolating themselves from it and construing an 'object–subject' dichotomy. An ultimate unity and a reciprocal penetration of nature and humankind, organically connected with each other and magically interactive, are taken for granted. The best expression to describe this type of world-perception is perhaps 'participation' in the cosmos. When the world and humans are seen to consist of the same elements, then people assume that they can have an immediate influence on the world and on the motion and action of things contained in it, including time.

One of the best-informed penitential writers, Burchard of Worms, was particularly distressed that these ideas were deeply ingrained in the popular mind and 'pass from father to son as if by right of inheritance'. Burchard's chagrin was fully warranted: such *traditiones paganorum* were in glaring contradiction to the church's teaching about divine providence, which alone is able to govern the world and define all its movements. We know from the penitentials – and other sources[8] – that many ritual feasts with chants and incantations were performed at the

Kalends of January to secure a bountiful harvest for the coming year. In the days around the winter solstice one could foresee the future and change it, by peering into the fire, or sitting on the roof of the house, or on an ox-hide at the crossroads.

The second condition of a good agrarian year was clement weather for the crop. That magic was applied for this is evident from the many denunciations in the penitentials of wizards who attempt to avert storms or change the climate.[9] Burchard describes, in his usual picturesque style, the rite for deliverance from drought and takes us right into an eleventh-century German village. When rain, which the peasants keenly need has not fallen for a long while, the women search out a great number of young girls, strip one of them naked and, placing her at the head of their procession, set out beyond the boundaries of the village. There they search for a certain herb, called *belisa* in German, which the naked girl has to dig out with the little finger of her right hand; its root is fastened to the little toe of her right foot. Then the other girls, with switches in hand, chase the naked one, dragging the *belisa* behind herself, to the nearest rivulet, where they sprinkle her with water and chant incantations for rain. Afterwards the girl is led back to the village, walking backwards 'like a crab'. Burchard of Worms suggests that women who have attended such rites should be told: 'If you did or agreed to do such things, you must fast on bread and water for twenty days'.[10]

The inducement of rain by a ritual action of innocent children is a rite very similar to practices among 'primitive' peoples (Tokarev 1959: 68). Medieval villagers were not too far removed from such animistic people – at any rate, not in terms of their perception of magic.

Other 'godless' people, swineherds, ploughmen and hunters, are known to Burchard to sing devilish chants over bread, herbs or some kind of knot, then to scatter these at crossroads in order to divert the plague from their animals towards the beasts of others.[11] Other penitentials also mention knots or ligaments, oaths and sorcerous formulas over herbs, in the woods or at crossroads, to protect cattle from murrain. By such practices some peasants attempted to deprive their neighbours of milk and honey, to entice abundance to their own cows and bees, and to cause damage to the household animals of others by magic words and 'evil looks'. Burchard denounces the magical incantations and gestures some women use over their weaving, their spinning and their cloths, these being supposed to aid their work.[12] The good bishop did not believe in magic and calls all these matters 'fuss' and 'illusion', but clearly, not all his contemporaries shared his views.

As a rule, medieval people were convinced of the efficacy of magic and applied it in many fields of their life;[13] the penitentials duly summon the entire arsenal of ecclesiastical repression against these beliefs and 'devilish practices'. One has the impression that, in an epoch of primitive technology and a lack of technical expertise, magic presented itself as an instinctive alternative to confronting nature. But, besides agrarian and household magic, directed at the productive forces of nature, many magical practices were applied to man. There seem to have been numerous techniques to influence the human body, its health and its senses. Women appear to have been the main practitioners in the preparation of drugs and cunning words against illness. They set children suffering from fever in the oven or on the roof,[14] burned grain in the house of a dead person in order to ward off disease from the deceased's family. Folk medicine and sorcery were daily practice in the Middle Ages, and many prescriptions survive which suggest that faith in the healing power of plants and other substances was combined with belief in magic and the influence of heavenly bodies on the health of the person (Cockayne 1864–6; Ettlinger 1943).[15]

The church did not prohibit the gathering of medicinal herbs if it was done piously while praying the Creed and the Paternoster, but it absolutely condemned it when accompanied by 'disgraceful incantations'.[16] Herbs were only part of the remedies; great medicinal powers were also attributed to different excretions of the human body, to carrion and garbage.[17] Water, earth, fire and blood were also used as remedies.[18] A highly successful method of treating a crying baby was believed to be this: a hole with two entrances was dug in the ground and the infant pulled through this tunnel.[19] Healing by contact with the power of the earth is a very characteristic trait of agrarian beliefs, and it was practised in innumerable forms.[20]

Black magic emerges from the penitentials with particular clarity. The typical elements of witchcraft – witches' sabbath, night-time flights of women, association with evil spirits – are all recorded in the guidance books for priests. Germany seems to have been particularly plagued by witches; here the penitentials record that there was widespread belief that some women, yielding to the deception of the devil and incited by the Evil One, join a crowd of demons in female form and on certain nights set off astride certain animals.[21] 'Popular stupidity calls such a witch [*striga*] a "holda".'[22] Holda, or Huld, is a female being with prophetic powers in Germanic and Scandinavian mythology and fairy-tale. In medieval Germany she was called Frau Holle, about whom people 'told all sorts of things, good and bad'.[23] She helps women in labour, is a good housewife and gardener, encourages industrious weavers and punishes the lazy. She makes the soil fertile, but she scares people when she races through the woods at the head of the *wilde schar*, the 'wild bunch' (Grimm 1939: 48, 188). In one penitential manuscript she is called *Frigaholda*, apparently identified with the Germanic goddess of magic, soothsaying, fertility and marriage, Frigg or Frîja. She, too, assisted women at childbirth and determined the fate of the newborn. She was the wife of Odin (Wotan) and mother of Baldur, and her name survives in the Germanic form of the Roman 'day of Venus' – Friday.[24] This goddess, known to both the Scandinavians and the continental Germanic peoples (especially the Lombards), was the protector of family life (Waschnitius 1913), but in Christian Germany she became a witch – a fate shared with other pagan deities.

As to the Latin term *striga* or *stria*, it occurs in many other documents besides the penitentials. The Salic law set compensation for a woman unjustly accused of being a *stria* – that is, a witch brewing a witch's brew in a cauldron. *Stria* are mentioned in the *Lex Alemannorum*, together with *herbaria*, preparers of potions. The Lombard law (Edict of Rothar) prohibited the killing of a *striga*, for Christians are not to believe that a woman is capable of devouring man's entrails. It has been proposed that the term *Frigaholda* in the manuscript just discussed is a misreading of the word *striga*, and that the whole passage, with the name *holda*, is an interpolation (Boudriot 1928, 54). Even if one accepts this interpretation, the fact remains that some copyist in the Middle Ages found the two mythical personalities, Holda and Friga, close enough to each other to conflate them, reflecting their proximity in the minds of the people.

It is worth dwelling upon these names because they offer us a rare insight into the conceptions of early medieval men about the powers and beings that occupied important places in their beliefs. Properly to understand the statements in Burchard's *Corrector* and other penitentials one has to consider the changes these 'beings' suffered when taken from popular culture into the texts of clerical authors. In the popular mind Holda was a peaceful kind of creature, which is indicated even by her name, related to *hold*, 'devoted', and *huld*, 'protection'.[25] For the compilers of guidebooks for confessors, Holda and other such figures of popular belief turned into evil spirits and appeared in exclusively negative terms. They were seen as sources of evil, phantoms begetting the devil in the heads of ignorant folk, distracting them from the path of truth. Jakob Grimm (1939: 188) recorded that belief in Holda was particularly strong in Hesse and Thuringia, the region where Burchard had grown up, and this explains why he was so well informed about these mythical beings and their role in the spiritual life of the people. This is one of the cases where we can see the bishop of Worms not being satisfied with repeating the passages of older penitentials, but adding material from his own observations.

In another chapter of the *Corrector*, Burchard discusses the beliefs of 'criminal women, having given themselves to Satan' and their nocturnal assemblies. He records that many of them imagine covering immense distances on different animals in order to meet for the sabbath. There for the duration of several nights they 'serve the pagan goddess Diana, their mistress'. 'Alas, if only they themselves had been the victims of their unbelief and had not enticed many others to the path of ruinous contagion!', exclaims Burchard. 'For incalculable numbers of people, seduced by their false fantasies, persuaded as to the truth of it all and believing it, deviate from the true faith, sinking into pagan delusion, thinking that there is some kind of other deities and higher powers, besides the one true God.' In fact it is the devil who appears in various forms and guises and deceives the minds subordinate to him by all kinds of apparitions. 'But who is so stupid and foolish', concludes Burchard, 'as to accept something seen in sleep as reality, not only spiritually but also corporeally?' Guided by the authority of the Bible, Burchard states that all those who believe in such delusions forfeit the true faith and should be subject to a two-year penance.[26]

In her capacity as the servant of the devil, the witch was eventually included in the world of Christian demonology, which, as we know, finally led to the catastrophic mass persecution of women in the early modern centuries. The authors of the *Malleus Maleficarum* borrowed heavily from medieval texts on witches' sabbaths and nocturnal flights but changed their overall assessment. For Burchard, as for his models (the fifth-century canon *Episcopi* and the eighth to ninth-century texts of Regino of Prüm), the fantastic exploits of flying women were absurd delusions and reprehensible superstitions, created by persons misled by evil spirits. Faithful Christians were not supposed to believe any of this, but the *Malleus* and its innumerable successors took it all for granted (Roskoff 1896: 1, 271). It is beyond the scope of the present study – because it lies beyond the confines of the Middle Ages, even if some popular writers like to call it 'medieval' – to discuss the reasons and causes of the horrible witch-hunts in the ages of the Renaissance and the Enlightenment.[27] Recent research has focussed on the collective psyche that leads to mass hysteria and persecution. It is obvious from the penitentials that many elements of those later events, popular belief in witches and in the ability of men and women to enter into a compact with the devil, were present in the preceding centuries. These beliefs did not originate with Christianity, for they are to be found among the most diverse cultures of the world (Marwick 1975), even if the hypothesis that the witches' sabbath was a survival of some cult of fertility has recently been seriously questioned.

The penitentials contain extensive information on beliefs about the activities of the ill-intentioned women 'led astray by Satan'. While the husband is peacefully sleeping in bed, in the arms of his wife, she is able to slip away through locked doors and join other women misled by the same delusion. They are able to destroy Christians, without any visible weapon, boil their flesh, eat it, insert into their bodies straw or woodchips instead of their hearts, and make them live again. Other human beings were also believed to be able to escape from locked houses, rise into the night sky and wage battles in the clouds, inflicting and receiving wounds.[28]

These beliefs, so consistently denounced by the church, seem to have been of great antiquity. The lore about battles between warriors in the sky recalls the Scandinavian myths about the *einherjar* fighting Odin's wars in Walhalla: heroes, fallen in combat, taken to the heavenly battlefields. As late as the fourteenth century, Rudolph of Schlettstadt still wrote about nightly assemblies and feasts to which people flew in hordes, anointing themselves with grease.[29] He tells a story about a Swabian nobleman, Svigerus, who had stained his soul by robbery, pillage and violence. This man once met on the road a whole army of defeated soldiers, who could find no peace by day or by night. Just as they had served the devil while alive, so after death they were tormented by demons. This was, apparently, the Christian transformation of the Germanic myth of the *einherjar*. Svigerus is placed among these hapless souls, for the same fate awaits him after his death.[30]

In the *Corrector*, Burchard also entertains the question whether the confessant believes that 'those commonly called Fates [*parcae*] exist' and that they determine the life of the newborn or can 'transform it into a wolf, that which vulgar folly calls werewolf or into any other shape'. 'If you believe what cannot happen because it must not happen – namely, that the divine image can be changed into any form or appearance by anyone except almighty God – you should fast on bread and water for ten days.' There is also penance for believing that 'there are women of the wilds, called *sylvaticas* who, they say, are in bodily form, and, when they wish, show themselves to their lovers and having amused themselves disappear'.[31]

It should be noted that Burchard speaks of a great number of 'fools seduced by evil spirits' who held these abberant beliefs and passed them down from generation to generation. The fairy-tale world of medieval Germany seems to have been quite diverse: it had inhabitants from Germanic mythology and from classical Rome; *parcae* and satyrs share its regions with Holda and werewolves. I doubt that it is of great use to describe these elements as 'survivals' of pagan cults, Germanic, Roman or otherwise. Their sources may have been many and varied. Of course, we should not forget that our informer is a well-read churchman, familiar with Greco-Roman mythology. Whatever their origins may have been, these diverse elements were fused in the rich soil of the popular mind, which assimilated and processed them in its own way, together with sometimes quite heterogeneous mythological and folkloric elements. The main point is that the very structure of this popular consciousness survived and was able continuously to reproduce highly consistent archaic traits, even within the context of Christianity and in spite of the ceaseless efforts of the church at the eradication of 'pagan superstitions'.

Burchard has a number of questions that are to be addressed to women alone. Their insidiousness gave him no peace.'Have you done what some women do at the instigation of the devil? When any child has died without baptism, they take the corpse of the little one and place it in some secret place and transfix the little body with a stake, saying that if they did not do so the little child would arise and injure many. If you have done so, or consented to or believed this, you should do penance for two years.'[32] If the mother died in childbirth, she too was handled in this way. Burchard knows of another illicit custom, punished merely by ten days' fast: when a child dies after baptism, some buried him so that they 'put in his right hand a paten of wax with the host and in his left hand put a chalice, also of wax, with wine'.[33] Such specific perceptions of the meaning of Christian rites were seen by the clergy as profanation, and properly punished.

Magical practices connected with the dead took some quite bizarre forms. A slain man was often buried with a certain ointment in his hand, 'as if by that ointment his wound can be healed after death'.[34] Clearly, this was no reference to the resurrection of the body, but rather to an assumed active life after death. 'Foolish women are accustomed to do such vanities' in the house of a dead person (so Burchard tells us) that they 'run to the water and silently bring a jar of water, and when the dead body is raised up, pour this water under the bier, and as the corpse is being carried out of the house watch that it be raised not higher than to the knees',[35] and this is done to preserve the health of the living. The penitentials strictly forbid sacrifices to the dead, pagan funeral rites, wakes and feasts at the burial. Burchard inquires: 'Did you sing diabolical songs there and perform dances which the pagans have invented by the teaching of the devil; and did you drink there and make merry... as if rejoicing over a brother's death?' He prescribes a fast of thirty days for such observances.[36] The church also denounced other, traditional expressions of grief such as setting one's hair on fire, marking the face by wounds or tearing clothes to pieces.[37] Some rites performed over the corpse were believed to open a window to the future.[38] The belongings of the dead man were of great magical importance: apparently, one could cause harm by tying knots in the belt of a dead man. Similar magic could be performed by hitting a dead man's chest with carding combs. An obscure practice involved the bier, which was taken apart while the corpse was borne out of the house.[39]

The most diverse examples of magic were observed by the sharp eyes of Burchard of Worms. As McNeill (1938: 43) noted, 'the stern bishop' had a 'fine intellectual interest' in these primitive and obscure observances. Of course, this interest was in no way accompanied by sympathy: the bishop's main concern was to save the souls of his flock. But he has done an excellent job in describing the many kinds of 'vanities' and 'foolishnesses' observed 'by many'. Therefore, in contrast to many of his predecessors, who merely copied older models, his *Corrector* is a rich treasure-house for popular practices and beliefs, which in all likelihood were alive and well known in his diocese during his episcopate.

Magic is connected to divination and soothsaying, and the denunciation of magicians and fortune-tellers runs through the penitential literature. *Mathematici*, foretelling the future from the course of the stars, are punished by five years' fast,[40] and jugglers (*caragii*), who 'can foretell the future from some kind of writings' are also denounced.[41] Divination was equated with murder by the church Fathers, and Byzantine emperors passed strict laws against *matematikoi*. Still, these soothsayers, who 'confused the minds of unstable persons' during their 'bacchanalia', seem to have been popular throughout the Middle Ages. Judging from the repeated prohibitions, particularly widespread was a kind of fortune-telling from Scriptures, 'falsely called' *sortes sanctorum*[42] (Riché 1962: 539). Oracles by the flight of birds (auguries) were also sought.[43]

As usual, Burchard of Worms discusses these practices most explicitly. In the *Corrector* he asks: 'Have you consulted magicians and led them into your house in order to seek out any magical trick or to avert it; or did you invite ... diviners to demand from them the things to come as from a prophet, and those who practice lots [*sortes exercent*] or expect by lots to foresee the future, or those who are devoted to auguries and incantations?'[44] The penitential ascribed to the Venerable Bede and the so-called *Penitential of Egbert* (*c*. 1000 A.D.) contain similar clauses, and both suggest that such practices were common among clergy and laymen alike.[45]

Burchard knows about oracles sought in codices or in tablets, from gospels and from psalters; he knows and condemns the practice of 'doing or saying anything by way of sorcery or magic in beginning any task' instead of invoking the name of God. He describes customs of fortune-telling by throwing grains of barley on the still-hot fireplace (jumping grains foretell danger) and of divining the fate of a sick person by looking under a stone on the way to his or her house (any living thing found under the stone indicates that the person will recover). Ten, twenty and thirty days of penance are imposed on those who practise such things.[46] He also denounces, 'what some are wont to believe', that the side from which a crow croaks when one starts a journey can foretell the success of the trip. Others trust the flight of a kind of owl (*muriceps* = mouse-catcher) in deciding about a lodging-place; others again avoid leaving the house before the cock crows,[47] and so on, and so forth.

One has the impression that every step of medieval people was accompanied by acts or gestures for the purpose of securing success and deflecting bad luck and disaster. Danger threatened from every quarter, and precautionary measures, be they divinations, incantations or the observance of signs and auguries, were of great importance. As if that were not enough, sorcery may become necessary, in order to counter one's enemies. Again Burchard: 'Have you done what some women, filled with the discipline of Satan, are wont to do, who watch the footprints and traces of Christians and remove a turf from their footprints and watch it and hope thereby to take away their health or life?'[48] The penance for this was two years' fast, in some penitentials even five. For the purposes of black magic, so it appears, 'diabolical characters' were made of grass and amber 'at the persuasion of the devil Jupiter'; these may have been runic texts of magic value. The same canon also mentions the observance of Thursday (Thor's day) in honour of Jupiter (Thor, Donar) (Boudriot 1928: 58).[49]

Burchard records a rather elaborate magical procedure, in which a woman smears her naked body with honey, rolls in wheat and then takes the grains that have stuck to her to the mill. There she 'makes the mill go round backwards against the sun' (a well-known magical or 'evil' movement!) 'and so grind the flour'. Bread baked from such flour causes, according to one text, her husband to become feeble and die, or, in another text, to become a better lover.[50] It is noteworthy that the authors of penitentials knew about many folk practices, but were not quite sure what the purpose of the magic was. Naturally, in popular imagination the same practice could serve both 'white' and 'black' magic.

Love magic attracted special attention from the confessors. Burchard knows of women who believe 'such improbable things' as that women can change the minds of men from love to hate or from hate to love.[51] Love potions and magical tricks were also used by adulterers in order to hinder their lovers from contracting lawful marriages.[52] Burchard records several esoteric prescriptions used 'by some women' to assure greater attention from their menfolk, including baking menstrual blood in the bread or feeding them with fish that has been suffocated in the vagina.[53] There are also references to clerics, even bishops, who try to use magical tricks to secure the forbidden affection of women.

These scenes of divination, soothsaying and magic, so vividly described in the penitentials, transport us into a world usually hidden from 'official' Christianity. Some of the customs recall ancient Germanic or classical ways of handling sacral powers; others are rooted in the darkness of great antiquity, while closely related to popular practices which have frequently survived into our own times. We encounter echoes of ancient myths and what V. Ia. Propp styled the 'historical roots of magic tales'. We recognize parallels to rites and beliefs recorded among 'primitive' tribes and peoples on faraway continents. Whatever the origins and parallels of these practices may be, the significant thing about them is their extraordinary, one might say striking, vitality in a period which is usually regarded as completely controlled by Christian spirituality.

If one does not classify the features of 'paganism' or 'demonism' according to the cardinal sins, as the authors of the penitentials usually do, but looks at their diverse manifestations as a whole and as representative of a general mode of thought and perception, the spiritual world of the common layman emerges. Even if this was different from official Christianity, it was by no means 'pagan'. The penitentials of the high Middle Ages rarely refer to pagan deities or those sacred places and idols that have been destroyed in the age of conversion. It is not against heathen 'religion' that the major battle is fought by the father-confessors. The parishioners come to church, pray to God, profess the Creed and go to confession. Of course, not all of them comport themselves in the most proper fashion, and we read about the punishment of those who do not leave their worldly affairs when going to church, chatter idly on their way or do not pray for those buried in the church-yard.[54] Others seem to have moved their lips merely for appearance, but not to have prayed during service, indulging rather in idle talk instead of offering their thoughts to the glory of God.[55] But these are just marginal complaints about the occasional vanity and unruliness of the faithful, not implying lack of faith, still less hostility to the religion of Christ. All in all, these parishioners behaved essentially as Christians.

However, this did not exhaust their spiritual life. The vulgarized and frequently distorted tenets of popular Catholicism included also a powerful layer of behaviour patterns, views of the world and ways of thought that had little in common with the tenets taught by the priests. The clergy does not seem to have been able successfully to counter this complex of superstitions and practices, as witnessed by the repetition of the questions and prohibitions about 'pagan' customs over series of centuries. It was possible to destroy or discredit the old gods, but not to eliminate traditional habits of thinking, embedded as they were in the eternally repetitive cycle of agrarian life and linked with the many techniques of 'managing' the matters of the world by way of magic.

This type of consciousness remained more or less unchanged over a very long historical period, reproducing again and again primordial mental structures.

However, in the period under study, this kind of 'magical world-view', if this is the right term, cannot be regarded as mere petrified survival of the past. In fact it had entered into an intricate interaction with Christian beliefs and ideas that had been assimilated, one way or another, by the common people. Traditional magic and Christianity did not form distinct layers or separate compartments in the medieval mind. A unity arose from their encounter – a unity surely not devoid of contradiction and ambivalence, but one in which old magical beliefs and Christian teachings found meaning and function precisely in their mutual correlation.

Even those peasants who did not go to confession knew full well that divination, sorcery and other practices were forbidden acts. Their relationship to magic, which they were unable to renounce, had been changed decisively in comparison to 'pagan times', when all this was unquestioned and an integral part of their world-view. On the other hand, magic expanded into Christianity's own territory. Mass, which they had to attend as passive onlookers, and the sacraments were perceived by laymen as magic rituals, whose theological meaning remained obscure to them. Magical thinking was well able to accommodate the cult of saints: as we have seen, saints, ideally embodying the lofty ideals of humility, asceticism and divine service, became miracle-workers in the eyes of the common folk, thus fulfilling a role that fitted well into the magical perception of natural and super-natural powers. Other aspects of Christian teaching were less easily accommodated. The prescriptions of the penitentials on diet, marriage, sexual practices – in a word, the Christian system of taboos – suggest some of the conflicts between the two world-views.

The rather elaborate lists of unclean or spoiled food, meat and beverages, contaminated by rodents, bird-droppings, insects or even carrion,[56] suggest that the clerical view of these matters was very different from that of the parishioners. In parts it probably reflected the rather primitive and unsanitary conditions in which the great majority of the populace lived. It is most likely that poor peasants were not much inclined to fastidiousness and did not care too much about handling food with dirty hands or bothering to keep bugs out of their kitchens. But it is also possible that they were unable to afford the luxury of letting the carcass of a fallen animal simply rot away. True, the penitentials contain exemptions for cases of extreme necessity and hunger, and relax categorical prohibitions.

However, in many cases it is obvious that the dietary rules belong to the struggle that churchmen fought against un-Christian magic. Potions and compounds prepared with the use of human excrement, dead mice or other animals were used for magic.[57] Especially strict was the prohibition of using the blood of animals, for it was known that pagans drank blood during their cults and used it as libation.[58] Such feasts, at sacred locations denounced by the church, were held as late as the eleventh century in Germany.[59] Apparently even rituals with human blood were not uncommon.[60] Similarly prohibited were common meals between Christians and non-Christians, pagans, Jews or not-yet baptized catechumens.[61] The rigorous definition of dietary taboos was in direct contradiction to the traditions of the population which could not be easily overridden even after conversion to Christianity. The notion that food could be 'clean' or 'unclean', especially in regard to ritual feasting, a very important part of pre-Christian social and religious life,[62] was totally alien to the people.

The civilizing function of the church is very conspicuous in regard to gluttony and drunkenness. As we know, the 'barbarians' knew no moderation in matters of food and drink: the Nordic sagas depict rather graphic scenes of mass drunkenness. The penitentials frequently cite statements of the church Fathers, above all, of St Benedict, that 'there is nothing so contrary to Christianity as intoxication and hard drinking'.[63] In Burchard's penitential a whole series of questions is aimed at these trespasses: 'Are you not in the habit of eating and drinking beyond need?' 'Did you not drink so much that you became drunk and vomited?' 'Did you drink out of boastfulness?' and so on.[64] Severe penance is prescribed in all penitentials for those who give themselves up to gluttony, who overeat, who are unable to wait for the end of the fast or the hour of the meal. Special punishment is meted out to those who induce others (out of 'false friendship' or 'hatred') to become drunk or who conduct themselves indecently while drunk. Whole sections of penitentials are devoted to clergy and laymen who – apparently owing to drink or food – are unable to hold the host in their mouth but spit it out, which was a very grave sin. Vomiting and other signs of gluttony and drunkenness are frequently mentioned. Apparently, these vices were very difficult to keep under control, maybe even impossible; and the laity was joined in them by its priests: clergy who mumble and are unable to perform the service due to drunkenness are referred to; monks, priests and even bishops feature as inveterate drunkards, brawlers and blasphemers. Their punishment was very severe, including defrocking. Extenuating circumstances were considered only if a priest was invited by a parishioner and, unaccustomed to drink, got intoxicated at the insistence of the host, or if he got drunk due to illness or weakness caused by fast.

To educate the people to moderation in food and drink was no mean task for the church in the process of the formation of feudal society, with its distinct regulation of the distribution of surplus foodstuff. The traditions of the pre-feudal age, based on largesse and demonstrative wastefulness had to be overcome not only for religious, but also for social and economic, reasons. In the feudal age, feasting became restricted to the warrior classes (Gurevich 1972: 225).

The 'educational' aims of the church in the sphere of sexual life had several aspects. First, the church insisted on restricting marriage among kinsmen. Several clauses in the penitentials are directed against incest. Sexual taboos among certain degrees of kinship existed, of course, in barbarian societies as well, but the Roman church expanded the circle of those prohibited to marry to the fourth or even the fifth degree. Besides imposing severe penance, the church insisted that sinful unions be broken up. The prohibitions also included spiritual, 'fictive' kinfolk: that is, godparents and godchildren. All penitentials contain prohibitions against the marriage of priests, but, as is well known, this issue was, and remained for centuries, a very controversial one.

The second goal of ecclesiastical 'sexual education' was to bring relationships into conformity with public morality and Christian values (Browe 1932; Noonan 1966). The sexual act was in principle regarded as sinful and was tolerated by the church only because God had commanded men to procreate and multiply. Proceeding from the antinomy of enjoyment *vs* continuation of the family (Flandrin 1969: 1394), the penitentials censure all manifestations of carnal desire; spouses, if lawfully married, could have intercourse exclusively for the purpose of producing offspring, not for 'the sake of passionate love'.[65]

The church considered itself obliged to meddle in the married life of the layman, including its most intimate aspects. The separation of life into public and private was unknown. Textbooks for confessors instruct priests to inquire whether the confessant made love during 'prohibited' times: before confession, during church holidays and fasts, during pregnancy, in the post-natal period, during menstruation, while under penance, and so on. Any of these was to be expiated by penance. Confessors incessantly warned their parishioners against sexual relations 'for desire' and against contraceptive practices.[66]

Carnal desire was a dangerous enemy of the church. Priests tried vigilantly to enforce the sexual taboos and to punish their disregard both in married life and, even more, in the totally prohibited extra-marital relations. Severe penance was imposed for seduction and rape, adultery and many kinds of 'perversions'. Penitentials contain descriptions and long enumerations of prohibited acts in great detail. Burchard of Worms is in this respect also very well informed, and his erotic vocabulary is very impressive indeed.

Sections of the penitentials on the observance of the vow of chastity and celibacy by the religious suggest that this also was a field fraught with many difficulties. Naturally, not only active trespasses and adultery were punished, but also the mere intention of 'fornication', even though the extent of the penance was different. From these passages, one receives a rather vivid image of men censured for illicit sexual relations, suffering extensive humiliation or, in other cases, fighting to repress the temptations of the flesh. On the other hand, the penitentials permit us to detect the many forms of aberration into which the strict anti-sexual prescriptions of the church have led its servants.

The incarnation of all temptation, drawn to and drawing others into the abyss of carnal sin was, in the eyes of the clerical authors, woman, servant of the devil, witch and pagan by her very nature. Burchard of Worms devotes dozens of chapters to sins committed by and with women. In the *Corrector* the connection, as seen by churchmen, between magical approaches to the world and sexuality is particularly well elaborated. In the sexual act the church has always seen the threat of penetration into the world of an authority beyond reason, undisciplined and threatening. Eroticism places the soul in an improper condition. Sex draws man away from God, but, because it is not possible completely to suppress it, the sexual sphere of life has to be kept under the strictest control and the Christian's mind has to be inculcated with the sinfulness and the inherent danger in it. Repressed sexuality in the Middle Ages gave rise to extraordinary mystical (and heretical!) experiences, but also to mass hysteria and gross perversions.[67]

This account does not by far exhaust the list of problems posed by studying the penitentials. These books offer insights into popular culture through the eyes of the father-confessors; hence they are sources for clerical ideas and intentions, besides at the same time shedding light on the beliefs and practices of laymen. The penitentials, written by and for the clergy – preoccupied, as all of them were, with the sinfulness of their flock – give, of course, a distorted and one-sided picture of the popular mind. The 'questionnaires' of the penitentials interpret all aspects of popular belief in categories of sin and trespass against Christian virtues, induced by evil spirits. The picture is distorted, because the integral whole of popular culture is, like a broken mirror, shattered in so many pieces.

The authors of these handbooks did not understand and did not wish to understand the 'exotic' culture of the lower classes, and certainly did not wish to give credit to it. Precisely this refusal to understand exposes the distance between the official ecclesiastical culture and the world of the common people. The latter was kept 'out of sight', or at any rate out of writing for many centuries. In the confessional this distance had to be bridged and the silence over popular culture broken. The parish priests were obliged to find out whether their 'children' were holding impious views or following nefarious customs. Of course we cannot tell how often confessants replied 'yes' to the questions we know were asked of them. Hence, there is no way to establish any kind of quantitive information on the number of trespasses against church morality and the actual frequency of pagan observances. But, assuming that the authors of penitentials, in spite of their adherence to tradition, did in fact know quite well the real conditions in the parishes and formulated their questions according to these, we may take their word that much of what they were concerned about actually existed. That is why the penitentials constitute such an important source for the historian of culture.

It is through the penitentials that we gain insight into the daily life of medieval villagers and townsfolk. We read about the means by which peasants tried to influence the weather, increase the harvest, cure the sick, foretell the future or charm a lover. Contemporary ethnographers and sociologists can observe many similar or parallel practices among present-day 'primitive' peoples and lower social groups; for the Middle Ages few other sources of information exist on these matters. Popular magic does not seem to have changed much over the centuries, maybe even the millennia, even if its forms have. But just because it is ever present and its function rather immutable, it would be a mistake to neglect the study of its history. It is most important not to isolate single features which seem to be interesting or quaint, but to see in the manifestations of popular magic that 'system of explanation of the world which defines its rhythm and determines its direction' (Leroi-Gourhan, 1964: 86). In this sense the study of medieval magical practices may lead to an understanding of the explanatory system that dominated the minds of men and women in those centuries.

The questions in the penitentials frequently refer to the same motifs and often to the very same characters that are known to us from folklore and fairy-tale of much later origin. Divination and sorcery, rites of passage and of fertility, werewolves, witches and soothsayers, all these belong to folklore.[68] But storytellers are rarely prosecuted and fairy-tales are not usually associated with mortal sin. The world inquired into and exorcized by the confessors is not the wonderful kingdom of fairies, but an 'underworld' of magic and ritual, part of the everyday life of the people, seen as a serious threat to the Catholic church. Folklore and folk-tale are not matters of faith but products of artful coping with reality, removed into a surreal time and space, separated from the real world by a boundary, rather fluid but well known to everyone. Popular magic, by contrast, was a means of actually mastering reality and determining social conduct. In it the church collided with an alien universe determined by powers which had no relationship to the Christian god or, perhaps, to any god at all. They were primordial and primary. These were the powers which united man and nature in a complex intercourse and continuous exchange.

The question of religion *vs* magic is a complex one (Tokarev 1959), and need not detain us now. Suffice it to say that magic is in some ways part of the religious experience. It is well known that the most attractive aspect of Christianity for the ordinary believer has been its ceremonial, very much permeated by magic. But, of course, not all magic is equal. The penitentials attacked that magic which was 'untamed' by the church, that was not 'baptized' and incorporated into the liturgical ritual.

One of the main differences between religion and magic is, to my mind, that religion 'humanizes' the world by imparting anthropomorphic character to it and its forces and by personifying the divine; while magic is rather a 'naturalization' of man, embedding him in the wholeness of the cosmos. In the still universal pre-Christian system of magical thought nature was not opposed to man and not perceived as an alien entity. It was seen as an all-embracing, living element, permeated with mysterious, potent forces, and man was included in it. The interaction between humans and the rest of nature was so intense and complete that they were incapable of looking at it, as it were, from outside. Man felt himself to be embedded in the powerfields and forcelines of the cosmos and followed its eternal rhythm. This perception explains why it was considered necessary to hold feasts and perform rituals for the continuation of natural order, such as 'helping' the moon recover its light.[69] Fields needed not only ploughing and sowing, but also proper libations; domesticated animals would not bear offspring without witchcraft; drought could not be stopped without young maidens 'enticing living water'. In this kind of thinking, magic and ritual are not means to supplement natural causality or practices applied to complement the natural movement of things; they are integral parts of the way the world moves, connecting natural and supernatural in an indissoluble whole.

Such was the magical view of the world – in the pre-Christian past. However, as we have seen, in the penitentials it appears in confrontation with the Christian image of the world, causing the previous self-evident unity to change into a strained relationship of connected but opposite poles. Man and nature are not identical any more; men still feel themselves part of nature but realize increasingly their alienation from it. The link between them ceases to be organic and becomes symbolic.

In medieval popular belief, animated nature exerts beneficial or harmful influence on people; hence it is necessary to recognize its mysteries and manipulate its forces appropriately. Witches, sorcerers, cunning men and women, were privy to these secrets and able to use them for their own ends – to help or to harm. A specific understanding of the powers in nature was of immediate importance for one's life.[70] One could receive assurances for success by observing the revolution of the stars, the flight of birds or other signs. A brew of herbs or of human excrement, or of certain animals' flesh and hide, could arouse love, heal illness or protect the members of the house. Chthonic powers were often called upon in these rites. The turn-of-the-year festivities in which people dressed up in animal skins and donned masks of calves or deer 'in pagan manner'[71] were visual demonstrations of their unity with nature. Popular assemblies and feasts, games and oblations usually took place under the open sky, at springs, in groves or at cross-roads. Several questions in the penitentials are directed at hindering this kind of identification of man and nature, attempting to tear people away from it, for the only clerically approved contact with a higher power was in and through the church of God.

Ancient, pre-Christian magical practices did not vanish. However, they existed now in an entirely new mental context. Their practitioners and participants had to become aware of the limits of magic and had to develop a critical attitude towards it. Not only on the rare occasions of formal confession, but all the time, the faithful had to realize the chasm between the different forms of behaviour prescribed by nature magic on the one hand and by Christianity on the other. Magic was too important for him to abandon it altogether, but at the same time, he was ceaselessly plagued by the thought of its being prohibited and sinful, and hence by the fear of eternal punishment for trespasses against divine commands.

The text of the penitentials betrays that the power which in the eyes of these 'sinners' and 'deluded persons' ruled the world was fate. Its personifications, 'the three sisters' (*parcae*), Holda, Freya and other such beings are frequently mentioned. Divination, soothsaying and magical activities are all connected with the basic underlying notion of fate. The sources under review do not permit us to analyse this concept and to find out, whether medieval people thought of 'fate' as a personal or as a super-personal principle, as a power defining the life of each person or of families, clans or peoples. In the Icelandic sagas and lays about gods and heroes, fate appears mainly as an ethical necessity, dictating the behaviour of the individual by expressing the norms of society which exerts pressure on its members (Piekarczyk 1971: 96; Gurevich 1979: 40, 51, 150). In the penitentials, fate presents itself in a different form and extends into that undifferentiated relationship between man and nature which characterizes agrarian societies.

Of course, this divergence may very well be due to the difference in

genre: saga and heroic poetry are mainly concerned with relations
between people and treat nature and man's influence over it with
indifference, seeing it as an unproblematic matter.[72] The authors of the
penitentials, by contrast, are most concerned with their parishioners'
attitude to nature, and wish to ensure that it does not conflict with the
belief in an all-powerful God.[73] The church attempted to eliminate the
intimacy between man and nature, for it was in conflict with Christian
tenets, according to which nature does not have any autochthonous
virtue but is merely a creature and a servant of the Lord. There was no
place for divine providence in the magical complex of man–nature.

The authors of the penitentials formulate rather harshly their disbelief
in magical connection between humans and the rest of nature. 'You do
not seriously believe', asks Burchard of Worms, 'that the roosters's crow
can drive off evil spirits better than divine intervention?' And his attitude
to the belief in witches is expressed in this question: 'Do you indeed
believe that anyone but almighty God is capable of changing the form
of a creature?' Magical rites were regarded by the clergy as attempts to
'evade' or 'by-pass' the judgment of God.[74]

Medieval believers thus faced a serious question: to which of the two
powers should they bow? They were confronted by a very serious
dilemma, forced to opt for a definite mode of behaviour. Magic of the
pre-conversion era had imposed on pagans such a universal script for
behaviour as left no space for choice or for self-evaluation. The notion
of sin transformed the spiritual life of the faithful in a very profound
manner. Once their priest defined sin for them and asked them about
trespasses in the confessional, they had to acquire the habit of self-
analysis even outside the annual (or less frequent) confession. It is not
the everyday life and its magical or other practices that changed, but the
new conditions arising from the conversion of the formerly pagan
peasants and warriors, which, as we have seen, had placed all this in an
entirely novel context.

The penitentials contain numerous clauses against the cult of natural
and other than Christian supernatural powers. It is, however, not
surprising that these cults surfaced not only in the early Middle Ages
(see above, ch. 2), but throughout the centuries. They referred to tangible
experiences of people living in an agrarian world, while the theological
abstractions of 'official' Christianity were not easy to grasp. Magical
practices satisfied more than one need: the religious-ceremonial, the
philosophical and the aesthetical, all at the same time. It is noteworthy
that the clerical authors of the penitentials are unable to define what
exactly their parishioners do when they gather, 'at the devil's behest' at
their assemblies in field or forest; do they pray, make sacrifices, play or
feast? In magical observances many different social and spiritual relations

are merged inseparably. This was totally alien to the clergy, who could not understand why at a wake or funeral people were feasting and dancing, instead of shedding tears, while during the church service they were inattentive and disorderly, like children.[75] But the historian of culture may see in these fragmentary pieces of information a precious hint at a most important archaic feature: ritual laughter. We obtain a glimpse of these medieval men's and women's attitude to death. Ritual laughter was in fact an ancient form of piety, turning death into a new birth, a 'magical means to create new life' (Propp 1976: 177, 188). Piety it may have been, but certainly not of the type the Christian priests expected from their flock.

The divergence between clerical civilization and popular consciousness also entailed a different perception of time. Time for agrarian people is nature's time, a succession of annual cycles, marked by the change of the seasons. In the peasant reckoning of time, nothing is new, everything repeats itself from birth to death, passing through the natural stages of life. Time is at the same time mythical and eternal. This perception of time implies a particular understanding of past, present and future. They do not form an irreversible, linear sequence, but rather are arranged next to one another, in a united mythological sphere. The past may recur again, and the future can be foretold well before it happens. Things to come already exist somewhere; hence they can be explored and changed by way of magic. The penitentials, as we have seen, attack both the festivities connected with seasons (Kalends of January) and the attempt to foretell the future or tamper with time. In Christian belief time is God's creation and governed exclusively by divine will; mortals can neither foresee it nor change its course. By contrast to mythical–natural 'circular' time, the time of the church is essentially linear and historical. It has a definite direction, and when its course is run it will come to an end. The world undergoes change in the course of time and the past cannot be repeated, even if certain parallels between earlier and later events can be established – as was frequently done in the typological interpretation of the Old Testament in terms of the New. Sermons and church iconography must have made common believers aware of this historical type of time; and here, once again, they were faced with a conflict, this time between their own magical–natural time perception and the linear–progressive reckoning of the ages in the divine history of salvation.

Considering all this, I venture to doubt the validity of Bakhtin's proposition about the 'turning off' of time in the medieval Christian world-view, which is to be contrasted with the historicity of popular culture in the carnival (Bakhtin 1965: 277, 351, 429, 436–9, etc.). On the one hand, Bakhtin correctly points to the cosmic character of popular world-perception, to its 'unity in time', to the 'uninterrupted duration' of the 'popular body' and to its 'historical immortality'. But how can these notions be reconciled with the alleged historicity? A cardinal parameter of cosmic world-perception is the cycle and its eternal return, and not directional time focussed on unique events and particular occurrences. Time in this sense individualizes; but popular culture was most definitely opposed to individualization, as Bakhtin very clearly demonstrated. The carnival was a break in the normal flow of time, rather like a notch on the wheel of eternal repetition, a point on the circle, but certainly not a unique moment giving a historical dimension to the course of time.

The idea of linear time and the singularity of events, in sharp contrast to eternity, led to a certain devaluation in Christian teaching of time, so that it became a symbol of imperfection, transitoriness and vanity – characteristics of the mortal vale of sorrows. On the other hand, for the archaic world-view, time does not exist as an abstract category separated from concrete reality. However, this does not mean that the two kinds of time perception did not interact; as a result of their interpenetration there emerged a specific medieval historical understanding characterized by a synthesis of variability and unalterability. To the extent that people assimilated Christian teachings, they became aware of their own partici-pation in the divine history of salvation – that is, in a progression of time towards a definite end, the Day of Judgment.[76] It must have been precisely through this notion, the fear of punishment for sins and of the day of reckoning, that people gradually came to accept the idea of 'history' and the linear progression of time towards its divinely prescribed end (see below, chs. 4 and 5).

Thus, the contradiction between two highly divergent systems of world-perception did not remain, as it were, an external one between clergy on the one side and the common fold on the other; rather, it became internalized in the consciousness of medieval people. It led to the emergence of what may be termed parochial Catholicism, accom-modating the popular interpretation of official belief and considerably more sympathetic to the spiritual needs of the illiterate parishioners than high theology could ever have been.

In the text of the penitentials this contradiction appears as a deep chasm between the 'path of truth' along which the priests wish to lead their flock and 'pagan errors' to which the devil tries to lure them. Reality was much more complicated.[77] But, since we never hear the answers to the question suggested by the penitentials or the exchanges between father-confessor and confessant – containing, as they must have done, explanations, self-justifications, evasions and so forth – we have no access to its study. The penitentials present the contradiction between the two kinds of images of the world as one between opposing wholes, and we cannot ascertain how and to what extent *homo naturalis* was in fact transformed into *homo Christianus*.

Another limitation, or rather distortion, of the penitentials is that the 'superstitions' and 'evil practices' are, by the very nature of these books, treated as individual trespasses by the confessant. Only rarely do we find reference to the collective character of sinful acts. Confessional practice was based on the assumption of individual responsibility, while, clearly, the pagan practices, magic rituals and non-Christian feasts were embedded in the collective consciousness. The great strength and cohesion of collectives in agrarian societies, such as village communities, is proverbial, and we might assume that many of the 'sinful' acts denounced by the church were fully approved by the communities, in which they were seen as valid norms. The stability of these communities implied continuous reproduction of their collective consciousness, which bound members to their norms. The individual adjusted his or her thinking and conduct, mostly unconsciously, to these norms, for they had a great value and significance as expressions of belonging.

This fact contains, to my mind, one of the essential reasons for the failure of the church to extirpate the mental habits and magical practices of the common folk, however alien they might have been to Christian teaching. No doubt, parish priests had powerful means of compelling sinners to admit their unorthodox behaviour and perform the prescribed penance, but could repentance and ensuing correction mean a break with all old habits, once and for all? Did the 'sinners' not remain part of the same socio-psychological environment as before, when they had been induced to act in a way approved by the community but denounced by the church? Except by the relatively infrequent punishment of excommunication, the church could not even attempt to sever the ties between an 'erring' individual and the collective that at least condoned these 'errors'. The references to recidivists and the repetition of the same prohibitions over many centuries suggest that clerical authors were aware of the difficulties parish priests faced in tearing their 'children' away from the illicit ways of popular ideas and actions.

However one-sided and distorting the mirror of the penitentials may be – and what historical source does not have its own bias? – they reflect real aspects of medieval popular religious culture. Were medieval parishioners Christians or adherents of the officially abolished, but in fact surviving, paganism? They were, of course, Christians. Confession, demanding from believers a constant analysis of their behaviour, turned their spiritual eyes inward to their moral being and could not fail to exert a significant educational influence, even if such self-analysis was imposed on them by the probing questions of the priest. In the course of time the skill of introspection necessarily developed. Medieval Christianity both offered and demanded this kind of self-appraisal by institutionalizing it in the confessional.

Ruth Benedict and other anthropologists have proposed a classification of ethical models as cultures of shame or cultures of guilt. In the former, the behaviour of an individual is determined by the fear that any breach of social norms will cause his associates to look at him askance; his or her self-evaluation depends on the judgment of the collective. In the latter, the ethical consciousness of the individual is based on an internalized system which determines right or wrong personal conduct, regardless of the knowledge or censure of others. Of course, this classification maintains ideal types, and in every actual society one will find diverse norms informing social custom.

In medieval Europe we can detect elements of both types. In pre-Christian barbarian societies shame prevailed over guilt. The hero of the Germanic–Scandinavian epic looks at himself through the eyes of the collective; his behaviour will be judged by actions and not by intentions; guilt is proved not by admission but by legal procedure. The central category of 'barbarian' ethics consists in honour and glory. Conduct is above all formalized and not internalized.

Aspects of this culture of shame remained valid in the Christian epoch. The judgment of the group to which one belonged was still an important factor; a good example for this would be knightly honour. The daily supervision of the conduct of commoners in the parish was based on the same kind of collective censure. However, the individual is increasingly held to evaluate his own acts, regardless of the views of others. This self-analysis is always a dialogue, both formally as the believer asks himself the questions learned in the confessional, and metaphysically as it takes place in front of the highest, omniscient judge.[78]

These are the elements of popular spirituality, as they emerge from the study of the penitentials. It has, beyond doubt, to be called Christian, but this should not be taken to mean that it was identical with the Catholicism of papal decretals, synodal canons or theological *summae*. The closer look at this popular Christiantity which we have attempted through the penitentials may help us to understand the importance of miracles in the saints' lives, discussed in the preceding chapter. Once we have seen how central was the need for exerting influence on the weather, on health, on human actions and sentiments through magic, we can appreciate how the miracle-working power of the saint fulfilled, in a Christianized version, these very same expectations. In hagiography the saints were endowed with supernatural powers, and thereby appropriated to themselves – and the church – the forces that used to reside in pagan magic. But we have also seen how contradictory were different aspects of ecclesiastical and popular views: about man and nature, time and eternity, individual and collective responsibility. It will be our task to explore the co-existence of these conflicting traits in medieval minds through the study of other genres of Latin letters addressed to the common believer.

The study of P. Adam (1964) on the life of French parishes came to my notice only after the completion of this book. He notes that the difficulties encountered by the church in the earlier Middle Ages characterized the parishes of the fourteenth century as well. Most of the clergy were ignorant; the parish priest was in fact a peasant himself; many a *curé* was absent from his parish for long periods. Churches were often in poor repair, cemeteries turned into market-places where comedians performed; the village youth danced and brawled and kept their amorous meetings. He registers religious indifference, absence from Sunday service, obscene behaviour in church and the practice of magic and superstition all around.

When speaking about magical rituals, one should point to the fact that the official church itself performed 'magical' liturgies – such as the blessing of fields, tools, carts, food, and so on – while it denounced the essentially identical practices of the laymen. Hence it is obvious that it was not magic itself, nor the 'magical view of the world' shared by clergy and laymen alike, that bothered the churchmen, but merely the 'authority' which performed the rites. If it was securely in their hands, clergy did not object to magic and believed in it, just as simple peasants did.

Since my writing much new research has been done on witchcraft and witch-hunts (Macfarlane 1970; Thomas 1971; Kieckhefer 1979; Muchembled 1979; 1979a; Naess 1982). These works demonstrate that the widespread accusations of witchcraft in the early modern centuries, though formulated by learned theologians and lawyers, was based on the age-old fears of the lower social strata of the dark forces beyond their control. This explains why peasant or urban women (or occasionally men) were accused of witchcraft by neighbours who bore a grudge against them. At the end of the Middle Ages the traditional ecclesiastical teaching which had earlier denounced belief in witches was transformed into a theory in which witches featured as major tools of Satan. Combined with social conflicts during the disintegration of the medieval village community, this new attitude fostered that mass hysteria which led to the murder of many thousands of people accused of witchcraft.

4

THE *DIVINE COMEDY* BEFORE DANTE

Notions about the world beyond the grave are an integral component of the 'image of the world' that lies at the basis of one culture or another. They may add up to an unusually rich picture, and they can be 'null' when heaven is empty and all that is found on the other side of life is non-existence. In any case, both worlds – of life and of death – are present in a culture's consciousness and determine its essential characteristics.[1] Christianity ascribes to the otherworldly realm the reward and punishment for a completed life. The world beyond the grave, according to this world-view, is the real world, and the earthly world is its pale likeness, the soul's temporary abode on the path to its true homeland. The fears and hopes begotten of the expectations of the transit to that Other World persistently haunted medieval man and compelled him to fashion certain ideas about its arrangement.

To study the attitude of medieval people towards death and their notions about the Other World leads to an understanding of an important aspect of their consciousness. They populated the realm of the dead with their own aspirations and nightmares and thereby embodied their collective mental complexes and obsessions in the scenes and images of the Other World. Inevitably, moreover, and probably without understanding this themselves, medieval people carried over into the structure of the Other World the ideas about time and space, about human personality, and about the relationship of spirit to matter, which were the main parameters of their vision of the world.

We can study these notions in a relatively detailed way, since pictures of the Other World appear time and again in art and literature throughout the Middle Ages. They were an integral part of church iconography and frequently recurred in the consciousness of visionaries who spoke about their otherworldly travels. However, the visual representation of the death and resurrection of the soul in sculpture, manuscript illumination and engraving, on the one hand, and literary 'visions' on the other, offer two different patterns for interpreting the transit to the Other World and its structure. As a result, it is appropriate to discuss iconography and literary representation separately.

Even before entering the church the believer beheld scenes of the end of the world, the resurrection of the dead, and the Last Judgment on the portals and tympana. These pictures were at once attractive and terrifying, inspiring trepidation and awe before God and fear of his wrath and punishment. The medieval craftsmen who built and decorated the churches did not work on their own; they were guided by instructions from the clergy and were supposed to embody sacred texts in their artistic creations. The scenes on the façades of churches were inspired by Revelation and the Gospel of Matthew, but they had to be translated into the language of visible images. For a correct interpretation of these difficult passages of Scripture the works of medieval commentators and theologians were consulted.[2]

However, masons, sculptors and stained-glass craftsmen were not restricted to a slavish illustration of canonical texts. The transition from word to representation confronted them with new and complex problems, not only of a purely technical nature, but of a semantic one as well. It was necessary to express a series of symbols visually: the essential problem was in composing the individual moments of the sacred narrative. As Emile Mâle (1958: 389) notes, the visionary perception of the East, deprived of harmony and plasticity, was clothed in finished forms by the Latin spirit of the West, and this transition was inevitably accompanied by losses. But not only by losses, for the builders of the cathedrals also introduced new motifs and original interpretations and placed the emphases in their own way. To a great extent, these innovations were dictated by the scholarly commentaries whose instructions the craftsmen followed. At the same time the popular world-view also found its expression in them, naturally not in the conception and design of the whole, but in many details and methods of interpreting the material.

The picture of the drama of the end of the world unfolded on church façades in a series of consecutive acts which the believer learned to apprehend as succeeding one another in time. The first act, in conformity with Revelation (6:2–8), is personified by the horsemen of the Apocalypse, the harbingers of the approaching Judgment. In the tympanum Christ is usually depicted on a throne in the manner of a judge, surrounded by angels who herald the coming Judgment. At Christ's right and left stand the Virgin Mary and John the Baptist – the intercessors before God in behalf of the sinful human race.

At the sounding of the angelic trumpets the graves gape and the dead proceed from them. This scene of cemeteries come-to-life unfolds under Christ's feet. Among the resurrected, usually seen naked, some figures wear crowns and tiaras. This is to show the equality of all men in the face of God's judgment, from the commoner to the pope and the emperor. According to medieval theologians, everybody will be resurrected as a thirty-year-old, at the age at which Christ conquered death by rising after the Crucifixion. All the people leave their graves young and handsome, regardless of the age at which they died.

The scene of the Last Judgment, occupying the next tier of the portal, corresponds not so much to the words of Scripture as to later commentaries. In its centre the archangel Michael is depicted with scales in his hands. Alongside stands a wretched soul, trembling in anticipation of the verdict. In one bowl of the scales are its good deeds and in the other its sins, and the devil, playing the role of prosecutor, fruitlessly attempts to deceive God's justice by pressing down on the bowl of the sins. The grotesque blending in a single picture of high and low, of the terrifying and the ludicrous, of the spiritually beautiful and the corporeally deformed permeates this entire visual–semantic order. The idea of a physical weighing of man's deeds is, of course, much older than Christianity (Kretzenbacher 1958) and does not have a direct relation to the Gospels, but it was expressed by theologians beginning with Augustine and John Chrysostom. The bodily personification of sins and good deeds – at Chartres they are depicted as small beings sitting on the scales – reflected in a most suitable way the popular understanding of the metaphor. In other instances (Bourges, Amiens) the Lamb of God is placed on the scales of good deeds, visually illustrating the thesis that the soul's salvation depends not on a man's merits, but on God's grace.

Right and left of the archangel Michael two groups are moving away from him. These parts of the representation are not synchronous with the action of the central scene, but offer an idea of what takes place after the Judgment. To Michael's right God's elect are rejoicing in their justification as they are directed towards the doors of paradise. St Peter, stationed at his post at the gates with keys on his belt, symbolizes the church, which alone opens the door to salvation. Paradise itself is not depicted explicitly, but the words that the blessed will come to the 'bosom of Abraham' receive their artistic expression: angels bring miniature people – the souls of the elect – to a bearded man sitting on a throne, and there they repose on his lap. Such literal and visual personification of the biblical metaphor satisfied the need of the believers to imagine abstractions and symbols by the only way that was accessible to their understanding. One may add that female figures on the portals of churches, symbols of spiritual and corporeal virtues, and the statues of angels were also supposed to convey the notion of the joys of paradise.

To Michael's left is the group of condemned sinners, who, bound by great chains, are dragged by demons into hell. In contrast to the shining smiles of the blessed, the faces and bodies of the damned are filled with despair and despondency. While the group of the elect moves ceremoniously and harmoniously towards the gates of paradise, the crowd of the damned is restlessly chaotic. It was precisely in the interpretation of the latter that medieval craftsmen could allow themselves the greatest degree of fantasy. Grimacing and laughing demons, with anthropomorphic and zoomorphic features, urge the damned on, seize them, and throw them over into the gaping cesspool of hell: the monstrous jaws of the Leviathan or a cauldron under which a fire blazes. Here too demons bustle, fanning the raging flames with bellows, beating the condemned with blows and slowly stirring the hellish soup. Unlike visionary literature, in which different categories of sinners experience distinct types of torments, in the sculptures the sinners' punishments are rarely differentiated. The common herd of the doomed is escorted by demons to hellfire. Occasionally avarice can be discerned by the purse hung on the neck of the condemned. Among the sinners one can see prelates and monarchs, sometimes (as at Rheims) in full vestments, with crown and mitre.

The artistic interpretation of hell, unlike the construction of the other scenes of the end of the world, was not based on theological texts. Moreover, the sculptural depiction of infernal tortures even contradicted the interpretations of theologians, who considered that the tortures of hell should be interpreted figuratively as possessing a symbolic meaning. According to Thomas Aquinas, the tortures of hell signify a mental grief, contrition. On the Bamberg tympanum all the consecutive stages of the Last Judgment – from the appearance of the Judge and the resurrection of the dead to the separation of the 'sheep' from the 'goats' – are reproduced simultaneously, with few characters, in an attempt to reproduce the emotional reactions of the blessed and the damned. But elsewhere toads and snakes devour the condemned; monstrous, fantastic beasts teem in hell with colossal paws that squeeze the heads of crying and wailing sinners, rend their bodies with claws, and bite into them with the sharp teeth of their jaws; demons bustle like cooks around the hellish cauldron with the damned being boiled inside it; small figures hide from the demons under the long clothing of the archangel; and the bodies of the damned are appallingly crooked and doubled-up, their faces grotesquely twisted with sobbings or shaken by mad laughter. All these scenes and figures were dictated not so much by scholarly literature as by the fantasy of the sculptors and the carvers, who drew material from all sides: from the *Elucidarium* as well as from homilies and hagiography, from folklore and stories about visions.

Just as preachers instructed the faithful that demons hourly and everywhere lay in wait for them, so also various details of the sculptural universe in churches depicted demons of all kinds, from the unspeakably frightful to the funny and pitiful. The fantasy of medieval craftsmen, once having achieved a certain freedom, knew no bounds (Neugass 1927). Looking at the numerous artistic versions of the Last Judgment, one cannot avoid the impression that the belief of medieval people in the reality of hell did not preclude their obtaining an aesthetic satisfaction from creating and contemplating their depictions of it – a satisfaction probably accompanied by a kind of catharsis. There were many variants of the pictures of the end of the world in various churches and in different stages of artistic development. On the tympanum of Autun, scenes of the Last Judgment are distinguished by an exceptional dynamism and expressionism. The creator of this sculptural ensemble (whose name, Gislebertus, is carved into the lintel) achieves a most powerful effect by elongating and breaking up his figures, thereby making them present the widest spectrum of feelings. The viewer beholds a storm of gestures, and it seems as if we hear the groaning and wailing of the condemned mixing with the hooting of the demons dragging them into hell. The apostles surrounding the stern Judge also tremble. Nothing is at rest, save the colossal figure of Christ, which draws our attention by its sheer symmetry, and yet from his slightly separated hands issues a tense movement which permeates the entire composition. Another peculiarity of the Autun tympanum is the fact that the resurrected abandon their graves with an expression of ecstasy or terror. Mâle (1924: 417) suggests that Gislebertus believed in predestination: the resurrected, he argues, already know whether they have been chosen for salvation or condemned to hell's tortures.[3] Inscriptions over the heads of the righteous and the sinners accordingly say 'Thus will be resurrected he who did not lead a godless life' and 'Let him shudder from terror who has fallen into earthly delusions, for the manner of his terrible fate is depicted here' (Nesselshtraus 1964: 184; Darkevich 1972: 135ff.).

It is easy to understand why pictures of the torments awaiting the condemned were much more varied than those of the paradisal bliss of the blessed, which were more strictly subordinated to church canon. Yet all these scenes constituted the connected links of a single consecutive narrative, and they all referred to that moment of the completion of humankind's history in an undetermined future which was constantly expected, at times with particular tension. Thus, church iconography and sculpture, in accordance with the promises of the Gospels and the teaching of theologians, put off the judgment of the completed earthly life until the 'end of time'. Representational art of the twelfth and thirteenth centuries did not know purgatory but interpreted the realm beyond the grave as a dichotomy of hell and paradise (Mâle 1958: 438). According to the observation of G. and M. Vovelle (1970), purgatory found a place in church iconography only at the end of the Middle Ages.

Such is the eschatological conception lying at the basis of the treatment of the Other World in the decoration of churches. I do not discuss other forms of art, since the people, whose culture I am trying to investigate, received their spiritual education precisely from the scenes carved on church portals and capitals or depicted in stained-glass windows. Book illumination, exceptionally rich and instructive in this regard, was not really accessible to them, just as the book itself was not.

In the mind of the medieval viewer scenes of the Last Judgment represented on the church portals were combined with stories about otherwordly sojourns that had a wide circulation in all segments of society. Many of them were written down in the specific literary genre of 'visions'. Verbal images from otherworldly visits and apocalyptic scenes of visual art intersected in the spiritual space of medieval people; hence their interpretation demands that we confront the two forms in their mutual relationship.

Otherworldly narratives are one of the most popular and fascinating types of medieval literature. The transformation in the crucible of medieval man's fantasy of subjects and images inherited from the East, Antiquity, and early Christianity went further in this genre than in almost any other, perhaps even more than in figurative art. Many otherworldly narratives were translated into vernaculars, recopied for centuries and disseminated in oral retellings, which in turn were again written down in a new form. This branch of medieval Latin literature lived according to the laws of both scholarly literature and folklore; in it these traditions were united.

The grandiose pictures of Revelation and Dante's *Comedy* are separated in time by more than a thousand years, during which the thoughts of Christians were ceaselessly turned towards hell and paradise in hope and despair. The usual form of medieval otherworldly visions was a story about a man who miraculously found himself in the lands of the Other World, after which he returned to life and revealed what he had seen 'there'. This otherworldly travelling was made possible by death, and the story about it was made possible by the resurrection of the person who had been vouchsafed such a miraculous experience. Sometimes the story was put into the mouth of a sinner tormented in hell who had received permission to relate his tortures and warn people still in this world.

A prerequisite of the development of this genre was that in medieval consciousness the radical boundary dividing life and death had to be at least partially transparent. In ancient literature the realm of the dead was visited by travellers who in some fashion had wandered there while yet alive. In medieval Latin compositions, to come upon that world meant to die, and to describe it to the living meant to return to life or to appear to someone in a vision. The mode of intercourse of the two worlds, the earthly and the otherworldly, was the miracle, be it resurrection or visitation, both the manifestations of the omnipotence of divine power.

A great number of such descriptions has come down to us. Scholarly inquiries into medieval visions are usually guided by the attempt to establish the extent to which the thought and figurative system of Dante were prepared and anticipated by his predecessors. From this viewpoint, the records of medieval dreams and visions do not possess an independent value – they deserve attention only in retrospect, as the 'prehistory' of the *Divine Comedy*. Another perspective in which medieval visions are examined is that of the 'survival' of Antiquity and early Christianity. Scholars uncover in them elements from ancient mythology, from Homer or Virgil, from Cicero's 'Dream of Scipio' and the works of Lucian, or from biblical prophecies. Both these approaches, sometimes even combined (Labitte 1842; Ozanam 1873; d'Ancona 1874; Rüegg 1945), are completely legitimate and useful. Their shortcoming is that the Middle Ages are seen as just an 'interval' between Antiquity and the Renaissance, an age which lived on the scraps of ancient culture and is worth studying to the extent to which it 'prepared' the Renaissance. Were it not for Dante, historians of literature might not have paid any attention to medieval visions. But even when medieval studies are pursued in their own right the criteria for selecting and evaluating the material are frequently drawn from the more 'respectable' ages, such as Antiquity or the Renaissance.

In fact, it is worthwhile to focus on medieval otherworldly visions as an independent object of study and as a specific phenomenon of the medieval world-view. It is possible and valuable to define their peculiarities and to search for their sources not outside the boundaries of the age, but inside it. For this, however, one must shift the customary viewpoint and examine these texts not merely in a scheme of filiations and borrowings, but with respect to the medieval experience and to the consciousness of an age extremely concerned with existence beyond the grave. Thus, I should like to anchor medieval visions in their own particular age, when they arose, and when they were perceived not as products of a literary tradition, but as revelations and breakthroughs into the transcendent world. Their artistic merits, the richness of the fantasy and the originality of their authors are for this inquiry rather secondary matters: one can say beforehand that in this respect they were inferior to both Revelation and the *Divine Comedy*. It is, in contrast, of primary importance that accounts of visions, as a rule, were written down by clerics and served definite practical aims, edifying or political. A narrative about an otherworldly visit served in the hands of the clergy as an effective means of influencing the faithful. The threat of posthumous retribution might have been more powerful than a sermon on abstaining from sins. Several authors included in the description of hell's tortures episodes with historical personages, mainly rulers, just as Dante did later. Such episodes were intended to frighten and warn successors against repeating the mistakes and sins of their condemned forebears.

A literary work can be studied in different contexts. One can examine its connections with preceding and subsequent works in order to establish the tradition to which it belongs, to trace the commonplaces reproduced in it and to discover what innovations an author has added to the tradition. For medieval Latin literature, orientated towards *imitatio*, this method is particularly fruitful (Curtius 1973). But besides a study geared to the scheme 'predecessors-work-successors' and concentrating on 'image', *'topos'* and 'tradition', another approach is possible, one that could be termed synchronous. Such an inquiry focuses on the cultural work as conditioned by the state of mind contemporary with it. It explores a text's relationship with current existence, the various stimuli the author received apart from the inherited artistic canon (which in itself is actually also included in contemporaneity), and also the possible influence of the work on its surroundings, its actual socio-cultural function. In proceeding this way it becomes obvious that each work presupposes a definite reading, a deciphering of it by a distinct circle of readers and listeners.

Medieval visions, intended for the widest audience, will interest us here as an essential component of medieval Latin literature in which the fundamental views of the people about the world were embedded into the context of ecclesiastical tradition, receiving from it new colouring and meaning. Such a formulation of our problem implies a clear limitation of source-material. On the one hand, I shall exclude visions preceding the Middle Ages, such as the *Book of Enoch*, the *Apocalypse of Ezras*, the *Apocalypse of Peter*, and others, and also otherworldly pictures found in early medieval vernacular poetry. On the other hand, the *Divine Comedy* will also remain beyond the limits of my examination, and not only because it was not written in Latin. This grandiose summation of all medieval Latin literature of otherworldly travels does not, strictly speaking, belong to the genre of visions of the otherworldly realm; even though it was begotten by them, at the same time it completed and surpassed this type of narrative. The modern reader tends to 'compare' medieval narratives about otherworldly visits to Dante's work in searching for criteria of judgment. This may be inevitable, but in the present context I should like to avoid regarding the *Comedy* as an artistic standard to which all its predecessors clearly did not 'live up',[4] but to see it as a specific phenomenon, a comparison with which offers the possibility of revealing the distinctiveness of medieval visions.

Although the church Fathers of the early Middle Ages kept repeating that the *parousia*, the 'end of time', the fulfilment of the 'night of this world' and the approach of the 'day of the world to come' was imminent, early otherworldly visions never reached the eschatological intensity and high dramatic effect of Revelation, their main model.[5] Still, the two worlds were in contact with each other, as the saints demonstrated. The saint lived among the people, but in him dwelled the Supreme Will, by whose power he worked miracles. The saint was directly associated with the Other World, and in a certain sense in this life he already belonged to the heavenly realm. There were also people who visited the 'other side' and returned to tell the living what awaited them beyond the grave. For Gregory I their testimonies possessed exceptional value, since they offered graphic and 'experiential' *(per experimentum)* evidence for afterlife and retribution beyond death.

Several instances are recorded in his *Dialogues*. A paterfamilias died before the priest Severus, who had been detained in a vineyard, could reach his bedside. When Severus learned that the man who had summoned him had already died without receiving final absolution, he began to repent loudly, reckoning himself his murderer. God heard the saint's entreaties, and the deceased man was brought back to life. When asked where he had been and how he had returned, he answered that immediately after his death he had been grabbed by 'loathsome people', from whose mouths and nostrils flames shot forth, and dragged into 'dark places', then suddenly a handsome youth appeared and ordered his release, since, owing to Severus' request, God was turning over the deceased to him. After spending seven days in penance, the man died 'a happy death'.[6]

Gregory I habitually reduces the spiritual to the level of the materially sensible in order to adapt it to the understanding of the audience for which his *Dialogues* were intended (cf. Golenishchev-Kutuzov 1972: l4lff.). The same applies to his descriptions of otherworldly visions. The nobleman Reparatus visited the Other World and saw an immense pyre prepared for the priest Tiburtius, who was still alive and had the reputation of being a dissolute and sensual man. Reparatus sent a messenger to him, but at that very moment the priest died.[7] It is unclear where the hell which this man visited is located, and Gregory I divulges nothing definite about its arrangement, except that in it a single fire blazes, the condemned are subjected to various torments in conformity with their sins, and their torments will never end.[8] Obviously, in the sixth century no clear picture yet existed of the otherworldly realm; even the highest clergy were satisfied with a general idea of the opposition between paradise and a fiery hell.

Subsequently in visionary literature the motif of the otherworldly torment of the sinner in conformity with the character of his transgression received especially graphic form: false witnesses and perjurers are struck by demons in the tongue; gluttons are tormented by hunger, drunkards by thirst; ill-begotten children killed by their mothers loom continually before their eyes as reproach and accusation, and so on. A comrade-in-arms of Charlemagne, renowned for his avarice, is stretched out on his back while evil spirits pour melted gold down his throat, saying; 'You coveted this in life and could not be sated, so here you go – drink to your heart's content!'[9] Delight in this world is transformed into torment in the other; the tormentor becomes tormented. In hell the *ius talionis* reigns. Just as the righteous in paradise are joined together in groups according to the type of their lives and conduct, so too sinners who have committed similar sins are brought together by evil spirits and subjected to analogous torments: the proud are tormented with the proud, debauchers with debauchers, the greedy with the greedy, liars with liars, the envious with the envious.[10]

People who visit the Other World and return to life, as a rule, die for good soon thereafter. Obviously, God requires their brief resurrection only to tell the living through them about the secrets of the Other World. Such is God's mercy: some are returned to their bodies after death and are terrified of the torments of hell which they have experienced and which they previously did not fear because they did not believe the rumours about them.[11] Pope Gregory's faith in the possibility of visiting the Other World and returning thereafter to life was unwavering. After all, he learned about various instances from those very people who had been there themselves. A certain Stephen, a man of high rank, told the pope that he had died in Constantinople and then, while his body was as yet unburied, found himself in hell. There he saw much in which he previously had not believed. When Stephen was led before the chief judge, the latter did not receive him: 'Not that one! I ordered the blacksmith Stephen delivered to me!' And swiftly this Stephen was returned to his body and his neighbour, the blacksmith Stephen, died at that very hour.[12] The demons had apparently mistaken the address.

A more definite picture of the Other World was given by another witness to Gregory the Great. This soldier, who had died and come back to life, related that he was led along a bridge suspended over a black and fetid stream. The righteous easily crossed over to the other shore, reaching fragrant meadows where people dressed in white strolled and bright dwellings stood, among which one building seemed to be of gold. But the iniquitous who attempted to cross the bridge fell into the fetid river. The above-mentioned blacksmith Stephen stumbled while crossing the bridge and frightful-looking men emerged from the stream to drag him into the abyss. However, at that very moment handsome, winged men grabbed Stephen and began to pull him upwards, so that a struggle flared up between the evil and the good spirits. Thus, explains the pope, the evil flesh struggled in Stephen with his good deeds.[13] It is unclear what the function of the stream was to be and whether it belongs to hell or purgatory. The bridge over the dark stream dividing the shore of the blessed from the shore of the condemned or those awaiting resolution of their fate became from the time of Gregory I a traditional and essential component of the picture of the Other World.

News from the Other World can help alleviate the lot of the sinners suffering in hell, since the living, learning of their torments, will pray on their behalf and perform good deeds, thereby lightening their punishment. This theme is elaborated with particular intensity by Hincmar of Rheims, the author of the *Vision of Bernold*. In the Other World Bernold encounters more than forty bishops in the most pitiful condition, now shivering from unbearable cold, now languishing from heat. The visionary communicates to the clergy and laity the supplication of the sufferers to pray on behalf of their souls, which immediately renders them a beneficial service: he finds them washed, shaved and suitably clothed. Charles the Bald, wallowing in filth and being devoured by worms, repents that while alive he did not heed the advice of Archbishop Hincmar. Bernold passes on his supplication to pray for him, and this ameliorates the emperor's lot.[14] A monk, condemned posthumously for concealing money from the brothers, appears to one of them in a dream and reveals that things are easier for him now, thanks to the mercy of the abbot who had condemned him. A bishop, sent to the baths by his doctor, encountered there a deacon, who had died years before, working as an attendant. He was told that the deacon, in punishment for his sins, was posthumously given this degrading task. He begged the bishop to pray for his soul, and a few days later he was not seen any more.[15]

A prayer on behalf of the deceased can help him, if his guilt is pardonable. So it happened with one youth who had joined a monastery unwillingly and while alive had done no good and was habitually foul-mouthed and sarcastic. As he was dying during a plague, the monks gathered around him and began to pray for his soul. But the dying man interrupted them: 'Go away, go away! I have been given over to a dragon that is devouring me, but he cannot devour me on account of your presence. He has already swallowed my head. Stand back, so that he will not torture me any longer. Let him finish me off, if that is what I am destined to. Why do you make me suffer this suspense?' He was unable to cross himself, since he was being squeezed by the dragon's coils. Nevertheless, the brothers' prayers alleviated his struggle with the monster, and in the end it fled, unable to endure the prayers. Having recovered, the sinner repented and lived a holy life.[16] The idea that the prayers and intercession of saints can alleviate the lot of sinful souls condemned to hell's torments was repeated in many stories of other-worldly visions, even if it did not express the official teaching of the church (Aigrain 1953: 232). A 'theology of feeling' contradicted the theology of doctrine.

Many of the later descriptions of the Other World follow the same
outline as in the *Dialogues* of Gregory the Great. Descriptions of
otherworldly visits are also found in the works of Gregory of Tours, a
contemporary of Gregory I. The abbot of a monastery who was distinguished by unusual humility, dreamt that he visited places where there
flowed a fiery stream at which an enormous multitude of people thronged,
like bees gathering at a hive; they were plunged into the fiery stream,
some up to the thigh, others up to the shoulder, and a third group right
up to the chin, and they were all crying and moaning as they were
tortured. Above the stream hung a bridge so narrow that one could
barely place one foot on it. On the other shore of the stream there
towered a large white house. It was explained to the abbot that those
who do not care for their flocks fall from the bridge, while the diligent
cross over to the other shore safely and joyously arrive at the house seen
there. At these words the abbot woke up and from that time became
very strict with his monks.[17] The vision served as a warning to him
against inordinate softness, which could lead to a lack of discipline
among the brothers and ultimately to the ruin of their souls.

Another vision mentioned by Gregory of Tours belongs to the category
of 'political visions', which were rather numerous in the Frankish period.
Nicetas, bishop of Trier, saw in a dream a tower with a multitude of
windows, so high that it approached heaven. On top of the tower stood
the Lord himself surrounded by angels, one of whom was holding a
large book in his hands. The angel enumerated in order the Frankish
kings, both past and future, and described the character of each king's
rule and the duration of their lives. The bishop retold all this and,
according to Gregory, the entire prediction came to pass.[18] The 'book
of life' mentioned here is an obvious borrowing from Revelation.

In describing paradise, the imagination of our authors, just like that
of the artists who decorated the churches, seems much paler than in the
representation of hell's torments. St Salvius fell ill and breathed his last,
whereupon his cell was shaken and illuminated by a bright light. The
monks began to prepare the saint's body for burial and to pray, but the
next morning he came back to life and lamented to God that he had
been returned from heaven to this unhappy world. He told the monks
that after his death angels had lifted him up to heaven, so that he saw
under his feet not only this mournful earth, but even the sun and moon,
the clouds and stars. Through a shining door he was led into a chamber
with a floor gleaming like gold and silver and of ineffable size, while the
light in it was unspeakable; such a multitude of people of both sexes
was found in it that it was impossible to take them all in with a single
look. The angels made a path for Salvius to a place where there hung a
cloud shining more brightly than light, and from the cloud resounded a

voice 'like the sound of many waters' (Rev 1:15). Salvius was greeted by men dressed as clerics and laymen – saints and martyrs. Towards Salvius wafted an aroma of unheard-of sweetness, so that he no longer desired to eat or drink. And he heard a voice: 'This one is to be returned to the world, for he is necessary to our church.' Although the voice could be heard, its speaker was invisible. Salvius fell prone, grieving that after all he had seen and heard in heaven he was compelled to return to earth, and he entreated God that he should be allowed to remain close to him. But the voice ordered him to go in peace, promising that he would yet be in that place. Gregory of Tours assures those to whom this story might appear improbable that he heard it from Salvius' own mouth.[19] What a striking combination of extreme humility with utmost arrogance! The saint himself testifies about his own election. It is significant that the description of paradise in human words appears impossible, and therefore Gregory constantly falls back on such expressions as *ineffabilis, inenarrabilis, nimius.*[20]

There are also reports of visions in Bede's *Ecclesiastical History of the English People*, one of the most extensive being the vision of the Irishman Fursey.[21] He fell ill, and one night his soul was parted from his body, so that it was vouchsafed him to behold the angelic host and listen to its singing. When he glanced at the world he had left behind, he saw a dark valley and above it four fires floating not far from each other. The angels accompanying him said that these fires will consume the world. One of them is the fire of falsehood, for people do not fulfil the vow given during baptism to renounce Satan and all his works; another is the fire of cupidity, for people who place the love of earthly riches above the love of heaven; the third is the fire of discord, for people who do not fear to harm those close to them even on account of trifles; the fourth is the fire of impiety, for people who think nothing of robbing and cheating the weak.

Fursey also saw demons flying in the flame and attempting to direct it against the righteous. The accusations which the evil spirits bring against Fursey and the counter-arguments brought forth by the good spirits are also enumerated – which suggests that a trial took place over the saint's soul. He encountered there saints from his own tribe, and they revealed to him many useful and instructive things. Then the saints withdrew to heaven and the angels accompanying Fursey set about restoring his soul to his body. Again he had to pass through the fire, but when he entered the passageway formed through it, the evil spirits grabbed one of the souls suffering in the flame and shoved it directly at Fursey, so that he received burns on his shoulder and chin that remained with him until the end of his life. Fursey recognized that fellow, since after his death he had received some of his clothing. An angel flung the fellow back into the fire, but an evil spirit said to Fursey 'Do not reject him whom you once received! After all, by taking the sinner's things you became a participant in his sin!' After his soul returned to his body Fursey lived out a long life.

It has been suggested that Fursey's vision is of great interest to the psychoanalyst, since it attests tortures of conscience and an awareness of sinfulness that produced in him such an intense feverish and ecstatic condition that he took burns possibly received during an illness for marks of hell (Rüegg 1945: 294).

Another vision related by Bede is that of Drycthelm.[22] On the left side of some huge valley he saw a frightful fire blazing, while on the right side unbearable cold reigned and a storm of snow and hail raged. Along both sides an innumerable multitude of human souls was tossed between the heat and the cold; when they could no longer endure the heat, the wretches found themselves in the clutches of the cold, but finding no relief in it, they were again thrown into the flame, and so on endlessly. Drycthelm thought that this was hell, but his guide, divining his thought, answered him, 'This is not yet hell.' In another place in front of him rose up columns of a loathsome flame that erupted noisily from a huge well and again fell back into it. Drycthelm discerned that the tongues of the rising and falling flame were full of human souls – they flew up like sparks and again were swallowed by the abyss. An unbearable stench prevailed there. Suddenly he heard behind him desperate cries accompanied by wild laughter, as if a coarse throng were making short shrift of a captured victim, and he made out a crowd of evil spirits who were dragging moaning and crying souls into the blackness with hoots and shouts. As the wretches were plunged into the blazing chasm the screams of the victims and the joyous exclamations of the demons fused into one. Among the condemned Drycthelm recognized a cleric from his tonsure, and also a woman.

Several dark spirits flew out of the fiery abyss and surrounded Drycthelm; their eyes blazed and he felt the vile flame that issued from their jaws and nostrils. The demons threatened to seize him with fiery tongs, but they did not venture to touch him. A guide came to his rescue and led him out on the side of the winter sun's rising. In the light of day he saw a great wall that seemed endlessly long and immeasurably high, without windows or doors or a ladder, but nevertheless in some incomprehensible fashion he found himself on top of the wall. There he found a wide, beautiful field so fragrant with the aroma of flowers that the stench of the gloomy furnace disappeared. The light permeating these places surpassed the sun's light in brightness. An innumerable multitude of people dressed in white strolled through the field in immeasurable joy. It occurred to Drycthelm that this was the kingdom of heaven which he had often heard about from the preacher, but again the guide read his mind: 'No, this is not the kingdom of heaven, as you imagine.' For further on they saw places where the light shone much brighter and the fragrances were even more pleasant and stronger than in the former places, and sweet singing resounded from there. Here, however, the guide turned back, having explained to Drycthelm the meaning of what he had seen. The valley in which the flame rages and the unbearable cold reigns is nothing other than the place where the souls of those who put off repenting and atoning for their sins right up until their deaths are subjected to trial and expiation. But since they repented, even if only on their death-bed, on Judgment Day they will all enter the kingdom of heaven; many of them will be helped by prayers for the dead, penances, fasts and especially masses read on their behalf. The fetid fiery well is the entry to hell, and he who falls into it will never escape. The souls of those who performed good deeds while alive, but did not attain such a degree of perfection as to be deserving straightaway of entering the kingdom of heaven, are admitted into the flowering field that they visited; nevertheless, on Judgment Day they will be vouchsafed the joys of heaven. But those who have attained perfection in all their words, deeds and thoughts immediately enter paradise after leaving the body. Drycthelm returned to life with great reluctance.

This vision is much more detailed than others of the same period. Bede's (or his informant's) picture of the Other World is more clearly described than those of his predecessors. Together with hell, whose entrance the traveller visited, and paradise, whose sounds and smells he was granted to enjoy from a distance, other places exist as well; one of them could be called purgatory, although the theologians of the early Middle Ages still had not elaborated the concept of purgatory. Here souls are actually tested and cleansed before entering paradise. Apparently, Bede, as also Gregory of Tours, experienced difficulty in describing paradise – it is too beautiful; its felicity cannot be rendered in human words. In the topography of the Other World there are certain coordinates tinged with significance: top and bottom, east and west, right and left. The symbolic orientation according to the lands of earth is present in other visions as well (Silverstein 1935).

Bede also records the vision of a soldier who had led a wicked life and had no desire to repent.[23] Finally, he fell seriously ill and revealed to his friends that now nothing would help him. At his words there appeared in his house two handsome youths, who took up positions at the head and the foot of his bed. They gave him a beautiful but very small book to read, in which the soldier found all his good deeds recorded, but they were few and insignificant. Silently the youths took the book away and immediately a horde of frightful-looking spirits flew in, surrounding the house and filling up the greater part of it. They also took up positions around his bed and the one who seemed the eldest, to judge from his dark and frightful face, gave him another book to read. But this time it was an awful-looking codex of colossal proportions and incredible weight. Reading the misshapen characters, the soldier discovered in it records of all his evil deeds, in act and word and design. The devil said to the beautifully dressed youths, 'Why are you sitting here? After all, you yourselves know that he's ours!' They responded, 'You are right. Take him and add him to the number of the condemned', and disappeared. Then the two most vile spirits came up to the soldier – one at his head and one at his feet – and plunged daggers into him. Now, he concludes his story, they are proceeding with their torture, and as soon as the knives meet I shall die and go to hell. Let the awful perdition of this soul, Bede concludes, serve as a lesson to others. As far as the books brought by the good and evil spirits are concerned, they are composed by divine approbation so that one may know that all our thoughts are kept and weighed by the great Judge and will be produced for us upon our deaths by either angels or adversaries.

The theme of a trial over the deceased's soul during which an angel reads a book containing a list of the man's good and bad deeds goes back to Revelation, but it was re-worked by Bede in his own way. In Revelation (5:1–3) there is a book with seven seals in which the fate of the world as a whole is recorded and which will be opened only at the Last Judgment. But Bede focusses on the salvation or damnation of the individual man – his own personal list of merits and sins is brought against each man. Let me also note another essential feature of the visions: the condemnation or justification takes place at the moment of a man's death; it is not postponed until the end of the world.[24]

More precisely, the picture of the Last Judgment in the visions is bi-partite. As we saw, in the vision of Drycthelm Bede mentions the terrible sinners who are directed into a fiery hell immediately after death and are already condemned to remain there for eternity, and he mentions those who are subjected to trials and cleansing by tortures but will enter the kingdom of heaven on Judgment Day. So also among the righteous he distinguishes between those not yet found worthy of paradise and those who have abandoned the shell of their bodies and are already in it. In other words, it seems that two judgments are posited: one is individual and takes place immediately after death, while the other is postponed until the Second Coming: a compromise decision, indefinite, but symptomatic in the highest degree. Two eschatologies are apparently juxtaposed: a 'small', personal one, and a 'large', universal one. This duality appears more distinctly in vision literature than in church iconography, which knows only the judgment at the end of the world.

It is in this respect that I cannot agree with the conclusions of Philippe Ariès (1976, 1977) as to attitudes towards death in the West. In his section on the medieval perception of death, Ariès refers to iconography, strangely disregarding vision literature entirely. By omitting from his survey an entire collection of texts having the most direct connection with the theme of his study, Ariès arrives at mistaken conclusions. In particular, he suggests that the idea of the Last Judgment was not popular before the twelfth century; there supposedly existed a notion that death signifies sleep lasting right up to the Second Coming, after which everybody save the most serious sinners (who will not be awakened and will be destroyed) will come back to life and enter the kingdom of heaven. Such a conception of death, unconnected with the idea of judgment, writes Ariès, eliminates the problem of the personal responsibility of the individual. Only beginning with the twelfth century does the idea of a divine judgment arise, and at the end of the Middle Ages the 'Book of Life', into which each man's merits and sins are noted, begins to be interpreted as some sort of individual ' passport' or 'bank account' produced at the gates of eternity. At this point, the notion of the Last Judgment becomes connected with a man's individual biography. Then Ariès turns to descriptions of the sinner's death-bed, which is surrounded by on the one side God the Father, Christ, the Mother of God and the saints, and on the other Satan and the demons (Tenenti 1952: 55, 59, 99ff.). Such engravings were widespread in the fifteenth century. Here God appears, according to Ariès, in the role not of a judge, but of an arbitrator or observer, and the fate of a man's soul depends on his conduct at his last hour.

Ariès, and after him Chaunu (1978), point completely correctly to the connection of the trial over the deceased's soul with the idea of individuality: instead of a common judgment over mankind at the end of the world, a separate trial is conducted over each man. Actually, the teaching that the appraisal of a man will be given at 'the end of time', when all mankind will stand before the Supreme Judge, was not linked with the idea of a whole and completed individual biography. Having lived out his earthly life, a man, in order to receive a final verdict, was required to wait for an indefinite duration of time. In other words, the end of his biography – salvation or condemnation – was cut off from that biography itself. Meanwhile, the introduction of a 'small' eschatology for each man, focussing attention entirely on his person isolated at the moment of judgment from other people, at the same time welded all the fragments of his life into one indissoluble unity. For according to this notion the deeds he performed during his life are appraised immediately after his life is completed, on the border separating life from death, and thereby the biography is completed without any temporal lacuna. Ariès, however, groundlessly puts off the origin of such notions until the twelfth or thirteenth century or even until the fifteenth or sixteenth. As we saw earlier, these ideas were already expressed with sufficient definition in the vision narratives of the sixth, seventh and eighth centuries, even though they actually penetrated into iconography only later.

Such an 'interiorization' of retribution for a completed life, the transfer of the centre of gravity from the common fate of mankind to the personal fate of the individual, is a characteristic feature of all medieval vision literature. The idea of a common retribution, of a judgment at which each man will stand before God simultaneously with all other people, did not disappear; this was the idea that found its artistic expression in church tympana depicting the Last Judgment. But the narratives about otherworldly visits stressed the individualizing side of the teaching about death and retribution.

To be sure, in applying the concept of 'individualism' to the Middle Ages one needs to use the term cautiously. Christianity made each man personally responsible for choosing the path of righteousness or of iniquity. Therefore, it is appropriate that a judgment over the soul of the individual should figure in vision stories. But at the same time the motives and actions of the individual are not evaluated as spontaneous expressions of his will; their source is placed outside his personality. Although they are precisely his thoughts, desires and actions, they are at the same time independent essences and do not depend on him. One can discover such a treatment of the soul and the judgment over it in an English monk's vision recorded by Boniface.[25] The monk related that in the Other World he heard from demons about all his unexpiated or forgotten deeds, and that all these shameful deeds complained about him in a loud voice. Each sin was personified and announced itself: 'I am your voluptuousness', 'I am arrogance', 'I am mendacity', 'I am idle talk'. Another proclaimed, 'I am the sight by which you sinned in looking at forbidden things', and another 'I am obstinacy and disobedience'. Voices resounded: 'I am indolence and sluggishness in sacred studies', 'I am the wandering thoughts and useless cares in which you have indulged too much both in church and elsewhere', 'I am somnolence', 'I am negligence and carelessness', and so on. The evil spirits demonstrated his sinfulness by adducing evidence and naming the places and very times of his sins. He met there a man whom he had wounded before entering the monastery and who was still among the living. Nevertheless, he was brought to testify against him: 'The bloody and open wound and even the blood itself cried out against him', charging him (the monk) with the crime of bloodshed.

Having gathered together and enumerated his sins, the demons

pronounced the monk guilty and doubtless their prey. But against them
his small, pitiful merits testified in his behalf. In turn they proclaimed,
'I am obedience', 'I am fasting', 'I am true prayer', 'I am care for the
weak', 'I am the psalm that he sang in praise of the Lord to atone for
idle talk.' And thus each merit pleaded on his behalf, and the angels
supported him, so that the merits themselves seemed even more significant. Finally, his body received its soul back and he returned to life,
although for an entire week he was unable to see anything with his
earthly eyes.

Just as confession induced believers to analyse and evaluate their own
morality, so also such a vision represented in its own way an attempt to
analyse personality. Hell and paradise struggle inside the human soul –
the monk reflects upon his merits and transgressions and compares them
them in order to bring them into a definite 'balance'. The chief role at
this trial is played not by the demon-prosecutors or the angel-interces-
sors, but by the conscience of the defendant himself. In keeping with the
conception of personality of the age, the aspects of his conscience appear
as personified and seemingly independent of him.

The material of vision literature contradicts yet another assertion of
Ariès and Chaunu: namely, that death in the early Middle Ages was
thought of as sleep lasting until the end of the world (cf. Neveux 1979).
According to those granted visions of the Other World, the world
beyond the grave is not at all immersed in sleep and immobility. In hell
eerie dynamism and agitation prevail; the physical and moral torments
suffered by the sinners have nothing in common with repose. Tranquillity
is possible only in the kingdom of heaven, but even paradise is not
immersed in lethargy: its inhabitants abide in ineffable joy, proclaiming
the heavenly Jerusalem with solemn hymns.

The Carolingian age witnessed the flowering of 'political visions'. In
these works, written by members of the high clergy, Charlemagne and
his ancestors and descendants often figure as prisoners in hell. In the
Other World of the *Vision of Wettin*, a recently deceased abbot, Bishop
Adalheim, who did not believe in visions, two counts and Charlemagne
himself are tortured, although the future cleansing of Charlemagne's sins
was foretold to him; and one finds there enormous riches snatched from
the poor.[26] In the *Vision of Eucherius* by Hincmar of Reims, Charles
Martel, guilty of encroachments on church possessions, is tortured in
hell – it was not for nothing that during the opening of his grave a
dragon flew out of it, but Charles's body was not there![27] In the *Vision
of Bernold*, Charles the Bald, who did not heed the clergy's advice while
alive, is found in a gloomy netherworld. Similar visions are described
also by William of Malmesbury, who placed in the gloomy regions of
the Other World bishops, evil counsellors, vassals of the king and even

somebody from the royal family; casks with boiling water have already been prepared for the living ruler in case he does not hasten to repent; finally, in paradise one of the pious kings prophesies about the subsequent order of the inheritance to the throne (Fritzsche 1887: 340–2).[28] The political goals and meaning of these visions are entirely obvious. The appraisals of various rulers deviate in different visions. Thus, in the *Vision of Rotchar*, Charlemagne is found not in hell, but in paradise among the saints; believers had prayed in his behalf (Levison 1921: 87ff.).

The idea of a 'small' Last Judgment held over the deceased's soul directly after his death appears in the 'political visions' with the same significance as in all other works of this genre. And in these visions one meets the motif of the cleansing of sins, although the word *purgatorium* is still absent and the binary structure of the Other World is not yet replaced by a tripartite one; the function of purgatory, apparently, belongs to hell or several of its compartments.[29]

The supply of early medieval visions is far from exhausted, yet there is really no need for more. Even with all their variations and individual particularities, the visions repeat the same motifs and images, distinguishing themselves merely by the skill with which they depict the torments of hell and the joys of paradise. Their repetition can easily tire the modern reader. Upon completing a survey of otherworldly narratives, one scholar noted: 'It cannot be denied that an element of monotony creeps in almost inevitably from the sheer fact of repetition. Perhaps there is some advantage in getting to know the geography of the Other World so well, but some of the novelty will be missing when we visit the place in this or another life' (Patch 1950: 320). True, but aiming at originality and diversity was foreign to medieval thought and literature. In the endless repetitions, in the variations on the same theme and in the handling of standard concepts and images, medieval man found confirmation of his beliefs.

In the numerous descriptions of otherworldly visits, we encounter several frequently recurring motifs: the bridge uniting the land of the blessed with the vale of the sinners and thrown across the stream holding the souls dragged into it by their sins; the books in which all a man's good and bad deeds are recorded; the struggle between angels and demons over the soul; the well emitting the hellish flame that burns the souls of inveterate sinners; the torment of constantly alternating cold and heat; the sweet fragrance, the delicate singing of the choirs of angels and the elect, the unparalleled brilliance of the clothing, the ineffable beauty of the chamber and wall of the heavenly Jerusalem, and the other inexpressible joys of paradise; the angel guardians and companions bearing the deceased's soul up to heaven; the soul's meeting with secular lords who have sullied themselves by their sins, especially crimes against the church, and with unrighteous clerics atoning in the Other World; the grief of a soul of the temporarily dead that it has to abandon the Other World and return to the sinful earth, and its resolve from then on to follow a righteous way of life; and so on. These stable motifs, although they vary and are reformulated every time, are clearly borrowed from the authors' predecessors.[30] We have before us the specimens of a genre of medieval Latin literature, with its particular stable commonplaces, that is in formation and gradually 'crystallizing'.[31]

In these motifs of vision literature the fears and hopes of early medieval people are transformed into artistic images joined together into entire pictures. While continuing to believe in their reality, the authors were at the same time also capable of experiencing an aesthetic satisfaction from grouping these motifs and images in the context of the narrative. As noted above, the same thing also took place in visual art. The artisans who decorated churches constructed their compositions in accordance with the laws of art. In iconography and vision literature, truth and fancy, faith and art entered into a specific interaction. Purely religious impressions and experiences were thereby transformed into artistic constructions without losing their initial nature. Two points of departure meet here, each of which can be understood only in the context that unites them, not on its own taken in isolation.

Although otherworldly visions reproduce a certain set of images and clichés, I doubt that the names of the visionaries are fictions; that the circumstances under which they had visions are completely concocted; and that the repeated references to witnesses who knew the visionaries are no more than literary devices. First of all, one should not forget that medieval man's entire way of life, ruled as it was by a common spiritual atmosphere and a particular psychology, completely prepared him for the experience of visions and for taking dreams and hallucinations, prophecies and fortune-tellings seriously. Visions and dreams were by no means attributed to the order of the illusory; they were rather seen as intrusions of a higher reality into daily life, by which one could penetrate the secrets of the Other World and catch a glimpse of the future. For medieval people the border between this world and the other was permeable in both directions. The reality of medieval men was more capacious than that of their modern successors; it encompassed many regions lying beyond the limits of earthly existence. Visionaries frequently assert that they have touched upon only an insignificant part of their experiences.

This does not mean, of course, that medieval men believed in everything indiscriminately and were completely lacking in any critical sense.

The monk whose vision was recorded by Boniface willingly related his otherworldly visit to pious people, but he was wary of scoffers.[32] Does not the very thoroughness with which early medieval authors note the sources of their information testify that they were not prepared to believe every story without requiring evidence? This concerns dreams as well. In the *Dialogues*, Gregory's pupil inquires whether it is necessary to attach meanings to dream. The formulation of the question is already significant; the answer is no less curious. The pope is by no means inclined to voice complete faith in everything that can be dreamt, and he divides dreams into several categories: dreams caused by a full stomach or by vanity; non-serious dreams; dreams begotten by wishes, or by wishes and the playfulness of the spirit together; dream-revelations; but out of the latter one should distinguish 'mixed' dreams, so to speak, those caused both by revelation and also by wishes.[33] In this way, of the six types of dream the pope was inclined to attribute to the order of genuine revelations, properly speaking, only one.

But how is one to distinguish just this variety? It is difficult to reconstruct the thought of medieval men on this score, but there is no doubt that the authors recording visions saw in them revelations deserving special attention and faith. One should remember that people had such visions at a decisive moment in life – on the threshold of death or, as they themselves and their contemporaries conceived it, already on the other side of the threshold, which they were able to cross at first only for a time. In contrast to the otherworldly regions in which travellers of antiquity or heroes of chivalric romances and Icelandic sagas sojourned, the Other World of the visions represents a picture, distinctively transposed on to the screen of theology, of the interior life of a man craving salvation and overcome by fear of posthumous punishments.

In speaking here of the actuality of some event, of course, nothing other is meant than its perception by early medieval men. In order to evaluate his own individual experience, practical or spiritual, this man had to correlate it with tradition. He could realize a particular experience only in categories of collective consciousness substantiated in religious and social ritual, in images of conduct or in literary convention. An event possessed authenticity only insofar as it could be placed under a corresponding model. It had to be identified with something going beyond the limits of the individual and the unique, and dissolved in the typical. Understanding of the essence of events consisted above all in the recognition of definite archetypes in them.[34]

The stereotypical form that visions received from many authors was the sole possible method of describing and realizing them. This did not reduce the vision to a purely 'literary' composition – in the modern meaning based on the opposition of life and literature. For already the visionary himself, attempting to communicate the secrets he had experienced in the Other World, could not help clothing his visions in traditional forms known to him. There can be no question that an ecclesiastical author intending to include a vision story in his work inevitably fashioned it according to generic rules by drawing upon ancient, early Christian and hagiographic motifs. A historical occurrence found significance for the medieval historian insofar as he was able to liken it to something else that had happened previously and could serve as a model and prototype. A general, a lawgiver or a spiritual leader was transformed by medieval authors into a 'new Alexander', a 'new Moses' or a 'new David'; the life of a saint in its main features was nothing other than an 'imitation of Christ'. In precisely the same way, a medieval author necessarily broke up a psychic experience, his own or someone else's, into semantic units meaningful for him, in accordance with an a priori scheme appropriate to the given genre.

In recording the vision of Bernold, Hincmar of Rheims identified the cleric to whom Bernold told everything he had beheld in the Other World and noted the respectability of the witness, who in turn had told the vision to Hincmar himself. 'I am convinced that this is the truth', writes Hincmar, 'for I read something similar in both the book of the *Dialogues* of St Gregory and in the history of the Angles [Bede] and in the works of the holy bishop and martyr Boniface, and also in the story about the *Visio Wettini* in the time of the emperor Ludwig.'[35] The testimony of the 'eyewitness' is easily included in the familiar and authoritative tradition and finds precisely in it a confirmation of its genuineness!

In essence, we encounter the same thing in those instances where medieval authors 'verify' their visions or the visions of others. The Virgin appeared to the mother of Guibert of Nogent, and she looked like the Virgin of Chartres Cathedral. A blind peasant whose sight was restored by St Foi recognized her in a vision because she corresponded exactly to the statue of the saint in the church. When a young monk from Monte Cassino beheld the archangel Michael carrying off the soul of his dead brother, he saw him 'exactly as he was usually depicted by artists' (Sumption 1976: 52). Hence it is obviously the wrong question to ask whether descriptions of the Other World are 'literary creations' or a fixation with the visions and dreams of concrete living people.[36] Early medieval man visited the Other World in his dreams and nightmares, attempted to describe these pictures and impressions, and for expressing them had recourse to the only possible and accessible language of traditional forms, which also made these pictures for him simultaneously full of higher meaning, artistically convincing and trustworthy.

In medieval notions about the Other World Christian dogma was capriciously interwoven with scraps of ancient or Eastern legends and with popular beliefs and stories. A. Rüegg (1945: 1, 197) calls these beliefs 'weeds in the garden of Christian thought'. Not only were they ineradicable, but even the most educated theologians, like Gregory the Great, widely exploited this extremely rich stock of primitive superstitions and legends in order to make Christian ideas about the soul, death and resurrection and about otherworldly retribution accessible to wide sections of the faithful. But the translation of the basic ideas of religion into the common language of the faithful was inevitably accompanied by their vulgarization, and hence they allow us to gain insight into popular fantasy through them. However great the dependence of Latin narratives about otherworldly visits on literary works, their connection with folklore was strong, for stories of otherworldly travels rested upon ancient beliefs and myths. If we knew more about popular beliefs concerning the Other World and what awaits the deceased's soul in it, we would be better able to analyse these borrowings. This is suggested by the unique inquiry by E. Le Roy Ladurie into the beliefs of the villagers of Montaillou. Some of them believed in metempsychosis, the transmigration of souls, while others thought that those who died wandered around in the bodily appearance of 'doubles' in deserted places near the village, pursued by demons. Hell begins somewhere in the backyards of the settlements. Besides those who believed that all souls would be saved on Judgment Day, others rejected that very Judgment and the resurrection of the flesh, maintaining that the world was eternal, without beginning or end. Some believed in the existence of an earthly paradise or other places of the departed's repose. Only a few accepted that masses and other good deeds were capable of saving the soul of a man who had gone to purgatory, or even the very existence of purgatory (Le Roy Ladurie 1975). Since a majority of these people were Cathars, it would be wrong to extend observations about their ideas to the medieval peasantry and the common people in general. A comparison of the opinions of Montaillou's population about the Other World with relevant descriptions of the Other World in church literature, especially in the great collection in Jacopo da Varagine's *Golden Legend*, reveals both similarities and differences of no small importance (Neveux 1979).

Syncretist notions about the other world were not subject to development: they were repeated time and again, reproducing the primordial stock of motifs and images. However, the literary genre of visions itself did change; authors marshalled the motifs and images into ever more refined literary schemes. In this respect one can speak about an evolution which reached its culmination in Dante's poem. If one compares the otherworldly visions contained in the works of Gregory I, Gregory of Tours, Bede or Boniface with the high medieval visions, their descriptions

appear unclear and very sparse in details. The otherworldly visions of
the early Middle Ages were usually inserted into historical or hagiographical works; their authors apparently did not attribute to them a self-
contained significance. Having related the visions of Salvius, Gregory of
Tours writes: 'I heard many more remarkable things from this man, but
since I want to return to the history I began, I leave them for the most
part by the side.'[37] In Pope Gregory's stories about holy men in his
Dialogues such stories have an edifying purpose: to scare the reader with
the tortures of hell and to encourage people to follow a righteous way
of life by the promise of otherworldly bliss. In these works didactic goals
clearly predominate over the aim of a detailed description of journeys
through paradise and hell.

In Western Europe, meanwhile, a particular genre of visions was
gradually taking shape, and visits to the Other World stood at its centre
of attention. The authors of such descriptions constructed more or less
well-thought-out systems.[38] They doubtless used the material of ancient
literature and the Christian tradition, beginning with Revelation and
including the stories of Gregory I and Bede, and they relied on popular
traditions as well. At any rate, we have before us finished literary
compositions. The element of spontaneity and ingenuousness, still present
in the earlier examples, has been reduced to a minimum.

A special place among these works belongs to the *Apocalypse of Paul*.
Since it is a translation of a Greek text dating back to the third century
and to the Eastern tradition (its supposed author was Egyptian), one
can in no way, of course, see it as an original work of Western European
thought.[39] This is clear also from its very contents, which sharply differ
from the visionary productions of sixth-to eighth-century Europe. The
editor of this work fittingly calls it 'a complete Baedecker of the other
world' (Silverstein 1935: 5). In the *Apocalypse of Paul* all the conceived
fears are consciously supercharged, and the tortures of the sinners,
arranged according to severity and character of transgression, are
described with exceptional thoroughness. Nothing, it seems, is omitted
from the torments to which a wretched soul, having fallen into the
clutches of the devil and his retainers, might be subjected. If the author
intended to frighten readers, there is no doubt that he completely
achieved his goal.

The descriptions of otherworldly punishments given by early medieval
Western writers pale before the developed and extremely detailed
technologies of torment in the *Apocalypse of Paul*.[40] In the visions
mentioned earlier the sufferings of sinners were not exclusively physical:
tortured in the fire of hell and in the clutches of loathsome demons, the
victims suffer no less from grief. While in the Other World depicted by
Gregory I or Bede the struggle for the soul of man continues, the

Apocalypse of Paul concentrates on the executioner and flayer heaping tortures upon tortures.[41] By contrast to Revelation, where the end of the world is accompanied by calamities of cosmic proportions and colourful grandeur, the *Apocalypse of Paul* paints torture-chambers. A sense of proportion, it seems, is decidedly missing. The criteria on which this impression is based are not really external: I have been attempting to establish them in reference to the contents and spirit of Western visions, which also aim at steering readers away from a sinful life, but without leaving them in a state of despair and hopelessness. For example, in the vision of a monk recorded by Ansellus Scholasticus (*c.* 940), Christ frees sinners from hell thanks to the prayers of the clergy, leaving there only the most serious sinners (Fritzsche 1887: 347–8), whereas in the *Apocalypse of Paul* it is said of the sinners being tormented in hell: 'It would have been better for them not to have been born at all' (Silverstein 1935: 196).

The author concludes a long story about all the possible sufferings prepared for sinners in the Other World with the words 'Thus did St Paul describe many punishments, and their number is one hundred and forty four. Even if there had existed from the beginning of the world one hundred men, each of whom possessed an iron tongue, they would not be able to speak about a single one of hell's tortures.' These words seem to hark back to Book VI of the *Aeneid*: 'If I had a hundred tongues and as many mouths, I would not be able to name all the penalties and number the punishments!'[42] In another redaction the terrors continue to be condensed. To Paul's question about the total number of hell's tortures an angel answers: 'The tortures of hell are one hundred and forty-four thousand, and if from the beginning of the world there had existed one hundred men and each had had four iron tongues, they could not have enumerated the tortures of hell.' The matter of this count does not end here: Wulfstan develops the apocalyptic hyperbole in a sermon: the men who were supposed to depict hell's tortures have seven heads and seven tongues in each mouth (Silverstein 1935: 155, 202, 213). The author of the twelfth-century Irish *Vision of Tnugdal* (or Tungdal), trying to surpass his predecessors, declares that the terrors of hell could not be described even if one had one hundred heads and each head had one hundred tongues.[43] However, even this was still not the limit, for one sinner appeared in a vision to his widow and told her about his sojourn in hell, finishing his conversation with the words, 'Even if all the leaves on the trees were turned into tongues, they still could not express my torments.'[44] The medieval author's fantasy does not beget original images so much as it attempts to add something new to the canon, falling into a sort of 'vicious infinity'.

To be sure, in the *Apocalypse of Paul* the joys of paradise are also depicted, as the author 'not only desired to force the listeners to shudder, but also to comfort their souls with the hope of eternal bliss' (Shepelevich 1892: 7). Through St Paul's intercession sinners are delivered from otherworldly tortures on Sundays. The picture of the Promised Land in this work also has important peculiarities. The fear of hunger that was always with the common man of Antiquity and the Middle Ages found its expression and resolution in this apocryphal work: the realm of the divine elect is above all the realm of every sort of abundance. Here rivers flow full of milk, honey, wine and butter (Silverstein 1935: 137ff.), while in other visions the saints and the righteous are sated by a ray of light sent by God. Just as in regard to otherworldly torments, the author of the *Apocalypse of Paul* also thinks substantially and materially in his depiction of otherworldly bliss.

The *Apocalypse of Paul*, which exerted considerable influence on later works in this medieval genre, differs both from early visions and from many of its followers in the great severity and cruelty of its images. For example, in the ninth-century vision of Bishop Anskar the Other World is not dominated by tortures: its inhabitants experience depression and fear, but are not subjected to physical trials.[45]

Medieval people were very much concerned with hell's location. Gregory I found it difficult to respond to a question on this point: some assume that hell is somewhere within the earth's limits, while others incline to the opinion that it is under the earth. Proceeding from the etymology of the word *infernum* ('quia inferius jacet'), Gregory himself thought that hell was located just under the earth.[46] It was widely believed that the earthly world and the Other World were in direct communication. Gregory related that a certain Eumorphius before death sent his servant to inform the military commander Stephen that '...our ship is ready to take us to Sicily'. At that moment Stephen died.[47] 'Sailing to Sicily' was a synonym for departing to the Other World, since the craters of Sicilian volcanoes led directly to hell, according to contemporary beliefs (inherited from Antiquity). The Gothic king Theodoric, an Arian and opponent and persecutor of the orthodox church, was enticed into the crater of a volcano in the Lipari Islands, dragged there by his victims Pope John and the patrician Symmachus.[48] Much later, sailors continued to show their passengers that volcano, calling it the 'Hell of Theodoric'. One hermit, secluded on an island not far from Sicily, saw a loathsome demon on a boat transporting the bound and tortured soul of King Dagobert I in order to throw it into the volcano, but the king was saved by the intercession of those saints upon whose churches he had bestowed much property while still alive.[49] How could one not believe such stories, when many people had heard with their own ears the groans and screams of the damned suffering in Vesuvius?! Throughout the centuries it was assumed that Etna and Vesuvius were the entrances to hell and that people who died not far from them were dragged away by demons and thrown into the gaping craters.[50]

The belief that hell and paradise are located somewhere on distant islands which one can reach, although not without difficulty, was also rooted in the consciousness of the inhabitants of the European North. The stories about the voyage of St Brendan make this particularly clear. Brendan lived at the turn of the fifth–sixth centuries and completed a series of voyages from the western part of Ireland to the shores of Scotland, to Britain, possibly also to Brittany, and to the Orkney, Shetland and Faroe Islands. In the following centuries stories about Brendan's voyages acquired a fantastic form, in which narratives about travels to remote lands were fused with eschatological visions. Dreams about the Promised Land and fears begotten by the expectation of the 'end of time', the spirit of travels and asceticism, love of the fantastic and reminiscences from ancient literature, folklore and religion were combined in these narratives, which assured the tale of St Brendan's voyages the widest, truly European popularity. In its basis this narrative borders on medieval visionary literature.[51]

The *terra repromissionis sanctorum* in the stories about the travels of the Irish monks is a direct contrast to the everyday world of men. The Promised Land abounds with every blessing and is a land of eternal flowering and fruiting; neither hunger nor fatigue is experienced in it.[52] Sheep there are the size of bulls and grapes the size of apples, and the fish are such that the monks thought one of them was an island. On one island they found a monastery whose inhabitants did not age, suffer from illness or cold, or at any time lack for good water and bread, which was supplied to them mysteriously from an unknown source. On another island food, drink, and rest awaited the sailors, and their table was laid miraculously for three days. The idea of abundant food and drink and the satiation of the hungry never leaves the author of Brendan's narrative; he is literally possessed by it.[53]

But the monks also met much that was frightening during their travels. The land of felicity and abundance does not seem to be separated spatially from the abodes of the forces of evil; the path to paradise can lead to hell just as well. Here bustle demons attempting to lead the brothers into temptation, and one of the monks is consumed by the fire of hell. Among the 'islands of the blessed' the travellers encountered a floating island of blacksmiths forging the souls of sinners, and then they came to the rock on which Judas Iscariot himself was sitting. On Sundays, owing to the Lord's mercy, he would rest from hell's tortures, but at the end of the day he was surrounded by demons and dragged into hell. After seven years of travelling Brendan and his surviving companions returned home with a load of precious stones. Some modern authors, concerned with pre-Columbian discoveries of America, ascribe the honour of being the first to reach its shores to St Brendan. Ignoring the specific character of medieval visionary literature, they attempt to read the tale of his wanderings as if it were a log-book.

In fact, the treatment of space in the visions is highly distinctive. I have mentioned already the symbolic 'topography' of visions, dividing right and left, east and west. In order to reach hell it is necessary to go towards the north; the gaze of sinners awaiting punishments is turned towards the north. But we are hardly dealing here with space in a real sense. One should rather suppose that the topographical terminology is applied to non-spatial phenomena: fears and hopes are expressed in similar 'geometricized' images. For 'north' in the visions is not a part of the world, but the concentration of the soul's despairs, just as 'east' is the embodiment of the expectations of salvation. The space of the visions is above all the exteriorization of the 'mental space' of medieval men. Only in reference to the symbolic aspect of the 'map' of the Other World can one fruitfully explore its general spatial structure.

First of all, in contrast to Dante's strict tripartite division, the visions of the preceding period resemble church art, insofar as they display a dichotomous structure. This is not, however, quite clearly defined: on the two poles are paradise and hell, but between them there is a series of transitions gravitating towards one or the other. Dante establishes the Other World with great precision, so that the reader of the *Comedy* can easily imagine his entire creation. Not so with authors of earlier visions. Travellers through the Other World visit different 'places'. How are they related to each other? In what sort of order are they arranged? All this remains completely unclear. Perhaps the sole attempt to structure the Other World is the introduction of the image of the bridge thrown across the stream: along this bridge, or rather plank, narrowing from vision to vision, the souls must pass; some succeed, since they are righteous, and others are dashed down under the burden of their sins into the fiery stream of cleansing. The meadows of the soul's repose are contrasted with the vale of suffering. In other respects the Other World of visions is a conglomerate of uncoordinated points not at all organized into one. They are connected only by the path along which the angel leads the travelling soul of the visionary from one *locus* to another.

This holds true not only for the early visions, but also for the relatively late *Vision of Tnugdal*.[54] In its forceful descriptions of otherworldly bliss and punishments scholars perceive the outlines of the plan of Dante's construction. After travelling through hell Tnugdal does not come immediately to paradise, but passes through places where the souls of the 'not very evil' (*non valde malorum*) are subjected to 'moderate punishments', as well as fields where reside the souls of the 'not very good' (*non valde bonorum*); this is a purgatory of sorts and the threshold of paradise. The *Vision of Tnugdal*, distinguished by the rhythm of the scenes and the proportionality of the distribution of tones, is extremely far from the records of the 'spontaneous' visions of the preceding period. Nevertheless, the idea of the spatial integrity of the Other World is still absent. Following an angel guide Tnugdal 'comes upon' various 'places' that are connected by nothing except the logic of the increasing punishments or rewards. Hell and paradise are no more than an aggregate of disconnected places (hills, valleys, swamps, pits, buildings, etc.); they are divided by unexplained voids unevenly surmounted in the narrative. The skin-sewn boat of Brendan and his companions sailed *per diversa loca*.[55] The Other World properly speaking, is not a united space; it is discrete, just as the space of the mythological world is discrete (Lotman, Uspenskij 1973: 288).

This 'patchwork' of space is especially visible in the *Apocalypse of Paul*, where shifts from one place of the Other World to another are usually expressed thus: 'and the angel transferred [or 'conducted'] me to...' Or the separate uncoordinated episodes are joined by such words as *et iterum vidi, posthaec*, etc. The spatial structure of the Promised Land in the *Voyage of St Brendan* is discrete in the same way (the monks sail the sea from one island to another).

The mythological and 'psychological' characteristics of the space of the Other World are also manifested in its distinctive 'irrational topography'. On the one hand, the places of the elect's bliss and of the sinners' tortures are contrasted in visions, when paradise is placed in the heavens or on 'happy islands' and hell under the earth. On the other hand, paradise and hell can be found in relative proximity, in lands separated from each other by several days' journey by sea. Sometimes they are really quite close. Bernold was led to a 'dark place' to which sweet aromas reached 'from a neighbouring place' and from which a ray of light was seen: the inhabitants of hell see the light of paradise and smell the fragrance of the 'abode of the saints' repose'.[56] In the *Elucidarium* Honorius of Autun wrote that the elect in paradise will observe those rejected by God and rejoice in their torments, even if they see among them parents, spouses or children; in a similar way the sinners at the Last Judgment will see the felicity of the elect, and thus the sufferings of the one and the bliss of the other will be intensified.[57] On the whole, the Other World of visions is comparatively cramped and not very large; one can make a complete round of it in one day, at most a few.

It would seem strange to speak about time and its course in the Other World, where eternity reigns. Nevertheless, in visions there is more about time than eternity, however paradoxical this may appear. Irish visions especially frequently speak about the measurement of time in hell. Owing to God's mercy, sinners are given a respite from their tortures every Sunday. The author of the *Voyage of Brendan* extends this mercy to Judas himself: although he is subjected to terrifying trials in two hells, a hot one and a cold one (on Tuesday, Thursday and Saturday he is tortured in 'lower hell', and on Monday, Wednesday and Friday in 'upper hell' – Rüegg 1945, 1: 329), on Sunday and feast-days he rests on a sea-cliff, because while alive he too performed a few good deeds. According to the *Vision of Adamnan*, clerics who had broken their vows and committed frauds of every sort are alternately now borne up to heaven, now plunged into the depths of the netherworld (Boswell 1908: 39, 42). In the *Vision of Baront* the souls suffering in hell are sent manna from paradise that restores their powers; they receive it daily 'around the sixth hour'. Liturgical time is counted in the Other World, too.[58]

The Irish king Cormack MacCartey, whom Tnugdal saw in the Other World sitting solemnly on a throne, and to whom an innumerable multitude of people brought precious gifts, was also plunged daily for three hours into the tortures of hell. The angel accompanying Tnugdal explained that gifts were brought to the king by paupers and pilgrims to whom he had given alms, but that the king must undergo tortures for having sullied himself by violating his conjugal fidelity, by murdering and by breaking oaths – all his remaining sins have been forgiven.[59] In the vision of the monk Alberich of Monte Cassino the punishments for lay sinners are set at three years, but the punishments for clergy who did not lead them on the true path are set at sixty and eighty years, depending on their rank (Rüegg 1945, 1: 412).

In paradise even birds observe the canonical hours by singing, and with the onset of the time for liturgy the candles light themselves. Here Sunday and other church holidays are observed. Before crossing from a lower heaven to one of the higher ones in the paradise of Adamnan the soul must wait for twelve to sixteen years. All this may seem less surprising when we learn from the *Vision of Baront* that in paradise there is also a church in which the clergy celebrates mass.[60]

Time also flows in Dante's Other World, but its flow is connected with the traveller's own reckoning.[61] It is the time of the observer rather than the 'objective' time of existence in hell and purgatory; it is not the Other World's inhabitants, but the stranger from without who 'measures the year by earthly calends'.[62] (On the complexity of the combination of time and eternity in Dante, see Andreev 1977: 17ff.) In the otherworldly regions of medieval visions this difference does not exist – both worlds are equally subject to the pace of canonical hours.[63]

To be sure, notions about earthly time were not always directly transferred into otherworldly visions. At any rate, Irish fantasy was not satisfied with such a transfer. In one of the narratives about an other-worldly sojourn Tejgu and his companions made a round of the Earthly Paradise in what seemed to them only one day, but its inhabitants explained to them that they had been there an entire year without, however, having grown hungry or become thirsty (Patch 1950: 38, 43, 47, 58ff., 94, 150). St Barint, who told Brendan about the 'Promised Land of the saints', also cited the words of the divine messenger who had appeared there to him and said: 'You have been a year on this island and still have not tasted bread or drink, and not once were you overcome by sleep, and you did not see night here.' But the meeting with this divine messenger took place on the fifteenth day of Barint's stay on the island.[64] In the same way Bran, son of Febal, who came with his companions to the Earthly Paradise ('Land of Women'), fancied that they had spent one year there, but in fact many years had gone by. One might think that in such instances a subjective experience of time is meant. But when the travellers, seized by homesickness, returned to the shores of Ireland, one of them, despite the warning of an inhabitant of the 'Land of Women', stepped onto land and was immediately turned into a pile of dust, 'as if his body had already lain many hundreds of years in the earth'.[65] Time elapsed differently in the earthly paradise and on earth, and what was a year in the 'Land of Women' was centuries in Ireland. Evidently time in general possesses unequal qualities here and there: on earth it leads to the destruction of all things, which in the world of the blessed are imperishable. The contiguity of time with eternity changes its nature. Approximately the same thing happens with travellers in the Other World as is supposed to happen with travellers on a spaceship proceeding to distant regions of the galaxy: their time elapses otherwise than on earth. In his *Pantheon*, Godfried of Viterbo narrates the journey of several monks who reached the Earthly Paradise by way of the ocean. There one day was equivalent to one century on earth, and after their return home they did not find any of their contemporaries alive; the laws had changed and old churches and towns had been destroyed. Other monks, who had the good fortune to visit paradise, asked permission to remain there for fifteen days, but learned with amazement that they had already been there seven centuries! How could this be, they asked; they were told that fruit from the Tree of Life and water from the Fountain of Youth partly endowed them with eternal life. They were also told that their names had been entered into the book of funeral masses, and therefore when forty days have elapsed after their return to earth they will turn into dust and find eternal rest. And thus it came to pass (Patch 1950: 159ff., 166).[66]

Earthly time and otherworldly time are directly inverted in those instances when the years of earthly life are compared with centuries and millennia in the Other World. One monk who left his order wilfully and did not receive absolution before death chose his own otherworldly punishment: a two-millennia stay in purgatory. Some time after his death he appeared to a bishop and told him that, owing to prayers for his soul and alms dispensed by the bishop, two years had been reckoned for him as two thousand years of otherworldly torture and now he was completely delivered from them.[67] A distinctive 'folkloric' treatment of time was common for the pace of time both 'here' and 'there'. This is the time of tale, epos and myth, a time far from being linear and unidirectional. In extrapolating earthly time to the Other World, medieval man affirmed the measure of his own life, making it the sole standard of temporality. Thus, time in the Other World turns out to be exteriorized spiritual life.

Christianity promises retribution at the 'end of time'; the Last Judgment is supposed to take place in the future, after the completion of the earthly age. As we have seen, this is reflected in church iconography. But literary visions say nothing about the future coming of Christ. Their interest in the Last Judgment is highly restricted; it is clearly focussed on rewards and punishments prepared for the soul after its separation from the body. The book with the list of merits and sins will not remain behind the seven seals until the 'fulfilment of time'. It is opened for each one of the deceased, and a lawsuit immediately arises between good and bad spirits over his soul. Visionaries wander through the Other World while remaining in earthly time, in the current moment. Retribution awaits a man not sometime in the future, but right now. One cleric from Clairvaux fell into an ecstatic state and saw himself standing before the divine tribunal. At the right hand of Christ he saw an angel with a trumpet which had already been blown once at the Lord's command. Christ was on the verge of ordering the angel to sound his trumpet a second time when the Mother of God interceded. Knowing that the world will perish after a new sounding of the trumpet, she saved it by her supplication.[68] A rich German burgher named Boxhirn saw in a vision Christ solemnly sitting in state amidst a multitude of people on Judgment Day. When Boxhirn drew near him, Christ proclaimed that he deserved to die and be cast down into hell, for he had never given alms to the poor.[69]

Those who return from the Other World sometimes tell about the tortures that they have experienced: the devil has already placed his sharp-clawed paw on them. Fursey emerged from the netherworld with burns on his body; another visionary saw his place waiting for him in hell; various sinners before dying tell of the agonies being inflicted on them by demons. The Other World is close spatially as well as temporally. Through the power of fears and hopes the Other World is transferred in visions from the future to the present. More precisely, it is in the future, but the future is really at hand in the present; the visions offer a unique possibility of experiencing this 'future at hand'.

We have seen that something similar took place with the cult of saints. By belonging immediately to both worlds, the saint was also included in two temporalities. As a man, he was a captive of the imperfect earthly world, but his saintliness was not of this world – it was a reflection of eternity – and in this sense while alive he dwelled in the Other World too. As a saint, while he was alive eternity was included in earthly time; he was its bearer among people, more perceptible and, owing to his miracles, more convincing than any other higher power.

That which according to theology is confined to linear time uninterruptedly flowing from the past through the present into the future – from the creation of the world and Christ's passion toward the end of the world and final reckoning – tends in visions and hagiography to be condensed into a single temporal projection and simultaneity. Fear of future retribution brought nearer what was to come and converted it to contemporaneity, just as on the church portals we encounter the phenomenon of the 'spatialization' of time arraying past, present and future side by side. As a result, this model of the world is seemingly 'flat' in time, deprived of temporal depth. The weight of the centuries that have elapsed from the creation is not felt, for memory, unburdened by a knowledge of sacral history, extends only for several generations, yielding then to legendary tradition, epos and tale. Also absent is a notion of a protracted future, since the expectation of the imminent end of the world continues to be latently present in this consciousness, now and again being realized as socio-psychological cataclysm. The idea of the Last Judgment is pushed aside by the thought of otherworldly retribution following immediately after the individual's death and of reprisal by the higher powers overtaking the offender immediately after transgression.

Hincmar of Rheims in his story about Bernold's vision leads him along the path of otherworldly wanderings to the abode of the saints' repose, where there stands a church in which Hincmar himself is preparing to celebrate mass. King Charles, who is suffering in hell, entreats Hincmar to pray for him, promising always to be obedient to him if he will aid him, and the cleric's prayers alleviate the fate of the king's soul. In which time does this take place? In the present? But Hincmar is still alive and reads mass in Rheims. In the future? After all, Bernold is already seeing the archbishop in paradise. However, after this he is able to relate his miraculous vision to the very same archbishop! The vision takes place in a special time in which present and future are not found in a relation of linear consequentiality, but are united in some mythical continuum.[70]

By studying time and space as 'categories' of medieval culture

(Gurevich 1985), one can state that both of them, at any rate if one departs from the scholastic thought of theologians, were generally not abstractions, but had a definite concreteness. A secular periphery surrounded holy places. Sacral periods and moments violated and rhythmically broke down the daily course of time. The appraisal of sacral time and space was principally other than that of profane times and places. Everything sacral belonged to eternity, and therefore the segments of space and time connected with it were distinguished by durability and imperishability. Sacred time does not flow and does not disappear; it is at rest, reflecting eternity. Eternity, as opposed to customary time, does not know consequentiality; it exists 'all at once', and sacred persons are not subject to the course of history. In the sculptural decoration of churches personages of the Old and New Testaments, pictures of the creation of the world, the Fall, the expulsion from paradise, Christ's passion, and of the Last Judgment are accommodated in one space. But the sacred space of the church is broken up, and each of its constituent parts corresponds to a definite stage of sacred history.

Works of medieval Latin literature, including narratives about otherworldly visits, do not permit time and space to be painlessly distinguished as conceptual categories, so deeply rooted are they in a single whole and unbroken vision of the world. The consequentiality of time is, as it were, bunched up or completely ignored. At the moment of a vision one can observe and experience not only present and future, but past as well. Caesarius of Heisterbach records a series of visions in which ecclesiastics were privileged to behold different gospel episodes: the Nativity and the star heralding it, the baby in the manger and Christ at age three, and Christ bound amidst Jews threatening him with death and finally crucified.[71]

Theologians developed dogma about eschatology and repeated that the Last Judgment, intended to complete earthly history, will be accomplished at the 'end of time'; but for the ordinary believer it was hard to imagine retribution somewhere in the indefinite, distant future. When his thought was turned towards the end of the world, he brought that moment nearer to the present and fell into a panicky expectation of an immediate final judgment. Thus, the 'personalistic' arrangement of popular consciousness, which at first glance one supposes one ought to seek rather in the eschatology of the élite, not of the masses, was paradoxically intensified. As a matter of fact, official dogma adhered to the teaching about a judgment at the 'end of time' of the souls of all people who ever lived, while visionary literature repeated the motif of an individual judgment directly after death. Each man's soul is confronted with books containing his sins and merits; these lists are produced by demons and angels at the moment of death. The fate of the individual's soul is decided in isolation from the fate of others both in time and in essence. As if torn from the history of salvation, a man is placed privately before the supreme tribunal. Ariès correctly notes this circumstance, which undoubtedly expressed a definite stage in the formation of personality. The key question is whether this stage occurred in the Middle Ages or later. As noted above, Ariès dates the idea of the individual judgment to the end of the Middle Ages, thereby connecting it with the breakdown of medieval culture proper. But early medieval visions leave no doubt that this idea was around as early as the sixth century. In other words, 'popular personalism', if I can put it that way, was an integral feature of the medieval world-view and not at all a symptom of its disintegration.

Following Ariès, R. Chartier analyses the iconography of the fifteenth century in such a way that images of a collective judgment are seen as expressing a traditional idea going back to Revelation, whereas pictures of a particular judgment over each soul are seen as expressions of the new individualistic view (Chartier 1976: 55). Chartier does not concern himself with sources of the scenes in which angels and demons compete at the bed of a dying man. Had he sought them, he would have noticed that the scene of the individual judgment was not at all novel in the late fifteenth century – it was already described by Bede! Accordingly, the juxtaposition of both variants – one with demons and angels producing records of sins and merits at the death-bed, the other with Christ enthroned, the weighing of the soul and an angel and a demon awaiting the outcome – must be interpreted as a paradoxical co-existence in the medieval mind of traditional eschatology and the notion of retribution after the individual's death.

Actually, the contradictory co-existence of the idea of the Last Judgment at the end of time with the idea of an immediate individual retribution is present in the Gospels themselves. According to Luke, punishments and rewards are due immediately after death. Thus, Christ says to the thief crucified with him: 'Verily I say unto thee, To day shalt thou be with me in paradise' (Luke 23:43; cf. 9:7). The poor man finds himself in the bosom of Abraham, the rich man in hell, right after death (Luke 16:22ff.). In other Gospels, on the other hand, the Second Coming and the Last Judgment are emphasized (e.g., Matt 24:3ff.; 25:31–46; 26:29; 13:39ff., 49–50; 19:28). The discrepancies between the Gospels of Luke and Matthew include not only the time of the judgment, but also the fact that in Matthew the stress is on the collective judgment, whereas in Luke it is on the individual's fate (cf. Chaunu 1978:76ff., 93). Most likely, in the time when these texts were written down the contradiction was not perceived. After all, the first Christians lived in expectation of the approaching *parousia*. Revelation concludes with an impatient cry: 'He which testifieth these things saith, Surely I come quickly. Amen. Even so, come, Lord Jesus' (22:20). The end of history was thought to be close: although no one but God knows the dates, Christ promises that many of those still living will be witnesses of his Second Coming (Matt 16:28).

The situation was somewhat different when in medieval Christianity the Last Judgment was put off until an undefined future in no way connected with the individual's biography. While reading the reports of otherworldly travels, one gains the impression that this contradiction of notions about the judgment was not sharply felt either in the medieval period: both ideas could be combined on the level of ordinary religiosity. This was not the case in theology, and in 1331–2 Pope John XXII found it necessary to state explicitly that neither would the righteous find eternal life nor the condemned go into hell until the resurrection of the dead at the 'end of time'. Such an affirmation of biblical truths suggests that the views reflected in visionary literature were widely held. Surely the pope's letters were meant as a sort of answer to the *Divine Comedy*, in which the deceased were already arranged in compartments of hell, purgatory and paradise.

This distinctive aspect of the ordinary believer's consciousness was connected with his general orientation towards the close, concrete, and visually perceptible. He easily materialized the spiritual and supernatural, transforming abstract concepts and qualities into bodies and independent essences. The human soul was also subject to this process of the materialization of the pretersensual.[72] Vision literature is very much concerned with the state of the soul which, temporarily separated from the body in order to visit the Other World, returns to its corporeal casing. First of all, it experiences grief, both from having seen the tortures of sinners and from having to leave paradise and spend some more time in the imperfect and sinful world. Reanimation is accompanied by a fundamental break in a man's life: he turns towards the way of truth, departs to a monastery, distributes his property to the poor or exhorts his companions to abstain from sin. To some visionaries, however, it seems improper to tell mortals about the Other World, and if they do so all the same, then they entreat the Lord not to be angry with them for the lack of restraint and explain it by a simple-hearted desire to tell near ones about the Other World exclusively for their souls' salvation, and not at all out of vainglory.

During an otherworldly sojourn the soul acquires supernatural powers of understanding and sight. Immediately the whole world is opened up before it. Travelling through paradise, Tnugdal was able for a moment to apprehend in a single glance the entire circle of the earth, not only what was lying before him, but also everything behind his back. This vision is of a distinctive sort, for Tnugdal, having seen everything at once, acquired a clear and full knowledge about all he had seen.[73] A poor woman, while in another world, read a prophetic inscription, even though she was illiterate.[74] But the return of the soul to its abandoned body does not take place without leaving a trace. In some instances spiritual and physical powers are diminished: the visionary temporarily loses his normal sight; his memory grows weak.[75] In other instances, however, returning to life is accompanied by new faculties which the individual did not possess earlier and which serve as proof of the veracity of his story. For example, an undistinguished youth named Armentarius, suddenly taken to heaven and returned after three days to his relatives, revealed which of them would soon die. Beyond the grave he acquired the ability to speak in any language.[76] Others brought back to life frequently foretell the fate of those still alive.

This ability is also ascribed to the souls of several of Dante's other-worldly inhabitants. But on the whole the treatment of the soul in the *Comedy* is profoundly different from that in the medieval visions. For all the clarity of hell's tortures, Dante's focus is transferred to mental sufferings, as earthly passions continue to torment men in the Other World. As far as physical sufferings are concerned, it is necessary to remember that it is shades deprived of an earthly body that are subjected to them. They are merely a 'void which had the appearance of bodies'. The inhabitants of Dante's hell and purgatory do not refract a ray of light passing through them, so they immediately recognize a stranger from the land of the living.[77]

Theologians taught that the souls of the dead will be clothed in flesh before the onset of the Last Judgment, but the authors of medieval visions, by contrast to Dante, forgot about this. In their understanding, the soul, apart from purely non-material qualities, apparently also possessed physical characteristics. When Fursey's soul, having received burns in the Other World, returned to its body, Fursey retained for his lifetime marks on his chin and shoulder. It would seem that the Dominican Rudolph of Schlettstadt should have had clear notions about the difference between the body and the soul, but in his Memorable Histories he manifests a typical inconsistency in this regard. He often speaks of sinners whose souls demons have carried away, leaving behind only their bodies,[78] but to a knight who had come to confession it was foretold '...demons will seize your body and carry it away to hell'.[79]

Soul and body, disconnected for a short time, can see each other. Thus, Boniface tells of the soul of a monk who beheld with revulsion the body it had abandoned. At the moment when the soul of Baront abandoned its body, he saw the soul: it was similar to a small bird just hatched from the egg. After this it found a new body outwardly similar to the old.[80] The character of the tortures to which sinners in hell are subjected also testifies to a material and corporeal view of the soul. The 'bodies' of souls are burned, torn by pincers, melted in furnaces, devoured, boiled in cauldrons, etc., and they differ from human bodies only in their ineradicability. Melted, re-forged in the smithy of hell, and devoured by the devil, the soul is restored to life for new interminable trials. The *Vision of Tnugdal* records a fire-breathing monster with two feet, a pair of wings, a long neck, an iron beak and iron claws. Sitting on a frozen swamp, he swallows souls of sinners, digests them and excretes them as dung onto the ice, where they grow up again to experience anew the same tortures. A picture truly worth the brush of a Bosch or a Brueghel.[81]

Like the body, the soul needs nourishment. In the *Apocalypse of Paul*, rivers of milk, honey, butter and wine flow in paradise. Baront saw heavenly manna sent down to suffering souls. In other visions a ray from heaven satiates the souls of the elect. In the satirical poem about false visions mentioned above, a feast given by Christ to a visitor to the Other World is depicted (Edélstand du Méril 1843: 298ff.). They also entertain in hell: sinners are presented with goblets filled with fiery liquid; toads and snakes cooked in sulphur were considered the specific infernal food. Palpable, material characteristics attributed to the soul, and other details of the Other World, are seen by theologians as mere 'images of things' (*imagines rerum*), through which the features of the Other World can be made accessible to imperfect, limited human understanding. Gregory the Great and other thelogians were not inclined to accept such images as ultimate reality.[82] Their audience, not at all prepared to recognize fine differences between the corporeal and the spiritual, saw it differently: it was disposed to perceive literally everything described in visions (Ponomarev 1886: 102, 127ff., 139, etc.). While for most Latin authors otherworldly bliss carried a chiefly spiritual character, the ninth-century cleric who in the *Heliand* set the Gospel in Saxon verses rendered the joy of paradise as *welo*, 'ownership', 'property', 'well-being', the spiritual legacy of Christians as *fader ôdil*, 'inherited landed ownership' or as *fehu*, 'cattle', 'movables', 'wealth' (Peters 1915: 22).

The purification of the soul from its sins is one of the most important questions of eschatology. In theological tractates it was discussed in abstract-speculative form, in the visions intended for a wide public by means of visual examples and stories about 'genuine facts' attested by the visionaries. Preachers knew full well the needs of their audience. 'People are convinced not so much by words as by living examples', wrote Gregory the Great.[83]

Man was thought of as standing at a crossroads, one path leading to otherworldly bliss, the other to hell. He needed deliverance from the burden of sin. That is why the basic place in the visions is occupied by pictures not of hell proper, but of the sufferings that cleanse the sinner's soul and prepare it for the transition to bliss. A large part of the trials undergone by souls in the Other World is not merely punishment for sins, but also the means of deliverance from the threat of eternal tortures. Purgatory is not designated in the early visions as a compartment of the Other World clearly separated from hell and paradise, but in a sense hell and the earthly world are endowed with certain functions of purgatory.

As a matter of fact, purgatory, according to these visions, is the place where one repents and is cleansed of one's sins. But a man already performs penance while alive; and perhaps from here comes the intimacy of purgatory with the earthly world. Penance imposed on sinners in the early period was expressed most of all in causing bodily sufferings; by means of physical deprivations and tortures the soul also was supposed to be cleansed. Sometimes penance was indistinguishable from physical trial. When a repenting sinner was compelled to spend a night in a grave together with a corpse, he undoubtedly felt himself already in the Other World. On the other hand, since souls are subjected to tortures both in hell and in purgatory, sharp lines of demarcation were not always drawn between these parts of the other world. According to Caesarius of Heisterbach, some sinners who found themselves in the Other World took purgatory for hell and hell for purgatory. At the same time purgatory was close to the Earthly Paradise;[84] and in some visions there are intermediary places for the 'not too evil' and the 'not too good' (see above, pp. 117–18).

Although the word *purgatorium* appears rather late, I am not inclined to attach too much significance to the long absence of the term.[85] For the contours of purgatory itself can already be discerned in early medieval visions. One of the regular components of the Other World, the fiery stream across which souls are supposed to pass along a narrow foot-bridge, apparently fulfils purgatorial functions.

By Dante's time the situation had changed. Penance had in large measure acquired a character of mental remorse. Hence the cleansing of the sinner's soul while alive began to be more clearly distinguished from the burning out of his sins in the flame of purgatory. Simultaneously the Other World was in large measure 'freed' from notions of time, being more tightly correlated with the idea of eternity; this was conducive to emphasis on the contrast between purgatory, a place of temporary residence of souls, and hell, where the tortures of the damned will have no end. The dichotomous structure of the Other World began to yield to the tripartitite division so distinct and perfect in Dante.[86]

The basic difference, however, between the *Comedy* and the visions of the preceding period is not this. Dante's Other World is allegorized. Though allegory for medieval man was not equivalent to fiction, and it is unlikely that for Dante hell, purgatory and paradise were mere poetic metaphors, nevertheless, this impressive picture of otherworldly reality was created precisely by Dante, and the poet realized his role as its creator, a creator in the sense that no one except him was able to see it thus and to celebrate it in such verses.

The Other World of medieval visions was perceived otherwise. Any man who descended into the cave of St Patrick could be convinced of the existence of purgatory. In the same way every man who lived near a volcano could hear the commotion raised by demons preparing to receive a sinner, and all who succeeded in visiting the Other World saw the fire-breathing wells of hell, the gloomy stream, the abode of the elect separated from the vale of sinners, or the walls of the heavenly Jerusalem. But it was not necessary to go so far, for in church the believer regularly beheld many of these scenes, and one must suppose that these images played no less a role than the priest's sermon in the formation of the dreams and nightmares of visionaries.

When in the vision reported by Boniface the sins and merits appear at the monk's trial, they are not figures in an allegory, but elements of human character with real independent existence. Nor is the wound's crying out and charging him with the crime a figure of speech. When in medieval art or literature allegory appears, the abstractions acquire a visible aspect. For example, sins and merits acquire the form of virgins inhabiting a tower, which in turn symbolizes a man.[87] But in the monk's vision his vices and merits do not have any allegorical embodiment – they simply appear and present the case for the prosecution and for the defence. And thus simply and naturally were the sounds of psalms sung by clerics without piety collected by demons into a sack or devoured by swine into which the same demons had turned themselves.[88] Fantasy was not realized as such; the world created by it was perceived by medieval man as reality.

In conclusion I should like to return to the comparison of the other world in medieval art and in literature respectively. The temporal sequence of scenes in the Last Judgments in sculptures is opposed by widespread disregard of eschatology in the descriptions of visions, in which future and present are combined on one mythological plane. This opposition was obviously not perceived by medieval people, otherwise the deviations of the visions from the theological canon would have been suppressed or even branded heretical. In fact, the church was not perturbed by them, nor by the 'materialization' of souls in the vision literature.

By transference of the judgment over the believer's soul from the end of the world to the moment directly following his death, the personal aspect of salvation is reinforced: a particular list of merits and deeds is brought against each soul and a particular judgment takes place over it. The completion of mankind's history is pushed aside in this consciousness by the individual believer's death and by the thought of his personal salvation. Biography triumphs over history.

One should also consider that the scenes represented in the 'Bible in stone', on church portals and capitals, were 'read' by parishioners synchronically rather than diachronically. Visual art tends to orientate the viewer towards joining various scenes into a simultaneous picture, and believers, familiar with travels through paradise and hell, were also inclined to transfer their mythological notions to what they saw upon entering the church. Let us remember that the mass celebrated there also attuned them to precisely such a perception of sacral history. Thus, popular consciousness, weakly receptive to an eschatological conception of time, accommodated in contemporaneity, during the life of each man, the entire content of salvific history, bringing together the fleeting moment of eternity, easily crossing over from the world of the living to the realm of the dead and back, and grotesquely endowing the soul with material qualities.

The image of a complete individual biography in its Christian understanding – as the fate of the soul – arose well before the end of the Middle Ages. At the same time, scenes of the Last Judgment were not forgotten either, as church iconography depicted them persistently. The fact that both judgments – the private one at the hour of death, and the communal one over humankind at the 'end of time' – coexisted in the medieval world-view expresses the original duality of Christian teaching about death and otherworldly retribution. This duality appeared most radically in the medieval epoch, when the Christians' impatient and exultant expectation of the imminent arrival of the kingdom of God yielded to fear of the severe retribution prepared for the majority of the dead.[89] The notion of the individual's personal responsibility for his fate and free choice of the path of salvation or of perdition does not belong to the transition to the Renaissance (as Ariès and his followers propose); it is present throughout the Middle Ages, however distinctively personality was understood in this era.

Is not the vacillation of the medieval mind between the idea of an immediate personal judgment and the idea of a collective judgment 'at the end of time' closely connected with the following peculiarity of the age's self-consciousness of personality? Medieval people felt themselves directly on two temporal planes – on the plane of transient individual life and on the plane of events decisive for the fate of the world: that is the creation of the world, Christ's sufferings, the Second Coming at the end of the world. Each man's fleeting life was intertwined with the world-historical drama and received from it new, higher and eternal meaning. 'This duality of the perception of time is an integral quality of the consciousness of medieval man. He never lives in only one earthly time; he cannot renounce the consciousness of sacral history, and this consciousness in a fundamental way influences him and his personality, for the salvation of his soul depends on his associating with sacral history' (Gurevich 1972: 127). The eschatological scenes depicted on the portals of churches in the twelfth and thirteenth centuries and the scenes narrated by otherworldly travellers do not belong to different stages of the development of the attitude towards death in the Middle Ages – they express the spiritual situation of the human personality in the two fold space of medieval culture.

The problem of the perception of death, of notions about the Other World and of the possibility of communicating with its inhabitants, as an essential component of the medieval picture of the world, is intensively discussed in a rapidly growing body of scholarship. Philippe Ariès' work (1977) was not the first in this direction, but he undoubtedly drew attention to this aspect of historical psychology. Recently M. Vovelle (1982) has emphasized that the study of this subject is not a mere fad, but an important avenue that opens new perspectives for the study of collective consciousness. Out of the great number of works devoted to the problem of death in the Middle Ages I should like to comment briefly on a few which, despite differences in approach, seem to attempt to survey the issue within a wider socio-cultural context.

P. Dinzelbacher's interesting analysis of medieval otherworldly vision literature (1981) is rich in concrete material. Space and time in the visionary's perception, contacts with otherworldly inhabitants, the description of the compartments of the Other World, the social function of visions and a 'sociology of visionaries' (that is, their social composition) are discussed in ways akin to my formulation of the question. The author also examines stories about the soul's travel through hell, purgatory and paradise, and records of the ecstatic visions of mystics of the later Middle Ages, which gives him the chance to compare these very different literary genres.

According to Dinzelbacher, in the earlier period non-nobles predominated among otherworldly visionaries – most of all monks, but also knights and peasants (some of the last had the most extended visions). At the end of the Middle Ages the nobility and bourgeoisie produced a large number of mystics experiencing visions. Between the sixth and the twelfth century only men had visions, but the situation changed from the thirteenth century. It seems to me that there are grounds for speaking about a certain 'democratic' tendency of visions in the early period that is expressed not only by the composition of the visionaries, but also by the pictures of the tortured souls of bishops, kings and nobles: this literature was orientated towards wide segments of the population, even if it could only reach the unlettered in a mediated form through re-telling.

Dinzelbacher's observations on the reflection of earthly social structure in notions about the Other World are extremely interesting. Paradise, as a realm of order and hierarchy, in contrast to hell, a realm of chaos, appears as 'ein sehr feudaler Himmel' (Dinzelbacher 1979; 1979a). In visions, as a rule, the issue is not the Last Judgment 'at the end of time', but the immediate judgment over the soul of the deceased individual. It is significant that he feels justified in speaking about purgatory in the works of Gregory I and Bede (cf. my comments on J. Le Goff 1981 below, and Gurevich 1983). My observation about the 'patchwork' of the depiction of otherworldly space in medieval visions (as an aggregate of uncoordinated *loci*) finds support in Dinzelbacher (1981: 125ff.), who also considers this feature characteristic of medieval consciousness in general.

Dinzelbacher's attempt to divide the vast corpus of visions into 'authentic' and 'ungenuine' ones is, however, doubtful. In medieval man's perception all these visions were genuine revelations offering the possibility of looking into the other side of life. The existence even then of vocal sceptics does not diminish the force of that assertion. The spontaneity of the visionary's perception is discussed above (pp. 124–5) and in the article about the two peasant visions (Gurevich 1984a). I only wish to emphasize that visions and dreams were necessarily modelled on the picture of the world of those who experienced them and in that sense are cultural facts (cf. Burke 1973; Le Goff 1977).

I cannot concur with Dinzelbacher's assertion (1981: 238) that vision literature in the early medieval period was accessible solely to educated people, that is, to the clergy and monks, since no one besides them was able to read, especially in Latin. Such a view underestimates the activities of the clergy and their influence through sermons on a wide spectrum of laymen. Let me refer again to a Scandinavian example: among the first works of church literature which the clergy found necessary to translate into Old Icelandic we find all the genres that I have been concerned with, including visions, and especially the *Vision of Tnugdal*. The audience for these translated works was clearly common Scandinavians, the overwhelming majority of whom were peasants. In the earlier period the function of literary translations was fulfilled through oral re-telling by the parish priest or monastic missionary, who would inevitably stress folkloric features to make the matter accessible to the unlettered. The fact that a folkloric basis is clearly present in visions and similar genres of medieval Latin didactic literature attests the pressure by the audience on the authors. These genres of medieval Latin literature can not be understood without considering the contact of various levels of social consciousness – from the scholarly to the popular.

While Dinzelbacher is a good introduction to a range of questions about the perception of the Other World, J. Le Goff's recent book (1981) is seemingly devoted to a more narrow theme – the origin of the notion of purgatory. In fact, however, he attempts to connect the move from a dyadic division into hell and paradise to a tripartite division including purgatory with general transformations in the intellectual life of the West in the eleventh to the thirteenth century, and to place changes in mentality within the development of the social system as a whole. Having carefully studied theological texts, Le Goff demonstrates the absence of the noun *purgatorium* before the 1170's and concludes that any concept of it was also absent. Purgatory arises on the map of the Other World only in the late twelfth century and becomes widely accepted in the thirteenth, finally receiving official recognition. The 'discovery' of purgatory signified a profound shift in the attitude towards death and the Other World: men believed that the fate of the deceased's soul could be altered by 'good deeds' and that its stay in the fire of purification could be shortened. Counting and reckoning were introduced in relation to the Other World, and a man simultaneously controlled both the earthly world and the world on the other side of the grave.

Le Goff does not attach independent meaning to reports of visions, but focusses rather on scholastic and theological literature. However, I believe that the perspective changes if we grant visions the significance that they deserve. Then it becomes obvious that a rather vague image of purgatory, not yet fully differentiated from hell, hovered in medieval consciousness long before purgatory was recognized by schoolmen and approved by the papacy. As we have seen, visions have no clear tripartite structure of the Other World, but purgatory is present in concept in this literature from the very beginning, even if it is not so called and not outlined as a separate realm. Therefore, I think that purgatory first arose not in the theology of the late twelfth century, but much earlier. True, it acquired distinctive outlines from the scholastics, acquired a name, and received an official right to exist. The difference between the visionaries and the scholastics is that between an indistinct complex of mental images not raised to the level of general concepts and a reflected, generalized system with precise categories worked out by disciplined scholarly reasoning.

The notion of an otherworldly place or places where souls are subjected not merely to torments but also to expiatory procedures arose already at the beginning of the Middle Ages, as a product of the irresistible need of believers to retain hope of salvation. Hence, it would be incorrect to attribute the initiative for the idea of purgatory to the scholastics. Accordingly, the change of the schoolmen's position with respect to purgatory, whose acceptance they had opposed for so long (for nothing is said about it in Scripture), is also difficult to explain exclusively by the general development of intellectual life during the growth of cities and the municipal estate. No little significance in this process should be attached to the pressure on the clergy by the masses of the population who needed to 'control' the otherworldly space in such a way that a man could retain a chance of salvation, even if he did not achieve it at the moment of death. The scholastics would undoubtedly have been receptive to stimuli coming from the mass of believers (compare what was said above about the position of the church in relation to the cult of saints).

My criticism is in no way intended to diminish my very high regard for Le Goff's study, but I should like to stress that the process of the 'birth' of purgatory must also be examined within the history of medieval popular culture, and not only in the context of the culture of intellectuals (cf. Gurevich 1983; 1984a: 328–34).

While Le Goff and Dinzelbacher are concerned with the medieval understanding of the Other World, M. Vovelle (1983) focusses directly on the perception of death through seven centuries of West European history. In a certain sense this important study appears as a competitor and opponent of the pioneering book of Ariès (1977), which embraces approximately the same period (Ariès begins even earlier, but touches upon the initial medieval period rather summarily).[90] However, the primary-source foundation of Vovelle is wider than that of Ariès, and his method is sharper and lacks the 'impressionistic' quality partially due to Ariès' one-sided selection of materials and arbitrary comparison of sources from different periods. Accordingly, Vovelle's conclusions are more balanced. The main difference between his book and that of Ariès is that Vovelle does not isolate people's attitude towards death from their social system; he does not believe in the autonomy of the collective imagination. The image of death is included within an all-encompassing social model which provides a general interpretation and, as a kind of specific 'ether', determines the weight and significance of all the forms of existence contained within it. Society is reflected in its image of death, but this reflection is distorted and ambiguous, and one must beware of attempting to establish a mechanical dependence of mentalities on the material life of society; one can speak only about mediated, indirect determinations. The development of society's regulations concerning death, in Vovelle's opinion (1976), must be examined within the entire complexity of their relations with economic, social, demographic, spiritual and ideological aspects of life.

A specialist on the study of the massive, uniform material of wills in eighteenth-century Provence (Vovelle 1978; 1980), which permits and requires the use of statistical methods, Vovelle in this generalizing work too attempts as much as possible to introduce number and measure into the study of such a 'delicate' socio-psychological phenomenon as society's regulations concerning death. In all parts of his book he includes a detailed analysis of demographic information, in order then to pose the question about the connection between this and the subjective expression of the conception of death in society. Recognizing the presence in a concrete period of a certain general spiritual climate, he nevertheless does not lose sight of the specific variations present in the social consciousness of definite groups and segments, and he continually returns to the problem of the resonance of one conception or another of death in the social environment. By contrast to Ariès, Vovelle (1979) does not speak about a collective subconscious, but he nevertheless emphasizes that a significant part of what society expresses about death remains unconscious. Religious, philosophical, scientific, and all other, arguments about death in a given society are in dialectical connection with a common stock of notions, beliefs, gestures and psychological states. Thus, the analysis of the attitude towards death is conducted on different, although also intersecting levels, where the unconscious yields to the conscious.

Vovelle describes the history of the changes in the attitude towards death as a slow development in which various models of conduct are combined, but this development is interrupted by convulsive, sharp leaps: cataclysms evoked by the Black Death of the mid-fourteenth century, the origin of the theme of the *danse macabre* at the end of the Middle Ages, the 'Baroque pathos' of death of the end of the sixteenth and the seventeenth centuries. In the history of the perception of death the 'time of the long duration' is combined with brief time, for various lines of development are characterized by unequal rhythms. Vovelle pays particular attention to the pitfall of silence in the history of death: throughout this very long era we hear almost nothing about the attitude towards death of the anonymous masses, and there is a real danger in assuming that the powerful forces of their world are speaking for them too.

Vovelle's book focusses on modernity, but it seemed to me essential to dwell on the work's initial methodological premises, since they help in understanding his innovative and at the same time well-founded approach to the study of the history of the image of death. As for the first parts of his book characterizing the Middle Ages, Vovelle distinguishes two models of death: death in its daily and mass perception and death in its Christian aspect. The first model proceeds from the belief in the existence of 'doubles' – corpses that represent a potential danger for the living, who therefore try to appease them. As E. Le Roy Ladurie showed in his study of the world-view of the peasants of Montaillou (1975), they believed that the souls of the dead, or rather their ghosts, wander around the settlement without finding repose. Possessing bodies, they require warmth and drink. Only with time, after expiatory sojourns around the village of the living, do the settlers of the village of the dead die a second time for good. Church doctrine about the Other World did not evoke particular interest among the local inhabitants, 'contaminated' by the heresy of the Cathars, and was known to them rather vaguely; but nevertheless concern for the soul's salvation and its deliverance from posthumous torments occupied an enormous place in their consciousness.

In characterizing the Christian model, Vovelle attaches greater significance than does Ariès to the role of religion in determining regulations in the attitude towards death. In his view, purgatory became popular much later; but I believe that he came to such a debatable conclusion on the basis of studying iconographic material and without taking literary facts into account. With certain reservations he accepts Ariès' thesis about the gradual individualization of the perception and experience of death throughout the later Middle Ages and he also speaks about the move from the idea of the collective judgment 'at the end of time' to the idea of the judgment of the individual at the moment of the sinner's death. As the reader already knows, I cannot agree with such a point of view. The two ideas are equally old and both were present from the beginning in Christianity. Vovelle, along with other scholars, does not understand the paradox of the co-existence in one consciousness of a 'large' and a 'small' eschatology (i.e. the idea of the Last Judgment after the Second Coming, and the idea of an immediate judgment over the soul right after the sinner's death), which contradicts our logic but at the same time sheds a particularly bright light on the medieval mentality.

For characterizing how the relationship of the world of the living with the world of the dead was understood in the Middle Ages the work of O. G. Oexle (1983) is very valuable. He shows that, according to notions then current, the dead continued to lead an existence and were found in mutual relations with the living. The dead were recognized as having legal capacity and capability: the deceased could figure in a lawsuit as plaintiff or defendant, and he could be a debtor or a creditor. The kin group and family also included the dead in their make-up. Between the living and the dead a constant interchange took place: through prayers and offerings for the soul's repose on the one hand, and through intercession and patronage on the other. The cult of the dead was very close to the cult of the saints, relations with whom where constructed on the same model. To mention the deceased was not simply to remember him: at the moment of the mention of his name it was as if he were present among the living. Thus, religious remembrance was also a definite social action joining the living with the dead as active subjects. On the other hand, refusal to bury the deceased symbolized his exclusion from society, to which the remaining dead continued to belong.

Such a tight intimacy of the living and the dead began to break down in the fourteenth century during the epidemics of the plague. Losing their mutual obligations *vis-à-vis* each other, people also ceased to observe them in relation to their own dead. This process, which continued in the following centuries, Oexle prefers to call not the 'dechristianization' or 'secularization', but the 'desocialization', of the individual. A visual indicator of the dissolution of the connection between the living and the dead was the displacement of cemeteries to beyond the city walls, while earlier they had been located within the city limits.

Finally, I should like to stress that, in contrast to several historians concentrating on the perception of death and on notions of the Other World, I believe it is necessary not to be concerned with this question as such, but to examine it as one of the components of the wider problem of the medieval world-view. It is more correct to study the theme of death and everything connected with it in this context, for it has no independent history. With the material of otherworldly visions one can discuss notions of space and time, the interpretation of the soul, definite aspects of the self-consciousness of personality, the understanding of history, and many other aspects of the medieval image of the world. While much of recent scholarship on this theme is very valuable, the theme of death is sometimes absolutized and taken in isolation from the spiritual universe of medieval man, and this is not helpful.

5

THE *ELUCIDARIUM:* POPULAR THEOLOGY AND FOLK RELIGIOSITY IN THE MIDDLE AGES

The genres of medieval Latin literature discussed in the preceding chapters confronted medieval man with various aspects of his spiritual life; but not all the components of Catholicism that were supposed to be instilled in the parishioners could be included in works of these genres. Basic religious principles required elucidation in a more systematized and coherent form. Yet theological works such as *summae* were clearly beyond the capacity not only of simple laymen, but also of a significant part of the lower clergy and monks. An enormous distance existed between high theology and the vulgarized, common version of Christianity, and a sermon's success depended in large measure on whether the preacher succeeded in bridging that gap. Tractates containing a simplified exposition of basic theological positions were created to solve this problem. Among them the writings of Honorius of Autun, composed at the turn of the eleventh and twelfth centuries, were exceptionally popular throughout Latin Europe for centuries. Honorius set himself the goal of popularizing theological principles by instructing those priests who were in direct contact with the faithful. His most famous works of this genre were: *De imagine mundi, Clavis physicae,* and the *Elucidarium.*[1]

The plan of the *Elucidarium* is distinguished by its harmony. In the first book, entitled *De divinis rebus,* sacral history is set forth as a teacher's responses to a pupil's questions. Here Honorius speaks about God and Creation, angels and demons, the creation of Adam, his Fall and punishment, Christ's Incarnation and life on earth, his redemptive sacrifice, his mystical body and the eucharist. The book ends with a discussion about bad priests. The second book (*De rebus ecclesiasticis*) is devoted to man's life from birth to death. It contains an account of the doctrine of good and evil, of Providence and predestination, of baptism and marriage, after which Honorius moves on to a digression about various 'categories' of people and their prospects for salvation. Then follows an analysis of the relations between God and man and discourses about guardian angels and demons, death and burial. The third book (*De futura vita*) treats the doctrine of paradise, purgatory and hell, the posthumous fate of the souls of the saved and the damned, and the Last Judgment. The work ends with a picture of the elect's eternal felicity. In this way questions of theology, Christian anthropology and eschatology are surveyed consecutively.

The inspiration of the *Elucidarium* comes from the author's concerns about the sinfulness of humankind, the greater part of which is facing eternal perdition. Honorius shares Augustine's teaching on predestination, but he simplifies it extremely and comes to almost fatalistic conclusions, abandoning Augustine's idea of the soul's quest for truth and of the necessity of God's grace and transferring the stress to the inscrutability of God's mercy towards the elect and his condemnation of the damned. The *Elucidarium* ignores the inner conflict of the introspective personality, the source of the believer's intense experiences, which constitutes the very essence of Augustine's reflections. Predestination is for Honorius God's will, already expressed before the creation of the world. In accordance with that, those for whom it is foreordained will enter the kingdom of heaven and be saved.[2] This formulation was orthodox from the viewpoint of Augustine's thought: predestination for salvation, but not for perdition (a thesis rejected by the church in the ninth century).[3] However, as we shall see further, Honorius also understands the inevitability of the perdition of the 'bad', those damned by God, as predetermined from before time. What stands out in the *Elucidarium* is the author's use of this rather crude version of predestination. According to Honorius, predestination lacks an individual character – it focuses on groupings: the representatives of definite social categories are chosen.

The problem of the soul's salvation, situated by Augustine in a purely spiritual scheme, is extended in the *Elucidarium* to a social scheme. What were, in Honorius' view, the prospects for salvation of different categories of people? After a discourse about priests and monks, among whom he distinguishes the righteous (the 'light of the world', the 'salt of the earth', the 'windows in the Lord's mansion through which the light of knowledge pours on to those remaining in the darkness of ignorance') and the unrighteous ('the most miserable of all people, for they are deprived of both this world and the Lord'), Honorius turns to secular estates. Knights and soldiers are condemned: they bring God's wrath upon themselves, since they live by robbery, the origin of all their wealth. 'Do merchants have a hope of salvation?' the pupil asks. 'A slim one', answers the teacher, 'since they acquire almost all that they own by fraud, perfidy and other dishonest methods. They make pilgrimages to holy places so that the Lord will increase their riches and preserve their property – and hell awaits them'. 'And what is the fate of various artisans?' 'Almost all of them will perish', the teacher answers without hesitation. 'Everything that they manufacture is based on fraud. It is said of them "there is no darkness, no deathly shade where the workers of iniquity could hide themselves"' (Job 34:22). 'Do jongleurs have any hope?' 'None, for they are servants of Satan. It is the same with those who confess publicly – they anger God by boasting of their crimes, and they shall perish. As for madmen, they are like children and shall be saved'.[4] 'And farmers?' 'The greater part shall be saved, for they live without guile and feed God's people by the sweat of their brow, as it is said, "Thou shalt eat the labours of thy hands: blessed art thou, and it shall be well with thee"' (Ps 127:2)[5] The pupil inquires about the fate of children. Children to the age of three who can still not speak will be saved, if they are baptized, for it is said 'Of such is the kingdom of heaven' (Matt 19:14). Of those beyond the age of five a part will perish, a part will be saved.[6]

A joyless picture, to be sure!

The idea that the overwhelming majority of people has no hope of salvation and is doomed to otherworldly tortures was widespread in medieval Latin literature. One bishop met a deceased hermit who revealed to him that he was one of 30,000 people who had died that day. Of them only he and St Bernard were taken into paradise, three more had entered purgatory, and all the rest were sent to hell (Tubach 1969: no. 3591). In another *exemplum* a preacher who appeared from the Other World made known that the wide path to hell was trodden by those under the care of bad parish priests who did not tend to their flocks; only a few will be saved (Klapper 1914: no. 22).

'Obviously, few will be saved', despondently concludes the pupil, and the teacher responds, '... "strait is the gate and narrow is the path, which leadeth unto life, and few there be that find it"' (Matt 7:14). Just as the dove picks out the pure seeds, so also Christ chooses his elect, hidden among all these categories, even among thieves. He knows those for whom he shed his blood.[7] Apparently Honorius was also privy to this knowledge, as he discourses without hesitation on the predestination of the souls of the members of all estates.

The damned are incapable of receiving the sacraments, for when they take up the host and drink the eucharistic wine transubstantiation does not take place. Just as the devil entered Judas once he had tasted the bread, so also every evil man at the moment of the sacrament eats and drinks the Lord's condemnation, not his grace.[8]

'Can one distinguish the good from the bad by some sort of characteristics?', asks the pupil. 'Possibly', the teacher responds with customary confidence: the elect, since they possess a pure conscience and believe in the future, have a joyous visage; their eyes shine; their step is light; and their speech is sweet. But the damned, burdened by an unclean conscience and experiencing a heartfelt bitterness, have a gloomy countenance; their words and deeds are unsure; their laughter is uncertain, as is their sorrow; their gait is heavy; and the venom which they conceal in their souls is poured out in their disagreeable and unclean speech.[9] However, this assertion is contradicted by an idea stated elsewhere in the tractate: 'Now good and bad are mixed together, and many of the bad will seem good and many of the good will be taken for bad'. Only on Judgment Day will the angels separate the righteous from the sinners, as wheat from chaff.[10]

Even though Honorius attaches great significance to predestination in deciding people's fates and governing the world, the devil also plays a prominent role in his system. God made him the 'industrious blacksmith of this world', compelled to serve the Lord's goals. Torments and misfortunes are the hearth of this craftsman, temptations his bellows, trials and persecutions his hammers and tongs, lying and deception his saws and chisels. By means of these tools he cleanses the heavenly vessel, that is the elect, and punishes the damned.[11] Earthly power and wealth serve as such tools, and both the elect and the damned can possess riches, health and power. But the possession of such riches by both the damned and the blessed has a contrary significance. An abundance of earthly riches is given to the damned 'for the sake of the elect', so that the latter will despise these transient valuables. For the damned, riches represent the opportunity to do evil against the elect and thus to turn them towards the path of truth. But the blessed use power and property for good deeds and also against evil people. Moreover, by possessing wealth and other earthly blessings they learn better to value heavenly blessings, for if the former are so pleasant how much more valuable will the latter be! In actuality, the evil are awash in every sort of pleasure and lack nothing, while the good are subjected to persecutions and deprivations, but before the Lord they will be the ones who are blessed and wealthy, while the evil will be poor and powerless.[12] Such is the simple dialectic or, rather, casuistry of our theologian.

Of course, the 'predisposition' of the common folk to salvation does not operate automatically. Every man should guard his soul, confess, repent of his sins, do good deeds and be faithful to the church. The 'social criticism' contained in the *Elucidarium* has an exclusively moral–didactic feature: the kingdom of heaven belongs to the meek and simple, but earthly powers, although they sometimes serve the devil, are not to be challenged but rather should be obeyed. In response to the pupil's question about the sources of earthly powers and statuses the teacher explains: 'Every power and dignity of both the bad and the elect is from God. For it is written, "For there is no power but of God"' (Rom 13:1).[13]

Honorius also undertakes the attempt at a distinctive 'social analysis' of the impending events of the Last Judgment during his account of the coming of the Antichrist. Born of a whore in Great Babylon, the Antichrist in the course of three and a half years will come to rule the world and will subject humankind to himself by four methods. First, he will suborn the nobles with riches, which he will have in abundance, because all hidden treasures will be thrown open before him. Secondly, he will subjugate the common people through fear, by displaying the greatest cruelty to the Lord's worshippers. Thirdly, he will enlist the clergy with his wisdom and unprecedented eloquence, for he will be skilled in every art and craft. Fourthly, he will deceive those monks who have despised earthly life with portents and prophecies, by ordering fire to descend from the sky and devour his enemies before his eyes and by raising the dead and compelling them to testify about him.[14]

The consideration of the problem of salvation in a social aspect is the characteristic feature of the *Elucidarium*, distinguishing it from other contemporary theological works, including the later works of Honorius himself. In the tractate *Speculum ecclesiae* he displays less pessimism as to the capability of various groups of the population to be saved. Soldiers figure here as the 'right hand' of the church. Merchants, although cautioned against abuses, merit his praise, since they serve all peoples and are subjected to every sort of risk during their travels. Everybody is indebted to them and should pray in their behalf. As for the peasants, his 'fellow-brethren and friends', he bids them obey their priests, not to transgress the boundaries of their fields, not to mow hay and cut wood outside the designated borders, and to pay the tithe conscientiously.[15]

Scholars of Honorius justifiably speak about the lack of originality and independence in his theology. However, this appraisal deserves correction insofar as his 'social' interpretation of salvation is concerned. On the other hand, it would be wrong to overestimate the weight of Honorius' statements on the predestination for salvation of the common folk, the farmers. Merely a few phrases are devoted to this in the *Elucidarium*. Let us not, however, lose sight of the specifics of the work. It is unwarranted to expect originality from a manual of theology which was intended to explain the basic truths of Christian teaching and whose author was supposed to limit himself to an account of dogmas, not entering into particular arguments. Orientation towards the already-known was a characteristic feature of theological literature, whose dogmatizing tendency is distinctly revealed in the *Elucidarium*. Therefore, if one still meets uncoordinated opinions and views of a certain originality, however scant, one cannot help but pay particular attention to them. There are very few such original positions in the *Elucidarium*, but it would be rash to overlook them. Even seemingly small nuances of meaning, and formulas departing from the mould would have served as essential signs for a medieval man schooled in endless repetitions within a monotonous stock of commonplaces.

As we see, Honorius' sympathies lie on the side of the common folk. The influence of the Antichrist on them is not connected either with bribery by earthly riches or with seduction by false teaching or miracles. The very fact that nobles can betray Christ to gain treasures offered to them and that the clergy and monks are given over to the charlatanry of Christ's enemy testifies by itself against the sincerity of their faith and rings out as an accusation.[16] Only the common people are 'God-bearers!' A critical attitude towards unrighteous priests and monks is repeatedly displayed in the *Elucidarium*.

Monks, priests, nobles, commoners – such is Honorius' 'social typology', generally inserted into a series of similar 'sociological schemes' worked out by church authors of the tenth to twelfth centuries (Fossier 1970: 144). This system does not contradict the well-known tripartite classification of *oratores, bellatores,* and *laboratores* which was widespread in literature of the period (Le Goff 1977: 80–90; Duby 1978: 300–10; cf. Gurevich 1977: 274–303). As a rule, this classification of society was not undertaken with the conscious aim of sketching a picture of classes, estates, orders and ranks, but rather arose involuntarily when authors spoke about the troubles of the world and the corruption of clergy and nobility and called them to pity and mercy towards the meek and oppressed. In Honorius' discussion of the possibilities for salvation of various categories of society, this scheme is lost in a rather unsystematic listing of priests, monks, knights, merchants, artisans, jongleurs, public penitents, madmen, peasants, children, etc. Social position and age, kind of work and spiritual health, moral qualities and productive roles, are mixed up in this list. Honorius could list them in this way because he was not really concerned with a social analysis but was troubled by an altogether different question: what manner of life and what condition of the soul favour the soul's salvation? The answer is unambiguous enough: besides upright clerics and monks, only the poor in spirit will be saved, namely small children, madmen and the greater part of farmers. This comparison of peasants with the spiritually poor and infants also sheds light on Honorius' appraisal of rural folk. The quality aiding their salvation is evidently not so much their labour or their closeness to the earth as their simplicity of soul, their lack of guile. In contrast to merchants and artisans, whose activity is inseparably connected with fraud and unjust enrichment and draws them into hell, peasants are upright. Thus, to a certain extent in the *Elucidarium* the earthly hierarchy is turned upside-down.

The tractate's discussion of the chances of salvation for various social groups does not imply the possibility of a choice of career. The medieval theologian's thought does not foresee transition from one social condition to another. Therefore, the unfavourable evaluation of one or another form of activity does not imply the necessary renunciation of the profession of soldier, merchant or artisan. On the ladder of ranks and dignities each man is supposed to occupy the station in life prepared for him by the Lord and to fulfil his designated function.

The idea of the church as a mystical community of Christians is developed in another place in the Elucidarium. The pupil asks: 'Why is the church called the body of Christ?' The answer: 'Just as the body obeys the head, so also the church is obedient to Christ, owing to the mystery of the transubstantiation of Christ's body. The head is placed over the body's members just as the Lord governs all the elect.' But further it turns out that Christ's enemies, those he has rejected, also participate in the sacred body of the church in a definite – negative – sense, as its 'waste'. Developing the analogy between the body and human society, considered in a sacred synchronism that embraces at once all the pages of history from Old Testament times right down to the end of the world, the teacher instructs that the prophets and apostles are the eyes; the church's dutiful members the ears and nose; the heretics the mucus; the Doctors the bones; the exegetes of Scripture the teeth; soldiers the defenders of the church, the hands; the farmers who feed the church the feet; and the unclean and sinful the dung devoured by swine-like demons.[17]

This joining of biblical characters and various categories of people in an entire organism governed by one law could easily be taken for a description of sculptural representations adorning churches – rows of prophets, kings, apostles, saints, sinners teeming under the feet of Christ the Judge, and demons dragging the damned into hell. Soldiers and farmers are an integral and important component of the 'body of Christ' ('hands' and 'feet'), as are the clergy and theologians. The teacher clearly defines the functions of the laity: soldiers are the 'defenders of the church' and peasants are its nourishers.

The fate of the damned is depicted in the Elucidarium in all its details. As soon as the sinner dies, frightful, terrifying and grimacing demons appear for his soul with deafening noise. Subjecting it to unbearable tortures, they wrench it from the body and pitilessly drag it into hell – precisely the same scene as the one recorded in otherworldly visions. Properly speaking there are also two hells, continues the author: upper and lower. Upper hell is the earthly world, full of sufferings, troubles, cold, hunger, thirst and various bodily and mental torments. In lower hell, situated under the earth, there are nine types of torture for evil souls. First, such an inextinguishable fire burns there that even the sea could not quench it; it burns without shining. Secondly, there is an unbearable cold in which even a mountain of fire would be turned into ice. Of this fire and cold is said 'the wailing and gnashing of teeth', because the smoke from the fire causes the tears to flow and the cold sets the teeth to gnashing. Next, the netherworld teems with worms and monstrous, hissing snakes and dragons, which dwell in the fire like fish in water. The fourth torture is an unbearable stench. The fifth is the whips, which the demons handle as blacksmiths use hammers. The sixth is the palpable darkness, about which it is said '...a land of misery and darkness, where the shadow of death, and no order, but everlasting horror dwelleth' (Job 10:22). The seventh torture is the shame evoked by the sins which are displayed before everyone and which cannot be concealed. The eighth is the terrifying view of demons and dragons sparkling in the fire, and the frightful howls of the victims and their executioners. Finally, there are the fiery fetters with which the sinners' limbs are bound.[18]

Such a concentrated characterization of hell's tortures is not met in previous theological literature. At most, Honorius could have borrowed various descriptions from Ambrose, Augustine, Gregory the Great, Bede, and other authors who worked in the genre of visions. However, he was the first to systematize them by uniting them into a complete picture of the Other World.[19] Comparing it with sketches of hell found in other-worldly narratives, we easily notice both similarity (the composition of tortures) and differences: the otherworldly visionaries focus on concrete, visual scenes, while in the *Elucidarium* there is a natural inclination to a more generalized discussion of the nature of the punishments awaiting sinners.

'Why do they undergo such sufferings?' asks the pupil. 'Sinners cast down into hell', answers the teacher, 'deserve these nine types of tortures because they scorned communion with the nine ranks of angels. Having wallowed in concupiscence while alive, they will burn in hellfire. Having grown numb on earth in the cold of evil, they will deservedly groan from the cold of the Other World. Because they were consumed by envy and hate, worms and snakes await them. The stink of luxury was sweet to them on earth, and so in hell they merit the torment of stench. They will be given over to ceaseless flagellation for having rejected the punishments they deserved in their earthly lives. On earth they liked the gloom of vice and disdained the light of Christ, and thus in hell they will be enveloped by a terrifying shade, for it is written, "...they shall never see the light" [Ps 48:20]. Because on earth they disregarded repentance of sins for which they felt no shame, in hell everything will be laid bare and revealed for eternal profanation. While alive they did not deign to listen and see good, and therefore after death they will contemplate only the terrifying and hear only the frightful. And just as on earth they dissipated themselves in the most varied vices, so also in hell fetters will bind their different limbs'.[20]

In hell sinners will be turned upside-down, back to back, and with the whole body stretched out. Lefèvre (1954: 170), unable to find in the works of theologians used by Honorius a similar posture of sinners in the Other World, suggests that this image was prompted by sculptures or paintings of the damned. Le Goff (1965: 602), sharing this idea, notes in particular the closeness of scenes depicted by Honorius to several motifs on the tympanum of the portal of the church in Vezelay.[21] One could also adduce several other parallels between the very visual and 'visible' descriptions of the Last Judgment in the *Elucidarium* and French cathedral sculptures of approximately the same time. The frightening pictures of sinners tortured and devoured by the devil on the portal of Autun, in Beaulieu, or in St Peter's at Chauvigny seem to be illustrations of Honorius' text.[22]

It is difficult to say to what extent one should seek the reflection of iconography in the figurative system of the *Elucidarium* or the influence of vulgar theology on medieval sculptors and artists, who drew ideas and notions about the Last Judgment from Revelation and visionary literature.[23] But it is worth emphasizing that the common character of the *Elucidarium* and the art-works of the eleventh and twelfth centuries was clearly due to the fact that both the 'Bible in stone' and the catechism were addressed to the same mass audience.

Painting the impressive picture of otherworldly punishments, Honorius does not confine himself to traditional teaching about the seven deadly sins but gives a more extensive list of transgressions. None of those condemned to infernal tortures will ever leave hell: the prideful, the envious, the cunning, the faithless, gluttons, drunkards, lovers of luxury, murderers, the cruel, thieves, robbers, brigands, the impure, the greedy, fornicators, lechers, liars, perjurers, blasphemers, scoundrels, the abusive, the quarrelsome.[24] This enumeration, as well as the picture of hell and the sinners' tortures, delivered in a priest's sermon must have terrified the parishioners and instilled in them a fear of the punishments awaiting all those who did not obey the church and did not keep the commandments. The very same emotions were supposed to be inspired by contemplating corresponding scenes on church and cathedral portals.

In describing hell and its tortures, Honorius does not forget to emphasize that the elect in paradise will observe these torments and sufferings: '…this is done so that they will rejoice all the more that they avoided the same'. And the damned at the Last Judgment will be given to see the blessed in glory, 'so that they will grieve more strongly for having scorned salvation'. After the divine judgment the 'optics' are altered, and the blessed will always see the tortures of the damned, but the latter are deprived of the possibility of seeing the elects' paradisal joys.[25] The pupil poses the natural question: 'Will not the virtuous be distressed at seeing the sinners in hell?' 'No', the teacher answers categorically: 'let even a father see his son or a son his father being tortured, or a mother her daughter or a daughter her mother, or a husband his wife or a wife her husband – not only will they not grieve, but this will be for them the kind of pleasant sight we get from seeing fish playing in a reservoir, for it is written, "The righteous shall rejoice when he seeth the vengeance"' (Ps 57:11). 'Will they not pray in their behalf?' the pupil inquires. The answer: 'To pray for the damned means to go against God, but the elect are one with the Lord, and they will approve of all his judgments'.[26]

The world of the *Elucidarium* is gloomy and joyless. Neither mercy nor love, but the justice of vengeance and man's unintelligible fate prevail there. Sympathy for the fallen and damned is not expected from the believer. The self-satisfied elect rejoice at seeing the tortures of the damned, even though their near relations are among them. In Honorius' dialogue God is not the personification of benevolence and forgiveness, but appears only as a merciless judge. Honorius' religion seems at times more Old- than New-Testamental, and the attributes of the stern God of the Bible are transferred to Christ himself. In creating a basis for the idea of a merciless, punishing God Honorius has recourse to casuistry. He says in the *Elucidarium* that Christ did not come into the world to save everybody. Although it is written that Christ 'died for the ungodly' (Rom 5:6) and tasted death 'for every man' (Heb 2:9), one should interpret this as meaning that the Son of God died for those elect alone who were still godless. 'For every man' means that he died for those chosen from among all peoples and tongues, not only of that time, but of all future times too. The Saviour said that he laid down his life for his sheep (John 10:15, 26); he did not say 'for every man'. Christ's mercy extends to the righteous, but the unrighteous are liable to his merciless judgments.[27]

Thus, 'none will be saved, except the elect', but no matter what they do they will not perish, 'because everything is turned towards a blessing for them, even their very sins'. But the pupil asks: 'If none but the predestined are saved, for what purpose were the rest created, and what is the fault for which they perish?' The teacher answers: 'The damned are made for the elect's sake, so that through them they will be perfected in their virtues and corrected from their vices, and so that they will appear more glorious in comparison with them, and so that by seeing their torments they will rejoice in their own salvation'.[28] If the Lord permits some children to die before baptism and thereby deprives them of the kingdom of heaven, then, says Honorius, a great secret is hidden here, but all the same one thing is clear: it is done as a blessing for the elect, who should all the more strongly rejoice in their own salvation, despite their transgressions, and realize that they are more pleasing to the Lord than those innocently condemned.[29]

Therefore, despite the fact that Honorius repeats the thesis of orthodox theologians about the predestination of the righteous and the 'self-condemnation' of the unrighteous, willingly wallowing in sin, the entire course of his argument depicts another picture: the world of people from the beginning is divided into good and evil, and the latter are irrevocably predestined by God to eternal perdition and his elect to eternal bliss. Moreover, according to Honorius' 'dialectics' the evil are created 'for the sake of the elect', and not for themselves.

This doctrine of predestination is developed within the limits of a narrative about the world's history – understood, however, not as a chain of events filling the lives of people and nations, but as a process of passing through the stages of creation, innocence, fall, abiding in sin, judgment, condemnation and redemption. In other words, history is considered from the point of view of the struggle between good and evil, a struggle whose outcome was determined in advance. Man is included in history. He does not actively participate in its pace and exerts no influence on its results – he is drawn by higher powers to an inevitable end. Free will (*liberum arbitrium*), to which Honorius had to refer, plays no essential role in this tractate, for the inclination of the individual to sin or his renunciation of it are seen to be predestined from eternity.[30] Nevertheless, the consciousness of the historicity of the world permeates the teacher's conversation with the pupil. Time moves from the act of creation, through the successive series of moments of sacred history to its fulfilment and return to eternity, just as the life of the individual unswervingly goes from birth to death.

Honorius invariably emphasizes the singularity and uniqueness of the events of sacred history, dwelling particularly on the question of their duration and temporal correlation. The pupil inquires: 'How long did the act of creation last? When were the angels created? How long did Satan dwell in heaven before being cast down? The teacher answers: 'Less than an hour'. 'How much time did Adam and Eve spend in paradise?' 'Seven hours'. 'Why not any longer?' 'Because hardly was woman created when she sinned. Man was created in the third hour and gave names to the animals. Women was created in the sixth hour and made man mortal immediately after she tasted the forbidden fruit. He ate the fruit out of love for her, and then in the ninth hour the Lord expelled them from paradise'. 'Why was Christ born at midnight, and why was he not born before the Flood or immediately after it? Why did he not appear during the period of the Law, or why did he not postpone his coming until the end of the world? How is one to understand the saying that he appeared at that moment "when the fullness of time had come"?'[31]

Having recourse to the numerical symbolism so popular in medieval exegesis, Honorius offers an interpretation of such questions as, for example, why Christ remained in the Virgin's womb for nine months, why he did not display signs of his holiness until he was thirty years old, how many hours he remained dead after his crucifixion, why he stayed in the grave for two nights and one day, at what time did he descend into hell, why he did not arise immediately after his death, etc.[32] All the temporal coordinates attracting Honorius' attention have a sacral meaning, into whose secrets the teacher initiates the inquisitive and reverential pupil.

The idea of man's dwelling in history, persistently presented in the *Elucidarium*, was essential for the work's influence on the consciousness of the masses. Its meaning is completely revealed if one recalls once again the features of the structure of medieval man's world-view in which Christian historicism was instilled. By the very order of conservative, primarily agrarian, life, and by all the ideological traditions going back to myth and ritual, this consciousness was orientated not towards development and change, but towards the reproduction of repetitious clichés and the experience of the world in categories of eternal return. The idea of the historicity and singularity of existence, to the extent which the people who read or heard Honorius' tractate were capable of perceiving it, suggested to them a new perspective, a principally new vision of life.

The form, however, in which the idea unfolded in the *Elucidarium* facilitated its assimilation by the people, in whose consciousness the archaic, pre-Christian picture of the world had not been definitively expunged. As already emphasized, in Honorius' view the history of humankind as a whole, and the life of the individual man in particular, are predetermined. Responding to the pupil's question about the omniscience of God, the teacher says that the whole of the past, present, and future lies before God's gaze, and that he foresaw everything before creating the world – the names of the angels and people, their morals, desires, words, actions, and thoughts. In God's predestination everything was contained, just as a house already exists in the mind of the builder before it is erected. Nothing takes place outside God's designs; there is no accident in the world of strict determination.[33] More subtle theological thought differentiated the concepts of *praescientia* and *praedestinatio*, but Honorius clearly confuses them.

It was easy to understand predestination as fate, and the category of fate had been close to the understanding of the common people since

barbarian times. Just as paganism believed that each man has his own
personified fate (in the form of some being or spirit, *fylgja, hamingja,*
accompanying him throughout his life and either dying with him or
passing on to his kinsmen), so also each Christian, as well as each people
and city, has his guardian angel guiding his thoughts and deeds.[34] But
at the same time demons beleaguer a man's soul, inclining it to different
sins and gladly reporting them to their prince. Each sin is represented
by its own particular demons, who in turn have under them countless
other demons. This entire hierarchically constructed hellish host impels
souls towards the path of sin. A ceaseless struggle goes on between the
guardian angels and the tempter demons. A man's body is like a church,
and this church is captured by either the Holy Spirit or the unclean
spirit.[35] The hierarchicized angelology and demonology of the *Elucidarium* also correspond to the social reality of the eleventh and twelfth
centuries and to the dogmatic scholasticism of the author, who syste-
matizes to the utmost the less regulated images which we met earlier in
visionary literature.

Man, the image and likeness of God, continues Honorius, is made
from spiritual and corporeal substances. In connection with this reasoning
he introduces the theme of the microcosm or the 'small world' ('micro-
cosmus, id est minor mundus'). The material substance of a man consists
of four elements. His flesh is made of earth, his blood of water, his
breath of air and his warmth of fire. A man's head is circular, similar to
the heavenly sphere, and his eyes correspond to the two heavenly lights,
while his head's seven orifices are like the seven heavenly harmonies. His
breast, rocked by breathing and coughing, is similar to the air shaken
by winds and thunder. The stomach receives all the liquids, as the sea
receives all currents. The legs support the body's weight, just as the earth
supports everything in it. A man's sight comes from the fire of heaven,
his hearing from the upper air, his smell from his lower parts, his taste
from water and his touch from earth. His bones have the hardness of
stones, his nails the strength of trees, his hair the beauty of grass, and
his feelings are like those of animals.[36] The concept of the 'microcosm'
in application to man and the structure of his body is not new and was
not Honorius' discovery. Without going back to the ancient East or the
Greek tradition, one need only refer to Isidore of Seville, through whom
this concept became accessible to medieval literature, beginning especially
in the twelfth century. But, as Lefèvre (1954: 115) observes, Honorius
displays a certain originality in demonstrating a minute and detailed
correspondence of the human body, its parts and feelings to the elements
of the world, the macrocosm. One can add to this that Honorius likens
the human body to the body of the church. In this way the pairs – the
physical world/the universe, the microcosm/man, and the sacred body/

the church – are apparently built on a general structure and consist of the same elements, visually demonstrating the unity of all God's creation. The scheme of Honorius possesses the clear merit of homogeneity and visibility. He develops the idea of the microcosm and macrocosm in the framework of the predestination of the created world to serve man and be subject to him.[37] The Lord made for man's sake not only the animals, foreseeing that after the Fall he would need them, but also flies and mosquitoes, so that they would cure him of pride with their bites, and ants and spiders, so that they might give an example of industriousness. The very name given to man is connected with the four sides of the world: the name Adam is composed of the first letters of their Greek designations (*anatole, disis, arctos, mesembria*).[38] Thereby it is considered demonstrated that man is inseparably linked with the universe and with all its elements and essences.

A comparison of the *Elucidarium* with the famous work of Honorius' teacher, Anselm of Canterbury, 'Why God became man' (*Cur Deus homo*) helps to clarify several of its characteristic features. Both are written as dialogues between a teacher and a pupil, but there is an essential difference. The pupil in Honorius' dialogue is not an interlocutor of the teacher; he is given a passive role. Only the teacher utters thoughts, and the pupil's questions are more markers for those things illuminated in the teacher's discourse or rejoinders in which he expresses delight at the teacher's judgments. In *Cur Deus homo* Anselm and Boso are, if not equals, at any rate both active interlocutors. Boso is not a fictitious bearer of rejoinders, but a real person, an educated monk, with his own thoughts and erudition.[39] Moreover, to Boso's lot fell the function of expressing the views and objections of the 'ungodly', so that Anselm might refute them. The active dialectical position of Anselm is in contrast to the monological position of Honorius, which excludes a comparison of different points of view. Correspondingly, Anselm's problem in the dialogue is convincing the pupil, but the teacher's task in the *Elucidarium* is merely lecturing. In the *Elucidarium* the pupil can only marvel at the truths revealed to him, while Boso expresses satisfaction at the persuasiveness of Anselm's logic.

Anselm's principle is found in the celebrated motto 'fides quaerens intelleçtum'. His goal is to transform faith into knowledge and to bring them into accord. Anselm pursues the problem of 'believing in order to understand' ('neque enim quaere intelligere ut credam, sed credo ut intelligam'). This principle, which he developed in his *Prosologion*, is successively brought forth in *Cur Deus homo* in an attempt to interpret rationally the myth about Christ and to provide a logical basis for God's Incarnation and redemptive sacrifice. Unwinding a chain of syllogisms with the goal of demonstrating the 'veritatis soliditas rationabilis', Anselm poses intellectual experiments, proposing a series of arguments proceeding from the premise that the Incarnation did not take place, or asking Boso whether he could kill Christ for humankind's salvation.[40]

Such questions and risky propositions are alien to Honorius. He aims at the truths of Christian belief without being over-concerned about the logic and demonstrations of his convictions. Instead of Anselm's pair of key concepts – *fides* and *intellectus* – we meet only in Honorius *fides*: a full faith, neither reasoning nor requiring understanding or an intellectual foundation. Honorius is dogmatic in the extreme. Intellectual material is given in the *Elucidarium* and in *Cur Deus homo* on completely unequal levels. The two tractates embody different styles of thinking.[41]

If in Honorius' depiction God is the stern judge, the merciless avenger, who has predestined to eternal perdition the greater part of humankind for reasons inaccessible to human understanding, then Anselm's God is the embodiment of wisdom, righteousness and compassion. He grants salvation to countless people, exceeding the number of fallen angels, and even to many of those guilty of Christ's death.[42] The idea of *Cur Deus homo*, that Christ's voluntary sacrifice possesses greater meaning than humankind's guilt before God, and thereby redeems and destroys its sins, was contrasted by Anselm to the interpretation of this sacrifice as the liberation of fallen man from the devil's power. Anselm's ideas were at the time accessible only to a few people trained in theology. In the scheme of his arguments the devil is seemingly pushed into the background. However, Honorius' picture of the world is deeply dualistic: paradise *vs* hell, God *vs* the devil, the elect *vs* the damned. Attention is not fixed on the harmony of the world, as in Anselm, but on the antagonism of two warring camps.

It seems to me that even a cursory comparison of the works of Honorius and Anselm permits one to evaluate somewhat better the *Elucidarium's* intellectual potential. It is not, comparatively, high, lacking that cultural reflection which distinguishes Anselm's works. At the same time it is extremely clear, easily and vividly written, abounding with intelligible and lively phrases and comparisons. *Cur Deus homo* and the *Elucidarium* were intended for different audiences. The former aimed at a learned audience, made up of educated and reflective people who were skilled in dialectics and were not satisfied with faith alone, but were interested in the discovery of rational foundations of truth. The latter work was directed at readers or listeners less needful of analysis and untrained in independent argument, being satisfied with simple and unambiguous dogmas and precepts.

Much of the intelligibility of the *Elucidarium's* content is undoubtedly explained by its form, linguistic structure and relative simplicity, and partly by the simplification of its account and its inclination to interpret speculative concepts by translating them into a system of visual representations. Quite often Honorius appeals to the emotions of his readers or listeners. In his depiction of paradise he mobilizes the brightest colours and most harmonious sounds. The bodies of the elect are transparent, like gleaming glass, and their nakedness is hidden by colours surpassing the flowers in freshness.[43] The opposition between the elect and the sinners is likened to a pictorial contrast: the artist applies black colours in order to distinguish more vividly scarlet and white. The painter uses all colours, but does not mix them into one; so too God loves each of his creations, but he allots to different creatures their proper places – to some the palace of heaven, to others the prison of hell.[44]

We have seen that Honorius uses many visual comparisons, which help in making theological questions accessible to the understanding of ignorant Christians. For example, the question of the insubstantiality of evil is explained with the aid of a comparison: blindness is the absence of vision and darkness is the absence of light, but neither blindness nor darkness is a substance. In the same way, evil is nothing other than the lack of good. Bread baked from poisoned flour is fatal, just as all of Adam's posterity is mortal on account of his transgression. The relationship of God the Father and God the Son can be understood by comparing it with the relationship of light to the sun. 'Why is God unable to leave sin unpunished?' asks the pupil. The teacher answers with a parable. When a slave fled from a lord he had robbed to a cruel tyrant, the emperor's son was sent from the palace into prison in pursuit of the fugitive, smashing the tyrant and returning the slave together with the plunder to the emperor's mercy. If a servant given an errand by his lord falls into a pit in spite of advice he has received, he is guilty, for he did not obey his lord and did not carry out his task – in exactly the same way the sinner seduced by an evil spirit is guilty. An unrenounced sin is like a wound from which the weapon that caused it has not been withdrawn. The Lord, like a mighty king, created a beautiful palace – the kingdom of heaven – and at the same time also a prison – the world – in which he fashioned a fatal abyss – hell. As a seal leaves its impression in wax, so also the image of God is imprinted on the angels. As if someone appeared in a window and immediately withdrew, so also a man is born and soon after his appearance in the world he dies. Pastors who follow an unrighteous way of life, even though they also teach the faithful, are like burning candles – they shine, but are consumed in doing so. But those priests who are righteous and do not preach are like smoke stifling a fire and eating away at the eyes.[45] And so on, endlessly.

The section devoted to the impending end of the world is especially abundant in comparisons. The meeting of the guardian angel with the elect's soul is likened to the meeting of the bridegroom with his bride, and the elect's body is likened to a prison in which the soul languished. At the resurrection of the dead at the Last Judgment the bodies are not obliged to take on their former aspect: just as a potter, having broken up a vessel and prepared from the same clay a new one, can change the handle or bottom, so also from the previous matter God can form another body, deprived of its former deficiencies. The Lord will come to the Last Judgment like an emperor entering a city. At the Judgment the impious will be dragged down by their sins, just as lead is drawn to the earth, and the righteous will be separated from the sinners, like wheat from chaff. As friends rejoice at those who are saved from shipwreck or a physician rejoices at healing a patient beyond hope, so also the angels and saints rejoice at seeing those who are justified at the Last Judgment. Just as an emperor, seeing on the road an ill man sitting on a garbage heap, has him raised up, washed and dressed, and gives him his name, adopts him and makes him his heir, so too the Lord draws us out of the filth of sin, raises us with faith, washes us through baptism, gives us his name and makes us his heirs. Christ is the sun of righteousness, and the church is the moon. The Lord's chariot is the four Gospels, and the horses harnessed to it are the Apostles, carrying Christ throughout the world by their preaching. From this vehicle heretics and schismatics have fallen out.[46]

It is not hard to see that there is little that is original in the greater part of these comparisons, as in almost all the contents of the *Elucidarium*. But let me emphasize once again that originality in general cannot serve as a principal criterion of the quality of a work of medieval literature, especially of theological literature, connected as it was with tradition and the authority of Scripture. To achieve the goals pursued by the preacher the use of habitual phrases and comparisons was preferable.

Along with the comparisons borrowed from different spheres of a man's life, which made the exposition of theological concepts more accessible to monks and priests untrained in theology (and through them to the faithful), one should also note the continued 'play' on words in contrasting a pair of concepts. The customary division of the world into poles, inherent in the Christian world-view – heaven and earth, paradise and hell, God and the devil, good and evil, the righteous and sinners – is successively carried out throughout the whole dialogue and was doubtless highly conducive to helping Honorius' audience understand and assimilate the truths he presented. In places Honorius coins literary formulas, formulas built on a rhythmical comparison of categories with contrasting meanings; such formulas, although serving to embellish the text, also possess a mnemotechnic function.[47]

It is difficult to speak about the ideological contents of a common theological manual, which by necessity embraced a wide range of questions and pretended moreover to embrace the entire Christian world-view. It is even more difficult to distinguish some specific features in it. Its facelessness was supposed to be perceived as a virtue: catechisms were written for stating church dogma and not some individual point of view. At most one can observe the tonalities and themes that received particular development in the *Elucidarium*.

What are these themes? First of all, the notion about the inevitable recompense for sins and merits. By exploiting the feeling of fear, easily aroused in medieval man, the church could very successfully instil in the faithful an idea of the necessity of a righteous way of thinking and a corresponding behaviour. The not inconsiderable efforts of the preacher were directed toward terrorizing readers with pictures of the cruel punishments and torments awaiting unrepentant sinners.[48] Mercy and forgiveness are not characteristic of the *Elucidarium's* Christ – this side of Christian doctrine, so important among the mystics and in the propaganda about evangelical poverty, is overshadowed by the idea of a stern and merciless judgment. At the Last Judgment the Lord will play the role of the judge, the devil will function as the prosecutor and man as the accused. But so that he be not condemned the priest, 'the vicar of the Lord', during confession on earth should play the role of judge, and the one confessing should be both prosecutor and accused. Penance is the sentence.[49] It was, as Nikolaj Berdjaev put it, truly a 'judicial religion'.

The interpretation of the liturgy in terms of war was highly significant for the popular consciousness in the time of the Crusades. In the eyes of Honorius and his contemporaries the mass they read was a fierce battle against the age-old perfidious enemy, the devil; and the priests celebrating it, whose vestments were but sacred armour, led the people to the 'eternal homeland'. Is this not the origin of the common symbolic syntax, the figurative construction and fantastic interweaving of feelings of helplessness and expectation of deliverance, all equally present in the era's art and theology? The end of the world, about which Honorius is so eloquent, seemed to his contemporaries not only inevitable, but close. That is why the thought about punishment at the Last Judgment so persistently haunted them and why they were troubled by concern as to whether they would be delivered from it. The parallels between the *Elucidarium's* pictures of the end of the world and the iconography of the Last Judgment are symptoms of an eschatological frame of mind that was widespread from the late eleventh through the twelfth century. The gloom of the apocalyptic visions of Romanesque sculptors, as well as of Honorius, attests that hopes for mercy and forgiveness were not great, because judgment had already taken place, properly speaking, before the beginning of time and will be carried out only at the end of the world. Souls were predestined from the beginning. Here is yet another twist of the theme of judgment in medieval thought! The Gospels and Revelation foretold retribution 'at the end of time'; in otherworldly visions the judgment was proposed immediately after the individual's death; but in the doctrine of predestination preached by Honorius a verdict was already prepared from the beginning.

Augustine's idea of predestination, proceeding from the experience of the individual's intimate relationship with God, accentuated the necessity of receiving from on high a grace unmotivated by a man's moral efforts (*gratia gratis data*), which on their own were completely insufficient for achieving salvation. In the Middle Ages this doctrine, despite Augustine's enormous authority, was not recognized by the church, though without an explicit break with Augustinism. The soul's predestination could in principle bring doubt upon the existence of the church as an institution bestowing through the sacraments salvation and recompense for the believer's merits and behaviour.

Augustine had not drawn such a conclusion. On the contrary, his interpretation of the church as the *numerus electorum, corpus Christi*, underscored the significance of the church as the *civitas Dei*. In addition, *gratia* acts, according to Augustine, not only as *praeveniens* (God's pre-election of a man for salvation), but also as *cooperans*, suggesting an interaction of the Lord's grace with the intense effort of the believer's spiritual powers to realize his goal. Honorius coarsens and simplifies Augustine's interpretation, and thus the general correspondence between his and Augustine's ideas did not appear completely orthodox from the church's point of view. Scholasticism of a later time also did not share these views of Augustine. The idea of predestination was revived only during the Reformation, in the doctrines of Luther and especially of Calvin.

In the *Elucidarium*, however, the doctrine of predestination lacks any anti-ecclesiastical direction. Honorius develops the thesis of the church as the mystical body of Christ, whose members are all the categories and ranks of people. He emphasizes the necessity of the believer's obedience and submission to the clergy and the importance of ecclesiastical rites. Having learned about the omniscience of the elect, to whose gaze is revealed all past, present and future, and all good and bad deeds, the pupil asks: 'Do the saints really know everything that I have done?'

The teacher answers affirmatively. 'But what is the purpose of confession and penance, if everything is known without them?' The teacher consoles the troubled pupil: 'What do you fear, what are you frightened of? Confession and repentance wash away sin, so that one needs grieve about it no more than about that committed in the cradle or about healed wounds. David, Mary Magdalene, Peter and Paul all sinned before the Lord, and yet they are all in heaven, and the angels rejoice at their salvation.[50] Thus, confession opens the door to the kingdom of heaven.[51]

Honorius is evidently not inclined to focus attention on the fact that between the ideas of predestination and of the omnipotence of the church there exists an imposing contradiction, revealed already in the ninth century in the controversies provoked by Gottschalk, about a 'twofold predestination'.[52] In any case, it is clear that this side of the question was not accessible to the understanding of the ordinary priest and even less to the layman into whose hands his catechism could fall. But such an essential moment could hardly have escaped the attention of the schoolmen of the twelfth and following centuries, who were more thoughtful and vigilant about the smallest nuances of theological thought. Their conspicuous silence (see above, ch. 1) about the *Elucidarium* may very well have been due to this circumstance.

The doctrine of free will and of internal perfection was less able to address the consciousness of the common believer of medieval society than the idea of a world determined from the beginning, a world in which good and bad men are distinctly delineated from each other and holiness or damnation are from time immemorial predetermined, where the circle of each man's obligations is distinctively outlined, each man carrying them out not as an independent individual, but as a member of a collective, an estate, a social category. Not ethical or spiritualistic problems, but adherence to external forms and an inclination to apprehend abstractions in a sensual image and to interpret a symbol literally: these are the features of ordinary religiosity fully present in Honorius' *summa*.

The *Elucidarium* may seem to put before the believer a somewhat different interpretation of the possibility of salvation from that which was revealed in other genres of medieval literature. There salvation was achievable through a righteous life and an opportune repentance, and pictures of hell's tortures were supposed to turn the faithful from sin. But Honorius stresses the predestination of some people and 'estates' to eternal perdition and of others to salvation, thereby seemingly lowering the significance of the Last Judgment. But one can overemphasize the contrast between the *Elucidarium* and other works; for Honorius is concerned with the necessity of repentance and submission to the church, and in stories about visions or in exempla the motif of the perdition of the majority of people is also clearly seen. One can instead speak about different emphases made in different genres. The *Elucidarium* is significant in the respect that in it a gloomy eschatology is intensified to the utmost.

Honorius gives the doctrine of predestination his own individual twist – the social hierarchy is inverted: first and foremost the common folk will be saved, those who are submissive to God and guileless and who live by the labour of their own hands and feed the church. One may say that Honorius transfers the problem of salvation from a spiritual plane to a social one, but one can very well formulate this the other way around: he expresses social estimation of the peasantry in theological terms, sublimating earthly categories and connecting them with the higher values of Christianity – election by God and the soul's salvation. As far as I know, such an appraisal of the place of the common people in the general scheme of the universe is unique in contemporary literature. Even Honorius abandoned this point of view in his later works.[53]

How is one to explain this praise of the common folk in the *Elucidarium*? Nothing is known for certain about the environment in which Honorius lived and wrote, or about his social origins. If, as a number of scholars suggest, he actually received his upbringing in Germany, then his thoughts about the place and meaning of peasants in the system of the socio-religious universe can be compared with the idealization of the rural population in German literature of the same time. Such works as *Unibos, Ruodlieb* and *Von Rechte* reflect the high self-consciousness of the peasantry, in contrast to French writings of the period, which slight the peasants in a haughty manner and with great disdain.

Medieval consciousness presents a world divided between two poles. The elect are juxtaposed to the rejected and damned as their essential antithesis. The bad exist 'for the sake of the good'; holiness is impossible and unintelligible without sin. Deepest despair is contrasted to brightest hope: pictures of the tortures prepared for the majority of humankind are counterbalanced by the promise of forgiveness to the humble. All medieval thought moves within the framework limits of this opposition, but the *Elucidarium* in particular is defined by it. The fear of damnation in opposition to the hope of paradisal felicity is depicted by Honorius with his customary visual concreteness and figurativeness. Along with the future resurrection of souls, particular attention is devoted to the resurrection of the body. All the resurrected, no matter their age when they died, will be raised as thirty-year-olds; their external appearance will be changed, and their previous physical flaws or deformities will disappear.[54] The whole world will be renewed: the previous one will disappear, but in its place a world without adversities and natural calamities will appear. The earth will eternally bear fruit and be fragrant with flowers; the sun will shine over it with unprecedented power. People will be as beautiful as Absalom, stronger than Samson and healthier than Moses.[55] Such a modelling of the approaching Earthly paradise must have found a ready response among the *Elucidarium's* readers, who were unable not to clothe their expectations of a better life in eschatological forms (Bicilli 1919: 110).

The study of the *Elucidarium* partly sheds light on the condition of the religious education of people in the Middle Ages. The development of theological thought in the twelfth to the fourteenth century obviously did not influence that education in any noticeable way. The complex of those notions that came together at the end of the eleventh century and at the beginning of the twelfth, and were in addition simplified and dogmatized, finding a reflection in Honorius' dialogue, was sufficient for the education of laymen throughout the following three centuries. According to Y. Lefèvre (1954: 336), this is explained not by the simple lag of the forms of mass consciousness behind scholastic speculation, but by its seeming 'immobility' (cf. Delaruelle 1975). In any case, there was a not inconsiderable gap between the two levels of medieval religiosity. The 'bread of theologians' was qualitatively distinct from the crumbs of 'folk Christianity'.

In an article on the *Vision of Tnugdal*, C. Carozzi (1981) makes several observations concerning the interpretation of the soul in Honorius' works. In his view, Honorius believes in the incorporeality of the soul and, accordingly, in the spiritual nature of the tortures it undergoes in the fire of expiation. There are indeed such statements in Honorius' works, possibly gleaned from a reading of John the Scot. However, in the *Elucidarium* – as Carozzi recognizes – it is plainly said that the souls of sinners are tortured *in forma corporum* (*E* III 9, (p. 446)). Carozzi wants to see in these contradictions a quarrel between the direction of scholastic thought represented by Hugh of St Victor and the one to which Honorius belonged. He thinks that this controversy has no relation to popular beliefs but represents a 'conflict of clerics over fundamental theological concepts'.

J. Le Goff (1981: 184–8) is not fully in agreement with Carozzi's position and thinks that the latter has exaggerated the importance of the fight between the 'materialists' and 'non-materialists' of the twelfth century. As Le Goff stresses, Honorius' point of view did not exert influence on the elaboration of the concept of purgatory by the schoolmen and did not block the introduction of that concept into scholastic thought. But Le Goff also finds the position of Honorius himself contradictory, since the *Elucidarium*, as just now mentioned, recognizes corporeal tortures of the souls being cleansed by, alternately, fire and unbearable cold. Le Goff calls this position 'paradoxical'. If I understand his thinking correctly, this paradox is generated by the clash of the metaphorical understanding of the Other World by Augustine and his followers with the stories of visionaries who visited the Other World and witnessed the torments experienced there by the souls of the dead. It is worthwhile to add to this that the paradox mentioned by Le Goff is of the same nature as the paradox of two Last Judgments – the collective one 'at the end of time' and the individual one immediately after death. Such paradoxes are an integral feature of medieval consciousness, and in both instances there is a clash between a theological conception and a notion rooted in popular culture and religiosity. The mutual influence of these two traditions evidently also generated this fundamental paradoxicality of medieval mentality.

One should also remember here that later, among the thinkers of the first half of the thirteenth century, one meets once again a distinctive contradictory combination of the idea of purgatory as a material place with the idea of purgatory in a metaphorical sense. Le Goff (1981: 329–30) rejects the interpretation of this contradiction in the works of William of Auvergne, who was simultaneously a theologian and bishop of Paris and who was concerned with admonishing his flock, as a sort of 'theory of two levels': for intellectuals and himself William admitted the existence only of a pseudo-fire, but for the mass of believers he developed a doctrine of the material reality of the cleansing fire. But this calls to mind situations in which one and the same author gives different interpretations of the same fact in works addressed to different audiences: for example, Gregory of Tours' story about the theological dispute between Catholics and Arians in the *History of the Franks* and his story about a comparison of the power of Catholic and Arian teaching by means of a trial by boiling water in the *Book of Miracles* (see above ch. 1). In such instances one must speak not about a conscious deception of the faithful and not about the 'two-facedness' of church authors, but about an understanding that the 'bread of theologians' was not to the liking of common believers, and about the extraordinary 'plasticity' of the doctrine of church teachers which proceeded from that understanding.

6

'HIGH' AND 'LOW': THE MEDIEVAL GROTESQUE

In the preceding chapters I have tried to show that medieval Latin literature reveals many rather unexpected aspects of that epoch's world-view – unexpected if compared to the traditional image drawn by historians of the 'Age of Faith'. These less-known sides of medieval culture are exceptional and unusual, and not easy to understand. The exceptional character of this culture lies in the strange combination of opposite poles: heaven and earth, spirit and body, gloom and humour, life and death. Holiness can be seen as a fusion of lofty piety and primitive magic, of extreme self-denial and a pride in being the elect, of worldly detachment and greed, of mercy and cruelty. Theologians affirm the hierarchy established by God only to condemn its highest earthly representatives and to exalt its lowest members. Learning is glorified and ignoramuses are treated with scorn, and at the same time foolishness, poverty of spirit, even madness, are reckoned the surest way to salvation. Life and death, extreme opposites in any world-view, are reversible, and the border between them is penetrable: the dead return to the living, and people temporarily dead may visit the Other World for a while. Judgment over the deceased, taught as taking place at the 'end of time', nevertheless is passed on each soul at the moment of death. As a result, collective consciousness, although inimical to individuality, created a basis for a kind of 'personalism': a man's biography is fulfilled at the moment of death and is not suspended, as in official eschatology, until the Last Judgment. In the Other World, where eternity reigns, earthly time flows.

These and other strange paradoxes in medieval Latin works are not marginal features but belong to the foundation of the culture that generated them. I have collected this material to demonstrate that paradoxicality, strangeness and contradiction were integral organic features of the medieval mind. The paradoxicality is intensified by the fact that we are not dealing with the ethnography of an exotic, 'primitive' culture. Medieval culture does not seem so foreign to us; we are bound to it by many threads. What we need is an intelligible apparatus for detecting and explaining the paradoxes. By explaining I mean a conceptual framework that will unite the contradictions discovered in the material without smoothing them over and cutting them off.

In the search for such a framework it is logical to turn to Mikhail

Bakhtin, whose name is connected with a turning-point in the study of medieval popular culture. His study of the carnivalesque and of popular laughter pointed to a layer of medieval culture that had been neglected. For even those who, before Bakhtin, studied carnival, farce, popular mystery plays and comedies, parody, and other manifestations of the medieval culture of laughter, did not grasp their meaning or their signal importance within the world-view. Such an underestimation, according to Bakhtin, was due to the fact that scholars unconsciously transferred to the past notions of their own time. In particular, the nature of laughter and the grotesque has changed so fundamentally over the centuries that now it is very difficult to perceive properly forms of laughter that have long since vanished and to understand their place in the consciousness of an age so distant from us.

Access to the peculiar essence of medieval culture is often precluded by the traditional tendency of scholars towards discovering in it some sublime principle. Historians take the Middle Ages at face value as believing that the body deserved only to be scorned and overcome and that man's true homeland was not on earth, but in heaven. Basing a 'philosophy of the body' ('the bodily lower stratum') on Renaissance material (the work of Rabelais), Bakhtin opened a new perspective in the study of culture. He applied his theory to medieval culture as well.

Bakhtin succeeded in deciphering 'a half-forgotten and already obscure language', the language of medieval forms of carnival and laughter. He demonstrated both their universality and the ambivalence inherent in them that at once affirms and denies. According to Bakhtin, the culture of carnival and laughter expressed a particular attitude towards life, 'laughter's aspect on the world', which was just as integral and essential to the medieval world-view as its serious, 'official' view. Bakhtin studied a particular type of laughter imagery, an aesthetic conception of reality: a 'grotesque realism' with its accompanying conception of 'the unready', 'the incomplete', 'the unexclusive', 'the open to the world', fruit-bearing, dying and reborn body – a conception fundamentally different from the culture of classical Antiquity or of modernity. 'Grotesque realism' expresses an ancient type of imagery that was present in ancient mythology and art and can be traced for many centuries. Although in the classical era it was driven down into the lower levels of society, into the non-canonical regions of art, it still continued to exist. In the medieval popular culture of laughter 'grotesque realism' blossomed again and broke through into the high spheres of art during the Renaissance, but then declined during the age of classicism (Bakhtin 1965).

Bakhtin's insights made earlier views on medieval culture at once outmoded. However, they raise crucial questions about medieval popular culture rather than answer them. For the place of popular culture in the general context of medieval culture remains unclear, as does its influence on official culture and vice versa. Although Bakhtin himself certainly did not equate 'popular culture of laughter' and 'popular culture' he did not explain their relationship or what composed medieval popular culture besides its carnivalesque aspect. Whether Bakhtin intended it or not, the impression remains that laughter was the leitmotiv of medieval popular culture. Hence, it has to be asked whether Bakhtin's interpretation of the grotesque is at all applicable to the material we have surveyed so far, since its connection with laughter and carnival is far from obvious.

Another problem stems from the fact that Bakhtin's observations rest upon sources from the end of the Middle Ages, the time of the rise of cities as the centres of an emerging new world-view. The carnival element he describes is entirely urban, and its centre is the town square. It is doubtful whether his theses can be extended to the peasantry and the villages of the earlier Middle Ages.

Bakhtin emphasized that he was not studying medieval culture as a whole, but only popular culture, and he speaks of a 'sharp break' between carnivalesque and official culture. He writes (1963: 173):

> One can say (with certain reservations, of course) that medieval man lived as it were two lives: one – official, monolithically serious and gloomy, subordinated to a strict hierarchical order, full of fear, dogmatism, veneration and piety, and another – carnival – vulgar, free, full of ambivalent laughter, blasphemies, profanations of everything sacred, lowerings and obscenities, familiar contact with everybody and everything. And both these lives were legitimized, but divided by strict temporal borders. Without taking into account the interchange and mutual influence of these two systems of life and thought (official and carnival), it is impossible to understand correctly the peculiarities of medieval man's cultural consciousness ...[1]

Bakhtin's understanding of medieval official culture is extremely one-sided: 'monolithically serious', 'gloomy', 'full of fear', dogmatized, filled with piety and veneration. When he underscores the 'frozen, petrified seriousness' of clerical culture, he is not dealing with the Middle Ages proper. Rather, he focusses on the transition between the Middle Ages and modernity, that is, the Renaissance, for which his source, Rabelais's novel, is indeed the best informant.

To be sure, high and low culture in Bakhtin's understanding are dialectically linked, for carnival, by inverting 'serious' values through laughter, thereby recognized them. By 'playing' with them, consciousness included them in its universe. Accordingly, the two cultures are internally linked. Popular culture was for Bakhtin fearlessly merry, inverting all stable attitudes and notions through laughter, and denying the idea of death and the end of a man's life in this world by resting upon the idea of the eternal renewal and recreation of existence. Official church culture and ideology, in Bakhtin's eyes, considered the world completed and entirely formed, perceiving it without laughter in a 'frightened and frightening' consciousness endlessly distant from play and laughter. The irrepressible, agitating element of the popular culture of laughter stood in absolute contrast to the static, solemn, heaven-orientated religious culture. The opposition of the two cultures appeared to Bakhtin as the opposition of motion and immobility, of life and mortification.

Having sketched a bright picture of the medieval popular culture of laughter, Bakhtin did not attempt to characterize its antithesis. Of course, that was not his aim, but he seems to have considered official culture sufficiently well known and unproblematic. But if we include official culture and investigate both popular culture and church culture within the framework of a single system, we are compelled to re-examine Bakhtin's contrast of the two cultures. In fact, which of them is distinguished by dynamism: carnival–popular or serious–ecclesiastical? Bakhtin traces the carnivalesque back to the distant past and reconstructs medieval popular culture from the image Rabelais had of it. But was this element not really some sort of extra historical constant that existed in its main features unchanged until the Renaissance? That 'serious' culture changed, despite the prevalence of dogma, is well-known, and one can correctly speak of a history of medieval philosophy, literature, art and science, as well as of a development of the church and its dogmas. Medieval culture was more complicated than it appears from Bakhtin's work.

The main problem in analysing Bakhtin's conception is this: if indeed medieval man lived in two such different, even contradictory, cultures, how were they combined in his consciousness? Bakhtin gave unequal weight to the two sides of medieval culture, and this can cause a misunderstanding of their relation to each other. The opposition of popular to ecclesiastical culture should not be understood simplistically, because it was not just an opposition. Bakhtin, of course, knew full well that carnival and laughter were closely connected to clerical culture, the carnivalesque being to a great extent the inversion of the official culture. The drunken whore playing the role of the Virgin, the fool in place of the bishop, the criminal on the throne, the ass in the church, the drunken liturgy – all these inversions of 'serious' religion and its rituals by no means ignored or denied the dominant religious culture; they rather proceeded from it and ultimately affirmed it. Carnival is a distinctive correlate of the serious culture present in it: it penetrates its substance and 'lowers it' for a short while, but not essentially. This 'lowering' assumes neither denial nor disregard, but a temporary overcoming of it through an inclusive inversion. The semantics of carnival are not external and extraneous with respect to official culture; rather, to a great degree they draw their elements from it.

Bakhtin describes the mutual influence – the confrontation – of official and unofficial culture as an ambivalence, a duality, in which the oppositions are dialectically connected, mutually changing places and retaining their polarity. In Bakhtin's conception, if I am not mistaken, ambivalence is somewhat akin to another of his key concepts: dialogue. The dialogue of two principles of medieval culture can be understood only if we do not consider them divorced and antithetical. It should be conceived of not as a debate between two metaphysically opposed entities, not as a 'dialogue of the deaf', but as the presence of one culture in the thought and world of the other, and vice versa. Carnival negates the culture of the official hierarchy by including it in itself, just as the 'serious' culture, in turn, includes the principle of laughter within it.

There are no explicit indications of carnival in the sources I have been studying. Rather, one can speak of 'carnival before carnival', about the presence of some semantic elements out of which the system of carnival later developed, such as dances, games, costumes, all sorts of inversions.[2] In the early and central Middle Ages carnival had not yet crystallized in time and space; its elements were diffused everywhere, and hence there was no carnival as such. However, the concepts of ambivalence and immanent dialogue are absolutely essential for understanding the whole of medieval culture, and the concept of the grotesque is no less important. Nevertheless, I should like to emphasize that, if medieval culture creates an importunate impression of strangeness and grotesqueness, this strangeness and grotesqueness are not at all equivalent to the comic and humorous, and are not reduced to them. Bakhtin opened up our view on medieval grotesque, but he erred, it seems to me, in interpreting it solely as comic grotesque.

The problem arising from the preceding analysis, and in a certain sense summing it up, is the ambivalence of the educated and popular principles in medieval culture, as they appear in works of Latin edifying literature.

I concentrated in earlier chapters on a single genre, moving from hagiography to penitentials, then to otherworldly visions, and finally to the *Elucidarium*. My further analysis will be based on the instructive *exempla* used in sermons. However, the problem of ambivalence or, if one prefers, of medieval grotesque will lead us beyond the limits of a particular type of writing. The summarizing nature of this part of my study requires drawing upon a wider body of material and returning to genres already discussed. The *exempla* will serve as a point of departure.

The synthesis of extreme seriousness and tragedy, on the one hand, and of the tendency to maximum lowering, on the other, was in essence part of Christian dogma, in which the concept of the Incarnation united the divine and the human in their extreme manifestation. Christ's humble birth, cruel passion, and humiliating death; his crucified, broken body as a symbol of the highest beauty; the cult of spiritual humility, asceticism, and poverty; the affirmation of spiritual power in physical powerlessness – these elements of ennobling 'disparagement' are combined in Christianity with a no less striking paradox, the incompatibility of faith and reason. 'The Son of God was crucified; I am not ashamed of it. And the Son of God died; it is by all means to be believed, because it is absurd. And he was buried, and rose again; the fact is certain, because it is impossible' (Tertullian *De carne Christi* 5).

The confrontation of body and soul and of earth and heaven was central to medieval aesthetics and was expressed especially in the grotesque, in both art and literature. The acquisition and perception of the grotesque were facilitated by the fact that the peoples of Europe had already possessed rather similar formal tendencies before Christianity: for example, in the 'savage style' of Germanic art, characterized by conscious violation of real proportions, an exaggeration of the dreadful and the deformed and an interest in the monstrous. The twisted and intertwined bodies of monsters in combat or the frightening animal figures of the pagan period compare easily with the gargoyles, demons and terrifying scenes of the Last Judgment in Romanesque and Gothic art.[3] Thus, we are not looking at marginal or strange rarities, but at a fundamental feature of medieval art and an integral part of medieval man's perception of reality.[4] The principle of laughter must be seen within the general context of the grotesque polarity.

E. R. Curtius notes the blending of the serious and the humorous and the fluidity of the borders between them as characteristic features of both late Antique and medieval literature. Humorous elements are found, sometimes rather unexpectedly, even in the grave scenes of hagiography. Evidently, the medieval public expected authors to introduce comic moments into these narratives.[5] Curtius (1963: 417–35) quotes several convincing examples of the device *ridendo dicere verum* in medieval literature and points to the need for further study on this problem. He merely states the occurrence of the blending (*ioca seriis miscere*), not analysing it in any depth. He apparently accepts that such a stylistic norm is sufficiently explained by the development of the Hellenistic and late Roman tradition, which contradicted the canons of classical aesthetics on the strict differentiation of high and low styles.

By contrast to Curtius, Bakhtin speaks not of a blending of high and low, but of a fundamental breach of all borders and oppositions, between the individual body and the world, the negative and the positive, the serious and the comic. The extreme proximity of 'high' and 'low', their inversion and mutual interchange, and the lively hyperbolization of reality lie at the base of the image of the 'grotesque body'. Bakhtin mentions the folkloric sources of medieval grotesque, finding them in different forms of medieval culture. 'Medieval and Renaissance grotesque, filled with the spirit of carnival, frees the world from all that is frightful and terrifying and makes it completely unfrightening and therefore completely merry and light' (Bakhtin 1965: 55). L. E. Pinskij (1961: 120) notes another aspect of medieval grotesque: 'Bringing the distant close, combining the mutually-exclusive, violating customary notions, the grotesque in art is kindred to the paradox in logic.'

Bakhtin localizes these fundamental features of laughter primarily in popular culture, sharply contrasting it with an official, clerical culture supposedly completely devoid of merriment. There seems to be some foundation for this – as, for example, when John Chrysostom states that 'Christ never laughed'. The Apostles and church Fathers condemned frivolous chatter and buffoonery, and the medieval church maintained this position and insisted on seemly conduct.[6]

Yet, already the ninth-century poet Notker the Stammerer defined man, following Aristole and Boethius, by his three characteristics: reason, mortality, humour ('homo est animal rationale, mortale, risus capax'). Notker considered man not only as capable of laughter, but as provoking it: 'Quid est homo? Risibile. Quid est risibile? Homo' (quoted Adolph 1947: 251). In the twelfth century John of Salisbury permitted moderate gaiety (Curtius 1963: 421), and from that time on parody and satire spread in medieval Latin literature. One should not forget, however the often considerable gap between general principles, enunciated by ecclesiastical authors, and actual practice.[7]

Notker's 'Aristotelian' list including the ability to laugh deserves attention. Laughter seems to appear here as the natural consequence of combining such contradictory attributes as reason and mortality, for only laughter can reconcile them. Laughter in the face of the unknown and terrifying, as a reaction to fear, is not that far from the concrete situations in which laughter appears in medieval Latin literature – as the manifestation of a particular psychological mechanism which enables man to face death and the forces of evil. Without destroying or conquering fear and without providing deliverance from it, laughter still relieved the unbearable tension caused by the awareness of death and posthumous retribution.

But the problem is not at all confined to the comic lowering of the exalted or the carnival inversion and blending of the serious with the humorous. Nor do the complementary characters of the sacred and the profane, which O. M. Frejdenberg (1936; 1973) demonstrated to have been since time immemorial merely the two sides of a single world-view, provide a complete answer to the paradox of medieval culture (cf. Mercier 1962; Gurevich 1982b: 153ff., 163ff.). Medieval grotesque was rooted in a specific kind of dualist view of the world in which heaven and earth stood face to face. The medieval mind brought these oppositions together, drew the unapproachable close, united the fragmented, and, occasionally, for a moment produced a very real synthesis. The earthly world in itself was taken completely for granted; the other world evoked piety, but it too was perceived as part of the same universe as the earth, and presented no riddle to medieval people. It was the meeting of the two that struck a note of marvel: each of the worlds was made vicariously foreign to the other. The paradox of medieval grotesque is rooted in this confrontation of both worlds.

The ambivalence of medieval consciousness is perhaps nowhere more visible than in medieval Latin popularizing literature. The work of clerics who had absorbed to varying degrees the elements of book-learning, these writings were directed at an illiterate popular audience and received input from its ideas and notions. The essence of medieval grotesque is revealed at the point where these two traditions come closest to each other.

In studying works of edifying literature one is constantly struck by a paradox: there is a clear contradiction between the general theme and its concrete realization. A clerical author concerned with his listeners' salvation writes down various stories to guide his flock on to the true path. The entire narrative is subordinated to this pious purpose. The demonstration of the power of the sacraments; the necessity of avoiding temptation; the denunciation of the devil's intrigues and the glorification of the saints; amazement at God's mercy; calls to contrition and repentance; demonstration of the superiority of spiritual simplicity and humility over pride; and, finally, the slight opening of the veil covering the Other World, with its punishments and rewards – these are the basic themes of the *exempla* used by medieval ecclesiastical authors. But these lofty, pious aims had to be realized in this sinful world, against the devil's intrigues, by people who as a rule pursued their own base self-interest. As a result, in the edifying short story sacred and secular, 'high' and 'low' were inevitably contiguous. These stories evoke from the modern reader an inadequate reaction, completely different from that of medieval readers or listeners and from the one which their authors intended to elicit.

The 'strangeness' of these stories for the modern reader lies in their
ability to make him laugh or wonder but not to take them seriously.
When Renaissance novellas mock the clergy's ignorance and depravity
or the laity's superstition, their being 'funny' is not unintentional. The
new age parted from the old through laughter. But the medieval Latin
short story originated in completely different circumstances. Its purpose
was not to ridicule or unmask; its aims were not destructive, but
constructive. Thus, their 'strangeness' demands our attention, for the
dissimilarity between medieval and modern culture appears here more
clearly than anywhere else. But is it possible to reconstruct the cultural
situation in which the medieval short story developed and flourished for
centuries?

The modern scholar's first reaction coincides with that of the modern
reader: he is inclined to take many of the *exempla* for comedy or parody.
But there are a good many difficulties here.[8] The sources of laughter and
irony differ from age to age; what appears to be laughable in one culture
may be taken very seriously in another. Keeping this in mind, it is not
easy to find examples in the texts under study of pure comedy or material
written solely to amuse an audience.[9] As a rule, episodes which make us
smile are set in a context of elevated and didactic aims. Did medieval
men perceive as humorous what now appears as only 'funny'? The
quarrels between the inhabitants of Tours and Poitiers over St Martin's
body (see above ch. 2) sound to us like comedy, only intensified by
Gregory of Tours' sober and pious presentation of the story. Here is a
strange confrontation of the two worlds, a confrontation these people
both craved and feared. It is grotesque, but if it is comical then it is only
so for modern readers, not for Gregory and his contemporaries. In any
event, even if in their time certain situations were perceived as comic or
parodic they also carried another, significantly more serious charge,
which was possibly the basic one.

Let me begin with the forces of evil that loomed so large in medieval
man's consciousness. There is a variety of views in modern scholarship
concerning the medieval perception of demons. Some scholars believe
that the devil was the incarnation of all evil and that demonophobia,
cultivated by the church, completely controlled the terrorized believers.
These conclusions are based both on textual evidence (Shejnman 1977)
and iconography (Villeneuve 1957). However, a thorough study of the
material leads to less simplistic conclusions. M. Gutowski's study (1973)
of comic elements in Polish Gothic art and its European parallels
demonstrates the role in religious art of elements of caricature and
parody: first and foremost, the forces of evil seem to be subjected to
ridicule.[10] (Cf. Randall 1957; Janicka 1962: 23, 36ff.).

Bakhtin links the devil with popular grotesque. In the diableries of the medieval mysteries, otherworldly vision and fabliaux, 'the devil is the merry ambivalent bearer of the unofficial point of view, of holiness inside out, the representative of the material bodily stratum. In him there is nothing frightening or alien' (Bakhtin 1965: 48). This assertion needs considerable correction, for, as we shall see, the humorous and the frightful are interwoven in the figure of the devil. Nevertheless, it is true that if Christ never laughed, the devil never cries. If he does weep, it is only for deception (Weinand 1958: 77).

In our sources great attention is paid to the forces of evil; hence it is tempting to verify Bakhtin's opinions on the basis of this material. Caesarius of Heisterbach's *Dialogue on Miracles* is particularly rich in reports of the devil's tricks. This is understandable: by his time the devil had already 'come into fashion'. Although he had also figured in early Christian literature, in medieval thought the devil acquired features previously absent, becoming a mighty ruler striving to subjugate all weak, vacillating souls and to compel them to render him homage. *Fac mihi hominium*, 'Offer me the oath of fealty', the devil badgers people, promising them help and every sort of boon in return. He once made such a proposition to a Cologne bell-ringer, threatening otherwise to leave him on the top of the tower where he had hurled him.[11] Although ecclesiastical authors regularly affirm that the devil is not equal in power to God, their 'latent Manicheanism' (Le Goff 1965: 205) permits the devil and his minions to grow into a frightful threat, an enormous force, lying in wait for man at every step. The devil is the incarnation of pride, treason and all other sins.

According to Christian theology, man stands at a crossroads leading to salvation or perdition, and being endowed with free will he makes his own choice. The church condemned the view that sinfulness and righteousness do not depend on the individual's will; but such notions were apparently widespread among a people reared more on the idea of fate controlling the world than on the abstract tenet of *liberum arbitrium*. In discussing the penitentials I have already touched upon a misunderstanding of this kind. The same motif appears frequently in sermons. Caesarius of Arles felt the need to refute the teaching of 'mathematicians' (astrologers) and Manicheans, who transferred responsibility for sins from man to the heavens: man himself does not sin; he is compelled to by the stars. In fact, explains Caesarius, the devil induces people to sin, but he can only tempt and induce them. He cannot compel them: they are free to accept or reject his blandishments.[12] Stress is laid on each believer's moral responsibility. But the idea of predestination remained popular for centuries. Popularizing theology, propagated by the lower clergy and monks, found reinforcement for this view in the *Elucidarium*. Caesarius of Heisterbach tells of the 'fatal delusion' of the

Landgraf Ludwig, who persisted in his sins with the justification that if he was predestined no sins could deprive him of the kingdom of heaven.[13]

However, 'ordinary' medieval religious consciousness was not satisfied with stating the dichotomy of sin and righteousness in a general form. The individual is not simply placed before a necessary choice – he is the object of the devil's ceaseless assaults. Like a fortress situated in enemy territory, he remains under constant siege. The forces of evil tirelessly seek out the smallest chance to penetrate the stronghold. Two angels are appointed for each man, a good one to protect him and an evil one to test him.[14]

If one compares the orderly hierarchy of the heavenly host sketched by Pseudo-Dionysius – in which angels occupy designated posts, with the notion of the angel constantly accompanying man to defend him from his antithesis the demon – the contrast is striking indeed. The theological system centralized heavenly powers, while popular fantasy particularized them. One commoner was granted the ability to see these companions at the moment when people entered or left church: people leading a virtuous life walked with bright, shining faces accompanied by a joyous angel, but sinners, with dark and gloomy faces, were led by the nose by demons, while an angel trudged forlornly some distance behind (Klapper 1914: no. 92).

Demonology is an important part of medieval theology. The image of the devil and his underlings constantly generated more and more stories about their tricks. Demons were a sort of medieval virus with which the whole sinful world was infected. Usually they were invisible to the naked eye: very few had the ability to observe them and discern their various aspects. As a result, certain people did not believe in demons until events forced them to do otherwise. One anchoress saw demons sitting on the shoulders and backs of monks in the form of monkeys and cats and mocking their gestures.[15] Caesarius of Heisterbach adds that he does not want to reveal the nun's name (a personal acquaintance), so as to save her from harm. Obviously, these monks were not without sin if the demons straddled them so.

A favourite theme of medieval art is the death-bed scene. In addition to the relatives and priest surrounding the dying man, and the saints, God the Father, Christ and the Virgin standing around the bed, loathsome demons bustle here as well. There are two planes in the picture. Mortal people are visible to everybody, but the heavenly powers and demons only to the artist (Tenenti 1952). This is the secret of the meeting of two worlds. Strictly speaking, there are even three planes here, for God and the saints on the one hand, and the demons on the other, do not notice each other, being focussed instead on the sinner's soul. The apparently empty bedroom is in actuality tightly crowded – here paradise, hell and the world are brought closely together. One only needs to know how to see their grotesque, terrifying proximity.

The *exempla* also present analogous instances of 'double vision'. One noblewoman, appearing in church decked out like a peacock, did not notice that on the long hem of her luxuriant dress a multitude of tiny demons was sitting. Black like Ethiopians, they clapped for joy and jumped like fish in a net, for the woman's inappropriate attire was nothing other than the devil's snare.[16] Having fallen into vanity, people do not see the demons swarming around them like flies, but this mournful picture is distinctly visible to the righteous. It is not impossible that such scenes were entertaining to Caesarius of Heisterbach's contemporaries, who found satisfaction in reducing the image of the forces of evil and in ridiculing sinners. But they also perceived another, deeper plane of these pictures, not humorous in any way. The amusing demonology of the Middle Ages always presupposes a terrible side.

Although a single demon is appointed for each man, that does not stop him from being set upon by an entire horde of demons. 'Do you see the large granary?' asked a sinful dying priest of his companion. 'There are more demons gathered around me than there is straw covering its roof'. Hearing this, the pupil in Caesarius of Heisterbach's *Dialogues* says to his teacher, 'But in that case, of course, there are more demons than sinners.' The monk answers, 'It is impossible to say how many there are at present, but it is clear nonetheless that at the end of the world, when the number of the damned is fulfilled, the number of sinners will far exceed the number of demons. For God cast down a tenth of the angels along with Lucifer, and they were transformed into demons. But nine times as many of the elect will take their place in heaven. And who can doubt that the number of sinners is incomparably greater than the number of the elect?'[17] According to Rudolph of Schlettstadt, one possessed man said that in Zurich there were 6,606 demons, who at God's command will fall on the townsmen and punish them for their pride.[18]

However, we are not dealing here with a quantitative profusion of demons, but with their unusual activism, cunning and aggressiveness. Demons stop at nothing to take control of souls. When a demon possessing a soul was asked whether he did not desire to renounce his evil ways and return to heaven, he responded without hesitation that if he had the choice between seducing a single soul and taking it into hell or being borne up to heaven, he would choose the former option. He added, 'Why does this surprise you? After all, such is my perfidy, and I persist in it so much that I am unable to wish anything good.'[19] This demon recognizes his perfidy and inability to set himself on the path of goodness. Even more striking, however, is another demon, who was ready to undergo any torture if only he would ultimately be returned to God. But this, according to Caesarius of Heisterbach, only testifies to the sort of blessing the demons lost with their fall, and not about the possibility of their returning to that blessing.[20] One demon came to confession in hope of absolution. The priest stipulated that his sins would be expiated if three times daily he would ask for God's forgiveness. This was too much for the demon, for he was unable to humble himself before the Almighty.[21] The devil, after all, is the incarnation of pride, which has forever deprived him of the possibility of being reconciled with God. These demons are not without a tragic dichotomy: they are attracted by good, but they lack the power to achieve it.

In Gregory the Great's depiction demons are extremely monstrous: black repulsive spirits, terrifying dragons enveloping men with their tails, swallowing their heads or shoving their snouts into their mouths and sucking out their souls, etc. Other authors have similar depictions, as do church sculptures and carvings.

It is impossible to see the devil in his actual form, as a spirit, with mortal eyes. Just as the elect's greatest felicity lies in contemplating God, so also the damned's greatest torture is beholding the devil.[22] But to the living the devil and his servants appear in any form: handsome men and beautiful women, priests, monkeys, pigs, cats, dogs or reptiles. Their capability for metamorphosis is unlimited. However, a demon assuming human form cannot be seen from behind, since demons do not have backs and always withdraw by walking backwards.[23] They are hollow inside.

Just as hell is the antithesis of paradise, so also the fallen angels are the complete opposite of the good angels, a sort of angels 'inside out'. The antagonism of the forces of good and evil in itself assumes the possibility of a 'carnival' interpretation of the latter. And although there are no misfortunes which demons do not strive to bring upon people, medieval authors nevertheless do not always depict demons in sombre tones: their demons do not lack duality and even a certain attractiveness.

Some stories about demons in Gregory the Great's *Dialogues* have elements of humour and comedy. One nun eagerly wanted lettuce, and she ate a leaf of it, forgetting to make the sign of the cross over the food. She was straightway possessed by a demon. The abbot Ecvitius was summoned, and he began to pray for her healing. As soon as the abbot appeared in the garden, where the possessed nun was in convulsions, the frightened demon, 'as if justifying himself', cried out, 'What have I done wrong? I was sitting on a leaf of lettuce, and she came and ate me'. The abbot indignantly ordered him to abandon the unfortunate nun, and immediately the demon withdrew.[24] On another occasion the priest Stephen, returning home fatigued, carelessly commanded his servant, 'Come on, you devil, take off my shoes'. And immediately the straps of his shoes quickly began to undo themselves, so that it became clear to Stephen that in fact the demon he had incautiously mentioned was untying them. 'Depart, miserable thing, depart! I summoned my servant, not you'. At these words the demon retreated.[25] Noting how 'extremely naive' these stories are, E. Auerbach (1965: 97–100) correctly locates in them 'a genuine atmosphere of tales of brownies and gnomes', where the marvellous is intertwined with the grotesque.

Similar short stories about demons appearing after a careless word are also found in Caesarius of Heisterbach. One angry father no sooner said to his son 'Go to the devil!' than the devil abducted his son. Something similar happened with a young girl: as she was drinking milk, her angry father mentioned the devil, who immediately took possession of her.[26] A servant who was bored guarding the monastery vineyard at night in jest summoned the devil to take his place. Without delay the devil appeared and agreed to stand guard on the condition that he receive a basket of grapes for his labours. But when the idler went to pay off the demon he found the vineyard completely bare.[27]

In these stories the demons 'take' a man at his word: he swears and mentions the devil, and immediately the latter appears. Is this the magic of the word so characteristic of archaic cultures? Perhaps. In any case, the devil only waits until he is summoned or his name is uttered by chance. Such careless utterances can have fatal consequences. One peasant wanted to 'know' his wife when she was menstruating. He threatend her with force, and she said angrily: 'Satiate your lust, in the devil's name'. She conceived and gave birth to a frightful monster.[28] Jacques de Vitry tells of a man who was unable to endure his wife and wanted to go on a pilgrimage. She asked him in whose care he was leaving her. 'I am entrusting you to the devil', he answered in his heart. When in the man's absence lovers came to his wife, the devil appeared and chased them away, saying that her husband had entrusted her to him. The man finally returned home and the devil hastened to turn over his wife to him, saying, 'I would rather be harnessed to a dozen wild horses than to such a savage woman' (Frenken 1914: no. 64).

Demons fear saints and flee from their presence. An evil spirit exorcised by St Fortunatus wandered along the city streets in the evenings, moaning, 'O holy man, bishop Fortunatus! What has he done? You have expelled a stranger from his haven. I search for a place to lay my head, and I find no refuge in his city.[29] The fear with which the demons regard powerful saints is mixed with respect. Gregory of Tours relates how a demon possessing the daughter of the emperor Leo refused to leave her in peace, crying out, 'I will not leave here unless the archdeacon of Lyons comes. I will not abandon this vessel for anything, unless he personally drives me out.'[30] According to Jacopo da Varagine, one woman, unable to be delivered of a child, sent her sister to get help from 'our lady Diana', But the devil (for pagan gods, according to the church, are only demons) answered, 'Why do you call upon me to do that which is beyond my power? Go to the Apostle Andrew, and he will help your sister.'[31] The demons themselves acknowledge the power of the saints.

Our authors compel demons to praise the saints. Thus, when the evil spirits that had possessed some people for neglecting to make the sign of the cross before drinking from a cup, and others for gluttony, perjury, theft, murder and other sins, learned of the approach of St Rusticula, the abbess of Arles, they went out to meet her, prostrated themselves, and begged her by the cross and the nails with which the Lord was crucified not to force them to abandon 'their dwelling-places'.[32] The pious author of the *Life of Rusticula* makes no comment on the demons' strange, uncharacteristic utterance. The demons' mention of the sacred objects that for them were the saints' most terrifying weapons must obviously be interpreted as a manifestation of their submission to St Rusticula.

Motifs coming from popular notions and beliefs contributed to the formulation of the image of the devil in medieval Latin literature. Is the devil not close to the naked and sore-covered black 'Egyptian' of the diableries, who argues with Bishop Narcissus over the soul of the prostitute Afra? The demon tries to persuade the bishop, who has baptized Afra, to relinquish her, since a whore is understandably his 'abode'. After a lengthy oral competition the devil is forced to humble himself before the bishop, and he prays him to show mercy and hand over to him some other soul. But hearing the singing of a psalm, he sobs and hurries off. After new disputes the sharp-minded bishop promises the demon the soul of the first person he meets and sends him into a desert where there are no people or animals, but only a dragon. Discovering the deception, the demon cries out, 'O mendacious bishop! You bound me by falsehood, so that I might kill my friend, for if I do not kill him, I will be forced to return to hell'. With the death of the dragon this scene from the *Conversion of St Afra* comes to an end.[33] The demon, bound by a vow he does not dare violate for fear of returning to hell, is a paradoxical and comic figure. But the episode is not restricted to the humorous: the main theme is the disgrace of the demon in his struggle with the saint for a human soul.

Readers of such stories were doubtless most amazed by good demons. A 'good' evil spirit is a rather strange combination, but however paradoxical it may appear, one does meet such creatures. One knight's squire was a handsome youth, who served him faithfully for a long time.

The knight suspected nothing, but the truth came out when the knight's wife fell seriously ill and nothing could cure her. The youth said that she could be cured by lion's milk and took upon himself the task of obtaining it, which he did within an hour. In response to his master's question he admitted that he had obtained the milk from Arabia, where he had milked the lion. 'You?' the shaken knight asked. Then he had to reveal that he was a demon. But why had he so faithfully served a man? 'It is a great consolation for me to be with human sons', was the demon's striking admission. The terrified knight refused his further services, although the demon assured him that if he permitted him to remain, nothing bad would happen. Obviously, the demon had no intention of ruining the knight's soul. He refused to be compensated, requesting only five solidi, which he returned to the knight, so that a bell might be purchased for the church and believers called on Sundays to mass. Having expressed such an extraordinary request, the good demon departed.[34]

Caesarius of Heisterbach offers other examples of *diabolica bonitas*. A demon carried the knight Everhard on his back to various countries, including the Holy Land, and returned him home unharmed.[35] Another demon, through the mouth of a possessed man, warned paupers about to attend a feast given by a rich man not to touch the food, since the dishes were prepared from the meat of calves five generations removed from a stolen cow.[36] A unique scrupulousness, worthy not only of a demon! Demons can render people other services as well. A demon possessing a man was able to disclose all the unconfessed sins of those present.[37]

These helpful and pious demons, whose behaviour erases or relativizes the antagonistic opposition between good and evil, may have entered medieval Latin literature from popular fantasy. Folk stories about good brownies and other fabulous spirits evidently contributed to their origin.[38] But in such stories one is struck by one common feature vividly distinguishing their grotesque paradoxicality: demons appeal to forces and symbols forever implacably inimical to them. Evil spirits entreat a saint by Christ's cross and nails; a demon squire returns his pay to acquire a bell for calling people to mass; a demon warns against eating meat tainted by crime; other demons crave absolution, and one has the suspicion that their salvation is prevented by church doctrine, not by the popular fantasy that created them.

The possibilities in the image of demons for transformation, play and freedom are such that this image begins to live in art with a particular life, partly independent of the imagination that created it and originally endowed it only with the ability to do evil. The medieval demon is still far from Mephistopheles, but it is impossible to deny him ambivalence.

I have just said that in the stories with 'good evil spirits' the opposition of good and evil is made relative, but that may not be so. Good is stronger than evil and triumphs over it, drawing to its side even evil's adherents, if only for a moment. For a demon cannot stop being a demon, and no amount of good deeds will return it to God. The temporarily violated balance of good and evil is inevitably restored, and Caesarius hastens to emphasize that the natural relation between devil and man is one of mutual hatred. The Lord placed enmity between them, and woe unto him who enters into a pact with the devil.[39] To many people the devil suggests such a pact, inducing them to render him homage.[40] However frightful and dangerous the demons are, it is within a man's powers to resist them. The devil is similar to a lion caught in a net: whoever avoids the circle of his reach will not be torn to pieces. The devil is unable to compel a man to sin if the man is not inclined to do so of his own free will.[41] Demons fear the sign of the cross and supplications to saints, especially the Virgin ('that woman' – demons neither dare nor wish to mention her by name). The nun Euthymia almost yielded to the demon pulling her by the right hand, since in her simplicity she assumed that one was not supposed to make the sign of the cross with the left hand. Another nun overcame a demon by giving him a good slap on the ear, at which the demon was sincerely offended: 'Why did you hit me so hard? I bothered your sister much more this evening, and she did not hit me.'[42]

Demons attempt to possess sinners' bodies and ruin their souls, and saints are accordingly concerned with driving demons out of the possessed. Almost all the heroes of hagiography are occupied in exorcism. At the approach of a mighty saint demons begin to cry out through the mouths of their victims, complaining of the tortures they are suffering on account of the saint.[43] In expelling a demon, the saint sometimes evokes from the possessed bloody vomit with which the demon departs from the body, and in other cases healing takes place in ways more humiliating for the demon.[44] Sometimes a struggle over the possessed's soul breaks out between a demon and an ultimately victorious angel.[45] Caesarius of Heisterbach describes a battle between saints and demons.[46] Speaking of the pious King Gunthram, belief in whose healing powers was widespread among the people, Gregory of Tours mentions that he has no doubts about this belief, for he himself has heard many times how demons, residing in possessed people, called upon the name of that king and confessed their evil deeds.[47] Demons also possess members of the clergy. One deacon even managed to meet with the devil himself. Stuck in an indecent pose, he saw the black figure of an enormous unrestrained bull of immeasurable thickness with flashing eyes. This, of course, was the devil himself, and he had already opened his jaws to devour the cleric when the latter overcame him with the sign of the cross.[48]

The interpretation of the devil and demons by medieval authors, beginning with Gregory I and Gregory of Tours and ending with Caesarius of Heisterbach and Jacopo da Varagine, is identical. The enemy of God and man, the devil makes every effort to steer souls into hell. As a result, the demons' tricks, however amusing they may be for a time, in the medieval perception cannot be deprived of a gloomy tinge. In these stories the humorous and the frightful are fused together. It may be that the humorous is interwoven into narratives about Satan's efforts to possess men's souls because those efforts, when successful, entail the most frightful consequences and an inexpressible, incomparable fear. The saying goes, 'The devil is not so frightful as he is painted', but the medieval devil was just as frightful as he was depicted in stories about visions and represented in church iconography. The jest, the mockery, the reduction of the image of the bearer of absolute evil to the comic, made bearable the tragedy of a situation threatening eternal perdition. In this psychological context laughter became the means of overcoming fear, the intensity of which is difficult for us even to imagine.[49]

The interpretation of the devil and demons by medieval authors was ambivalent and dualistic. It is doubtful whether laughter can conquer fear of the devil and make him 'unfrightful', as Bakhtin asserted, or even make him less frightful. But medieval consciousness, not for a minute relinquishing confidence in the absoluteness and permanence of the forces of evil, also found in them another side: it saw them as humorous, pitiful and even good-natured fools, humiliated by saints and angels. The frightful not only repelled; it also greedily attracted. The comic was extended to the world of evil and gave rise to a specific grotesque in which the unusual occurred in the domestic sphere. Monks pray or sleep in church, but among them bustle demons; a woman dresses herself up to appear beautiful, and on her hem demons frolic; a novice does not make the sign of the cross over her piece of lettuce, and a demon possesses her; a cleric mentions the devil, and he appears on the spot. Was this amusing for medieval people, who believed in the reality of demons? They surely laughed.[50] But what was the nature of their laughter? Laughter was an admission that behind life's most ordinary, commonplace phenomena there is invariably revealed something supernatural. Laughter was the emotional acknowledgment of the eternal antagonism of good and evil, sacred and profane, which lay at the base of the medieval world-view. 'Grotesque realism' (Bakhtin)? 'Vulgar realism' (Frejdenberg)? But this is a 'realism' that one could rightly also call 'vulgar, grotesque mysticism', for this ambivalent, serious–humorous attitude towards the forces of evil was an essential manifestation of popular religiosity.

L. P. Karsavin emphasized the complexity of the medieval attitude towards the forces of evil. Imagination, he wrote, worked at once in two directions: 'On the one hand, the frightful and repulsive are depicted with bright and concrete colors, but, on the other hand, the worldly-comical is done just as brightly and hyperbolically' (Karsavin 1915: 72). The latter is accomplished by medieval Latin authors extremely natural-istically. Stories of demons made pleasant and merry reading, but there was another side too in them: the comic element did not abolish the religious attitude towards the devil and did not make him religiously neutral (ibid.: 75).

The demon unites in himself absolute evil and buffoonery. It is not by chance that common, petty demons usually figure in literature and figurative art, and not the devil himself, who was a difficult subject to portray humorously.[51] There remained something in these demons from pagan spirits and elves, and the people's attitude towards them was ambivalent, vacillating between fear and hatred and good-natured humour. As the sources show, moreover, the violation of the strict demarcation dividing the realms of good and evil also attributed to some demons the attempt to do good and the impractical but real desire to be saved. The demon himself became ambivalent. The grotesque contained within itself both aspects of reality: without destroying the frightful, it found in it an opposing, comic side. Carnival also hardly abolished the horror. Phenomena of the fifteenth and sixteenth centuries shed light on the essence of the medieval grotesque as well. Such elements as the *danse macabre*, with its kings, popes, prelates, knights, ladies, townsmen and peasants dancing hand in hand with a grimacing and grinning death, were already latently present in the medieval grotesque and are closely related to its nature.

Here it is appropriate to recall that there was a tendency deeply inherent in medieval popular perception to translate the spiritual into the concretely sensible and the material. But such is also a characteristic of art. Evidently, medieval popular culture created favourable conditions for an intimacy of the religious and artistic assimilations of the world. Symbols were transferred into artistic images without ceasing to be symbols. This is yet another source of the ambivalence in medieval Latin literature.

Vulgar popular grotesque, making material the spiritual and erasing the borders between abstraction and object, not only reduced the Other World to the earthly but also dissolved the earthly in the supernatural. Caesarius of Heisterbach tells without marvelling what took place in a church in which priests sang loudly and without piety, 'in a secular manner': one cleric noticed a demon standing on high and gathering the voices of the singers into a large sack. And they thus 'sang' a 'sack full'.[52] Around a monk who habitually dozed off in the monastery choir demons scurried in the form of pigs. With grunts they picked up the words of the psalms, devoid of grace, that fell from the mouth of the sleepyhead.[53] Prayers and psalms were conceived of as material bodies.[53] A rich citizen of Cologne, hearing from a priest that the Apostles will judge the universe, became thoughtful and decided to buy stones for the future, so that on Judgment Day, when his good and bad deeds are weighed, the Apostles can put these stones in the bowl with the good deeds. He acquired an entire ship of stones, which he unloaded near the Church of the Apostles in Cologne. Soon the church was enlarged and the stones used for its foundation.[54] The course of this man's thoughts is extremely symptomatic. Giving stones to repair a church was itself a good deed to be taken into account in the Other World, but this citizen visually imagined his stones lying on the scales together with his other good deeds. A good deed in this system of consciousness possesses a physical body. As a result, we are not surprised to read that on a ship there was a man the weight of whose sins the sea could not support;[55] or that fervent piety raised a priest into the air during prayer and that he soared in the church without touching his feet to the floor;[56] or that demons failed to drag into hell the soul of the dying Charlemagne, since the stones put by St James on the scales outweighed the emperor's sins, the stones being understood in the vision of Bishop Turpin as the churches built by Charlemagne in honour of St James (Tubach 1969: no. 946). Nor is it surprising in this system of logic that during one deceased man's embalming no heart was discovered in his chest. After all, it says in Scripture: 'For where your treasure is, there will your heart be also' (Matt 6:21). They actually searched his moneybox and found his heart lying with his money (Klapper 1914: no. 159).

The sacraments are also perceived of as medicine. In particular, baptism can exert influence not only on the soul, but also on the body. Thus, a youth who had possessed from birth a dreadful deformity was cured after being plunged three times into the font as the Holy Trinity was invoked.[57] The host was used as a magical remedy.[58] This was the attitude not only of common parishoners, who confused the sacrament with popular potions, but also of some clergy. One of them attempted to use a host for seducing a woman. Wishing to excite her through kisses, he put a host in his mouth beforehand, for which *maleficium* he suffered a cruel and surprising punishment. One young girl, seeing that caterpillars were destroying everything she had planted in the garden, on the advice of a tramp broke up a host and sprinkled her vegetables with it, for which a demon possessed her. In the same way a noblewoman from near Bonn, fearing that the vicissitudes of weather might harm her crops, put a consecrated host in the earth, but to her horror the grain she expected was transformed into coagulating blood. 'For it was not pleasing to the Lord that his sacraments be used for worldly needs', notes Caesarius of Heisterbach.[59] But is this not contradicted by his stories of miraculous aid rendered by the eucharist in completely secular affairs, such as duels?[60]

Caesarius of Heisterbach notes that 'God's nature is such that he cannot be seen with the body's eyes, nor heard with its ears, nor touched by its hands,'[61] But he is unable to hold fast to the positions of learned religion. Revelations of faith ought to be presented visually and perceptibly, and the religious–artistic view, uniting a sacred symbol with a visible image, is constantly revealed in his dialogues in most unexpected ways. To those clergy who doubt Christ's presence in the host, the Lord reveals himself in a physical aspect, alone or with his Mother.[62] In the same way that the Lord punishes a sinner by striking the organ with which he sinned, he can also reward the virtuous.[63] The zeal of one copyist of church books was deemed worthy of a miracle: his hand had not turned into dust even twenty years after his death. One Cologne resident whose custom it was to pray continually, both on the way to church and on the way back home, appeared after death to his kinsman, and the latter marvelled that on his shins was written the verse 'Ave Maria gratia plena ...'.[64]

In analysing otherworldly visions we have seen how in them the soul was perceived just as materially as the body. One could, of course, formulate it in another way: popular views of the body and soul did not proceed from assuming their opposition. Something similar is found in Caesarius of Heisterbach. In a village there lived a sinful priest who was on friendly terms with a knight and shared all his godless pastimes with him. And one night the devil appeared to this knight in the form of his friend, the priest, and forced him to go somewhere through a field undressed and barefoot. His feet torn up and his body weary, the knight finally flew into a rage and clove the priest's head. Making it home somehow, he related the occurrence to his disbelieving friends and servants. That same night the priest himself accidently fractured his head on a lintel, drawing blood. When he met the priest in church, the knight was convinced that what he had experienced had not been a dream, but reality. The priest, accordingly, was simultaneously in two places; a demon had evidently stolen his soul. What was Caesarius' attitude towards this event? He expresses no surprise at all. For him the story's interest lies in the fact that a demon is always happy to cause friends to quarrel.[65]

The grotesque reduces the great to the small, profanes the sacred, and thus can come close to sacrilege. Take, for example, the bizarre situation where some schoolboys baptized a dog. Imitating the priests, they baptized the dog in a river, invoking the Holy Trinity, and the poor animal, unable to bear the sacrament, went mad. Caesarius of Heister-bach adds that the Lord had mercy on the children, knowing that they did not intentionally insult the sacrament, but did so out of the foolish-ness characteristic of their age. But when adults acted that way – two haunters of taverns smeared each other on the head with ashes in mockery of church ritual – God punished them severely.[66] Rudolph of Schlettstadt repeatedly tells of the use of the host as a means of bewitchment and of the sufferings Christ undergoes as a result. Jews, sticking into the host a knife or needle, evoke, according to him, a mysterious child's cry or a flow of blood, for which they are subjected to persecutions. Unbelievers even call the eucharist 'the Christians' little God'.[67]

Rudolph narrates several instances of blasphemy. A swarm of hornets attacked the vineyard of a peasant, and in a temper he desired that all the insects 'be in the heart of our Lord Jesus Christ and devour his insides, just as they have laid waste my vineyard'. And straightaway the hornets attacked the blasphemer and stung him so badly that he died the following day.[68]

There are other striking cases of blasphemy. Alberico da Romano, losing his falcon on a hunt, 'dropped his trousers and exposed his rear to the Lord as a sign of abuse and reviling. When he returned home, he went and defecated on the altar, on the same place where Christ's body is consecrated'. Karsavin (1915: 42) adduces this as evidence of a 'thirst for faith', a dread of losing one's faith and being subjected to doubts, and not as proof of a lack of faith and a complete denial.[69] Possibly: such an interpretation evidently does not contradict the fact that the profanation of sacred things and blasphemy can be understood as the carnivalized side of religiosity, not unlike the mocking of divinity and the parodying of religious ritual in some ancient and medieval cults (Frejdenberg 1973).

An instance of extreme proximity of the most lofty and sacred to the base and shameful is also found in Caesarius of Heisterbach. One baron who sided with the Albigensians 'out of hatred towards Christ' emptied his stomach on the altar in Toulouse cathedral and used the altar covering to wipe himself. Such behaviour also astounded the very enemies of orthodoxy. Other Albigensians placed a whore on the altar and indulged in debauchery in sight of the crucifix.[70] In Crusader-besieged Beziers heretics urinated on a Gospel and threw the defiled book from the wall onto the heads of the orthodox and, showering them with arrows, cried, 'Here, you wretches, is your law!' Christ, continues Caesarius, was not slow to take revenge, and the fortress was taken. The deeds of the Catholics who burst into the city seem no less paradoxical, for it was in Beziers that there occurred the notorious massacre of orthodox Christians along with heretics. When the Crusaders asked the abbot how to distinguish the righteous from the damned, he ordered, fearing that one of the heretics might pretend to be Catholic: 'Kill them. The Lord knows his own.' And a countless multitude of townspeople were annihilated.[71] 'Novit enim Dominus qui sunt eius' is an expression from one of Paul's Epistles, in which further on are the words: 'And the lord shall deliver me from every evil work' (2 Tim 2:19; 4:18).[72] The use of this citation in this case is somewhat unexpected, to put it mildly, but Caesarius himself, shaken by the heretics' blasphemies, reports the slaughter of Beziers without any comment, apparently not noticing how evil and good have changed places.

In sermons, pious dialogues and hagiography there is no place for the fool or jester, and so his role is played by the simpleton. However, the *simplex* of medieval Latin literature is by no means identical to the fool. For in his person one of the most important Christian virtues, spiritual poverty, is glorified: 'Blessed are the poor in spirit: for theirs is the kingdom of heaven' (Matt 5:3). *Simplices* are the 'salt of the earth'. However, the celebration of spiritual poverty also opens the way to a comic re-interpretation of the image of the simpleton.

The God-pleasing 'holy simplicity' that surpasses learned wisdom is allotted an honoured place in the works under consideration here. The sixth part of Caesarius of Heisterbach's *Dialogues on Miracles* is entitled 'De simplicitate' and offers striking examples of monks' lack of guile. Several of these stories are tinged with humour. One simple-minded nun who had grown up within the monastery could scarcely distinguish laymen from animals. Once she saw a goat clambering on the wall and asked a sister who it was. Knowing her simplicity and lack of experience, the sister answered in jest that it was an elderly laywoman, since with age laywomen grow horns and beards.[73] The priest Ensfried was so good and simple-hearted that one day, while on his way to venerate a saint, he gave the trousers right off his body to a persistent beggar. The episode drew a smile from the canon who noticed Ensfried's lack of trousers but did not know the reason for his nakedness. But Caesarius, informed of Ensfried's motives, is delighted with him: '...to part with one's trousers is greater than to divide one's shirt'.[74]

The Lord loves *simplices* and encourages them. One monk hurried so fast to church one night that out of sleepiness he missed the door and went through a window. He was not hurt, however, for angels caught him and carefully set him on the ground. Seeing the grief of one nun who had lost her crucifix, the abbot advised her; 'Search the corners of your cell and inquire: "Lord, where are you? Please answer!" and straightaway in some chink in the wall you will find it'. The abbot was joking, but the holy woman, not drawing a distinction between God and the crucifix, took his advice literally and found the cross exactly where the abbot told her to look. Another nun also forgot where she had left her favourite wooden crucifix. While she was crying Christ took pity on her, and she heard: 'Do not weep, my daughter. I am lying in the small bag you put under the cot.' The Lord even endures the familiarity and crudeness of his beloved *simplices*. One of them, tormented by temptations, prayed: 'Lord, if you will not free me from temptation, I will complain about you to your Mother'. Immediately Christ freed him from temptation.[75] A woman whose son was imprisoned abducted the Christ-child from a statue of the Virgin and returned it to the church only after the Virgin freed her son (Tubach 1969: no. 1024).

An extreme instance of simple-heartedness and trustfulness immediately rewarded by God is provided by an episode with a priest's mistress. After a sermon about sins and hell's frightful punishments for them, she asked the preacher in her agitation: 'What awaits the mistresses of priests?' In jest he answered: 'Nothing can save them, unless they enter a burning oven'. She understood this literally and waiting for a time when everybody was out of the house, crawled into a blazing oven where bread was being baked. At the moment when the fire consumed her, people near the house saw a small snow-white dove fly from the chimney. Nevertheless, because she had committed suicide, her remains were buried in unconsecrated ground. The Lord had judged otherwise: since she had killed herself out of obedience, and not out of any evil intention, at night candles would spontaneously light up on her grave.[76]

The following story of monastic simplicity is interesting for the fact that some humanist would undoubtedly perceive it as evidence of the gluttony in which clerics willingly indulge. A baron living near a monastery constantly encroached illegally on the monastery's property. Finally, after he had seized a large number of cattle, the monks decided to send a messenger to him with a request to return what he had taken. The choice fell upon one monk, who promised to try to return at least part of what had been seized. When he arrived at the baron's home, the latter invited him to dine. Because the monk eagerly set to eating the meat dishes, the baron asked him after the meal whether monks were permitted to eat meat. 'Under no circumstances', answered the monk. 'But why then have you eaten meat here today?' asked the baron. The monk replied: 'When my abbot sent me here, he ordered that I not refuse whatever little of our cattle that I could return. And since the meat you offered me undoubtedly belongs to our monastery, I was afraid that I would only be able to return with whatever I could get with my teeth. So I ate out of obedience, lest I return empty-handed'. The Lord does not repudiate *simplices*, adds Caesarius, and the baron, shaken by the monk's simple-heartedness and afraid of the Lord's punishments for acting against such holiness, returned everything he had taken from the monastery and promised in the future not to encroach on its holdings. Here is an example, concludes Caesarius, of how a transgression bad in itself was turned into a good deed as a result of the simpleton's good intentions.[77] 'Caesarius is not unaware of the episode's humour, and he calls this story 'as merry as it is marvellous'. But the humorous and amusing sides of his stories never stand on their own; they are invariably subordinated to edifying aims. The most ridiculous and even sinful deeds can be made holy and pleasing to God if they are accomplished by people with pure hearts and simple minds.[78]

Discourses upon God-pleasing simplicity are also connected with the theme of 'knowledge and ignorance'. To what degree are knowledge and capabilities inherent in a person, and to what degree are they given from on high? The thesis that God is the lord of knowledge, who can miraculously grant it and no less wondrously take it away, is illustrated by Caesarius of Heisterbach through the example of an illiterate deacon who found himself in a vision in a heavenly cathedral, where he was ordered to read the gospel in front of the Lord. After he had finished reading, he heard a voice: 'From this hour you will possess the knowledge and virtue to preach the word of God.'[79] An educated and literate priest, on the other hand, as a result of a flow of blood lost all his knowledge, 'as if it had flowed out of him with the blood'. From that time he did not know Latin and was incapable of understanding or uttering a single word of it. However, emphasizes Caesarius, the reason for this was not madness, for all his remaining habits and capabilities were preserved without harm. The reason lies in God's will, and in accordance with God's will literacy returned to him after a year.[80] Latin education, as we see, is more meaningful and related to God than other types of knowledge.

Demons were also capable of knowing Latin. A demon addressed Ensfried with a Latin verse of his own composition.[81] Karsavin (1915: 66) presents the story of a demon who possessed a crude peasant, whose tongue, to the demon's chagrin, was unfit for pronouncing Latin. The demon himself knew Latin no worse than the monk who refused to admit that he was a demon unless he would speak in Latin. Another demon entered a peasant who had never studied letters, but nevertheless he spoke from him in Latin so well that, according to Rudolph of Schlettstadt, he deserved praise.[82] Yet another demon expressed himself both in German and in Latin.[83] When a possessed young girl required the demon to read the 'Our Father', he did so, but with omissions and barbarisms. But this was not explained by his ignorance, for with a laugh the demon said, 'This is the way you laymen usually say your prayers'. The distortion of the sacred text made it blasphemous, and so the prayer was deprived of power and could not reach the Lord. The demon also knew the Creed, but twisted it by saying 'Credo Deum Patrem omnipotentem', and not 'Credo in Deum...', for, explains Caesarius of Heisterbach, the devil believes that God exists and that God's words are true, but he does not believe *in* him in the sense that he does not love him.[84]

The devil can also give man knowledge. To one Paris student not noted for his abilities the devil offered education on the condition that the student render him homage. In order to acquire omniscience it was sufficient to grasp a stone handed over by the devil, and the youth, previously ridiculed and considered by everybody as an *idiota*, actually became victorious in scholarly debates. But when he threw away the stone in fear of retribution, he lost all his learning along with it.[85]

Ignorance is obviously not always reckoned a serious deficiency, even for clergy. Gregory of Tours narrates an instance from his own experience. Because he was ill, mass was celebrated in his stead by a priest who evoked sneers from the listeners on account of the 'uncouthness of his speech'. But on the following night Gregory had a vision in which a man appeared and said to him that for glorifying the Lord 'pure simplicity' was more appropriate than 'philosophical playfulness'.[86] Caesarius of Heisterbach misses no opportunity to emphasize that the instigators of the Albigensians were *litterati*, who led the common folk (*illitterati*) astray.[87]

The ignorance of other clergy is truly striking, and whatever Caesarius of Heisterbach's intentions in telling of it, his stories reveal a curious aspect of medieval culture. The Cologne canon Werinbold was so 'simple' that he could not count; he could only distinguish pairs of objects. He counted the hams hanging in the kitchen in this manner, 'Here is a ham and its companion; here is another ham and its companion', etc. The servants took advantage of his ignorance to steal hams, and he was able to discover the loss only when they took a single ham. Hearing this story, the pupil in the *Dialogues* expresses the suspicion that Werinbold was stupid, rather than simple, but the teacher denies this. The Lord blessed his simplicity.[88] A priest so ignorant that he could not read mass except for a prayer addressed to the Virgin was removed from his post. In grief he called on the Virgin, and she helped him retain his parish.[89]

This does not mean that education was not considered significant. Like other authors, Caesarius of Heisterbach notes among the virtues of various clerics erudition (in church literature) and ability in Latin. The contrast between educated people and the uneducated and ignorant was basic throughout the Middle Ages. The inability to express oneself in

Latin, with few exceptions, was considered a deficiency and frequently mocked.[90] In a society in which knowledge long remained primarily sacred and books were rare and very valuable, the guardians of knowledge inevitably formed an élite isolated from the laity.[91] Examples of the justification of the ignorance of God-pleasing *idiotae* were all the more meaningful.

Latin authors considered a concrete, living example the most effective means of educating the faithful. Hagiography, sermons and homilies are replete with such examples from the lives of pious men and women. However, the saints of medieval Latin literature frequently conduct themselves rather peculiarly. Christian forgiveness is far from obligatory for them. We have already (ch. 2) dealt with the facts of the touchiness, anger and revenge of saints. But in our sources there are numerous episodes in which saints resort to physical violence to convince wayward and disrespectful believers. To a nobleman guilty of burning a church St Austrigisilus, bishop of Bourges, appeared in a dream. Asking him angrily why had he burned 'his house', he hit the nobleman's head so hard that it left a bruise. After waking up, the nobleman told his horrified servants what had happened and died.[92]

St Nicetas of Lyons also resorted to physical violence. When it became clear after his death that he had not bequeathed any of his property to the monastery in which he was buried, one very discouraged priest accused Nicetas of being stupid. That night Nicetas appeared to him accompanied by two bishops. Turning towards him, the saint uttered: 'Here is the one who does not know that I left here something more valuable, namely my own body'. Then he beat and nearly strangled the unlucky priest.[93] St Crispin and St Crispinian appeared one night to a bishop who had led into ruin the monastery built over their graves and tore off his right hand and foot. The bishop died, but before burial he three times rose from the grave to say that he was damned forever (Tubach 1969; no. 337). One Bonn canon never bowed before the altar in a church dedicated to St Peter and John the Baptist. And one night the Baptist appeared to him in a dream, bitterly reproaching him for disrespect and pride. Not satisfied with rebukes, the saint kicked the canon so hard in the stomach that the latter woke up beside himself with fear and pain. From that hour he began to ail, and he soon died. The canon's name, adds Caesarius of Heisterbach, was also John, and it was apparently for this reason that the saint felt himself particularly offended.[94] In the same way four of the patron saints of a monastery in Soissons, outraged by the impious encroachments of the count of Lotharingia, appeared to him in a dream and cruelly beat him: the sinner woke up covered with bruises (Geary 1979: 39). Patron saints of

churches and monasteries were not slow to punish people who encroached
on property given to them.

Even the Virgin and Christ himself conduct themselves no less aggress-
ively in several instances. A canon who had a vision of the Virgin before
death told his companions about it, for which he received an appreciable
slap in the face, unseen by anybody else. The reason for the Virgin's
anger, suggests Caesarius of Heisterbach, is that the dying man revealed
his vision out of vainglory. The Virgin also gave a good smack to a nun
who was on the verge of succumbing to the sinful enticements of a cleric.
In punishment for calling an old icon of the Madonna and Child a
'decrepit piece of junk', a noblewoman was condemned by the Virgin to
constant poverty. Deprived by her own son of all her property, the
woman became a beggar.[95]

Nor does Christ permit the Virgin to be insulted. When two gamblers
began to blaspheme and one of them abused God and his Mother, a
voice resounded, 'I could somehow endure abusing me, but I will not
suffer dishonouring my Mother.' And straightaway the sinner received
a wound from which he died.[96] In a Narbonne church there was an icon
of Christ crucified, and Jesus appeared to the priest Basil with the
request that his nakedness be covered: 'You are all arrayed in your fine
outfits, but look at me naked'. The priest did not understand the vision's
meaning, although it was repeated a second time. The third time Jesus
beat the priest cruelly and threatened to kill him if the crucifixion was
not covered with a cloth.[97] A no less 'frightful and marvellous event'
happened to a monk whose habit it was to sleep during liturgy. One
night, when he was supposed to keep vigil and sing psalms with his
brethren, he was awakened by Christ, who came down from the altar
and gave him such a blow in the jaw that he died three days later.[98]

Christ the Judge, rewarding every man at the Last Judgment for his
sins or merits, is a majestic figure, corresponding to notions of God's
justice ruling in the world. But a God dealing out slaps and correcting
sinners with kicks produces a strange impression. In addition to everything else, one is struck by the contradiction between the contemplative
immobility and solemn repose befitting heavenly dwellers and the bustling
dynamism of these same personages in stories of their violent exploits.
How is one to reconcile these slaps, blows and murders with the doctrine
of mercy, humility and love towards one's neighbour? John the Baptist
was usually depicted humbly kneeling by the side of Christ's throne or
bearing the cross, but listeners of such stories were supposed to imagine
him swearing and kicking. It is no easy task to move from contemplating
the crucified Christ, whose tortured and bloody body hangs lifeless on
the cross, to the figure of him with fists raised over the sinner's head.

Is all this blasphemy? Not at all; these are 'frightful and marvellous occurrences'. I think that ultimately such scenes are phenomena of the same order as the tendency of vision stories to interpret the Other World according to the image and likeness of the earthly world – to populate it with souls which are indistinctly similar to living bodies and to subordinate it to the flow of earthly time. For saints and Christ punishing insults follow the logic of the earthly world, and they act just as the people among whom these stories were current would have behaved. This is the unconscious lowering of the great and sacred to the small and earthly.

The instillation of piety and righteousness through slaps, mutilations and the saints' physical force are telling pieces of evidence for the character of lay religious perceptions. To the clergy it seemed most effective not to try to influence the emotional state of the faithful directly but to attempt to reorganize his internal world through the most primitive means of external activity, such as beatings and threats of reprisal in this or the Other World. Emphasis on palpable 'argumentation', which was in complete accord with medieval man's general inclination to substitute the corporeal for the spiritual and the visual for the abstract, parallels the aims of the clergy. These goals, as we already know, appear very clearly in the penitentials with their tariffs for sin and their penances, which were primarily physical deprivations and punishments. That these excesses induced fear and confusion in believers, but apparently did not lead them to doubt God's holiness, indicates that these are not only Gospel paradigms but Old Testament ones as well. An angered God intervenes in human affairs with blows, and the misfortunes brought down upon people make them submissive. A flood in Frisia that killed more than a hundred thousand people was apparently caused by the fact that one of the Frisians was guilty of sacrilege: he threw a consecrated host on the ground. The Virgin appeared to an abbot and announced that for the insult done to her son the country would be inundated.[99] Through the example of such a link between an enormous natural calamity and the transgression of one individual one can notice that in the popular version of medieval Christianity there was a certain affinity to Old Testament principles. The more spiritual religion of the New Testament was less accessible to the masses. Medieval religiosity wavered on the border between the 'punitive' religion of Yahweh and the loving religion of Christ.

The simultaneous spiritualization of the bearers of the sacred principle and their 'secularization' and bringing down to earth, which border on profanation and farce, was a recurrent feature of medieval consciousness.[100] This suggests once more that we are not dealing with occasional 'deviations' from orthodoxy or the vulgarization of lofty ideas by a population immersed in ignorance, stubbornly holding on to pagan traditions and inclined to naturalistic misinterpretations of Christianity. Rather, we encounter here an organic feature of a religiosity that perceived the sacred elevated in unity with the 'lower' and the crudely material. A fighting Virgin, a kicking saint and a violent Christ lost nothing of their holiness in the eyes of believers. These exploits inspired terror and only intensified worship. The paradoxical combination of the highest benevolence with extreme cruelty, maximal distantiation with closest proximity, brings us once again to the medieval grotesque.

Medieval Latin literature abounds in the kinds of stories discussed above. Some of them are funny, humourous and even playful, anticipating Renaissance novellas. But those short stories are completely secular in both tone and content, whereas narratives of clerical authors have a completely different character. Religious content, perceived extremely seriously, is transformed in them into the artistic in order to serve didactic goals. Both appear in a contradictory, even impossible paradoxical unity: paradoxical, because art assumes imagination, fantasy and a relativizing of the truth, while sermons require absolute faith and do not permit fancy. The grotesque nature of medieval culture seems to be precisely in this union.

The main content of the *exempla* is the miracle. These stories were also styled *miracula*. The *miraculum* is an unusual phenomenon, a violation of the usual course of nature, and therefore something marvellous and wonderful that evokes great interest, but usually not doubts. The miracle unites for a moment both worlds: it takes place here on earth, but it is worked by otherworldly powers. Caesarius of Heisterbach writes: 'We call a miracle that which takes place contrary to the customary, natural course of things, for which reason we marvel at it. There is nothing in a miracle that contradicts higher causes.'[101] The miracle is a breach of everyday life by essences hidden beyond its borders. Thanks to the miracle, eternity is manifested in human time. Precisely because a miracle overcomes the dissociation of the two worlds and reveals their connection, it possesses a higher truth and persuasiveness. The miracle seemingly 'explains' God's world in its integrity; it reveals it 'all at once' in those 'compartments' which in everyday life are in opposition.

In theology the earthly city and the heavenly city are completely separated, but in popular literature about miracles they are extremely close, in constant contact and association. It is possible to visit the Other World and to return to this world, and death can seem like sleep, for the path to the Other World is sometimes open in both directions. When the monk Mengos was dying, the abbot ordered him: 'Don't you dare die, Mengos, until I get there', but he had already stopped breathing.

The abbot repeated his command, and Mengos returned to life, 'as if he had woken up from a deep sleep'. He said that he had already been in paradise. Only after he had related his otherworldly vision did the abbot allow him to go in peace, and Mengos died.[102] The two worlds were so close in the medieval mind that some people even managed to carry on feuds of a typically earthly character in the Other World. Thus, two insolent peasants, whose families were implacable enemies, died at the same time and in accordance with God's will were buried in the same grave. But even there they continued to fight, kicking and scratching each other, until they were separated into different graves.[103]

The saint belongs at once to both worlds, since already while alive he is a 'citizen' of the heavenly city. Christ suddenly descends from the altar or is revealed in a host in his physical aspect; he, like his Mother and the Apostles, can at any given moment visit the living, offering comfort and the promise of otherworldly blessings or bringing reproaches and rebukes, even beatings or death. Satan and his demons are active among people, lying in wait for them at every step, sometimes literally tripping them up, and always ready to carry off a gaping soul into hell.[104] Without particular difficulty, availing themselves of the smallest negligence, demons can penetrate into a man and take control of him. They can make him do whatever they want: commit outrages, quietly converse with companions, prophesy, fight with priests or unmask unrepentant sinners.

Because the two worlds, despite their polarity, are so interwoven, their different laws are also difficult to distinguish. Not only a man's moral, but also his physical condition depends on otherworldly powers. Man commits sins at the devil's bidding, but illnesses are also thought to be inflicted by him. As a consequence, the best healer is a saint and the most effective remedies are not the ones suggested by physicians, but sacred objects and sacraments.[105] In a similar way natural phenomena are most easily explained as the intervention of either good or evil forces: harvests and good weather are from God, just as misfortune and adversity are either the Lord's wrath or the devil's machination.[106] Many miraculous things happen in the world, not all of which can be explained in terms of natural causes. I mentioned above the flood in Frisia in which more than one hundred thousand people perished for the guilt of one sinner. In another place hostility flared up between two families of knights. The representatives of one family went so far as to stain a church with the blood of their enemies, and the Lord punished the sacrilege: immediately the kinsmen of the slain slaughtered almost all the murderers.[107] Such is the logic explaining various phenomena.

The 'synthesizing' view of the world, uniting the Other World with this one, permeated not only the fable, epos and myth, but also the salvific stories of the clergy about saints, good and evil spirits and otherworldly visions. The opposition of the earthly and heavenly worlds and the antagonism of the forces of good and evil are not removed by this view. The one world cannot be conceived without the other; they can only be thought of together, in a tense, unending mutual interaction and hostility. As a result, the intimacy and interweaving of 'high' and 'low' generate grotesque situations. Medieval fantasy erases all the borders between the possible and the impossible, between the beautiful and the ugly, between the serious and the comic. More precisely, these boundaries are constantly being violated: everything is restored in order to be repudiated or cast into doubt. In this ceaseless movement from opposition to blending and from blending to opposition lies the force field of the activity of 'grotesque thinking'.

The righteous, whose joy in paradise is intensified many times over from contemplating the sinners suffering in hell; faithful servants of the Lord indiscriminately killing heretics and Catholics in the hope that the Almighty will separate them; lepers' snot turning into pearls after being licked by a pious priest;[108] a demon refusing to break a promise to a bishop, who in turn does not hesitate to deceive him; fanatical worshippers of a saint making an attempt on his life in order to secure for themselves the valuable relics; a demon faithfully serving a knight and desirous of giving a bell to a church; wild animals and birds 'praying for absolution' from saints; executioners helplessly frozen with swords raised to decapitate a saint; thieves penetrating a saint's tomb and unable to tear loose from the saint's arms which promise both punishment and forgiveness; a monk who dies forgetting about a penny he owed and returns to life only to pay off the debt; a hunting dog unjustly killed by its master coming to be venerated by the peasants as a holy martyr and healer of children (Schmitt 1979) – such episodes are abundantly strewn throughout medieval Latin popular literature. Is this not the ambivalent and paradoxical grotesque that combines so fantastically things and phenomena in direct opposition, material and spiritual, elevated and base, immobile and dynamic, inverting all established and customary notions of the tragic and the playful? Inverting and then restoring everything to its place. This grotesque can evoke merriment, but it does not destroy fear. Rather, it unites them in some contradictory feeling in which we are supposed to assume both sacred trepidation and merry laughter as an indissoluble pair.

But the medieval grotesque is contained not only in the specific relation of laughter and fear. The most important thing in it is the paradoxical intimacy and confrontation of the earthly with the Other World, when each of these worlds is alien to the one opposing it. Medieval grotesque is not opposed to the sacred and does not retreat from it; it rather represents one of the forms of drawing near to the sacred. It simultaneously profanes the sacred and confirms it. As a jesting couplet cited by Karsavin goes, 'Ego et ventrem meum purgabo et Deum laudabo' (1915: 39). The very essence of medieval grotesque is contained in this bowel movement expressed in liturgical language.

The grotesque in modern art and literature is a conscious creative device intentionally demolishing or breaking down the usual structure of a phenomenon and creating a particular fantastic world. This grotesque is a departure from the 'normal' view and pursues the goal of more sharply and deeply revealing the contrasts of life. Both the creators of the grotesque and their audience are fully aware of its conventionality.

Medieval grotesque is not an artistic device and not the fruit of the cultivated intention of the author. It is rather the norm for viewing the world. I exclude from consideration here explicit satire and parody, which certainly existed in the medieval period, and should like to focus attention only on those aspects of 'grotesque thought' which are revealed in the edifying works addressed to the widest circles of society, where satiric imagination is scarcely possible and where the aims of parody could not be pursued. We should concentrate on the grotesque way of thinking organically inherent in medieval society. It is an essential quality of the medieval world-view, just as integral a feature of man's attitude towards reality as his propensity towards the sacred. Therefore, medieval grotesque is always ambivalent and represents the attempt to apprehend the world in two hypostases – sacred and secular, sublime and base, serious and playful. Bakhtin indicates the enormous significance of grotesque in culture outside the church, in carnival and farce, but he reduced it to the principle of laughter and comedy. By contrast, my material suggests the hypothesis that the grotesque was a style of medieval man's thinking in general, embracing the entire culture, beginning from the lower, folkloric level and continuing up to the level of official church culture. Although I do not propose to bring these aspects completely together and fuse them into one, I nevertheless believe that between them there was much in common.

The differences between Bakhtin's interpretation of medieval grotesque and mine are largely conditioned by the various layers of the material we use. Bakhtin takes primarily the culture of the 'waning of the Middle Ages', and his chief source for analysing medieval and Renaissance comic elements is Rabelais. But the carnival element so impressively characterized by Bakhtin was localized in the late medieval city. I have used Latin literary works of the early and high Middle Ages which appeared for the most part in monasteries and episcopal residences and were addressed to the lower clergy and the laity, the majority of whom were peasants. It is possible that the differences between us arise to some degree from our studying different historical phases. My material does not refer to carnival and contains no evidence for its existence, even if there are, as mentioned earlier, indications of 'carnival before carnival'. The elements of the universe lying at the basis of carnival were still dispersed throughout the culture, whereas at a later stage of development they would crystallize in definite points of time and space and give carnival its well-known classic forms.

The differences in interpretation of the grotesque principle in medieval culture are also undoubtedly bound up with the conditions of our material's origin and existence. Popular grotesque, according to Bakhtin, lowers the serious and through laughter seemingly overcomes it; the element of laughter is opposed to the official-sacred. But such an attitude towards the serious and sacred was hardly 'primary'; rather, it was the result of the decay of an organic stage of religiosity. It could not have prevailed during the flowering of medieval religious culture, which embraced both the official and the unofficial spheres. In those centuries, in contrast to the decline of the Middle Ages, the grotesque assumed not the humourous but the serious aspect of the sacred. The specific relation of 'high' and 'low', and the unexpectedness of their combination – in the treatment of 'holy simplicity' and the everyday miracle – were the productive sources of medieval grotesque. The sacred is not cast into doubt here; it is rather strengthened by the principle of laughter, its double and companion, its constantly resounding echo.[109]

The further transformation of the didactic genre of medieval Latin literature is necessarily beyond the bounds of this study. In the later Middle Ages the closeness and even blending of the sacred with the secular were further intensified, though they led not to the spiritualization of life but to profanation, to the disappearance of religious content from traditional forms, to the 'constant, incessant lowering of the eternal to the finite,' and to the substitution of superstition for faith (Huizinga 1969: 214ff.).

I emphasized the need for particular caution in attempting to trace back to the distant past the 'classical form' of carnival as it existed in the sixteenth to the nineteenth century. Considering such facts as the artificial restoration of carnival in a number of large European cities (Cologne in 1823, Nürnberg in 1843, Nice in the mid-nineteenth century), modern scholars are increasingly unwilling to see archaic 'survivals' in customs and institutions which developed quite late. For example, carnival and the holiday of the Maypole had already been mentioned for some time (Moser 1961; Rosenfeld 1969). Y. M. Bercé (1976: 9) maintains that the thesis about the origins of rural holidays is a myth (cf. Goubert 1982: 295). In fact, the majority of elements of village culture emerged only as late as the reigns of Louis XV and Louis XVI.

In regard to my comments on the image of the simpleton, I should like to repeat that it is clearly two-sided. On the one hand, throughout the greater part of this book uneducated, simple people figure under the name *simplices*, in contrast to educated, erudite clerics and schoolmen. Our authors called *simplices* and *idiotae* those who were illiterate (at least in Latin) and incapable of entering into direct contact with Scripture, patristic literature, and the works of medieval thinkers. Most of the writings in the didactic–edificatory genre were created to cater for these 'simpletons'. Learned people disapproved of ignorance and highly esteemed their own learning. On the other hand, I also adduce material depicting the *idiota* as one of the elect. Not 'rhetoricians and philosophers', but 'fishermen and shepherds', were chosen by the Lord to carry his word, and the extreme simplicity (apparent stupidity) of some of them was transformed into sanctity.

These two seemingly contradictory images suggest that the simpleton was not only the object of the clergy's homiletic efforts, but also an integral and essential embodiment of medieval culture and an expression of the contradictoriness and grotesqueness of medieval thought. In order to address the faithful with a sermon or edifying *exemplum*, the clergy had mentally to adopt their point of view. Was this way of thought merely alien to them, or did they contain the simpleton in themselves? One must assume that the dialogue between the simpleton and the scholar is inherent in the mind of the theologian, of the university professor, of the prince of the church.

These considerations are connected with the observations of V. S. Bibler, who, after reading this book, insisted on the necessity of distinguishing between the real illiterate parishioner and the literary image of the *simplex–idiota*. If I understand him correctly, one can trace the path from the 'extra-cultural' *idiota* to the image of the simpleton by moving from those 'low' genres of medieval Latin literature which I have analysed in this book to the works of 'high' medieval literature. But this is another tale, for another scholar, for another night.

AFTERWORD

When the time came for Tristram Shandy to come into the world new mishaps were added to the ones of the previous nine months. Called to deliver the baby, Dr Slop could not untie the knots of his instrument bag, since his servant Obadiah had tangled them. During the futile attempts to cut the cords the doctor cut his finger badly and burst out with invectives aimed at Obadiah, whereupon Mr Shandy, whose habit of philosophizing was not stifled by the troubles accompanying the impending birth of his heir, remembered a list of curses from his collection of literary rarities. He brought this document to the attention of the unsuspecting 'papist' Dr Slop, who involuntarily read it aloud to the accompaniment of Uncle Toby whistling 'Lillabullero' and the intensifying bustle above in Mrs Shandy's room. The eleventh chapter of the third book of *Tristram Shandy* contains the genuine text of an excommunication formula composed by the Rochester bishop Ernulf at the beginning of the twelfth century. The fact that Slop adds Obadiah's name to the formula, the situation in which the formula is read, and the occasion which reminded Mr Shandy about it are all comical, as a result of which the excommunication itself sounds 'Shandyesque'.

Sterne was not the first to use ecclesiastical curses for satirical purposes. In John Donne's poems and elegies such ritual curses are frequent and clearly shocking to Catholic practices: they are hurled at potential violators of his mistress. But an excommunication formula could also be parodied in the Middle Ages, just as the mass, the Gospel and other sacred texts were parodied. The tradition was an old one, although its meaning had changed. The majority of Englishmen in the seventeenth and eighteenth centuries were not Catholics, and for Mr Shandy (as also for the Anglican pastor Sterne) Ernulf's formula was apparently no more than a curiosity. But medieval burlesques of church rites took place within the same world-view as generated those rites, and therefore, despite all their 'carnivalization', they had a completely different character. Medieval man, even while blaspheming and profaning, 'praised the Lord', and yet he could not exceed the limits of his religious world-view. At most, he could deviate from orthodoxy or invert it and fall into heresy. Non-orthodox use of an anathema hardly deprived it of its seriousness. The attitude towards the word, particularly towards ritualistic formalized speech, was essentially different in the Middle Ages from what it has been in modernity. Hamlet's 'Words, words, words...' would be completely foreign to medieval people.

A word was just as effective as a deed. Prayer acts automatically, because it is uttered. In attacking church ceremonial the Waldensians asserted that the sacraments could be performed by a dog, if it were capable of pronouncing the necessary words. It was not for nothing that the devil went around churches collecting in a sack unpronounced syllables of the psalms. Verbal formulas had an obligatory character. An oath uttered correctly was considered inviolable, but it lacked force if pronounced incomplete or with a lapse of tongue. Belief in the harmful effects of curses was just as strong. When directed against a man, a word was reckoned capable of bringing him benefit or harm. A medieval Icelandic law strictly punished those who composed poems about other people without their knowledge, for it could prove to be an encroachment on their well-being and health. The magic of the word, well known to ethnologists, was widespread in medieval Europe. A barbarian survival? Of course. But references to 'survivals' never explain anything. What is important is the context in which these vestiges are preserved, the reasons why they are preserved and the function which these fragments of the old culture fulfil in the new one.

Let us return to the excommunication formula used by Sterne:

> By the power of almighty God the Father, the Son, and the Holy Spirit, and of all the holy canons, the holy and pure Mother of God Virgin Mary, and all the celestial virtues, angels, archangels, thrones, dominions, powers, cherubim and seraphim, and of all the holy patriarchs, prophets, and of all the holy apostles and evangelists, and of the holy innocents, who in sight of the Lamb are found worthy to sing the new song, and of the holy martyrs, and holy confessors, and holy virgins, and together with all the saints and elect of God, we excommunicate this sinner and malefactor, we anathematize him, and we place him beyond the threshold of the holy church of God, so that he be given over unto eternal punishments with Dathan and Abiram and with those who say to the Lord God, 'Depart from us, we desire none of they ways'.[1] And as a fire is quenched by water, so let the light of him be put out for evermore, unless it shall repent him and make satisfaction. Amen.
>
> May he be cursed by God the Father, who made man! May he be cursed by the Son of God, who suffered for us! May he be cursed by the Holy Spirit, which was sent down to us in holy baptism! May he be cursed by the holy cross, which Christ mounted for our salvation in triumph over his enemy! May he

be cursed by the holy Mother of God and ever-virgin Mary!
May he be cursed by St Michael, the defender of holy souls!
May he be cursed by all the angels and archangels, principalities
and powers, and all the heavenly hosts! May he be cursed by
the venerable assembly of the patriarchs and prophets! May he
be cursed by St John the forerunner and baptizer of Christ!
May he be cursed by St Peter, St Paul, St Andrew, and all
Christ's apostles and other disciples, and also the four evangel-
ists, who converted the universal world by their preaching! May
he be cursed by the glorious company of martyrs and confessors,
who by their good works have been found pleasing to God!
May he be cursed by the choirs of holy virgins, who have
despised the vanity of the world for the sake of Christ's honour!
May he be cursed by all the saints, who from the beginning of
the world and to the end of ages are found pleasing to God!
May he be cursed by heaven and earth and everything holy
abiding on them!

Having begun with an exhaustive list of heavenly powers, from God
himself through all the saints, in complete conformity with the teaching
of Pseudo-Dionysius on the sacred hierarchy, the author of the 'Rochester
text' seemingly forgets about the sinner's soul and heaps an avalanche
of curses on his body:

May he be cursed wherever he be found, whether at home or in
the field, on a highway or a path, in a forest or in water, or in
church! May he be cursed in living and in dying, in eating and
drinking, while hungry, thirsty, fasting, drowsing, sleeping,
keeping vigil, walking, standing, sitting, lying, working, resting,
urinating, defecating and bleeding! May he be cursed in all the
faculties of body! May he be cursed inwardly and outwardly!
May he be cursed in the hair of his head! May he be cursed in
his brains! May he be cursed in his forehead, temples, brow,
ears, eyebrows, eyes, cheeks, jaw, nostrils, teeth, both foreteeth
and molars, lips, throat, shoulders, wrists, arms, hands, fingers,
mouth, breast, heart, all his intestines right down to the stomach,
hips, groin, thighs, genitals, shins, feet and toenails! May he be
cursed in all the joints and articulations of his members from
the top of his head to the soles of his feet! May there be no
soundness in him! May he be cursed by Christ, the Son of the
living God, in all the glory of his greatness, and may heaven
with all the powers which move therein rise up against him to
damn him, unless he repent and make satisfaction! Amen. So be
it, so be it! Amen. (Liebermann 1960, I: 439ff.).

In its detailedness and belief in the magical efficacy of the word this church formula, leaving the sinner 'not a single living place', fully rivals barbarian magical oaths. However, it was composed not at the dawn of the Middle Ages amidst a half-barbarian population, but during the 'Renaissance of the twelfth century', and its author was an English bishop, a contemporary of Anselm of Canterbury, the 'father of scholasticism'. The list's 'learned' thoroughness and sequentiality are completely in keeping with the spirit of contemporary scholasticism.

In an earlier eleventh-century formula, along with the curses extending to all organs and parts of the sinner's body, there is the following text:

> May he be cursed by the sun, moon, stars, birds, fish of the sea, four-legged creatures, grasses, trees, and all of Christ's creations! May his corpse be left to be devoured by dogs and birds of prey, and let him remain unburied! May the Lord send down on him hunger and thirst, anger, torments, and the assaults of evil angels, until he comes into the depths of hell, where there is eternal darkness, inexhaustible fire, eternal smoke, and grief without consolation, and where from day to day every sort of evil grows!

Then come curses in the names of biblical patriarchs and prophets, but even that is not enough. The formula continues: 'May his sons be orphans and his wife a widow! May his sons be driven from their dwellings and shudder in their destitution!' (Liebermann 1960: 1, 437)

Excommunication was supposed to set the universe against the sinner, from the sun and planets down to the grass of the earth. The unity of man with nature, in whose function he participates directly according to the popular view of the world, is dissolved, along with social bonds and connections with higher powers. The Gospel spirit did not inspire the composers of these formulas, but rather the spirit of Yahweh, who severely punishes the disobedient, even into the seventh generation.

Formulas of excommunication were not written down for amusement. They were the most powerful means of the church's influence on unsubmissive sinners, and as a rule it was an effective means. It was one of the most frightful punishments that could befall a man: to be excommunicated from the church meant to be declared outside society; all connections were severed, and the sinner's soul was doomed to otherworldly torture and perdition. Churchmen who composed such formulas took care that the curses they contained produced a corresponding impression on the faithful. The bishop, surrounded by twelve priests holding candles, read the text aloud in church, and as the formula was read they threw the candles down and trampled them to symbolize the sinner's deprivation of the light of salvation. In the expression of

Marc Bloch (1961: 87), fear of hell was a powerful 'social fact' of medieval life. As a result, we cannot explain these collections of frightful curses by reference to 'pagan survival'. In any case, these same curses continued to resound for many centuries thereafter, right down to the nineteenth century.

Do not the astonishing grotesque symbiosis of magical harmful formulas with purely scholastic circumstantiality and logicality, and the combination of biblical damnation (Deut 27, 28) with teaching about the divine hierarchy, represent the product of a particular 'meeting' of two cultural traditions – the folkloric, 'magical' with the 'learned', clerical? It may be termed fanaticism, bigotry, obscurantism (Shejnman 1977: 74), but it would be an unjustified simplification to reduce everything to the single-minded obscurantism of churchmen. Their power and influence are exaggerated by those scholars who, in accordance with a venerable tradition going back to the Enlightenment, construct a picture of relations between the medieval clergy and the people on the model of a trickster and a credulous fool. There certainly was enough deception and gullibility, but it is hardly possible to understand anything in the history of medieval culture and religiosity by adhering to such facile conceptions.

The study of excommunication formulas shows how over time their text was filled out with new details and made more circumstantial and systematized, how their logical proportion and universality increased, reaching an apogee in the twelfth and thirteenth centuries, and how moreover the anathema acquired an even greater bloodthirstiness (Little 1979). The composers and redactors of excommunication texts attempted to impart to them the most effective form, and for this it was necessary to turn to the stock of ancient popular incantations and to the same black magic which the church condemned and persecuted.[2]

An anathema was frightening. It was supposed to shake, terrorize, discipline and overcome the sinner. And we know that few of those who were excommunicated could endure the power of such a damnation, which set against them all the heavenly powers, nature and man, and created around them an unbroken zone of alienation. I intentionally used this formula in Sterne's comic setting in order to highlight more strongly the inadequacy of its perception by a man standing beyond the limits of the medieval sacred–magical sphere. This is 'another culture' already foreign to us; it is 'other'.

In qualifying these phenomena as manifestations of a 'foreign', 'other' culture with its own inherently specific notions and values, let us beware of looking down on it. (This arrogant, derisive view is not foreign to Mr Shandy.) Caution is scarcely superfluous if one recalls how frequently every sort of backwardness, intolerance and obscurantism is labelled 'medieval', no matter where it occurs or for what reason it is expressed. It would be much more productive to interpret medieval culture as 'another' culture, admitting that it is not our culture and that the criteria for evaluating it must be sought within itself. Only with such an approach can one count on entering into a dialogue with it. A dialogue assumes not a view from the top to the bottom and not a condemnation, but amazement and interest in understanding the interlocutor and deciphering his language. Such an approach allows one to see the human content in a past culture. It shakes off the unhealthy inclination to see in history a catalogue of errors and mistakes which have been only now overcome. Let us resign ourselves to the fact that medieval culture is other, and let us attempt to understand that 'other'.

I have before me Axel Munthe's *The Story of San Michele*, the notes of a Swedish physician who moved at the turn of the century to Italy and lived among its people. On Capri he had a house built by the local inhabitant Mastro Nicola. Once on Good Friday Munthe saw Mastro Nicola and his children continuing to work:

> Of course they knew how anxious I was to go on with the work full speed, but I would never have dreamt to ask them to work on Good Friday. Indeed it was kind of them, I told them I was grateful. Mastro Nicola looked at me with evident surprise and said that it was no festa to-day.
>
> 'No holiday to-day?' Did he not know that it was Good Friday, the day of the crucifixion of our Lord Jesus Christ? '*Va bene*,' said Mastro Nicola, 'but Jesus Christ was not a saint.'
>
> 'Of course He was a saint, the greatest Saint of all.'   'But not so great as Sant'Antonio, who has done more than one hundred miracles. How many miracles has Gesù Cristo done?' he asked with a malicious look at me.
>
> Nobody knew better than I that Sant'Antonio was not easy to beat on miracles, what greater miracle could he have made than bringing me back to his village? Avoiding Mastro Nicola's question I said that with all honor due to Sant'Antonio he was but a man while Jesus Christ was the Son of our Lord in Heaven who in order to save us all from hell had suffered death on the Cross this very day.
>
> 'It is not true,' Mastro Nicola said resuming his digging with great vigour. 'They put him to death yesterday to shorten the functions in church.' (Munthe 1930: 343–4)

Let us recall the doubts, noted above, of the people of a completely different age as to the sanctity of John the Baptist, who was not glorified by miracles, and the resigned judgment of Jacopo da Varagine: people are more inclined to venerate the saints close to them than a distant and unintelligible God.

But let us read more of Munthe's book. While visiting in Naples the pharmacy of Don Bartolo, famed for its highly sought-after anti-cholerical mixture, the effectiveness of which was guaranteed by San Gennaro, Munthe got to know the pharmacy's regular customers:

> Don Bartolo's clients seemed chiefly drawn from the many convents and churches round his street. There were always a couple of priests, monks or frati sitting on the chairs before the counter in animated discussion about the events of the day, and the last miracles performed by this or that saint and the efficacy of the various Madonnas. Seldom, very seldom, I heard the name of God mentioned, the name of His Son never. I once ventured to express my surprise to a shabby old Frate who was a particular friend of mine over this omission of Christ in their discussions. The old Frate made no secret of his private opinion that Christ owed His reputation solely to His having the Madonna for His Mother. As far as he knew, Christ had never saved anybody from cholera. His Blessed Mother had cried her eyes out for Him. What had He done for Her in return? 'Woman,' He said, 'what have I to do with thee?'
>
> '*Percio ha finito male*, that's why He came to a bad end.' (Munthe 1930: 163)

Already Thomas More in his *Dialogue about Tyndale* had mocked the plurality of Madonnas by retelling a conversation he had overheard: 'Out of all our Mothers of God I love most of all the Virgin of Walsingham', says one believer; but another one replies, 'But I love our Virgin of Ipswich' (Thomas 1971: 27). They were obviously worshipping not the Virgin, but an amulet, a miracle-working fetish, love for the Virgin depending on the curative power of this magic object.

What struck Munthe has also struck many others. It is not atheism or religious indifference: at the base of the opinions of both Munthe's characters, the simple builder and the monk, there is the same arrangement, I would say even polarization, of Christianity's sacred personages as we have observed in reading medieval Latin literature. Saints and the Virgin are intelligible and close.[3] One can expect help from them, and because they are perceived in a specific aspect, as the sources of miracles for which one can ask, they deserve veneration and enjoy love. The Trinity is distant and foreign. It is too abstract for this consciousness; one can 'do nothing' with it, since God and his Son do not accomplish any concrete miracles. The fourteenth-century English preacher John Bromyard tells of a shepherd who was asked if he knew the Father, Son and Holy Spirit. 'I know well the father and the son', he answered, 'for I tend their sheep, but the third fellow I don't know. There's nobody in our village with that name' (Thomas 1971: 165).[4] These people apparently had a certain durable stock of their own notions, and their world-view admitted only a definite, strictly limited selection of images and ideas – to everything else they remained deaf and unreceptive.

This recalls yet another modern piece of testimony seemingly drawn from another age. The peasants of Lucania, among whom the writer and artist Carlo Levi had to serve his exile under the Fascists, live outside history, 'in a shadowy land, that knows neither sin nor redemption', to which Christ did not come. In their world, subject to its own rhythm and time, there is no border between nature and people; everything is permeated by magical influences and the power of fate. Here the Madonna is venerated as an earth goddess, and 'church ceremonies become pagan rites, celebrating the existence of inanimate things, which the peasants endow with a soul, and the innumerable earthly divinities of the village'. The Italy which Levi saw is not even medieval, in his judgment, but such as it was in the time of Aeneas. He speaks of the confrontation of village and city, of a pre-Christian civilization and a post-Christian civilization (Levi 1947: 4, 117, 251).

Is it that the church failed to instil in the faithful even an elementary knowledge of Christianity? A difficult question, and simplistic answers are no longer satisfactory. Modern scholars are rather sceptical about the 'myth of the Christian Middle Ages'. This scepticism appeared in connection with a change in focus: medieval religious history, traditionally concentrating on the history of the church and its institutions, dogma, theology and mysticism, began to be dislodged in large measure by a sociology of religion and a transfer of the centre of attention from the 'top' to the bottom. The new works which this produced are primarily devoted to a period later than that which I am studying, but they must be taken into account.

J. Toussaert, the author of one of the chief studies of medieval religiosity, insistently cautions against an over-optimistic evaluation of the church's successes. The extensive material he collected regarding Flanders in the fourteenth, fifteenth and early sixteenth centuries, as well as evidence on church history in other countries of the West, suggests that the religious education of the masses was always very low, that the essential religious content remained incomprehensible, and that the faith of the majority of Europeans was primarily expressed in a mechanical performance of rituals. Medieval man did not choose to be a Christian; he was born and lived in this atmosphere, but his religious conduct, as a rule, was automatic. Toussaert (1960: 845) quotes the verdict of Gabriel Le Bras: in the history of the Catholic church there was no 'Great Age', the world was never Christian. Toussaert recalls the words of the outstanding Dutch historian Huizinga: '...the church struggled and preached in vain'.

Following Toussaert, J. Delumeau also shares Le Bras's scepticism: the 'Christian Middle Ages' are a myth, and hence arguments about the 'dechristianization' of Europe with the transition to modernity are also mistaken. This Christian folk religiosity existed along with magic and an 'animistic consciousness'; the average European was Christianized only superficially, and there is no reason to see the highpoint of Christianity in the twelfth and thirteenth centuries or its decline in the following centuries. The Reformation and Counter-Reformation, with all their conflicts, promoted a more consistent Christianization of the European population and a spiritualization of religiosity, at least in the cities. From Delumeau's point of view, the gap between urban Christianity and a rural religiosity poorly concealing the paganism of the basic mass of the populace was essential (Delumeau 1971: 227ff., 236ff., 243ff., 248ff.). Both the Reformation and the Counter-Reformation represented an energetic struggle against the polytheism and magic with which the medieval church had had to be reconciled in one way or another. In this endeavour both Luther and Loyola proceeded from the presupposition that the mass of the people was un-Christian. Thus, the period of the sixteenth to the eighteenth century is a period not of 'dechristianization', but of a 'second Christianity', more total and binding than the 'first', the medieval one (Delumeau 1975: 57ff.). Delumeau (1971: 330) concludes his book on Catholicism in early modern Europe with this question: was not Christianity under the *ancien régime* a 'mixture of practices and beliefs frequently far from the teaching of the Gospels'?

In turn, J. Ferté, who studied the religious life of the peasantry in the region of seventeenth-century Paris, asserts the superficiality of popular belief, the scarcity of living piety and an external adherence to rituals and gestures (Ferté 1962). Another scholar of popular religiosity, R. Manselli (1975: 194), is more cautious in his conclusions, but nevertheless speaks of an 'increasingly aggravated drama of misunderstanding' between the church and the people in the thirteenth century. F. Rapp evaluates the situation of the fourteenth and fifteenth centuries more 'optimistically' than does Delumeau. He suggests that the high spirituality of the educated people was diffused among common believers, who belonged to a 'civilization of another type', devoid of literacy, and although as a result Christianity was subjected to vulgarization it did not lose its 'authenticity'. The 'renewal' of Christianity in the sixteenth century was prepared in the preceding two centuries (Rapp 1971).

E. Le Roy Ladurie discovered roughly the same picture on the border between Spain and France at the turn of the fourteenth century: Catholicism, assimilated superficially and mainly from the external, ritualistic side, coexisted in popular consciousness with pre-Christian folklore and 'peasant naturalism'. The sole thing that really troubled these people was fear of otherworldly perdition. This was apparently the reason that many of Montaillou's inhabitants accepted Catharism (Le Roy Ladurie 1975). J. Sumption (1976) also writes about the dominance in the medieval village of a magical interpretation of religious rites and about the people's superstitions and superficial understanding of the basic elements of Christianity.

Noting the many differences between scholars, especially between Rapp and Delumeau, A. Vauchez hopes that their opinions do not exclude one another and depend to a significant degree on the point of view from which they have chosen to survey the material of the later Middle Ages. In this instance something else interests me: all these specialists concur in thinking that the Middle Ages proper, which preceded the age they studied, was not a time of undivided dominance by official Christianity in the spiritual life of the masses. But it is important here not to overlook Vauchez's observation: those who speak of an 'incomplete' Christianization or even of an 'unchristianized' Europe at the end of the Middle Ages obviously proceed from an implicitly assumed model of 'pure religion'.[5] But there are certainly other, more historically reliable conceptions of Christianity, including an 'impure' religion, not devoid of ambiguity. It is to such a conception that Vauchez attributes the 'religion of the earth', permeated by magic, the religiosity of the peasantry, parallels to which are not difficult to find in modern developing countries where Christianity has recently been introduced. This syncretism is alogical to Cartesian minds, but real at the level of daily practice. 'Religion of the chapel' *vs* 'religion of the meadows', learned religion in conflict with religion of simple folk – such is the conclusion flowing from all the recent studies of medieval religiosity. It remains to establish the exact contents of both (Vauchez 1973: 1048-50).

But that is precisely the point! Without imposing on the Middle Ages an ideal type of 'Christian belief', and not being satisfied with an élitist interpretation of the latter, one should reveal patiently and attentively the spiritual life of medieval man, the common man, the 'idiot'; and the sole way of demonstrating his culture is the systematic study of the sources.

Since the time of Karsavin, however, no essential advances in this field have been made. One cannot help noticing that even in recent studies on medieval popular religion few attempts are made to explore new layers of the sources. Their authors are satisfied with interpreting already-known material along the lines of their projects (Leclercq 1961; Delaruelle 1975; Vauchez 1975).[6] However, conclusions made by extrapolating from the condition of religiosity in the fourteenth to the sixteenth century, or from the carnival in the time of Rabelais, to the Middle Ages are rather problematic. The 'waning of the Middle Ages' is characterized by a series of new phenomena that do not belong to the preceding centuries: epidemics of fear and flagellation, immersion in mystical communion with God, the cult of the Mother of God, the spread of heresies, religious wars, hypertrophy of the image of death and obsession with ideas of Satan,[7] frenzied witch-hunts, the ferocity of the Inquisition, traffic in indulgences, and a break-down in the relative unity of church and society. These sketchy references may suffice to point to the dangers of not separating the cultural phenomena of the late Middle Ages from those of earlier periods. The questions of medieval popular culture must be answered by evidence from the period itself.

The method I have chosen to discover 'low-level' medieval culture, the separate analysis of certain genres, was imposed by the project itself. The danger for the historian is that he may take the evidence of the sources chosen by him for an authentic and comprehensive picture of the life he is studying. But any historical text contains information only about a certain fragment, an aspect, of reality, which will be determined in large measure by its genre and function. This 'intelligible lattice' is laid over the chaotic picture of a changing real life; only what corresponds to the source's internal structure is selected, while what remains outside is disregarded.

A study should conform to the internal logic of the texts united by the genre and should reveal that logic as much as possible. The attitude of the author of a medieval Latin literary work towards his audience was to a significant degree determined by the work's purpose and form: sermons and hagiography were to edify; a penitential served as a handbook for confessors; *exempla* achieved a didactic effect if they were entertaining and memorable; and Honorius of Autun's theological vulgarization was intended to offer a clear and intelligible exposition of dogmas. We have seen that the same motif and subject might receive unequal interpretations in works of different genres. The devil of the *Memorable Histories* and hagiography has little in common with that of the *Elucidarium*: in the one case the devil is not only frightful and perfidious, but occasionally both amusing and simple-hearted, while in the other he is completely terrifying. The eschatology of official religion, attributing otherworldly rewards and punishments to the 'end of time' and the Last Judgment, was in poor accord with the depiction of hell and paradise found in otherworldly visions.

Despite their important differences, the texts discussed in this book have much in common. All of them ultimately served the church's attempts to educate the laity, and almost all grew out of the interaction of literary and oral culture. But we should not forget that these texts reveal to us a very limited horizon. The parishioners appear only in the author's perception. What we meet in our texts is the consciousness of the priest himself, even if it was orientated towards his audience. As a result, let us be cautious of building on the basis of a few texts an entire picture of early medieval popular culture. At most, I have managed to reveal to some degree one of its slices. Any attempt to absolutize such conclusions would lead to error.

The problem is to detect in texts of medieval Latin literature the mode of medieval man's world-view, the structures of consciousness hidden behind it, and the social behaviour determined by it. I have focussed not on the degree of piety and devotion to Gospel ideals and not on the question of the degree of the parishioners' understanding of the mass, but on their picture of the world and system of explaining it. Naturally, the problem of popular religiosity is not exhausted by this approach to the question, for medieval culture was permeated with religious notions, with faith in the supernatural and in the power of magic. However, in my opinion this religiosity can be understood only within the wider context of medieval man's general notions about the world and himself.

My field of vision has included not the mass movements of heresies or crusades, but rather everyday life, daily religious–cultural practice, and the salient habits of consciousness and forms of behaviour of routine existence. Nor have I focussed on the paroxysms of collective hysteria which occasionally shook society and which were accompanied by the surfacing of irrational forces; rather, I have concentrated on parish life, defined by the constants of the common man's spiritual orientation and the dominants of popular culture.

I also wanted to discern in texts of edifying literature the human environment to which they were addressed and in which preachers and confessors acted. In mutual influence with that environment their compositions and sermons acquired a genuine life and had their contents actualized. My focus was not on samples of medieval Latin literature, however interesting they are on their own, but on the zone of their contact with the mass of laymen, a contact in which two types of consciousness influenced each other – the learned consciousness of churchmen and the folkloric, magical consciousness of the people. This contact implied both a dialogue and a conflict. The dialogue consisted in attempting to convince parishioners of the need to live in accordance with ecclesiastical norms and to make them obedient to these; and so churchmen inevitably appealed to the stock of the people's customary notions passed on from generation to generation. But there was also conflict: this stock of collective notions and mental habits frequently contradicted the tenets of clerical, spiritual culture. Considering, then, this crucial problem, I am forced to reformulate somewhat my approach to medieval popular culture. The question should not be of two isolated cultures, but of the constant influence and opposition of these two, for they can only be correctly understood in their interaction. One should study these cultural traditions not within their respective confines, but in their strained interlacing.

What was the outcome of this dialogue–opposition? If one remains within the range of my sources, it is difficult to give a clear and unambiguous answer. But perhaps it is more important to focus on the very process of this interaction. I propose that the dialogue of the two traditions remained the basis of the cultural and religious development of the West. As long as clerical culture was capable of incorporating elements of popular traditions and beliefs and displaying a certain flexibility in its relation with the culture of the *simplices*, Christianity was vigorous. Then this symbiosis was broken down and confrontation took over. Popular religiosity was forced into heresy: the Inquisition was made the main instrument of church politics; and massive persecutions of heretics and witches began. The dialogue was over.[8]

The phenomena discussed in this book did not constitute a distinctly formulated, thought-out and structured ideology 'designed' to make both ends meet and eliminate clear unconformities; nor did they add up to a complete cultural system with a distinct character. It was rather an amorphous world-view, with a constantly surfacing stock of constants and archetypes, that could unreflectively combine in itself opposing notions and beliefs. This obscure discourse of magic and ritual, of grotesque and inversion does not yield to rational classification and translation into a language of logic which excludes contradictions.[9] The spirit of university learning and scholastic reasoning was quite distant from all this. But it may be that the reasons for its ineradicability lie precisely in the diffusiveness, openness and incompleteness of the popular perception of the world.

In opposition to medieval learned culture – the 'religion of the Book', which also perceived the world as a 'book', as a strictly organized hierarchic text needing to be read and commented upon – folkloric culture was characterized by the repudiation of a final rigid fixation. Social memory consolidated itself in this instance in oral form, probably not only because letters were inaccessible to the bearers of this tradition, but also because there was no need for writing it down. For securing it in texts would have meant imparting to it an invariable canonicity and ending its existence as a living, changing and renewing organism; and it would also have led to the 'alienation' of popular tradition from its bearers. Its oral character – the organic feature of the 'culture of idiots' – ought to be evaluated not as a deficiency or a weakness, but rather as a guarantee of its power and its capability of opposing learned culture in the ceaseless dialogue that imparted vitality to medieval culture as a whole.

Historians of aesthetics, philosophy, literature and science look at this culture with an arrogant incomprehension, or, more frequently, take no notice of it at all. The values they study lie on another plane. But an élitist understanding of culture is not the only possible one. Creators of artistic works do not live in isolation from their social environment and do not create without an audience. In every society there exist modes of viewing the world which may not be explicitly formulated, but which exercise enormous influence on actual life, including 'cultural figures'. Models of behaviour, not necessarily expressed in literary works, are no less effective. Habits of thinking, the vision of the world and the meaning attributed to actions cannot be understood only by studying unique cultural creations. The deeper layers of culture and the consciousness in which they are rooted possess their own rhythm, which does not correspond to that of 'high' culture. The historical–anthropological approach to medieval culture and its actual functioning in society is only now being taken up by medievalists.

The issue is important not only for the history of the Middle Ages. This aspect of medieval culture promises to bring us closer to understanding that common base out of which different types of pre-capitalist civilizations emerged. Intellectual, learned culture is different in each instance, but its anonymous substrata, which it influenced, and from which it undoubtedly recieved certain impulses, traditions and clichés of behaviour, reveal an astonishing similarity. Do we not approach here the 'invariant' of the history of culture? It seems legitimate to suggest that in the cultures of the ancient and the medieval worlds one should differentiate between relatively static, repetitive and seemingly 'extra-temporal' structures and dynamic, individualized and unique phenomena. These two sets do not function as separated and uncoordinated features, even if they may appear to the observer, falsely, as such. Exploring their specific essences would lead to a better understanding of a culture that was unique and highly original, while also containing constant, ever-reproducing matrices of consciousness and behaviour.

I could have embarked on an analysis of popular culture in the period of transition from the Middle Ages to early modernity, to demonstrate that the layer of medieval social consciousness I have studied remained essentially unchanged. But since the conclusions remain the same, I will refrain from citing specialists on the cultural history of the fifteenth to eighteenth centuries. It would also be necessary to devote a separate study to the crisis of popular culture that expressed itself in such a powerful socio-psychological paroxysm as witch-hunts, which were connected with the offensive of the absolute monarchy and the post-Reformation or post-Tridentine churches against the world-view of the lower strata of society (Macfarlane 1970; Thomas 1971; Kieckhefer 1976; Muchembled 1979a, 1979b; Naess 1982).

While re-reading this book in preparation for its translation, I sensed more sharply than before the inadequacy of some of its key concepts. Is it at all accurate to speak of the medieval 'grotesque'? Some attentive readers of the book objected to the use of this concept. I could call upon the authority of Bakhtin, who introduced into scholarly circulation an expanded concept of the grotesque and gave it a sense outside art history. The reader will have noticed that my interpretation of the grotesque, which frees it from the obligatory connection with laughter and the 'culture of laughter', departs in many respects from that of my great predecessor.

I now have more serious doubts about another concept in the title and throughout the pages of this work: popular culture. I am less worried about the adjective than the noun; I regret not having found a more adequate intelligible apparatus for comprehending the phenomenon. Despite all its indefiniteness (or because of it?), the term 'mentality' (*mentalité*) is apparently more appropriate for describing it than is the term 'culture', although it too has many different meanings and may lead to endless debates. However, I hope, the subject of my book is clear enough, whatever its title.

NOTES

Editorial preface

1 A. Y. Gurevich, 'Space and Time in the *Weltmodell* of the old Scandinavian People', *Medieval Scandinavia* 2 (1969); 'Wealth and Gift-Bestowal among the Ancient Scandinavians', *Scandinavica* 7 (1968), 126–38.

2 B. Malinowski, *Argonauts of the Western Pacific* (London, 1922); M. Mauss, *Essai sur le don* (1925), trans. as *The Gift: Forms and Functions of Exchange in Archaic Societies* (London, 1954).

3 J. Le Goff, 'Au Moyen Age: temps de l'église et temps de marchand' (1960), translated in his *Time, Work and Culture in the Middle Ages* (Chicago–London, 1980), 29–42; G. Duby, *Guerriers et paysans* (1973), trans. as *The Early Growth of the European Economy* (London, 1974).

4 The book has been translated into Italian and Swedish, but not into French or English.

5 A. I. Gurevich, *Kategorii srednevekovoi kul'tury* (Moscow, 1972), trans. as *Categories of Medieval Culture* (London, 1985).

6 K. Clark and M. Holquist, *Mikhail Bakhtin* (Cambridge, Mass., 1984).

7 The first appeared in Russian in 1977; the most recent is 'Oral and Written Culture of the Middle Ages: Two Peasant Visions', *New Literary History* 16 (1984), 51–66. Cf. ch. 4 of the present study.

8 J. Le Goff, *La Naissance du Purgatoire* (1983); transl. as *The Birth of Purgatory* (Chicago–London, 1984); cf. A. I. Gurevich, 'Popular and Scholarly Medieval Cultural Traditions: Notes in the Margin of Jacques Le Goff's Book', *Journal of Medieval History*, 9 (1983), 71–90, and J. Le Goff, 'The Learned and Popular Dimensions of Journeys in the Otherworld in the Middle Ages', in *Understanding Popular Culture*, ed. S. Kaplan (Berlin, 1984), 19–34.

9 A. I. Gurevich, 'Medieval Culture and Mentality according to the New French Historiography', *European Journal of Sociology* 24 (1983), 167–95.

10 I should like to thank Professors Aron Gurevich and János Bak for their assistance.

Foreword

1 For full bibliographical description of works cited, see Abbreviations (pp. xi–xii) and References (pp. 259–71).

2 In all honesty it should be noted that an attempt was made to overcome the traditional, inadequate approach to popular religiosity more than seventy years ago (1915) by the eminent Russian medievalist, L. P. Karsavin, whose work has been undeservedly neglected ever since.

3 Translations from Latin, Russian and German are – unless otherwise stated – all ours. For Slavic names, we chose a generally comprehensible transliteration, for which we beg the indulgence of specialists (Trans.).

1 Popular culture and medieval Latin literature from Caesarius of Arles to Caesarius of Heisterbach

1 In Acts 4:13 Peter and Paul are described as 'homines sine litteris et idiotae'.

2 According to Owst (1961: 23), it was precisely the medieval sermon, full of examples drawn directly from life, understandable to all and simple in language and style, that served as the foundation of European literature. The renaissance of literary realism was due much more to this genre than to the renewed interest in classical letters.

3 Therefore one can speak of the Middle Ages as 'an age of ink' (Averintsev 1977: 208) only with the greatest reservations and by limiting one's view to the élite culture. But even in regard to clerical culture this is not quite tenable: symbolic acts such as the eating of scrolls bearing a sacred text or the drinking of wine into which written characters were dipped (*ibid.*: 189, 204) are hardly indicative of a book culture. They are rather signs of a culture in which the book remained a sacred object full of mystery. For the Middle Ages, the book was not only a source of information: people looked upon it as an instrument of magic. A person could be healed by placing a book on his head, fortunes were told and sorcery practised with books. The book may have been used in this way because of its sacred character: 'the book' usually meant Holy Scriptures. But even pieces of parchment without any writing on them could serve magical functions. If a seal was applied or appended to them, they received the same force as the decree that could have been written on them but in fact was passed on verbally. For a land-deal to acquire legal force, a piece of parchment was placed on the plot to be transferred before being appropriately filled out (Gurevich 1985: 173). On the culture of the common people as a non-literate one, see Ginzburg 1980: xiii–xiv.

4 For the relevant canons of church councils of 1229, 1234 and 1246, see Richter 1976: 51, n. 22. This ban included also the *conversi*, the lay members of monastic orders. Neverthless, translations came to be made, because laymen – and even some clergy – knew no Latin (Coulton 1940: 23ff., 27ff). Walter Map wrote: 'Shall then the pearl be cast before swine, the word given to the ignorant, whom we know to be unfit to take it in, much less to give out what they have received? Away with such a thought…!' (*De nugis curialium: Courtiers' Trifles*, ed. and trans. by M. R. Jones, R. A. B. Mynors, C. N. L. Brooke (Oxford, 1983), 125).

5 As is well known, Augustine was amazed that Ambrose read 'without moving his lips' (*Confessions* VI, 3). It is characteristic that in their writings medieval authors often addressed the 'listeners' (Crosby 1936: 88–110). On the spread of silent reading in the later Middle Ages, see Saenger 1982. Apparently the situation was somewhat different in Byzantium, where contact with the book was more intimate (Kazhdan 1973: 136).

6 See *S. Brunonis episcopi signensis sententiae libri VI* (PL 165: 1071), cf. *Bernardi abbatis adversus Waldensium sectam liber* (PL 204: 813). Sermons were preached differently to *simplices* than to the educated; the 'simple and infant' are to be nourished by 'simpler doctrinal milk'. For ecclesiastical prescriptions about the need to preach to the common folk in a language comprehensible to them, see Linsenmaier 1886: 7ff., 10, 40, 75ff. Cf. Owst 1965: 255ff., 351. The conversation of St Boniface with a young Frank,

whom he asked whether he had learned the Bible so well that he could not merely repeat it by heart in Latin but also give its meaning in his native tongue, is recorded in *Vita Liutgeri*, MGH SS 15, 1: 68.

7 This applies not only to literature in the narrow sense. Customary law remained unwritten for centuries and its eventual recording was never complete. Written records co-existed with oral tradition. Oral preaching predominated over the written word.

8 In the treatise *De pignoribus sanctorum* (*On the Relics of the Saints*), Guibert of Nogent tells of a young man of humble origin who died on Good Friday, whereupon his neighbours, 'thirsting for something new', began to bring gifts to his grave and light candles over it, venerating him as a saint. Soon his fame spread far and wide and attracted crowds of pilgrims to his tomb; 'all of them were peasants, with not a noble person among them'. Seeing the flow of offerings, the abbot and the monks 'allowed themselves to be convinced by spurious miracles' (Sumption 1976: 146ff.)

9 *Gesta Alberonis auctore Balderico*, MGH SS 8: 257.

10 'The difference between the priestly order and the common people is as great as that between light and darkness', wrote Honorius, conventionally called Augustodunensis (of Autun) ('De offendiculo' c. 38; MGH Ldl 3: 51). The association of Honorius with Autun is a debated issue but need not here detain us. Even though he might have been a German who studied and lived in England, I shall use his conventional epitheton.

11 One of the *exempla* (no. 101) in Jacques de Vitry's collection treats of the priest Maugrin, 'valde illiteratus' (Frenken 1914: 146–7). Not understanding a single word of the sermon, delivered by a travelling scholar, the priest announced to his servant that the visitor was mad. Some time later the scholar complained about the ignoramus to the bishop, who summoned Maugrin and pretended to confess to him; in actual fact he spoke in Latin 'ex dialectica et aliis facultatibus'. Not suspecting the plot, the priest absolved his bishop.

12 MGH Epp. Kar. 2: 183.

13 *DM* iv, 36.

14 One who places generally accepted truths in doubt and advances new arguments is, in this frame of thinking, a heretic, a 'confutator veritatis et novorum introductor argumentorum' (*Vita Columbani* ii, 10; MGH SS rer. Mer. 4: 127).

15 The usual and most convincing proof of the truthfulness of a communicated fact was a reference to an eyewitness or some object linked to the event.

16 In the later Middle Ages questions from laymen on liturgy and ritual often placed priests in a difficult position, and special works were written to help them out in such 'ticklish' situations (Young 1936: 224–5).

17 This little collection from the thirteenth century was only recently edited (Kleinschmidt 1974) and, as far as I am aware, not yet been utilized by historians of medieval mentality. An extension of the range of sources would not significantly add new information to this inquiry. An index of motifs contained in the *exempla* (Tubach 1969) shows how highly repetitive they in fact are. Quite soon one arrives at a 'saturation point' and experiences only *embarras de richesses*.

18 Most enlightening in this regard are the thoughts of Likhachev (1967: 49ff.) on the differences between genres in ecclesiastical literature, as these reflect their practical aims and their 'service' character.

19 *S. Gregorii Magni registrum epistolarium* XI, 34 (CCSL 140A: 922).
    Gregory also tells about St Benedict of Nursia that he as a young man
    refused to be educated in Rome, seeing therein a danger to his soul: 'In
    the desire to please God alone, he turned his back on further studies'
    (*Dial.* II, Praef., 2)

20 It is worth noting that while in the early Middle Ages *sermo rusticus* meant
    vulgar Latin, in later centuries the term came to be used for the vernaculars,
    as opposed to Latin (Beumann, 1972: 41–70).

21 It is sufficient to refer to Jerome's well-known dream in which he was
    chided for being 'not a Christian, but a Ciceronian' ('Ad Eustachium'
    XXX, *The Letters of Jerome* I, trans. C. C. Mierow (London, 1963), 166).

22 *De doctrina Christiana* IV, x (24) (CSSL 32, 2: 133).

23 MGH SS rer. Mer. 1, 2: 586.

24 *S. Gregorii ep. Turonensis De miraculis S. Martini epistola* (PL 71: 911–12).

25 *S. Gregorii ep. Turonensis Libri miraculorum*, Proem (PL 71: 705–6).

26 *S. Gregorii ep. Turonensis Liber de gloria beatorum confessorum*, Praef. (PL
    71: 829–30); *Hist. Fr.*, Praef. Actually, he is not far from the truth, for his
    grammar was atrocious, his syntax monstrous and his handwriting
    barbarian. It reads as though the author was not guided by literary diction,
    but let colloquial popular speech flow into his pen, with all its alogisms,
    solecisms and contradictions. Auerbach (1965: 103–12) discussed Gregory's
    style, mainly on the basis of the *History*; had he included an analysis of
    the hagiographic writings, his verdict would have been even harsher (cf.
    Bonnet 1890: 76–80 and *passim*).

27 *Hist. Fr.* Praef. prima.

28 *Ibid.* x, 31.

29 Janson (1964: 144) noted that this passage follows a topic from Irenius'
    In Rufinum; but even if the wording of this plea is borrowed, its contents
    reflect Gregory's own concerns.

30 *Registrum epistolarium* XII, 6 (CCSL 140A: 974–5).

31 *Ibid.* XI, 10 (CCSL 140A: 873–6).

32 *S. Caesarii Arelatensis Sermones* VI, 4–5 (CCSL 103: 32–3).

33 *Ibid.* XCI, 8 (p. 378).

34 *Ibid.* VI, 7 (p. 34).

35 *Vita S. Caesarii episcopi* I, 4 (MGH SS rer. Mer. 3: 433ff.).

36 *S. Caesarii Arelatensis Sermones* I, 21 (CCSL 103: 17).

37 *Ibid.* XLIV, 3 (pp. 196–7).

38 *Hist. Fr.* II, Praef. secunda: *Prosequentes ordinem temporum, mixte
    confuseque tam virtutes sanctorum quam strages gentium memoramus.*

39 *Ibid.* v, 43; VI, 5, 40; x, 13.

40 *Libri miraculorum* (as n. 25) I, 81 (PL 71: 777–8).

41 On the mutual connections between folklore and the Latin writings of
    medieval authors such as Gregory the Great or Jacopo da Varagine, see
    Golenishchev-Kutuzov 1972: 138ff., 212, etc. Cf. also Poliakova 1972;
    246ff.

42 See below, ch. 4.

43 The thoughts of Likhachev (1973: 48) on the genetic connections between
    folklore and medieval literature are most pertinent to this point.

44 We are not here concerned with all types of edificatory *exempla*, for this
    genre included very different kinds of stories. The novellas of Caesarius of
    Heisterbach or Rudolf of Schlettstadt, just as the *Dialogues* of Gregory
    the Great or the brief lives of Gregory of Tours, clearly bear the stamp of

being closely related to popular tradition. Other collections of *exempla* tend to ascribe allegorical interpretations to the facts which they narrate, transforming little scenes from life into parables; here the contact with popular fantasy is lost, replaced by borrowings from scholarly literature. This is the case with most of the *exempla* edited by Klapper (1914) and Welter (1927), and the anecdotes in the sermons of Jacques de Vitry or in the treatises of Thomas of Chantimpré. Also part of this 'scholarly trend' are, by and large, the *Gesta Romanorum*, the collection of Peter Alfonsi and the writings of Gervase of Tilbury or Walter Map. These works were addressed to an audience other than the common people.

45 *DM* IV, 1; VII, Prol.; XI, 1; XII, 1.

46 Caesarius describes the vision of a Cistercian, who in the state of ecstasy was vouchsafed the sight of heavenly glory, angels, patriarchs, prophets, apostles, martyrs and also monks of different orders who ascended to heaven. He was astounded and depressed when he did not find any of his brethren near the throne of the Lord and took the liberty of asking the Virgin Mary about it. She reassured him that the White Monks were so dear and precious to her that she was protecting them under her mantle, where they were indeed seen, when she lifted her arms lightly (*DM* VII, 64).

47 *DM* VI, 7; XI, 56.

48 The novice tells: 'magis exemplis quam sententiis scire desidero' (*DM* VIII, 1).

49 Caesarius quotes the *Dialogues* of Gregory the Great as readily as he does the Scriptures.

50 Caesarius reports that he heard the story of a priest whose tongue was torn out by heretics but replaced miraculously by the Virgin Mary from someone who had met that priest and seen his new tongue (*DM* VII, 23; Scott-Bland: I, 490).

51 *DM* X, 66.

52 Kleinschmidt 1974: 63–8 (nos. 15–17), 73 (no. 21), 82–4 (no. 26).

53 The interest in Rudolf's stories is attested by the fact that they were copied by a historically interested sixteenth-century nobleman and some of the tales about spirits and demons found their way into his nephew's *Chronicle of Zimmern*: see Kleinschmidt 1974: 3–35.

54 *Ibid.*, 84–5 (no. 27).

55 *Ibid.*, 108–9 (no. 46).

56 Obligatory annual confession for every believer was prescribed by can. 22 of the Fourth Lateran Council (1215), *Sacrorum conciliorum nova et amplissima collectio*, ed. J. D. Mansi (Venice 1769; repr. Graz 1960) XXII, 1007ff.

57 See can. 38 of the Second Synod of Châlons (813) and can. 32 of the Sixth Synod of Paris (829): *Ibid.* XIV, 101, 559–60.

58 Wasserschleben, 300; cf. *Ancient Laws and Institutes of England*, ed. by [B. Thorpe for] the Record Commission (London 1840), 343ff.

59 Schmitz, I, 761. Lea (1896: 368) quotes a medieval distichon which adapted the Aristotelian (Ethics III) sequence of questions to those to be asked during the confession: 'Quis, quid, ubi, per quos, quoties, cur, quomodo, quando, / Quilibet observet animae medicamina dando.'

60 Schmitz I, 162, 241–2. Medieval Latin authors knew about people who yielded to the temptation to commit a sin after learning about it from a father confessor (*DM* III, 47). There are some entertaining stories about 'unqualified' confessors; one of these imposed identical penances on two

people, on one for incontinence and on the other for continence (*DM* III, 40). There is another about a man who on his death-bed confessed to having committed all possible sins; however, the priest found out that he had done absolutely nothing wrong, but the previous vicar made the parishioners recite the entire general confession, and this man admitted to all transgression in the book (*DM* III, 45).

61 Penitential 'of Monte Cassino': see Schmitz I, 400; cf. McNeill 1938: 429.
62 Wasserschleben, 387–8. Cf. its model, the Penitential of Columban, in McNeill 1938: 251–2.
63 He writes: 'Canonum iura et iudicia poenitentium in nostra diocesi sic sunt confusa atque diversa et inculta ac sic ex toto neglecta...' (Hauck 1952: 439).
64 Violation of the secrecy of the confessional was regarded as a major sin and a crime. The following story is contained in a manuscript collection of *exempla*. A knight killed a man and nobody knew about it. He disclosed his deed in confession to a priest, who, in expectation of a reward, informed the prince of the murder. Thereupon the prince pardoned the knight but had the priest blinded and his tongue cut out (Tubach 1969: no. 1203).
65 Penitential of Finnian, cap. 17 (Wasserschleben, 111; Schmitz I, 504): 'in corde et non in corpore unum est peccatum, sed non eadem penitentia est' (cf. McNeill 1938: 90).
66 It seems that Roman tradition opposed these practices from the outset and regarded anyone who fasted for a reward as unworthy to be called a Christian (Schmitz I, 326; cf. 148, 768). The rule that the killer of a penitent had to complete the victim's penance above and beyond his own for homicide is contained, among others, in Burchard's *Corrector*, cap. 24 (Wasserschleben, 636; cf. McNeill 1938: 329 (no. 25)).
67 Schmitz I, 698–9.
68 'De magnatum penitentia', in King Eadgar's penitential rules (Mansi, *Concilia* (as above, no. 56) XVIII, 525).
69 Schmitz I, 781; II, 412, 414, 782.
70 *S. Gregorii Magni Regula pastoralis* I, 1: 'ars est artium regimen animarum' (PL 77: 14).
71 Schmitz I, 91, 243, 429, where distinction is made between free and bond men, the latter, not being their own masters, being granted reduction by half of their penances.
72 Schmitz I, 88, 99, 563; in some penitentials the *homo intellegibilis* is distinguished from the *simplex*, the *literatus* from the *non literatus* (*ibid.*, 788–9).
73 In some penitentials the decision about the duration of penance is left to the priest, because, in the words of a thirteenth century penitential, 'apud Deum non tam valet mensura temporis quam doloris...' (Schmitz I, 807).
74 See the detailed classification of sins in *Poenitentiale Merseburgense* (Schmitz I, 700–1); cf. Schmitz II, 761–2. See also Bloomfield 1967: 69–70.
75 I use the term for the sake of simplicity, although medieval catechisms were not series of questions given into the hands of catechumens in the course of instruction, as modern ones are, but couched in the form of a 'dialogue' between a teacher and a pupil. Essentially, however, their aim was the same.
76 In another work, Honorius refers to the *Elucidarium* as an *opusculum* of his.
77 See above, n. 10.

78 In his prologue, the author compares his work to a building erected on the 'rock of Christ' and supported by four columns: the authority of the prophets, the virtue of the Apostles, the wisdom of the Fathers and the meditations of the masters. He writes that the purpose of the *Elucidarium* is to share the received treasures with others, both in the present and in the future. In spite of his misgivings about arousing envy, Honorius does not seem to have suffered from inordinate modesty. The new critical edition (Lefèvre 1954) makes this work now easily accessible to study.

79 In a twelfth-century manuscript this work is characterized as a 'very useful book that opens the minds of both lay and learned men by replying to their questions'. In the fourteenth century the Spanish inquisitor Nicholas Aimerich called it 'a book of great age, often published, deposited in many libraries and known to all' (Lefèvre 1954: 60, 485).

80 As Le Goff (1986: 87–97) demonstrated, common people are almost entirely absent from early medieval writings, and this silence eloquently characterizes their place in the society and culture of the age. If peasants appear in the literature, comments on their spiritual life are rather ambiguous. So, for example, the *Vita Wilhelmi abb. Hirsaugensis* (MGH SS 12: 217) tells a story in which the abbot found, upon questioning a poor couple who lived in a miserable hut in the forest about the Catholic faith, that they were completely ignorant of religion. Manselli (1975: 126–7) noted that the mere fact of the abbot's asking these questions implied that he knew of the ignorance of common folk. But one can read this passage in another way as well. The hagiographer Haimo was surely uninterested in the religiosity of some rustics, his aim being to extol the deeds and sayings of the holy abbot, who, upon hearing the peasants' replies exclaimed, 'What can be surprising about your poverty in external matters when you are lacking the blessing of God within!' and proceeded to give them a brief instruction in the faith. The purpose of the anecdote was, clearly, edificatory and not 'sociological'.

81 Naturally, such disrespect towards the saints was in no way an expression of some kind of medieval 'agnosticism', but rather a symptom for popular distrust in Christian rituals – in contrast to pagan practices – and even more in those clergy who performed these rituals and stood for the dogmas of the church.

82 On the applicability of the concept of genre to medieval literature, see Likhachev 1967, 1970, Vagner 1974 and Mikhailov 1976.

2 Peasants and saints

1 *Hist. Fr.* I, 48.

2 *Gregorii Turonensis Vitae patrum* XIII, 3 (PL 71: 1067). The clash of two armed groups instigated by an argument over St Patrick's body is narrated in Irish hagiography (Bieler 1975: 20).

3 *Hist. Fr.* V, 14.

4 *Petri Damiani Vita s. Romualdi*, c. 13 (PL 144: 966, 967).

5 *Vita Rigoberti*, c. 25 (MGH SS 7: 76).

6 *Hist. Fr.* VIII, 34.

7 *De miraculis s. Martini*, no. 12 (PL 71: 996).

8 *Hist. Fr.* VI, 6.

9 *DM* VIII, 52.

10 *Vitae patrum* II, 1 (PL 71: 1018).
11 *De miraculis s. Martini* II, 60 (PL 71: 968). Cf. *Liber de gloria beatorum confessorum* VI (PL 71: 834); *Odonis abbatis Cluniscensis II. De vita s. Geraldi Auriliacensis comitis. Praefatio*: '...qui signa quidem quae vulgus magni pendent...' (PL 133: 642).
12 St Theobald set out to put an end to the civil strife raging in Champagne, but a demon, attempting to impede him, stole a wheel from his wagon and threw it into the river. The saint ordered him to serve as his wheel, and the demon did not dare disobey him (Frenken 1914: no. 59).
13 *Miracula Martini abbatis Vertavensis*, c. 1 (MGH SS 3: 568).
14 *Vita s. Goaris confessoris*, c. 7 (MGH SS 4: 418).
15 *Hist. Fr.* VII, 29.
16 *Ibid.* IV, 16; V, 14.
17 *Ibid.* VII, 31.
18 *Libri miraculorum* I, 37 (PL 71: 738–9).
19 *Dial.* I: 7, 2.
20 *Libri miraculorum* II, 21 (PL 71: 814).
21 *De gloria beatorum confessorum*, c. 80 (PL 71: 887–8).
22 *Libri miraculorum* I, 90 (PL 71: 784–5).
23 *De gloria beatorum confessorum*, c. 99 (PL 71: 901–2).
24 *Ibid.*, c. 81 (PL 71: 889). 'If anyone should think that this was an accident,' notes Gregory, 'it is strange that his neighbours suffered no damage.' For the punishment of a peasant for failing to honour St Genulf, see Töpfer 1957: 53.
25 *Miracula s. Leutfredi*, c. 2 (MGH SS 7: 17).
26 See below, ch. 4.
27 *Libri miraculorum* I, 89 (PL 71: 783–4).
28 Kleinschmidt 1974: 91–2 (no. 32). Saints did not tolerate disrespectful handling. A sack of grain, placed on the grave of St Ecvitius by a villager who was not interested in whose body was reposing there, was miraculously thrown out, 'so that all would know the services of the saint' (*Dial.* I, 4, 2–3). A chicken sacrificed by a poor old woman to St Sergius was stolen, but the thieves could not enjoy it: during the cooking the bird hardened all the more, and the feast ended in embarrassment: *Libri miraculorum* I, 97 (PL 71: 790–1).
29 *Vita Remigii ep. Remensis* XVII, XXV (MGH SS 3: 307, 321–2).
30 *Ibid.*
31 *De gloria beatorum confessorum*, c. 62 (PL 71: 873).
32 PL 71: 879–80. Cf. PL 79: 885; *Libri miraculorum* II, 15, 16, 18 (PL 71: 810–12).
33 *Libri miraculorum* I, 105 (PL 71: 797).
34 *Ibid.* II, 17 (PL 71: 811–12).
35 *Vita Fridolini*, c. 30 (MGH SS 3: 367–68).
36 *De miraculis s. Martini* I, 29 (PL 71: 934).
37 *Libri miraculorum* I, 64 (PL 71: 763); cf. I, 74, 105.
38 On the mythological and folkloric sources of Byzantine hagiography, see Poliakova 1972: 248ff.
39 MGH SS 3: 31. However, the authenticity of this report has been doubted.
40 MGH SS 2: 410.
41 MGH SS 1: 268.
42 *Heliand und Genesis*, ed. W. Mitzka (Tübingen, 1965).

43 *Vita Remigii ep. Remensis auctore Hincmaro*, MGH SS 3: 314.
44 *Libri miraculorum* I, 80 (PL 71: 776–8). One Arian priest wanted to stage a miracle and put up a Goth to feign blindness and then, at the priest's words, to recover his sight. As a result, he actually went blind: *De gloria beatorum confessorum*, c. 13 (PL 71: 837–8).
45 *HE* I, 25.
46 *Ibid.* IV, 22.
47 *Jacobi a Voragine Legenda aurea*, ed. Th. Graesse, 3rd edn (Breslau, 1890), 70 (p. 316).
48 *De gloria beatorum confessorum*, c. 81 (PL 71: 889–90).
49 *Miracula s. Leutfredi*, MGH SS 7: 17.
50 *Vita Gamalberti* V, 6 (MGH SS 7: 189).
51 *Vita Pardulfi*, c. 1 (MGH SS 7: 25): '…ex agricolarum cultoribus fideli genealogia'; cf. *Vita Richardi*, c. 4 (MGH SS 7: 446). The situation changes, properly speaking, only towards the end of the Middle Ages, when a cult of saints from the common people forms, provoking the church's suspicion and hostility.
52 *Vitae patrum* VI, 2 (PL 71: 1031). Cf. also an attack by the people on the bishop: *ibid.* VI, 4 (PL 71: 1032).
53 *Vita Remigii*, c. 22 (MGH SS 3: 315–16).
54 *Vita Amandi ep.*, c. 1, 13–15 (MGH SS 5: 437–9); cf. *Vita Columbani*, c. 2, 25 (MGH SS 4: 149ff.); *Vita Eligii ep. Noviomagensis*, c. 20 (MGH SS 4: 712).
55 *Vita Walarici*, c. 22 (MGH SS 4: 169). On the expulsion by peasants of priests 'propter insolentiam morum', see *Vita Richardi confessoris Centulensis*, MGH SS 4: 390.
56 *Vita Desiderii Cadurcae urbis ep.*, c. 8 (MGH SS 4: 568).
57 *Vitae patrum* X, 1 (PL 71: 1055–6).
58 Even monks rebelled against strict abbots. When St Lupicinus made arrangements to introduce restrictions into the brothers' food, so that satisfying the belly might not impede their service to the Lord, discontent began among them, and twelve men revolted and left the monastery: *Vitae patrum* I, 3 (PL 71: 1013–14); cf. *Vita s. Romani abbatis* c. 12–13 (MGH SS 3: 138–9).
59 References to 'false prophets' are found in a still earlier source, Sulpicius Severus' *Life of St Martin*. He mentions a youth in Spain who declared himself the prophet Elijah; the people took him for Christ, and one bishop even 'worshipped him as the Lord', for which he was deprived of his rank. At the same time somebody else declared himself John the Baptist. All these 'pseudo-prophets', says Sulpicius, presage the coming of the Antichrist. Once a demon appeared to St Martin in imperial clothing and crowned with a diadem; he called himself Christ and demanded the saint's veneration. Martin, however, did not give in and retorted that Christ would appear to him as one crucified, and not in imperial splendour. The devil was forced to go back whence he came, leaving behind in the cell a terrible stench. Martin himself, concludes Sulpicius, told him of this meeting, 'so that nobody might fancy that this is a fable': *Sulpicii Severi De vita beati Martini* XXIV, 8 (ed. J. Fontaine, 308ff.). Of interest in this story is the establishment of a direct connection between the pseudo-prophets and the devil. It is unclear who these impostors were, from Sulpicius' point of view: deluded sinners or demons?
60 *Hist. Fr.* IX, 6.

61 Schmitz I, 317; II, 424, 429, 496.
62 Cited by Bede in *HE* I, 30.
63 *Hist. Fr.* X, 25.
64 *Summa de judiciis omnium peccatorum* VII, 21: '...nullus presumat diabolica carmina cantare, ioca saltationes facere...' (Schmitz II, 496); *Poenitentiale Eccles. Germ.*, c. 91: 'fecisti...saltationes quas pagani diabolo docente adinvenerunt...' (Schmitz II, 429); *Benedictus Levita* VI, 96. See Homan 1965; 48–9. See also below for heavenly punishments befalling dancers, according to the edifying exempla.
65 Acts 8: 9.
66 *Hist. Fr.* X, 25.
67 *Ibid.* VII, 44; VIII, 33.
68 *Ibid.* IV, 34.
69 MGH Conc. 2, 1: 34.
70 Adelbert's condemnation is interpreted somewhat differently by J. B. Russell (1964: 241ff.). Russell's work is the most detailed study of this episode, but I differ with him in interpreting the meaning of Adelbert's activity, which Russell sees as an attempt at church reform and not as an appearance of 'eccentrics', obsessive types, 'lunatics' and psychologically unbalanced people.
71 MGH Epp. sel. 1: 112 (no. 59).
72 MGH Epp. sel. 1: 117ff. (no. 59). From a letter of cardinal-deacon Gemmulus to Boniface soon after the close of the Rome synod, it is clear that Adelbert and Clement were excommunicated: see *ibid.*, 127 (no. 62). The synod's participants demanded the burning of Adelbert's works, but the pope, while recognizing that they deserved it, nevertheless ordered that they be preserved in the archives for further study. The condemnation of these heretics took place by default; they were not summoned to the synod.
73 MGH Conc. 2, 1: 35.
74 MGH Epp. sel. 1: 105 (no. 57); 112 (no. 59).
75 *Ibid.*, 102ff. (no. 57); 120ff. (no. 60); 127ff. (no. 62); 1599ff. (no. 77).
76 The reliability of the report of 'Anonymous of Mainz' about the murder of Adelbert by robbers (MGH SS 2: 355) is doubtful. See Hauck 1922: 526.
77 *Admonitio generalis* c. 78 (MGH Capit. 1, 1: 60).
78 *Ibid.*, c. 16, p. 55.
79 Under the Carolingians warnings against the abuse of miracles became especially frequent and insistent ('...quia signa plerumque diabolico instinctu fiunt'; MGH Conc. 2, Suppl.: 155), against venerating false martyrs and dubious saints (MGH Capit. 1: 55, 56), and against excessive interest in acquiring relics. Charlemagne (*rex et sacerdos*) claimed the right to control strictly all the church's activity and religous life in general. Let us add further that precisely to the eighth century belong the enactments of penitentials about punishments for persons who maintain relations with heretics. See the Penitential of Columban, c. 25: 'Si quis laicus per ignorantiam cum...haereticis communicaverit...Si vero per contemptum hoc fecerit, id est postquam denunciatum illi fuerit a sacerdote ac prohibitum' (Schmitz I: 601).
80 For 'false priests', 'people who fear not God' and 'false bishops' discovered by Boniface, see MGH Epp. sel. 1: 107, 124–6, 195, 205 (nos. 58, 60, 61, 87, 90).

81 *Ibid.*, 129 (no. 63). On heretical sects stirring up the people and seducing a good portion of them, see *Vita s. Bonifacii auctore Willibaldo* VIII–X (PL 89: 620–4) '...magna ex parte populum seduxerunt'. On Adelbert, see *IX*, 29; *X*, 30.
82 MGH Epp. sel. 1: 111 (no. 59).
83 *Annales Fuldenses*, MGH SS rer. Ger. 7: 36–7. The later story of Sigebert of Gembloux (MGH SS 6: 339) is based on the Fulda annals.
84 However, there is such an allusion in Sulpicius Severus (see above).
85 A saint who saved the population from hunger by filling a vessel with an inexhaustible supply of bread ordered his followers not to divulge this miracle (*Vita Iohannis abbatis Reomagensis*, MGH SS 3: 512). Gregory of Tours admits that once in his youth he himself paid for vain pride. When a storm overtook him on the road, he protected himself with relics which he had with him. Gregory fancied that this was granted to him not only because of the saint's protection, but also on account of his own merits. God immediately punished him; his horse fell under him and Gregory was seriously hurt.
86 Cf. a similar instance of the veneration of Tanchelm, the leader of Flemish heretics at the beginning of the twelfth century (Sidorova 1953: 87–8).
87 MGH Epp. sel. 1: 112 (no. 59). Boniface complained to the pope about Samson, another heretic of Irish origin (like Clement), who taught that one can become a Christian without baptism, by a simple laying on of hands by a bishop: *Ibid.*, 177 (no. 80).
88 *Ibid.*, 175.
89 MGH Capit. 1: 222. *Indiculus superstitionum et paganiarum* c. 6: 'De sacris silvarum, quae nimidas vocant'; c. 7: 'De his, quae faciunt super petras'.
90 C. P. Caspari, *Eine Augustin fälschlich beigelegte Homilia de sacrilegiis* (Christiania, 1886), ch. 2.
91 *De gloria beatorum confessorum* c. 2 (PL 71: 830–1).
92 *Gregorii Magni Epistolae* IV, 23; VIII, 1, 18, 30; IX, 11 (PL 77: 692, 904, 921, 932, 954–5; cf. *Hist. Fr.* II, 10.
93 *S. Caesarii Arelatensis Sermones* LIII (CCSL 103: 233–4); cf. *Vita S. Caesarii episcopi*, I, 55 (MGH SS rer. Mer. 3: 479–80).
94 *Vita Willibrordi*, c. 10 (PL 101: 700); quoted by Adam of Bremen, *Hist. Hammaburg. eccl.* (MGH SS 7: 124ff.).
95 *Vita Amandi ep.* I, 13, 24 (MGH SS 5: 437, 447).
96 *Vita Lucii confessoris Curiensis*, cc. 12ff. (MGH SS 3: 5ff.).
97 *Miracula Martini abbatis Vertavensis*, c. 5 (MGH SS 3: 570ff.).
98 Schmitz II, 424.
99 *Ibid.* II, 430.
100 On the Frisian cult of trees which Boniface attacked by ordering the cutting down of a huge tree venerated by the pagans, see *Vita s. Bonifatii auctore Willibaldo* VIII, 22, 23 (PL 89: 619–20); cf. *Vita Walarici abb. Leuconaensis*, c. 22 (MGH SS 4: 168–9).
101 MGH Epp. sel. 1: 174 (no. 80).
102 *Ibid.*, 69 (no. 43).
103 *Indiculus superstitionum et paganiarum* I, 2 (Homan 1965).
104 Adelbert came *de simplicibus parentibus;* one of the false saints mentioned by Gregory of Tours was a runaway servant; the pseudo-Christ who robbed the rich and gave the loot to the poor was obviously a peasant by

origin. Pope Zachariah's letter names among the 'sacrilegious priests' 'numerous tonsured runaway slaves', 'slaves of the devil pretending to be servants of Christ...': MGH Epp. sel. 1: 175 (no. 80). But, as I mentioned, church saints of the time were almost always noble and prosperous people, and not infrequently of royal blood: see *Vitae sanctorum generis regii* (MGH SS 2); cf. Prinz 1965: 489ff.

105 Definitions of them in the sources: 'homines nudo corpore saltantes atque ludentes', 'mulierculae debacchantes'.

106 The church considered that people whose behaviour deviated from the norm were possessed by demons. One of the most widespread miracles performed by saints was the exorcism of demons from *energoumenoi*. Hence the church's apprehensions about holy ecstatics with large followings. Raoul Glaber also depicts the preacher Leutard as possessed: see *Les cinq livres de ses histoires*, ed. M. Prou (Paris, 1886) II, 11–12 (pp. 49ff).

107 MGH Epp. sel. 1: 175 (no. 80).

108 This feature of heavenly dwellers is traced not only in hagiography, but also in *exempla*: see below, ch. 6.

3 Popular culture in the mirror of the penitentials

1 See, however, the books of Dobiash-Rozhdestvenskaia (1911; 1914) which have not lost their relevance in the course of time. The works of Georges LeBras on parish life in early modern France also contain valuable insights for the medievalist. See also Ferté 1962 and Rapp 1971.

2 'The veritable bacchanalia of crude jollity with the performance of such rituals and festivities which may be regarded as pagan feasts flourished in and around churches': Dobiash-Rozhdestvenskaia 1914: 133–4. On dancing in churches and churchyards, and the constant struggle of the ecclesiastical authorities against these customs, see Gougaud 1912.

3 The most profound analysis so far of everyday religiosity in a medieval village was presented by Emmanuel Le Roy Ladurie (1978). The picture he has drawn of the life of a Pyrenean village is, of course, not typical, because the deep penetration of Catharism in Montaillou had altered the religious and cultural cohesion characteristic of medieval parishes. But the relationships between the villagers and between parishioners and local clergy emerge in such a clarity and in such unique detail that no medievalist can overlook them.

4 See above, pp. 24–31.

5 '...sacerdos Christi vicarius, judex, homo et accusator et reus; poenitentia est sententia': *E* II, 71 (p. 432).

6 *Excarpsus Egberti*, c. 130 (Schmitz II, 695); cf. McNeill 1938: 229, 330.

7 See the Penitential of Halitgar of Cambrai (Schmitz II, 727); cf. McNeill 1938: 305; or the penitential of Burchard of Worms (Schmitz II, 423); cf. McNeill 1938: 330.

8 Among others, the penitentials of Regino of Prüm and Burchard of Worms (Schmitz II, 423, 432); cf. McNeill 1938: 229, 270–1, 318, 334–5.

9 Schmitz I, 308, 460, 811; II, 422, 425; cf. McNeill 1938: 334ff.

10 Burchard's Penitential, c. 194 (Schmitz II, 452); cf. McNeill 1938: 330.

11 Schmitz II, 423f; cf. McNeill 1938: 330. Tying of magical knots accompanied by spells was practised by the Germanic peoples from ancient times: witness the well-known 'First Merseburg Spells'.

12 Schmitz I, 459, 463; II, 424, 446, etc.; cf. McNeill 1938: 330. One could also enhance one's economy through the help of goblins by preparing boys'-size bows and shoes, leaving these in the barn, so that the 'goblins and satyrs' might have fun and bring wealth and richness: *ibid.* II, 434; cf. McNeill 1938: 335. Others expected advantages from 'those three sisters whom antiquity called Fates' (*parcae*): a feast was prepared for them, and if they came and ate of the food then the household was to flourish: Schmitz II, 443; cf. McNeill 1938: 338.

13 Magic belonged not only to the world of *simplices*; many highly educated minds of the Middle Ages believed in it: see Thorndike 1923.

14 Schmitz II, 430, 535, 556, 667, 682; cf. McNeill 1938: 198, 229, 246–7, 318, 350.

15 An apparently reliable method of protecting oneself against gossip was to eat a radish during the night: Payne 1904.

16 Schmitz II, 424; cf. McNeill 1938: 330–1 (c. 65).

17 Schmitz I. The prohibitions are particularly extensively discussed in early Irish and Anglo-Saxon penitentials: Schmitz I, 619; II, 437, 448, etc.

18 'Mulier quae sanguinem viri pro remedio suo biberit...' is assigned penance in the *Poenit. Valicell.* II, 69 (Schmitz I, 382).

19 Schmitz II, 448. On many other procedures of medieval 'paediatry', see also Schmitt 1979: 104–9.

20 Broëns (1960) presented interesting hypotheses on the rebirth of archaic ('pre-indoeuropean') beliefs in Mother Earth and other cults of the dead connected with chthonic deities. Cf. also Bordenave, Vialelle 1973.

21 Schmitz I, 460; cf. McNeill 1938: 331.

22 To counter such beliefs among his parishioners, Burchard included a passage by Regino of Prüm and the early medieval canon *Episcopi* in his penitential. These texts were to feature later in the infamous *Malleus maleficarum*, but, of course, with an opposite meaning and in an entirely different context: Vogel 1974: 761.

23 Cf. *Deutsche Sagen*, ed. by J. & W. Grimm (Berlin, 1956), 35ff.

24 Cf. Old English *frigedag*, Old High German *fiatac*, Old Frisian *fri(g)endei*, Old Norse *Frjadagr*, and so on.

25 Old English and Old High German *hold*, Old Icelandic *hollr*, Norwegian *hull*, Icelandic *hollur*, meaning 'dear', 'good', 'beloved' and related positive qualities.

26 McNeill 1938: 332–3 (c. 90); cf. Schmitz II, 429.

27 The same applies also to the Inquisition, in regard of which historians 'tend to have a rather poor memory' (Losev 1978: 134), for they usually connect it only with the Middle Ages. As is well known, the Inquisition's heyday (in Spain, Italy and elsewhere) was in the sixteenth and seventeenth centuries; hence it may in fact be called a 'child of the Renaissance' (*ibid.*). On the persecution of 'witches' in the late Middle Ages and during the Renaissance, see *ibid.*, 135.

28 Schmitz II, 446–7.

29 Kleinschmidt 1974: 93–4 (no. 33).

30 *Ibid.*, 95 (no. 34).

31 Schmitz II, 442; cf. McNeill 1938: 338 (cc. 151–2).

32 *Ibid.* II, 442; cf. McNeill 1938: 339.

33 *Ibid.* II, 450; cf. McNeill 1938: 340 (c. 185).

34 *Ibid.* II, 431; cf. McNeill 1938: 334 (c. 97).

35 *Ibid.* I, 461; II, 430; cf. McNeill 1938: (c. 96).

36 *Ibid.* ii, 429; cf. McNeill 1938: 333 (c. 99).
37 *Ibid.* i, 338; ii, 338, 344.
38 *Ibid.* i, 61.
39 *Ibid.* ii, 430; Bourdieu 1928: 49–50.
40 *Poenit. Valicell.* i, 80: 'Si quis mathematicus fuerit, id est per invocationes demonum mentes hominum tolerit aut devacantes fecerit, V annos peniteat in pane et aqua.' The text later equates the 'mathematicians' with 'incantatores qui demones invocant': Schmitz i, 303.
41 Schmitz i, 581; cf. McNeill 1938: 229.
42 *Ibid.* i, 327, 379, 414; ii, 324, 336, etc.; cf. McNeill 1938: 229, 276, 288, 305, etc.
43 *Ibid.* i, 414; ii, 181, 236, 321, etc. In spite of ecclesiastical prohibition of fortune-telling and soothsaying, many medieval scholars and other churchmen, even monks, resorted to them: Thorndike 1923.
44 McNeill 1938: 333; cf. Schmitz ii, 422.
45 Schmitz ii, 694.
46 *Ibid.* ii, 425, 431–2; cf. McNeill 1938: 334–5.
47 *Ibid.* ii, 441–2; cf. McNeill 1938: 337–8.
48 *Ibid.*; cf. McNeill 1938: 339.
49 *Ibid.* ii, 429, 444ff.; cf. McNeill 1938: 334.
50 *Ibid.* ii, 451–2; cf. McNeill 1938: 340–1.
51 *Ibid.* ii, 452. The sorceresses are described as attempting 'mentem hominum mutare' (*ibid.* ii, 425).
52 *Ibid.* ii, 445, 447, 502.
53 *Ibid.* i, 459; cf. McNeill 1938: 340; cases of sorcery practised by jealous women have been described in several Icelandic sagas: cf., e.g., *Njal's Saga*, chs. 6–7.
54 Schmitz ii, 251; cf. McNeill 1938: 340.
55 *Ibid.*, 441; (cf. McNeill 1938: 337) see also above, pp. 7–8. We shall see later that the evil forces recruited adherents among monks who did not follow attentively the sermons, but dozed off (see below, p. 195) and other 'lax Christians'.
56 Schmitz i, 448, 668–9; ii, 437.
57 *Ibid.* i, 317.
58 *Ibid.* i, 320: 'If anyone ingests the blood of animals alive or dead or killed [for a sacrifice] ...'; cf. *ibid.* ii, 182, 338, 448. The textual history of these prohibitions suggests that the condemnation of drinking the blood of animals weakened around the fifth century but regained strictness in the sixth to the seventh, when missionary activity among the Germanic peoples began.
59 Schmitz i, 415; ii, 344.
60 The Penitential of Columban, c. 24 (Schmitz i, 600) equates the drinking or eating of blood by anyone who has been warned not to do so, with 'sacrilege and participation in the Devil's feast' and implies that such things are done 'in the service of demons'. Cf. also Schmitz ii, 303, 305; ii, 424, etc.
61 Schmitz i, 416, 618.
62 On the relation of pre-Christian and Christian views on food and its role in social life, see Piekarczyk 1968: 96ff.; Hauck 1950. On feasts among barbarians and the function of banquets in these societies and in feudalism, see Gurevich 1970: 76–7; 1972: 87, 189, 206, etc.
63 Schmitz ii, 494.

64 *Ibid.* II, 427–8; cf. McNeill 1938: 332.
65 *Ibid.* I, 508, 789.
66 For the very same reason all methods inducing abortion or causing the death of the foetus were strictly condemned (Flandrin 1969). Just as decisive was the persecution of infanticide, usually done by 'over-laying' of babies, i.e. smothering them in the common bed of the family.
67 The mystic ecstasies of visionary religious women (and nuns) often imply the barely disguised sexual experience of their 'marriage to Christ' (Bicilli 1919: 19ff.). On medieval misogyny and late medieval 'demonization' of women, see Delumeau 1978: 305–6.
68 A Spanish penitential mentions among the personages condemned by the church a certain *orcus*, and Schmitz (I, 711) mentions that in Iberian carnivals there was a cyclops-type figure by the name of *orco*.
69 The eighth-century Frankish list of superstitions (cf. Homan 1965; McNeill 1938: 419–21) records that at the time of lunar eclipse the peasants encouraged the moon by shouting 'Vince Luna!' (MGH LL 2, 1: 222).
70 A similarly 'analogical' perception of the interrelationship between man and nature is, incidentally, also characteristic for highly educated medieval authors: Sprandel 1972: 24ff.
71 Schmitz I, 311, 413, 479.
72 Nevertheless, these works also contain much information on folk magic and reflect exactly the same attitude to nature that we have noted in the study of the penitentials.
73 It has been argued that the Germanic peoples in the Middle Ages did not see that conflict between divine providence and 'fate' which modern scholars register. In the monuments of Old English, Scandinavian and German literature fate was supposedly thought of merely as a principle of creation established by the deity and expressing the constant changeability of human affairs (Weber 1969). The fault of this conclusion originates, to my mind, in the very approach which studies only one distinct term and overlooks all other complex references which might illuminate the problem from another side.
74 Potions and magic objects are seen by the ecclesiastical authors as attempting to divert *judicium Dei*, and their users are to be punished *ut magi* (Schmitz I, 811).
75 'Nullus presumat diabolica carmina cantare ubi luctus et planctus debet resonare...' (Schmitz II, 496; cf. McNeill 1938: 333).
76 Fear of a terrible divinity or of the forces of evil, fear of human adversities and natural catastrophies, and above all of the terrifying Last Judgment and damnation, permeated the popular mind of the Middle Ages and frequently led to mass psychoses. 'Intimidating and intimidated thoughts' (Bakhtin) were not only characteristic of official Christianity but were also integral parts of popular culture. Pessimism as to salvation and damnation was ever-present. Hence it is difficult to concur with Bakhtin, when he writes (1963) of 'fearlessness' in the medieval popular mind. The overcoming of social and cosmic fears in the carnival represents rather a psychological compensation of sorts, a kind of relaxation of tension by people who were under constant pressure from forces beyond their control. Only after the completion of the manuscript of this book did I gain access to the excellent study of Delumeau (1978) on the all-encompassing fear in the late medieval and early modern centuries; much the same, and more, could be written on the early and high Middle Ages.

77 This synthesis of Christian and pagan elements must have been present in those popular, carnivalesque, feasts which were held on certain saints' days, and against which the church authorities kept fulminating: '...si quis balationes [= saltationes] ante ecclesias fecerit, seu qui faciem transformaverit...' (Schmitz II, 337; cf. McNeill 1938: 276, 293; cf. also 229). A similar syncretism can be detected in the oft-banned form of fortune-telling from sacred writings or by saints' names (*sortes sanctorum*): Schmitz II, 231, etc.; McNeill 1938: 000, etc.

78 The Dominican John Bromyard reports on sudden fits of parishioners, who would feel the need immediately to confess their sins and beg their priest: 'Ask me right now, listen to me!' (Owst 1961: 237).

4 The *Divine Comedy* before Dante

1 Of significant interest in this regard are recent studies focussing on the problem of the perception and experience of death in various historical eras: see Tenenti 1952; Vovelle 1972, 1974; Ariès 1976, 1977; Chaunu 1978; Neveux 1979; and the special issue of *Annales E.S.C.* 31 (1976), no. 1.

2 A prime place among these interpretations belongs to the *Elucidarium* of Honorius of Autun, which will be discussed in the following chapter. The works of Vincent of Beauvais, hagiography and other works also played an essential role.

3 On predestination, see below, ch. 5.

4 The extent to which this aspect of the study of medieval literature is ignored can be seen even in such a fundamental work of that of I. N. Golenishchev-Kutuzov (1971), in which Dante's connections with the Graeco-Roman world, the Bible, medieval thinkers and Arab culture are shown. Only there is nothing about the vast literature of 'otherworldly journeys'! The author dispenses with them in one note criticizing the views of A. N. Veselovskij (1866), who fell into an 'exaggeration of popular origin and tradition in medieval literatures' (Golenishchev-Kutuzov 1971: 478, note). But should not one first point out or study this popular origin and only then judge whether it is exaggerated? In a commentary on Dante, Golenishchev-Kutuzov haughtily calls all medieval works about otherworldly journeys 'feeble' (*Dante Alig'eri* 1968: 467). But can one not put the question: how was the *Divine Comedy* perceived in Dante's time? After all, at the beginning of the fourteenth century the medieval period was not over, and everybody knew and remembered numerous stories about otherworldly visits from the souls of people who died and then came back to life – works of a favourite and widely disseminated literary genre already centuries old by Dante's time. People of his time were tormented anew by the thought of what awaited man after death. Miraculous otherworldly sojourns were preached from the pulpit and in the evening were related at home, and for medieval man there was no subject more vital and captivating. Dante's poem, for all its originality and uniqueness, stands at the end-point of a path along which such literature had passed. A comparison of the *Comedy* with medieval otherworldly narratives shows all the more clearly that which is principally new in Dante's world-view and artistic method. At the same time this analysis would help reveal the popular roots of pre-Renaissance culture. It is clear that such an approach by no means supposes a 'return' of Dante to the

medieval world-view. Dante departed from the world-view of the Middle Ages, but it was precisely from that view that he departed.

5 St Eutichius the Martyr appeared to a bishop and proclaimed three times: 'The end of all flesh has come!' This prophecy was quickly thereafter corroborated, according to Pope Gregory I, by heavenly signs, as well as by the ravaging of Italy by the Lombards, the depopulation of cities, the pillaging of churches and monasteries, the desolation of fields and property, so that wild animals appeared in those places in which formerly people had dwelled. The pope does not know about the situation in other countries, but in Italy he is convinced that the world no longer awaits the end – it is experiencing it! (See *Dial.*: III, 38, 2–3; IV: 43, 2.) In any case, one can speak about a feeling of the 'ageing of the world' (*mundus senescit*) widespread among medieval writers, although in many such expressions one might suppose a commonplace going back to the apostolic epistles and to the works of Augustine (Curtius 1963: 38).

6 *Dial.* I: 12, 1–3.

7 *Ibid.* IV: 32, 2–4.

8 *Ibid.* IV: 44, 1–45, 2.

9 *Visio cujusdam pauperculae mulieris*, in Wattenbach-Levison, *Deutschlands Geschichtsquellen im Mittelalter: Vorzeit und Karolinger*, ed. H. Löwe, I, (Weimar, 1967), 317–18. This vision records also the punishment for Ludwig the Pious, considered responsible for the death of his kinsman, King Bernard of Italy: the emperor's name disappeared from the wall surrounding paradise, access to which is permitted only to those whose names are written on the walls in gold letters: 'Illius interfectio istius oblitteratio fuit' (*ibid.*, p. 278).

10 *Dial.* IV: 36, 14.

11 *Ibid.* IV: 37, 2.

12 *Ibid.* IV: 37, 5–6. This story is borrowed almost literally from Lucian's satire 'The Lover of Lies, or the Doubter'. But in Lucian's Hades the court is composed of pagan gods and mythological creatures, and presiding over it is Pluto, who proclaims upon seeing Cleodemus (mistakenly having reached the underworld): 'His thread is not yet finished, so let him go!' He ordered that his neighbour, the blacksmith Demylus, be brought to court: see *Lucian*, with an English translation by A. M. Harmon, Loeb Classical Library (London–New York, 1921) III, 359. It is highly significant that Gregory's reinterpretation of the story is accompanied by a weakening of the initial sense of parody and satire.

13 *Dial.* IV: 37, 8–14.

14 PL 125: 1115–19. Cf. *Visio cujusdam pauperculae mulieris* (as no. 9 above), p. 317.

15 *Dial.* IV: 57, 2–6.42. The pope considers it necessary to add that one has more hope of being saved while alive than of salvation from others after death: cf. *ibid.* IV: 60, 1.

16 *Dial.* IV: 40, 3–5.

17 *Hist. Fr.* IV, 33.

18 *Vitae patrum* XVII, 5 (PL 71: 1082ff.).

19 *Hist. Fr.* VII, 1.

20 In German poetry, especially in the *Heliand*, the heavenly kingdom is often depicted with the aid of terms borrowed from domestic, economic and rural life. 'The prosperity of a householder stands before the spiritual gaze

of the poet when he speaks about otherworldly blessings' (Peters 1915: 22).

21 *HE* III, 19.

22 *Ibid.* v, 12.

23 *Ibid.* v, 13.

24 Young boys in a church reading books on whose pages black and blood-red letters are visible figure in the vision of an English cleric described by Prudentius (*Ann. Bertiniani*, ad. a. 839, ed. G. Waitz, MGH SS rer. Germ. 5); sins are recorded with the red letters. The boys are the souls of saints, who pray for the forgiveness of people's transgressions. In the vision of the Italian Alberich (*circa* 1129 in Dante, *Divina Commedia* (Padua, 1882), v. 287–328), during the quarrel over the soul, a demon takes out a book in which all its sins are recorded, but an angel pours on to its pages a bottle of tears shed by the righteous and washes away the writing (cf. Fritzsche 1887: 339, 354–7).

25 *S. Bonifatii et Lullii epistolae*, ed. M. Tangl, MGH Epp. sel. 1: 7–15 (no. 10).

26 *Visio Wettini*, MGH Poet. lat. 2: 267–75, 301–33; cf. Fritzsche 1887: 337–9.

27 'Visio Eucherii' (E. Baluze, *Capitularia regum Francorum*, 2 vols. (Paris, 1677) II, 109); cf. Fritzsche 1887: 339.

28 PL 125: 1115–19; cf. Fritzsche 1887: 340–2.

29 Cf. the work of J. Le Goff, *La naissance du Purgatoire* (Paris, 1981), and my critical comments in A. Ja. Gurevich, 'Popular and scholarly medieval cultural traditions: notes in the margin of Jacques Le Goff's book', *Journal of Medieval History*, 9 (1983), 71–90. See also my comments on his views below, pp. 148–9.

30 In particular, as already noted above, a vague image of purgatory now arises, now disappears in various descriptions. The same otherworldly realms are either places of the soul's eternal punishment or the threshold of those places into which souls come after a more or less protracted cleansing or after Judgment Day. A settled idea of purgatory, as already stated above, was formed rather late (at the end of the twelfth or the beginning of the thirteenth century). In iconography it was consolidated only towards the fifteenth century.

31 On the commonplace of visions, see Patch 1950. In many cases these commonplaces are close to the otherworldly motifs of fairy-tales: see Suits 1911.

32 Moreover, there were people who generally did not believe in the resurrection of the soul. Gregory of Tours tells of a cleric with such doubts (*Hist. Fr.* x, 13). There were also false visions. In the satirical 'Song about False Visions' a liar is ridiculed who told of his visit to the Other World, where he was entertained by Christ himself, with John the Baptist serving as cupbearer and St Peter as chef (Edélstand du Méril 1843: 298ff). In the story about St Patrick's visit to purgatory, whose entrance is located in a cave on some northern island, mention is made that this story evoked suspicion among the common people: '...if that were in fact the case, then everybody could visit it and return' (Wright 1844: 65). Caesarius of Heisterbach wrote about St Patrick's Purgatory: 'If anyone doubts the existence of purgatory, let him go to Scotland [i.e. Ireland] and enter the purgatory of St Patrick, and he will have no more need to doubt the

punishments waiting in purgatory' (*DM* XII, 38). Froissart asked an English knight whether the stories about the miracles performed at St Patrick's cave have any foundation, and he answered affirmatively (Patch 1950: 114).

33   *Dial.* IV: 50; cf. *DM* VIII, 4. Along with the classification of dreams in Caesarius of Heisterbach there is also a classification of visions. The two sides of a ladder leading from heaven to earth, he writes, depict the two types of visions – the corporeal and the spiritual. Together with the *visio corporalis* and *visio spiritualis* he dwells on the *visio intellectualis sive mentalis* (*DM* VIII, 1). On dreams as a literary genre and as a component of medieval culture, see Le Goff 1977: 299–306, and P. Burke, 'L'Histoire sociale des rêves', *Annales E.S.C.*28 (1973), 329–42.

34   Cf. the thoughts of Ju. M. Lotman on the 'aesthetics of identity' (Lotman 1964: 173ff.).

35   PL 125: 113.

36   The problem is considered in just this way by Glendinning (1974), who investigates dreams in the Icelandic 'Saga of the Sturlings'. He attempts to separate the 'genuine' dreams from the 'ungenuine', winnowed from tradition or thought up by the saga's author.

37   *Hist. Fr.* VII, 1. In the same way, Bede, having decided to tell his readers about Fursey's otherworldly visions, refers them to the work in which they are described in detail, while he himself thinks it most expedient to confine himself to a paraphrase of a single episode: see *HE* III, 19.

38   One of the earliest works of this genre is the 'Vision of Baront' (eighth century). In a dream Baront was carried off into hell by two frightful demons, where he was whipped before being saved by the archangel Raphael. In the Other World his chief sins were revealed to him and their atonement was appointed. Penance, usually imposed in life by a priest, is set by St Peter in the Other World (*Visio Baronti*, MGH SS 5: 379ff.). Regarding this vision, Levison (1921: 86) notes: 'The question here is really about the delirious fantasy of a monk, and not about a conscious invention, and owing to its spontaneity this small, little-noticed monument sheds more light on the religious notions of the time than many other works.'

39   The *Apocalypse of Paul* was widespread (in translation) both in the Near East and among the Slavs and in the West. The period of its highest popularity begins in the eighth century; the greater part of its extant Latin redactions belongs to the tenth–twelfth centuries (Silverstein 1935: 3ff., 12).

40   Cf., however, the interminable list of trials in the Irish vision of hell: *Life of Brenainn son of Finnlug. Lives of Saints from the Book of Lismore*, ed. W. Stokes (*Anecdota Oxoniensia*) (Oxford, 1890), 254ff.

41   Augustine decisively condemned the 'absurd Apocalypse of Paul, rightfully rejected by the church and full of fantastic fables' (C. Tischendorf, *Apocalypses apocryphae* (Leipzig, 1866), xiv).

42   In turn, these words from the *Aeneid* echo the 'ship list' of the *Iliad* (II. 489): 'Even if I had ten tongues and ten throats...'.

43   *Visio Tnugdali*, ed. A. Wagner (Erlangen, 1882), 35.

44   *DM* XII, 19.

45   *Vita Anskarii auctore Rimberto*, ed. G. Waitz, MGH SS rer. Germ. 55 (Hanover, 1884), c. 3 (p. 22).

46 *Dial.* IV: 44, 1.
47 *Ibid.* IV: 36, 8–9.
48 *Ibid.* IV: 31, 2–4.
49 *Gesta Dagoberti* I, 44 (MGH SS 2: 421).
50 Caesarius of Heisterbach cites the stories of eyewitnesses who, finding
    themselves near volcanoes, heard the conversations of demons preparing
    to receive sinners: *DM* VII, 7–9, 12, 13.
51 The dating of the manuscript of the *Voyage of Brendan* is approximate
    (possibly to the tenth century): see *Navigatio sancti Brendani abbatis*, ed.
    C. Selmer (Notre Dame, Ind. 1959), xxviiiff.
52 When Brendan's crew was already at full strength, three more monks came
    to him and entreated him to take them on the voyage, 'so that they would
    not die of hunger': *Navigatio sancti Brendani*, p. 11.
53 Medieval fantasy occasionally located its utopias somewhere in the East.
    One can conjecture that the descriptions of otherworldly paradises were
    also connected somehow with utopian hopes. However, even if notions
    about every sort of abundance are also transposed into these transcendental
    regions, I do not note a universal equality. The earthly hierarchy is also
    preserved on the other side of life: the social system is not subject to doubt
    and earthly ranks and status are preserved.
54 See above, n. 43
55 Cf. *Sulpicii Severi De vita beati Martini* VII,, 6 (ed. J. Fontaine, pp. 268ff.)
    (on the journey of a dead man through the Other World): '...deputatumque
    obscuris locis et vulgaribus turbis...'.
56 PL 125: 1117.
57 *E* III, 19–21. For more details, see below, ch. 5.
58 Demons preyed upon Baront in hell 'right up to the third hour', when he
    was rescued by Raphael, who struggled with the demons for his soul right
    up 'to Vespers': *Visio Baronti*, c. 17 (MGH SS 5: 379ff., 391).
59 *Visio Tnugdali*, pp. 42ff.
60 MGH SS 5: 368–94. In another vision mention is made of a church in the
    Other World so capacious that all humankind could fit in it at the same
    time (Wright 1844: 42).
61 *Inferno* XV.38; XXI.112–14; XXX.83; *Purgatory* XV.1–6.
62 *Purgatory* XVI.26–7.
63 Dante's appearance in hell roused its inhabitants: 'It introduced a short
    moment of historical dramatism into the immutability of eternal destiny'
    (Auerbach 1976: 200). Dante puts himself at the centre of his otherworldly
    narrative. But the journeys of medieval visionaries through the Other
    World in no way affect its population, and the travellers are only detached
    observers, passive spectators.
64 *Navigatio sancti Brendani*, p. 67.
65 *The Voyage of Bran, Son of Febal to the Land of the Living*, II (London,
    1897), 2–35; J. D. St. Seymour. *Irish Visions of the Other World* (London,
    1930), 62ff. The *Voyage of Bran, Son of Febal* is dated to the eighth
    century. I do not dwell in detail on the very interesting Irish otherworldly
    stories, since they do not belong to Latin visionary literature and require
    an independent study.
    Cf. the *Speculum historiale* of Vincent of Beauvais (quoted Wright 1844:
    31): a young boy visiting purgatory saw adults being boiled in cauldrons
    until they were transformed into new-borns. Then they became adults and

once again were boiled down to childhood, whereupon the whole procedure started up once more. Thus, time for those people acquired a sort of bi-direction.

66 A knight mentioned by Walter Map thought he spent three days in the Other World, but it turned out to be really two centuries. A hero of a chivalric romance, returning to his homeland after travelling in the Other World, learned that more than three centuries had gone by. For another romance character two hundred years in the Other World seemed like twenty (Patch 1950: 232, 245, 261, 263).

67 *DM* II, 2.

68 *DM* VIII, 5. Christ yielded not so much out of pity for sinful humankind, continues Caesarius of Heisterbach, as out of pity for the Cistercians, giving them more time to prepare themselves for the passage to the Other World (*DM* XII, 58).

69 Kleinschmidt 1974: 74 (no. 22).

70 On the 'paradigms' of mythical time, see Meletinskij 1976: 171ff.; cf. Mikhailov 1976: 161ff.

71 *DM* VIII, 5ff.

72 In stories about meetings of the living with the dead in Icelandic sagas, which basically reflect a still pagan conception of death, a deceased man appearing from the grave is just a physical body. Only the destruction of the body – e.g., by burying or dismembering it (the most sure method is by decapitating the 'living dead' and sticking the head to his thighs) – leads to his 'full' death. Incorporeal spirits are unknown in the sagas, as is the notion of the Christian soul.

73 *Visio Tnugdali*, pp. 52–3.

74 *Visio cujusdam pauperculae mulieris*, p. 278.

75 MGH Epp. sel. 1: 8–15 (no. 10).

76 *Dial.* IV: 27, 10–13.

77 *Inferno* VI.36; XII.96; *Purgatory* II.79–81; III.88–96; V.4–6, 25–7; XXI. 133–6.

78 Kleinschmidt 1974: 48 (no. 18), 69 (no. 18), 111 (no. 48).

79 *Ibid.*, 119 (no. 54). As Thomas of Chantimpré tells it, one man in a tavern doubted that the soul continues to exist even after the body's death. As a joke he sold his soul to one of those present, and when the festivities were over the devil (for who else could have bought the soul?) seized it and the body – 'After all, he who buys the horse gets the bridle, too!' (Coulton 1930: 131). With the same words the devil seized the bodies of sinners whose souls he already possessed (Klapper 1914: no. 158; cf. no. 163).

80 *Visio Baronti*, c. 5 (MGH SS 5: 381). In a story of Paul the Deacon, the soul of the Frankish king Gunthram abandons its body in a dream in the form of a lizard and finds in the depths of a mountain treasures hidden there 'already in ancient times'. Together with the corporeal image of the soul, we note in this story the traditional visionary motif of the bridge thrown over the stream which leads to the Other World (here as a sword along which the lizard crosses over the stream).

81 There is nothing to be surprised at here, since in depicting the hell's scenes Bosch was inspired not by the *Divine Comedy*, almost completely unknown in northern Europe, but by the *Vision of Tnugdal*, as well as by 'marketplace diableries'.

82 Just as theologians interpreted stories about the Earthly Paradise with a certain caution. Augustine mentions three views on this score: that the Earthly Paradise is literally real; that is must be understood spiritually and figuratively; and that sometimes it must be taken as a physical fact and at other times interpreted spiritually. He himself inclined to the latter compromise. Such was also the opinion of other theologians (Patch 1950: 143ff.).

83 *Dial.* IV: 1, 5.

84 *DM* XII, 23, 24.

85 Ultimately Bede's expression 'locus in quo examinandae et castigandae sunt animae' (*HE* V, 2) communicates the essence of purgatory just as well as the term *purgatorium*.

86 However, the presence of an immediate connection between the consolidation of the idea of purgatory and the changes in the social structure at the end of the Middle Ages, which several French scholars assert (Chaunu 1978: 95ff.), seems to me to be doubtful.

87 A man's soul is invariably a passive object of this conflict. But 'psychomachia' was interpreted this way in the early Middle Ages. In the twelfth century Alan of Lille in his poem *Anticlaudianus* essentially changes the theme: the man himself, summoning his merits for help, fights against his sins (PL 210: 481ff.). This new interpretation displays as clearly as possible the specificity of the preceding conception of man and his spiritual world, as well as the measure of his absorption by society and concerning his weak autonomy. The allegorism of the struggle of sins and merits 'carried away' the moral virtues and imperfections of the personality beyond the bounds of its internal world and imparted to them an independent existence or, in any case, divided the personality into two adversaries – body and soul – fighting between themselves. For an account of the struggle of the soul with the body, see the poem about the vision of Fulbert (Edélstand du Méril 1843; cf. Batiushkov 1891).

88 *DM* IV, 9, 35.

89 The conviction existed in the Middle Ages that the greater part of souls will perish and only a few will be saved: see below, ch. 5.

90 For critical remarks, see Borst 1980. My polemic with Ariès is contained in Gurevich 1982.

5 The *Elucidarium*: popular theology and folk religiosity in the Middle Ages

1 The sub-heading *Dialogus de summa totius Christianae theologiae* apparently does not belong to the author.

2 *E* II, 28.

3 Honorius explains that the damned 'propter se ipsos pereunt, cum malum sua sponte eligunt, diligunt et vellent sine fine vivere, ut possent sine fine peccare': *E* II, 29

4 *E* II, 52–60.

5 *E* II, 61: '*Discipulus* – Quid de agricolis? *Magister* – Ex magna parte salvantur, quia simpliciter vivunt et populum Dei suo sudore pascunt, ut dicitur: "Labores manuum qui manducant beati sunt." '

6 *E* II, 62.

7 *E* II, 63.

8 *E* I, 195, 196. Such an interpretation of the sacraments deviated from the orthodox tradition and was condemned even by Augustine: PL 38: 453.

9 *E* II 66.

10 *E* III 59.

11 *E* II, 9.

12 *E* II, 11–12, 15–16.

13 *E* II, 17.

14 *E* III, 33.

15 *Sermo Generalis* (PL 172: 865–6).

16 For the Antichrist's resurrection of the dead will be a fraud: the devil will enter their bodies and compel them to walk and talk, as if they were living: *E* III, 34.

17 *E* I, 179.

18 *E* III, 12, 14.

19 Cf. the distichon on hell's torments in Vincent of Beauvais: 'Nix, nox, vox, lachrymae, sulpur, sitis, aestus, / Malleus et stridor, spes perdita, vincula, vermes.' (*Speculum historiale* CXIX) A mid-fifteenth-century manual for exorcism contains questions addressed to souls who appeared from purgatory and hell. Here are several questions put to an emigrant from purgatory: 'How long have you been in purgatory?' 'Which torments turned out to be the most salvific for you?' 'Why have you appeared?' Questions to the soul of a damned sinner dwelling in hell: 'Why have you been condemned to eternal tortures?' 'Why have you come? Do you want to frighten the living? Do you secure the damnation of pilgrims, which we are on earth? Would you not prefer never to have been born to having to undergo hell's trials? What are the most frightful torments in hell? Is not the loss of seeing Christ in person the most painful of all tortures?' (Delumeau 1978: 79)

20 *E* III, 15.

21 On the connection of Honorius' works with the artistic culture of his time, see Mâle 1924: 409; 1958: 400, 426; Endres 1903. As for the posture of those tortured sinners in hell, one can refer to the following parallel: in the Icelandic 'The Story about Thorstein the Goose-Flesh' the ancient hero Starkad stands in the netherworld on his head and is completely engulfed by hellfire (Gurevich 1979: 148, 166).

22 Hamann 1955, 2: 144–8, ills. 130–6; Le Goff 1965, ills. 74, 76, 77, 142; Darkevich 1972: 135ff.

23 Honorius' ideas on the significance of painting and sculpture are collected by Endres (1903: 13ff.). On the symbolism of church iconography in connection with Honorius' work, see Sauer (1902).

24 *E* III, 18.

25 *E* III, 19.

26 *E* III, 20, 21. Thomas of Chantimpré repeated roughly the same thing in the second half of the thirteenth century: the saints experience joy at seeing the tortures of sinners, even if their kinsmen are among them, and one can have no doubt about this, like other fools. The saints, unaffected by any but sublime emotions, are not susceptible to grief and worries, and a complete unity with divine justice is required of the perfect Christian (Coulton 1930: 109).

27 *E* II, 64, 65.

28 *E* II, 29.

29 *E* II, 42.
30 The question of free will is different in the late works of Honorius: see *De libero arbitrio*, PL 172: 1223–4.
31 *E* I, 36, 90, 91, 121–4, 128, 129.
32 *E* I, 127, 137, 156, 157, 159, 161–6.
33 *E* I, 13, 15; cf. II, 22–5.
34 *E* II, 88.
35 *E* II, 92, 93. It is curious that one of the medieval French translators of the *Elucidarium* included in the text a discussion absent in the original about witches flying through the air, soothsayers, sorcerers and other servants of the devil: see Lefèvre 1954: 299ff.
36 *E* I, 59.
37 Honorius had built on the thought of predecessors – Macrobius, Ambrose, Augustine, Rabanus Maurus – particularly in searching for numerical correspondences, to which he, like most medieval theologians, attributed symbolic significance. Honorius returns to the theme of the microcosm in *Sacramentarium* and in *De imagine mundi* I, 82 (PL 172: 140, 773): see Endres 1906: 108.
38 *E* I, 64, 65, 67.
39 Boso was the abbot of the Norman monastery of Bec (1124–36), and his biography is preserved (PL 150: 723–32). *Cur Deus homo* is cited according to the edition: Anselm of Canterbury, *Cur Deus homo. Warum Gott Mensch geworden*, ed. and trans. J. Schmitt (Munich, 1970).
40 *Cur Deus homo* I, 10; II, 14, 15.
41 The character of the dialogues in these tractates, as well as in medieval literature in general, needs study. On the dialogue in Anselm of Canterbury and Honorius, see Grabmann 1909: I, 317ff; 1911: II, 130. On the dialogue as a principle of thought and of structuring a literary genre, see Bibler 1975; Batkin 1978: ch. 3.
42 *Cur Deus homo* II, 15, 9, 20.
43 *E* III, 81, 106. Honorius' love of light, tonalities of colour and the beauties of nature are also striking in reading his other works: see Sanford 1948: 406, 412.
44 *E* I, 46; II, 6.
45 *E* I, 5, 23, 54, 102, 113; II, 2, 40, 41, 52, 72.
46 *E* III, 1, 7, 46, 51, 53, 59, 114, 118, 121.
47 For example, *formositas–deformitas, libertas–captivitas, deliciae–miseriae.* Cf. *E* III, 119: 'Sicut igitur hi amici Dei nimium felices perenniter in Domino gloriabuntur, ita e contrario inimici ejus nimium miseri et infelices jugiter cruciabuntur et, sicut isti maximo decore illustrantur, ita illi maximo horrore deturpantur. Sicut isti summa agilitate sunt alleviati, ita illi summa pigritia praegravati', etc. On the 'poetic streak' in Honorius, see Endres 1906: 18, 127ff. On the rhythmical prose in the *Elucidarium*, see Lefèvre 1954: 209, 213. On the 'homoeoteleuton' – the assonance of endings, which links grammatically homogeneous words in works of ancient and medieval prose – see Averintsev 1977: 223–31.
48 James Joyce's novel *A Portrait of the Artist as a Young Man* can give some notion of the extent to which the description of the punishments awaiting sinners influenced a more modern Catholic: his hero Stephen Daedalus hears a sermon based on the *Elucidarium* or, in any case, a source extremely close to it. The consequence of this sermon is a deep

crisis of conscience. An age, a structure of the personality other than in the Middle Ages; the sermon itself is altered and psychologically deepened, and in it stress is laid not only on the physical trials threatening the sinner in the Other World, but also on his moral condition and on his personal relationship with Christ. Nevertheless, the reaction evoked by these pictures and images is for the most part evidently the same.

49 *E* II, 71.
50 *E* III 107–14.
51 In the *exempla* there is more than one mention of people whose sins were completely forgotten by the priest after confession, as if they had never been at all.
52 Gottschalk taught that there is a twofold predestination – not only for salvation, but also for perdition ('praedestinatio gemina ad vitam et ad mortem'), from which it followed that the sacraments and good deeds were powerless, and obedience to the church meaningless – which was precisely the accusation of his enemies.
53 Cf., however, the high estimate of the labour of farmers and their chances for salvation in the *Sermones vulgares* of Jacques de Vitry (died *circa* 1240): *Sermo LX ad agricolas et vinitores et alios operarios*, text in Welter 1927: 457–67. See also the eleventh-century *Vita Dagoberti* (Duby 1978: 211ff.).
54 Cf. above, ch. 4, on the depiction of the resurrected in church sculpture.
55 *E* III, 11–16.

6 'High' and 'low': the medieval grotesque

1 Here Bakhtin (1965: 8) writes about the 'sharp break' between two lives, official and carnival. Cf. his similar statement: '…ritual-visible forms…organized on the principle of laughter, were extremely sharply, one can say principally, distinguished from serious official, i.e., church and feudal-governmental, cult forms and ceremonials. They offered a completely different, emphatically unofficial, extra-ecclesiastical, and extra-governmental aspect of the world, man, and human relations; on this side of everything official they built a sort of second world and a second life, in which all medieval people participated in varying degrees and lived for definite periods of time. This particular type of two-worldness must be taken into account in order to understand correctly medieval cultural consciousness and Renaissance culture.'
2 Medieval *exempla* contain numerous stories about divine punishment inflicted on impious dancers: an entire group of such sinners is condemned to dance without stopping for an entire year; a young girl carried away by a dance is abducted by the devil; the devil appears as a musician to the tune of whose music people dance unsuspectingly; lightning strikes some dancers and the church they insulted (Tubach 1969: nos. 1063, 1415, 1419, 1420, 1424). See E. E. Metzner, *Zur frühesten Geschichte der europäischen Balladendichtung. Der Tanz in Kölbigk. Legendarische Nachrichten, gesellschaftlicher Hintergrund, historische Voraussetzungen* (Weisbaden, 1972).
3 With the Christianization of Scandinavia there was apparently no opposition to the use of pagan artistic forms, such as the heads of dragons, in the decoration of churches.

4 In the *Preface to Cromwell* Victor Hugo sagaciously and accurately indicated the role of the grotesque in the art of Europe after the end of Antiquity. Particularly fruitful is his observation on the all-embracing significance of the grotesque, which permeated all spheres of medieval life, including its customs and law (cf. Souriau 1897: 137–45).

5 A scholar of Byzantine hagiography arrives at contrary conclusions, asserting that the hagiographical has an 'invariably serious tone' and 'does not know irony' (Poliakova 1972: 255).

6 John Chrysostom: 'Or is laughter evil? No, laughter is not evil, but excessiveness and inappropriateness are evil…Laughter is placed into our soul so that the soul may rest, and not so that it may be spilt' (quoted by Averincev 1977: 274).

7 There is a story about St Gregory doing the unheard-of thing of bursting out laughing while saying mass. When asked why, the saint answered that he had seen a terrifying demon seated on the railings with a piece of parchment writing down everything people chattered about during the service. But they babbled so much that the piece of parchment could not contain it all. In order to stretch the piece out the demon grabbed hold of it with his teeth and pulled with such force that it tore in two, and he fell over backwards. That was what set the saint to laughing (Klapper 1914: no. 33).

8 As an example of the difficulties of distinguishing comedy, satire and parody in medieval Latin literature, one can point to the enigmatic philological tractates of the enigmatic grammarian known as Virgilius Maro. Some scholars see in him and his works about Latin a reflection of the specific linguistic situation in the barbarian kingdoms in the seventh century (Fortunatov 1946). Others believe that he was a cabbalist, and that he extended the methods of cabbalist mystical interpretation to Latin grammar (Curtius 1963: 312n., 439n.). However, Bakhtin (1965: 18) and Lehmann (1963: 9ff.) consider these works parody.

9 I do not use works that have a specific satirical or parodic direction; there is no riddle in them. See Gilman 1974; Lehmann 1963.

10 The artistic interpretation of the forces of evil cannot be dealt with in this book, but one warning seems necessary. The essential shortcoming of works devoted to the theme of the devil in medieval iconography is in the confusion of different periods. The image of demons in medieval art underwent a long evolution, and one cannot speak indiscriminately about monuments from the early period and from the fourteenth and fifteenth centuries at the same time. Demons on the margins of illuminated manuscripts and on the portals and capitals of Romanesque and Gothic churches, on the one hand, and demons in the paintings of Breughel, Bosch and other Renaissance artists, on the other, are to be treated very differently. Medieval art proper was much more restrained and laconic in treating demons and the devil than was the succeeding period, in which one observes simultaneously the violence of demonology and the decline of its seriousness. Medieval artists strove to reveal the devil's image, 'how he was in fact', and in this sense they were convinced that they were not inventing anything. Artists of the Renaissance and Reformation revelled in invention, piling up newer and newer details and creating original compositions. The theme was common to both ages, but the way they looked at the Other World and, consequently, the artistic language which

they used, were very different. The brilliantly distorting fantasy of Bosch and Breughel generates nightmarish pictures of infernal horror, but they are completely tinged by their artists' subjective vision, even in those instances where they derive from texts of medieval otherworldly visions, e.g., the *Vision of Tnugdal*. This reservation is important, since the tendency to judge the Middle Ages in the light of later centuries is not uncommon. To use the works of Botticelli, Michelangelo, and Dürer to reconstruct medieval man's conception of the devil and demons is just as mistaken as to reconstruct the Middle Ages from the mass witch-hunts of the fifteenth to seventeenth centuries: cf. Delumeau 1978: 232ff.

11 *DM* v, 56.
12 *S. Caesarii Arelatensis Sermones* CCLIII, 3 (CCSL 104: 260).
13 *DM* I, 27.
14 *DM* v, 1.
15 *DM* v, 50; cf. IV, 32, 33, 35. One monk saw a snake, which of course was the devil, crawling along the back of his neighbour, who had fallen asleep during mass. On the head of another sleeping monk sat a tom-cat. Grunting pigs scurried around a monk who habitually dozed off in choir.
16 *DM* v, 7.
17 *DM* v, 8.
18 Kleinschmidt 1974: 98 (no. 37). Sixteenth-century tractates on demonology fixed the general number of demons at 7,400,000, headed by more than 70 princes, in turn subordinated to Satan himself (Delumeau 1978: 251).
19 *DM* v, 9.
20 *DM* v, 10. According to Sulpicius Severus, St Martin declared to a demon, with whom he had fought for sinners' souls, that the Lord could forgive even him, if he would agree to repent. But the demon was unable to do just that. The legend of the demon craving reconciliation with God was also widespread among the Slavs: see Kretzenbacher 1966.
21 *DM* III, 26.
22 *DM* v, 28.
23 *DM* III, 6.
24 *Dial.* I: 4.
25 *Ibid.* III: 20.
26 *DM* v, 12 and 26.
27 *DM* v, 43.
28 Kleinschmidt 1974: 96 (no. 35). Similarly, when a women kept giving birth to daughters, her husband in anger ordered her next time to have a goat or dog instead of a daughter – and so it happened: *Ibid.*, 114 (no. 51); cf. also *ibid.*, 97 (no. 36).
29 *Dial.* I: 10; III: 21. A demon possessed a peasant and compelled him to squeak and bleat. A nun, to whom that same man had come with a present, ordered the demon to leave him immediately, but the demon replied, 'If I depart from him, to whom shall I go?' Just then a pig was passing by, and the nun told him to take up residence there, which he did, killing the pig and then disappearing.
30 *De gloria beatorum confessorum*, c. 63 (PL 71: 873). In the same way a demon possessed the daughter of an Italian count and declared to the priests, 'There is no way that you can get me to leave. But there is a man named Gallus, who has already expelled me from Tuscany, where I had

dwelled for a long time, and he destroyed all my churches. Unless he comes in person, I will not depart from here.' St Gallus drove him out of the girl and sent him into hell in the form of a frightful black raven (*Vita Galli confessoris*, cc. 16–21 (MGH SS rer. Mer. 5: 265–7).

31 *Legenda aurea*, II, 3.

32 *Vita Rusticulae sive Marciae abbatissae Arelatensis*, c. 13 (MGH SS 4: 345–6).

33 *Conversio sanctae Afrae*, cc. 6–7 (MGH SS 3: 58–160).

34 *DM* v, 36.

35 *DM* v, 37.

36 *DM* v, 38.

37 *DM* III, 2. A village priest seduced the wife of a knight, and when the latter was told about it, being a wise and distrustful man, he ordered that the guilt be verified. Knowing that in a neighbouring village there lived a possessed man who revealed the secret sins of those present, the knight invited the priest on some pretext to go there with him. Fearing disclosure, the priest hastened to confess in a stable to the knight's servant and begged for penance to be assigned him. In response to the knight's questions the demon replied that the priest's confession had destroyed the sin. Cf. *DM* III, 3.

38 There was also nothing crafty about a demon who faithfully served in human form a rich man, who gave him his daughter in recompense. But the demon fled from her, since she nagged him day and night. In parting with his father-in-law, he admitted that hell was his homeland, but that he had never met in hell such discord or suffered such evil as he had experienced in just one year with his wife!: Frenken 1914: no. 60.

39 *DM* v, 54.

40 *DM* II, 12; XII, 5, 23.

41 *DM* v, 52.

42 *DM* v, 44, 45.

43 *Libri miraculorum* II, 30 (PL 71: 818); *De miraculis S. Martini* IV, 21 (PL 71: 999).

44 A demon possessing and cruelly tormenting a man would not obey the commands of St Columbanus. Thinking for a long time, the saint thrust his hand into the man's mouth, grabbed hold of his tongue and in the Lord's name ordered the demon to depart immediately. The demon was expelled along with a noxious vomit: *Vita Columbani* I, 25 (MGH SS 4: 99). St Martin, exorcising a demon, did not permit him to depart through the mouth and compelled him to exit through the rear: *Sulpicii Severi De vita beati Martini*, c. 17 (ed. J. Fontaine, pp. 290–1).

45 *De miraculis s. Martini* IV, 37 (PL 71: 1005); *Hist. Fr.* VI, 29.

46 *DM* x, 29; cf. XI, 16.

47 *Hist. Fr.* IX, 21.

48 *Vitae patrum* VII, 4 (PL 71: 1044); XVII, 3 (*ibid.*: 1081). When a horde of 'Ethiopians' attacked the monastery, the monks turned to the powerful remedies of a sermon and the eucharist, and the demons cried out, 'Tomorrow, tomorrow...be patient, be patient, wait a little...Woe is me!' They were unable to endure the rites of the church: *Vita Columbani* II, 29 (MGH SS rer. Mer. 4: 140.

49 But even the theme of otherworldly retribution was sometimes presented

in the *exempla* with irony. Fear of hell's tortures turned some from sin, but one student used to comfort was set right by a preacher who informed him that the beds in hell were very hard (Tubach 1969: no. 544).

50 Caesarius of Heisterbach in these stories uses the expressions: '...ad sua ludibria illos [monachos] trahebat...'; '[conversus] illuderetur a diabolo'; 'daemonos illic dormitantes irrideant...'; 'diabolum ioculariter vocavit...'.

On the representation of forces of evil in medieval art, see the pages in the volume *Le diable*, 1979.

51 *DM* IV, 9.

52 *DM* IV, 35.

53 Jacques de Vitry mentions a stupid peasant who thus imagined hymns. He went to a neighbouring town intending to buy some cantilenas, for the feast-day of his village's patron saint was approaching. A trickster sold him a sack full of choice canticles, but in fact he had filled it with wasps, which in the end repeatedly stung everybody gathered in front of the church (Frenken 1914: no. 78).

54 *DM* VIII, 63.

55 *DM* III, 21.

56 *DM* IX, 30.

57 *DM* X, 42.

58 *DM* IX, 11ff: the power of the eucharist is also extended to animals, insects, and even to insensible objects.

59 *DM* IX, 6, 9, 25.

60 *DM* IX, 48: in a duel between two knights the winner was not the physically stronger one, but his opponent, who had eaten a host before combat.

61 *DM* II, 5.

62 *DM* IX, 3, and others.

63 During a storm in the region of Trier the genitals of a bell-ringer were set on fire by lightning, for he was a fornicator (*DM* X, 29). A litigious fellow, who 'sold his tongue in lawsuits', died with a gaping mouth, which could not be closed by any means (*DM* VI, 28). For the same reason the tongue of another lawyer vanished as he died (*DM* XI, 46).

64 *DM* XII, 47, 50.

65 *DM* V, 40. Cf. Karsavin 1915: 132.

66 *DM* X, 45, 53.

67 Kleinschmidt 1974: nos. 1–6, 8–10, 13, 25, and others. In the same way blood flowed from a crucifix when stones were thrown at it and one of its hands was cut off: *Ibid.*, 59 (no. 12).

68 *Ibid.*, 88 (no. 29).

69 Cf. the story of a woman who, 'having lifted up her hem, exposed her rear to the saint', for which she was punished with terrible sores (Sumption 1976: 41).

70 *DM* V, 21.

71 *Ibid.*

72 Caesarius' report, repeatedly used in literature, is hardly true, but it is interesting for elucidating its author's mentality.

73 *DM* VI, 37.

74 *DM* VI, 5. On the theme of 'lost trousers' in medieval Latin literature, see Curtius 1963: 433–5.

75 *DM* VI, 9, 30–2.

76 *DM* VI, 35.

77 *DM* VI, 2.

78 In the Middle Ages it was also possible to misunderstand the expression 'like milk from a bull'. St Fechin, when he was still a child, worked as a shepherd. There was a fast, and he grew hungry. Not distinguishing the animals' sexes, he attempted to milk a bull by squeezing its genitals. Seeing that no milk was flowing, Fechin blamed himself: 'The Lord has deserted me, since women can milk this cow, and yet I cannot.' 'And lo a miracle, an unusual thing: the bull gave milk in abundance like a cow. This was possible only for Him Who produced honey from stone and butter from rock!': Ch. Plummer, *Vitae sanctorum Hiberniae* (Oxford, 1910) II, 79.

79 *DM* X, 3. The Virgin can also teach Latin. Thus, she instructed in Latin an illiterate Slavic doorkeeper who did not even know German: Klapper 1914: no. 54.

80 *DM* X, 4. A Parisian master of theology (Alan of Lille), praised for being able to interpret the letters of Paul better even than the Apostle himself, was punished with the loss of all his knowledge, so much so that he could not even make out separate letters: Klapper 1914: no. 153.

81 *DM* VI, 5.

82 Kleinschmidt 1974: 87 (no. 28).

83 *DM* III, 2. A demon possessing an illiterate woman exhibited a knowledge of Latin texts in front of clerics: DM v.13.

84 *DM* III, 6.

85 *DM* I, 32.

86 *De miraculis s. Martini* II, 1 (PL 71: 941). As we saw above (ch. 1), the confrontation of the cultivation of the educated with the directness of simpletons is frequently repeated in the works of Gregory and other church authors. It was a widespread 'commonplace'.

87 *DM* v, 21, 22.

88 *DM* VI, 7.

89 *DM* VII, 4; cf. VII, 5. Caesarius narrates a lawsuit between two priests that took place at the papal court. One of them was threatened with losing his parish on account of his ignorance, which obviously hindered him from saying mass. The other litigant was an educated, eloquent man who had encroached upon that church, although he already possessed a series of prebends. He was attempting to secure it with a shower of artfully constructed speeches, which were interrupted by his simple-minded opponent, who declared that he did not know Latin. But the pope permitted him to speak as he could, and he related his poverty and won his case. Having condemned the greed of the educated cleric, the pope left the parish in the possession of the illiterate priest, since the latter had, from the pope's point of view, an undoubted advantage, namely his simple soul and speech: *DM* VI, 29.

90 See the story of the miraculous healing by a saint of a Briton from dumbness. On the saint's feast-day a flow of blood began from this Briton right in church. The monks were about to chase him out, so that he would not stain the holy place, but straightaway the dumb man began to speak inarticulate sounds, and then he started to speak 'in his own coarse British tongue'. 'I am a freed man, I am a freed man' ('Libertinus sum, libertinus sum'). He wanted to say, 'I am free' ('Liberatus sum'). Thus was his tongue unbound: *Vita Austrigisili ep. Biturigi*, c. 13 (MGH SS 4: 207).

91 A modern scholar of medieval Latin education concludes that the age was significantly less 'Latin' than is usually thought from its written sources (Richter 1976: 80).

92   *Vita Austrigisili ep. Biturigi*, c. 10 (MGH SS 4: 206).
93   *Vitae patrum* VIII, 5 (PL 71: 1044). Cf. *Hist. Fr.* IV, 16.
94   *DM* VIII, 52.
95   *DM* VII, 33, 44, 55.
96   *DM* VII, 43.
97   *Libri miraculorum*, I, 23 (PL 71: 724–5).
98   *DM* IV, 38.
99   *DM* VII, 3; 55. A man in shining clothes accompanied by two others appeared to an anchorite in Antioch. With a wave of his hand half the city was destroyed and everybody perished, men, women and cattle. His companions restrained him from destroying the entire city: Klapper 1914: no. 103.
100 On the stability of notions of the vengeance of saints in the fifteenth and sixteenth century, see Delumeau 1978: 61. In Berry there existed a spring dedicated to 'St Evil', close to which people asked for harm or death to come upon their enemies. Not far from it there was a chapel of 'St Good': *ibid.*, p. 62.
101 *DM* X, 1: '...Miraculum dicimus quicquid fit contra solitum cursum naturae, unde miramur. Secundum causas superiores miraculum nihil est.'
102 *DM* XI, 11.
103 *DM* XI, 56.
104 A poor man crossing a bridge heard a voice, 'Drown him, drown him, don't delay!', and another, 'Even without your invitations I would do what you bid, except that sacred objects hinder me. As you know, he is guarded by the blessing of the priest.' The man saw nothing during this exchange. Making the sign of the cross, the poor man continued on his way, and the *pars adversa* did not overpower him: *De gloria beatorum confessorum*, c. 31 (PL 71: 851–2).
105 A man ill in his kidneys was cured by a saint. According to Gregory of Tours, the man 'was liberated from diabolical misfortune': *De miraculis s. Martini* III, 14 (PL 71: 974). Because they considered illness the result of sin or the intervention of the devil, church councils forbade physicians from visiting the sick before the arrival of a priest and threatened Christians who used Jewish physicians with excommunication. These prohibitions, however, were not observed.
106 At the devil's instigation a wind came up and blew dust and chaff into a boy's eyes, but his mother from inexperience did not guard him with the sign of the cross, with the result that the boy went blind: *De miraculis s. Martini* III, 16 (PL 71: 975).
107 *DM* VIII, 26.
108 *DM* VIII, 32. Here Caesarius of Heisterbach offers yet another story equally repellent to modern tastes, but no less pious. A Salzburg bishop offered the body of Christ to a leper, but the latter threw it up. Fearing the profanation of the sacrament, the bishop put his palm under the leper's mouth and swallowed what had been disgorged. Later the pious prelate understood that the leper was Christ himself, whose custom it is to test his elect: *DM* VIII, 33.
109 In conclusion I should just like to comment on the article of Ju. M. Lotman and B. A. Uspenskij on the nature of laughter in medieval Rus'. Correctly and very timely criticizing the mechanical extension of Bakhtin's ideas about carnival-laughter culture to 'regions where their very application

should be the subject of a special study' (Lotman–Uspenskij 1977: 152, n. 2), and emphasizing the absence of ambivalence in the Rus' 'world of laughter', the authors point out (*ibid.*: 154): 'In contrast to the ambivalent popular carnival laughter, according to Bakhtin, blasphemous diabolical laughter does not loosen the world of medieval notions. It constitutes a part of the latter. If the "Bakhtinesque" laughing man was outside medieval values by being neither naked nor perishing, but merely living, then the laughing blasphemer was inside the medieval world...' This judgment is completely accurate in relation to the blasphemous medieval man; as we saw, the same can also be said about Western 'blasphemers'. Let us leave to one side the difficult question of whether there was more blasphemy inverting the medieval structure of the world, and thereby affirming it, in Western or in Eastern Europe, and where it played the more essential role. But it must be mentioned that in the West the 'devil's' (that is, the witches' or heretics') universe was just as far from the culture of laughter as in Rus'.

Lotman and Uspensikj (*ibid.*: 153) interpret the 'Bakhtinesque' laughter of the Catholic region as essentially 'religionless' and 'governmentless'. Proceeding from this interpretation of Bakhtin (which admittedly has some foundation), they are naturally inclined to differentiate West European laughter and the laughter of Rus'. However, if one does not rush to assume an opposition of official and carnival cultures, it is possible that the similarities between the popular cultures of the West and Rus' would seem somewhat greater. I hope that I have shown in this part of the book that the laughing man of the medieval West, like the 'blasphemer', did not fall out of the prevailing system of values. Medieval laughter, as it appears in my sources, was clearly not restricted to priests and monks, but had deep roots in the widely diffused medieval world-view. Expressing important aspects of the popular element, this laughter can hardly be qualified as 'religionless'. Medieval man lived, at one and the same time being saved and perishing, and expressed his contradictory, ambivalent world-view, especially in laughter.

Afterword

1 Dathan and Abiram rebelled against Moses and were swallowed up by the earth (Numbers 16:1–35).

2 In 1465 one excommunicated Englishman expressed his contempt by pointing out that the harvest in his field was no worse than his neighbours' harvest, which would be impossible if the Lord had intervened. *Ergo* the excommunication has no force (Thomas 1971: 46). Excommunication was understood as a magical incantation. Even in the eighteenth century the peasants of Franche-Comté required the Besançon archbishop to excommunicate solemnly the insects and rodents that had devoured their crops (Vauchez 1973: 1048).

3 Some scholars tend to connect the veneration of the Virgin, which increased in the later Middle Ages, with a change in the attitude towards women in Western society.

4 There is almost certainly an allusion to this same text in a novel of Iris Murdoch. A conversation of two modern clerics: 'I no longer believe.' 'What don't you believe in?' 'I don't believe in either God the Father or

God the Son.' 'And what about the other fellow?' 'Without them he either doesn't exist or has no relation to Christianity' (Iris Murdoch, *Henry and Cato* (London, 1976), p. 141).

5 Cf. the critical observations of Davis (1974: 308ff.) on studies of popular religiosity which proceed from the notion of 'deviation' from a norm or ideal, and on interpreting the mass of believers as passive receptors of dogma who did not in turn exercise influence on the content of Christianity.

6 There are few exceptions. One such is J. Le Goff's study (1977: 236–79) of the legend of St Marcellus' expulsion of the dragon of Paris: in this legend one can discover the mutual influence of folkloric and church culture. Another is the study by Le Goff and Le Roy Ladurie of the woman–serpent Melusina, whose story expressed the frame of mind and aspirations of knighthood: (*ibid.*: 307–31). Of exceptional interest for the study of medieval peasant culture is J.-C. Schmitt's innovative monograph on the cult of St Guinefort, the healer of children. This cult, censured in the mid-thirteenth century in one of the *exempla* of Etienne de Bourbon, fantastically identified the saint with a wolfhound of legend. The legend summarized by Etienne de Bourbon (it is known in various versions in other sources) tells of a knight's hound that guarded a cradle with his child. A snake attacked the child, but the dog saved the infant and bit the snake to death. Seeing the dog's bloody snout, the knight imagined that it had killed the baby and thus he slew it. As a result, the peasants of the castle's environs (north of Lyons) began to worship the dog as a saint: mothers brought new-born and sick babies for healing to the trees under which the dog was buried. Etienne de Bourbon, being an inquisitor, secured the prohibition of this 'idol-worship', but the cult of St Guinefort was preserved with certain modifications down to the last quarter of the nineteenth century. In Schmitt's opinion (1979: 241), the cult disappeared with the decline of traditional peasant folkloric culture and its antagonist – clerical civilization. In my view, the study of a saint appearing now as a man, now as a dog, sheds additional light on the grotesque way of thinking of medieval people.

7 In the later medieval period the devil emerges as an equally strong partner and adversary of God, and at times he seems even stronger than God; demonology develops into demonophobia. The existence of demons began to be considered the most convincing proof of God's existence: 'no demons, no God'. In answer to a question as to the number of Gods she recognized, one woman answered: 'Two, God the Father and the devil' (Thomas 1971: 469ff., 476). In the opinion of Roskoff (1869: I, 317), the thirteenth century saw the beginning of the *Teufelsperiode*. Cf. Delumeau 1978: 233–53.

8 Unfortunately, I became acquainted too late with Muchembled's interesting study (1978) of the process of the displacement of popular culture from the sphere of 'high culture' at the end of the Middle Ages and the beginning of modernity.

9 I must concur in Karsavin's sense (1915: 35ff.) of the 'antinomy' of medieval collective consciousness.

BIBLIOGRAPHY

Adam, P., 1964, *La Vie paroissale en France au XIVe siècle* , Paris

Adolf, H., 1947, 'On Medieval laughter', *Speculum* 22: 251–3.

Aigrain, R., 1983, *L'Hagiographie, ses sources, ses méthodes, son histoire*, Poitiers.

Altman, Ch. F., 1975, 'Two types of Opposition and the Structure of Latin Saints' Lives', *Medievalia et Humanistica*, NS 6: 1–11.

Andreev, M. L., 1977, 'Vechnost' v "Bozhestvennoi komedii"' ('Eternity in the Divine Comedy'), *Vestnik Moskovskogo Gosudarstvennogo Universiteta* 1: 17–27.

Ariès, Ph., 1976, *Western Attitudes to Death: From the Middle Ages to the Present*, trans. P. M. Ranum, Baltimore.

1977, *L'Homme devant la mort*, Paris.

Auerbach, E., 1953, *Mimesis*, trans. W. R. Trask, Princeton.

1965, *Literary Language and its Public in Late Antiquity and in the Middle Ages*, trans. R. Mannheim, London.

Averintsev, S. S., 1977, *Poetika rannevizantiiskoi literatury* (*Poetics of Early Byzantine Literature*), Moscow.

Bakhtin, M. M., 1963, *Problemy poetiki Dostoevskogo*, 2nd edn, Moscow; trans. C. Emerson as *Problems of Dostoevsky's Poetics*, Minneapolis, 1984.

1965, *Tvorchestvo Fransua Rable i narodnaia kul'tura srednevekov'ia i Renesansa*; trans. H. Iswolsky as *Rabelais and his World*, Cambridge, Mass., 1968.

1976, 'Problema teksta' ('The problem of text'), *Voprosy literatury* 10: 122–51.

Batiouchkof, Th. [Batiushkov, F.], 1891, 'Le Débat de l'âme et du corps', *Romania* 20: 1–55, 514–78.

Batkin, L. M., 1978, *Italianskie gumanisty: stil' zhizni i stil' mysleniia* (*Italian Humanists: Their Style of Life and Thought*), Moscow; trans. as *Die historische Gesamtheit der italienischen Renaissance. Versuch der Charakterisierung eines Kulturtyps*, Dresden, 1979.

Bercé, Y.-M., 1976, *Fête et révolte: Des mentalités populaires du XVIe au XVIIIe siècle. Essai*, Paris.

Bernoulli, C. A., 1900, *Die Heiligen der Merowinger*, Tübingen.

Beumann, H., 1959, 'Der Schriftsteller und seine Kritiker im frühen Mittelalter', *Studium Generale* 12: 497–511.

Beumann, H., 1972, *Wissenschaft vom Mittelalter. Ausgewählte Aufsätze*, Cologne–Vienna.

Bibler, V. Ts., 1975, *Myshlenie kak tvorschestvo (Vvedenie v logiku myshlennogo dialoga)* (*Thought as Creation: Introduction to the Logic of the Imaginary Dialogue*), Moscow.

Bicilli, P., 1919, 'Elementy srednevekovoi kul'tury' ('Elements of medieval culture'), in *Gnosis*, s.l.

Bieler, L., 1975, 'Hagiography and Romance in Medieval Ireland', *Medievalia et Humanistica*, NS 6: 13–24.

Bloch, M., 1953, *The Historian's Craft*, trans. P. Putnam, New York.

1961, *Feudal Society*, trans. L. A. Manyon, 2 vols., London.

Bloomfield, M. W., 1967, *The Seven Deadly Sins*, East Lansing, Mich.

Boglioni, P. 1979 (ed.), *La Culture populaire au moyen âge*, Montreal.

Bonnet, M., 1890, *Le Latin de Grégoire de Tours*, Paris; repr. Hildesheim, 1968.

Bordenave, J., & M. Vialelle, 1973 *Aux Racines du mouvement cathare: La mentalité religieuse des paysans de l'Albigeois médiéval*, Toulouse.

Borst, A., 1973, *Lebensformen im Mittelalter*, Frankfurt–Berlin.

1980, 'Zwei mittelalterliche Sterbefälle', *Mercur* 34: 1081–98.

Bosl, K., 1965, 'Der "Adelsheilige", Idealtypus und Wirklichkeit. Gesellschaft und Kultur im merowingischen Bayern des 7. und 8. Jahrhunderts' pp. 167–87: in *Speculum historiale. Festschrift Johannes Spörl*, Munich.

Boswell, C. S., 1908, *An Irish Precursor of Dante: A Study on the Vision of Heaven and Hell ascribed to the Eighth-Century Irish Saint Adamnan*, London.

Boudriot, W., 1928, *Die altgermanische Religion in der amtlichen kirchlichen Literatur des Abendlandes vom 5. bis 11. Jahrundert*, Bonn.

Broëns, M., 1960, 'The Resurgence of Preindoeuropean Elements in the Western Medieval Cult of the Dead', *Diogenes* 30: 75–103.

Browe, P., 1932, *Beiträge zur Sexualethik des Mittelalters*, Breslau.

Burke, P., 1973, 'L'Histoire sociale des rêves', *Annales E.S.C.* 28: 329–42.

1978, *Popular Culture in Early Modern Europe*, London.

Carozzi, C., 1981, 'Structure et fonction de la Vision de Tnugdal': pp. 223–34 in *Faire croire: Modalités de la diffusion et de la réception des messages religieux du XIIe au XVe siècle*, Rome.

Chartier, R., 1976, 'Les Arts de mourir, 1450–1600', *Annales E.S.C.* 31: 51–75.

Chaunu, P., 1976, 'Mourir à Paris (XVIe–XVIIe–XVIIIe siècles)', *Annales E.S.C.* 31: 29–50.

1978, *La Mort à Paris, XVIe–VIIe–XVIIIe siècles*, Paris.

Cockayne, O., 1864–66 (ed.), *Leechdom, Wortcunning and Starcraft in Early England*, 3 vols., London.

Cohn, N., 1970, *The Pursuit of the Millennium. Revolutionary Millennarians and Mystical Anarchists in the Middle Ages*, London.

Coulton, G. G., 1930, *Life in the Middle Ages*, vol. I, Cambridge.

1940, *Europe's Apprenticeship: A Survey of Medieval Latin with Examples*, London.

Crosby, R., 1936, 'Oral Delivery in the Middle Ages', *Speculum* 11: 88–110.

Curtius, E. R., 1963, *European Literature and the Latin Middle Ages*, trans. W. R. Trask, New York–Evanston.

D'Ancona, A., 1874, *I precursori di Dante*, s.l.

Dante Alig'eri [= Alighieri], 1968, *Bozhestvennaia komediia*. Perevod Lozinskogo, izd. podgotovil I. N. Golenishchev-Kutuzov (*The Divine Comedy*, trans. Lozinskii, ed. I. N. G.-K.), Moscow.

Darkevich, V. I., 1972, *Putiami srednevekovykh masterov (In the Footsteps of Medieval Masters)*, Moscow.

Davis, N. Z., 1974, 'Some Tasks and Themes in the Study of Popular Religion': pp. 307–36 in *The Pursuit of Holiness in Late Medieval and Renaissance Religion*, ed. C. Trinkaus and H. A. Oberman, Leiden.

1975, *Society and Culture in Early Modern France*, Stanford.

Delaruelle, E., 1975, *La Piété populaire du moyen âge*, Turin.

Delehaye, H., 1899, 'Note sur la légende de lettre du Christ tombée du ciel', *Bulletin de la classe des lettres et sciences morales…, Académie Royale de Belgique*.

1906, *Les Légendes hagiographiques*, 2nd edn, Brussels.

1921, *Les Passions des martyrs et les genres littéraires*, Brussels.

1930, 'La Méthode historique et l'hagiographie', *Bulletin de la classe des lettres et sciences morales…, Académie Royale de Belgique*, sér. 5, t. 16.

Delumeau, J., 1971, *Le Catholicisme entre Luther et Voltaire*, Paris.

1975, 'Au Sujet de la déchristianisation', *Revue d'histoire moderne et contemporaine* 22: 52–60.

1978, *La Peur en Occident (XVIᵉ–XVIIIᵉ siècles): Une cité assiégée*, Paris.

Dinzelbacher, P., 1979, 'Klassen und Hierarchien im Jenseits': pp. 35–40 in *Soziale Ordnungen im Selbstverständnis des Mittelalters*, Miscellanea Mediaevalia 12,1, Bonn.

1979a, 'Reflexionen irdischer Sozialstrukturen in mittelalterlichen Jenseitsschilderungen', *Archiv für Kulturgeschichte* 61: 16–34.

1981, *Vision und Visionsliteratur im Mittelalter*, Stuttgart.

Dobiache-Rojdestvensky [Dobiash-Rozhdestvenskaia], O., 1911, *La Vie paroissale en France au XIIIᵉ siècle d'après les actes épiscopaux*, Paris.

1914, *Tserkovnoe obshchestvo vo Frantsii v XIII v. (Ecclesiastical Society in Thirteenth-Century France)*, Petrograd.

Duby, G., 1961, 'Histoire des mentalités': pp. 937–66 in *L'Histoire et ses méthodes* ed. Ch. Samaran, Paris.

1980 *The Three Orders: Feudal Society Imagined*, trans. A. Goldhammer, Chicago.

1981, *The Age of the Cathedrals: Art and Society, 980–1420*, trans E. Levieux and B. Thompson, Chicago.

Dupront, A., 1961, 'Problèmes et méthodes d'une histoire de la psychologie collective', *Annales E.S.C.* 16: 3–11.

Édelstand du Méril, M., 1843, *Poésies populaires latines antérieures au douzième siècle*, Paris.

Eggers, H., 1963, 'Non cognovi litteraturam (zu Parzival 115, 27)': pp. 162–72 in *Festgabe für Ulrich Pretzel*, Berlin.

Endres, J. A., 1903, *Das St. Jakobsportal in Regensburg und Honorius*, Kempten.

1906, *Honorius Augustodunensis. Beitrag zur Geschichte des geistigen Lebens im 12. Jahrhundert*, Kempten–Munich.

Erickson, C., 1976, *The Medieval Vision: Essays in History and Perception*, New York.

Ettlinger, E., 1943, 'Documents of British Superstition in Oxford', *Folk-Lore* 54: 227–49.

Ferté, J., 1962, *La Vie religieuse dans les campagnes parisiennes (1622–1695)*, Paris.

Fichtenau, H., 1957, *The Carolingian Empire: The Age of Charlemagne*, trans. P. Munz, Oxford.

Flandrin, J.-L., 1969, 'Contraception, mariage et relations amoureuses dans l'Occident chrétien', *Annales E.S.C.* 26: 1370–90.

Fortunatov, A. A., 1946, 'K voprosy o sud'bakh latinskoi obrazovannosti v varvarskikh korolevstvakh (po traktatam Virgiliia Marona Grammatika)' ('On the problem of Latin erudition in the Barbarian kingdoms (according to the treatises of Vergilius Maro Grammaticus)'), *Srednie veka* 2: 114–34.

Fossier, R., 1970, *L'Histoire sociale de l'occident médiéval*, Paris.

Fournier, P., 1911, 'Le Décret de Burchard de Worms, ses caractères, son influence', *Revue d'histoire ecclésiastique* 12: 451–73, 670–701.

Franz, A., 1960, *Die kirchlichen Benediktionen im Mittelalter*, 2 vols., Graz (repr. of Freiburg edn, 1909).

Frejdenberg, O. M., 1936, *Poetika siuzheta i zhanra (Poetics of Subject and Genre)*, Leningrad.

   1973, 'Proiskhozhdenie parodii' ('Development of parody'), *Tartu Riiklitu Ulikooli toimetisted/ Uchenye zapiski Tartuskogo gos. universiteta/ Acta et Communicationes Universitatis Tartuensis (Trudy po znakovym sistemam) 6.*

Frenken, C., 1914, *Die Exempla des Jakob von Vitry. Ein Beitrag zur Geschichte der Erzählungs-Literatur des Mittelalters*, Munich.

Fritzsche, C., 1886–7, 'Die lateinischen Visionen des Mittelalters bis zur Mitte des 12. Jahrhunderts', *Romanische Forschungen* 2: 247–79, 3: 337–69.

Gaiffier, P. B., 1968, 'Mentalité de l'hagiographie médiévale d'après quelques travaux récents', *Analecta Bollandiana* 86.

Gasparov, M. L., 1971, *Antichnaia literaturnaia basnia (Fedr i Bavrii) (Antique Literary Tales: Phaedros and Babrios)*, Moscow.

Geary, P., 1979, 'L'humiliation des saints', *Annales E.S.C.* 34: 27–42.

Geremek, B., 1978 (ed.), *Kultura elitarna a kultura masowa w Polsce późnego średniowiecza (Elite Culture and Mass Culture in Late Medieval Poland)*, Wrocław.

Ghellinck, J. de, 1948, *Le Mouvement théologique du XIe siècle*, Brussels–Paris.

Gilman, S. L., 1974, *The Parodic Sermon in European Perspective: Aspects of Liturgical Parody from the Middle Ages to the Twentieth Century*, Wiesbaden.

Ginzburg, C., 1980, *The Cheese and the Worms: The Cosmos of a Sixteenth-Century Miller*, trans. J. and A. Tedeschi, Baltimore.

Glendenning, R. J., 1974, *Träume und Vorbedeutung in der Islendigna-Saga Sturle Thordarsons*, Berne–Frankfurt.

Golenishchev-Kutuzov, I. N., 1971, *Tvorchestvo Dante i mirovaia kultura (Dante's Art and World Culture)*, Moscow.

   1972, *Srednevekovaia latinskaia literatura (Medieval Latin Literature)*, Moscow.

Goubert, P., 1982, *La Vie quotidienne des paysans français au XVIIIe siècle*, Paris.

Gougaud, J., 1914, 'La Danse dans l'église', *Revue d'histoire ecclésiastique* 15: 5–22, 229–45.

Grabmann, M., 1909, *Die Geschichte der scholastischen Methode*, 2 vols., Freiburg.

1946, 'Eine stark erweiterte und kommentierte Redaktion des Elucidarium des Honorius', *Miscellanea Giovanni Mercati* (Vatican City) 2.

Graus, F., 1961, 'Die Gewalt bei den Anfängen des Feudalismus und die "Gefangenenbefreiungen" in der merowingischen Hagiographie', *Jahrbuch für Wirtschaftsgeschichte* 1: 61–156.

1965, *Volk, Herrscher und Heiliger im Reich der Merowinger*, Prague.

1974, 'Sozialgeschichtliche Aspekte der Hagiographie der Merowinger- und Karolingerzeit': pp. 131–76 in *Mönchtum, Episkopat und Adel zur Gründungszeit des Klosters Reichenau*, ed. A. Borst, Sigmaringen.

Grimm, J., 1939, *Deutsche Mythologie*, ed. K. H. Strobl, Vienna–Leipzig.

Grundmann, H. 1958, 'Litteratus–illiteratus. Die Wandlung einer Bildungsnorm vom Altertum zum Mittelalter', *Archiv für Kulturgeschichte*, 40: 1–65.

Guariglia, G., 1959, *Prophetismus und Heilserwartungs-Bewegungen als volkskundliches und religionsgeschichtliches Problem*, Horn–Vienna.

Guiraud, J., 1892, 'Le Commerce des reliques au commencement du IXe siècle: pp. 73–96 in *Mélanges G. B. de Rossi*, Paris–Rome.

Gurevich, A. Ia., 1970, *Problemy genezisa feodalizma v Zapadnoi Evrope (Problems of the Origins of Feudalism in Western Europe)*, Moscow; trans. as *Le origini del feudalesimo*, Rome–Bari, 1982.

1972, *Kategorii srednevekovoi kul'tury*, Moscow; trans. G. L. Campbell as *Categories of Medieval Culture*, London, 1985.

1975, 'Iazyk istoricheskogo istochnika i sotsialnaia deistvitel'nost': srednevekovyi bilingvizm' ('The Language of Historical Sources and Social Structure: Medieval Bilingualism'), *Riiklitu Ulikooli toimetisted/Uchenye zapiski Tartuskogo gos. universiteta/Acta et Communicationes – Universitatis Tartuensis... (Trudy po znakovym sistemam)* 7: 98–111.

1977, *Norvezhskoe obshchestvo v ranee Srednevekov'e. Problemy sotsialnogo stroia i kul'tury (Norwegian Society in the Early Middle Ages: Problems of Social Organization and Culture)*, Moscow.

1979, *'Edda' i saga (The 'Edda' and saga)*, Moscow.

1981, 'O novykh problemakh izucheniia srednevekovoi kul'tury' ('Concerning New Problems in the Study of Medieval Culture'): pp. 5–34 in *Kul'tura i iskusstvo zapadnoevropeiskogo srednevekov'ia*, Moscow.

1982, 'Au Moyen Age: conscience individuelle et image de "au-delá" ', *Annales E.S.C.* 37: 255–75.

1982a, 'On Heroes, Things, Gods and Laughter in Germanic Poetry', *Studies in Medieval and Renaissance History* 5: 107–72.

Gurevich, A. J. [= Ia.], 1983, 'Medieval Culture and Mentality according to the New French Historiography', *Archives européennes de sociologie* 24: 167–95.

1983a, 'Popular and Scholarly Medieval Cultural Traditions: Notes on the Margin of Jacques Le Goff's book', *Journal of Medieval History* 9: 71–90.

1983b, 'Die Darstellung von Persönlichkeit und Zeit in der mittelalterlichen Kunst (in Verbindung mit der Aufsassung vom Tode un der jenseitigen Welt': pp. 87–104 in *Architektur des Mittelalters. Funktion und Gestalt*, ed. F. Möbius and E. Schubert, Weimar.

1984, *Kategorii srednevekovoi kul'tury*, 2nd edn, Moscow.

1984a, 'Oral and Written Culture of the Middle Ages: Two "Peasant Visions" of the Late Twelfth to Early Thirteenth Centuries', *New Literary History* 16, 1: 51–66.

1985: *see* Gurevich 1972.

Gutowski, M., 1973, *Komizm v polskiej sztuce gotyckiej (The Comic in Polish Gothic Art)*, Warsaw.

Hagendahl, H., 1959, 'Piscatorice et non Aristotelice. Zu einem Schlagwort bei den Kirchenvätern': pp. 184–93 in *Septemtrionalia et Orientalia: Studia B. Kalgren dedicata*, Stockholm.

Hamann, R., 1955, *Geschichte der Kunst*, 2 vols., Berlin.

Harmening, D., 1979, *Superstitio. Überlieferungen und theoriegeschichtliche Untersuchungen zur kirchlichen theologischen Aberglaubensliteratur des Mittelalters*, Berlin.

Hauck, A., 1922, *Kirchengeschichte Deutschlands*, vol. I, Leipzig.

1952, *Kirchengeschichte Deutschlands*, 3rd edn, vol. III, Berlin–Leipzig.

Hauck, K., 1950, 'Rituelle Speisegemeinschaft im 10. und 11. Jahrhundert', *Studium generale* 3: 611–21.

Hermann-Mascard, N., 1975, *Les Reliques des saints. Formation coutumière d'un droit*, Lille.

Hertling, L., 1931, 'Hagiographische Texte zur frühmittelalterlichen Bußgeschichte', *Zeitschrift für katholische Theologie* 55: 109–22, 274–87.

Hildebrand, H., 1851, *Untersuchungen über die germanischen Penitentialbücher*, Würzburg.

Homan, H., 1965, 'Der *Indiculus superstitionum et paganiarum* und verwandte Denkmäler', (Ph.D. thesis, Göttingen).

Hügli, H., 1929, *Der deutsche Bauer im Mittelalter dargestellt nach den deutschen literarischen Quellen vom 11.-15. Jh.*, Berne.

Huizinga, J., 1924, *The Waning of the Middle Ages*, trans. F. Hopman, London.

Isambert, F.-A., 1977, 'Religion populaire, sociologie, histoire et folklore', *Archives de sciences sociales et religions*, 43: 161–84.

Jakobson, R., 1966, *Selected Writings*, vol IV, The Hague.

Janicka, I., 1964, *The Comic Element in the English Mystery Plays against the Cultural Background (particularly Art)*, Poznan.

Janson, T., 1964, 'Latin Prose Prefaces: Studies in Literary Conventions', *Acta Universitatis Stockholmiensis* 13: 1–179.

Jones, W., 1975, 'The Heavenly Letter in Medieval England', *Medievalia et Humanistica*, NS 6: 163–78.

Karsavin, L. P., 1914, 'Simbolizm myshleniia i ideia miroporiadka v srednie veka (XII–XIII vv.)' ('Symbolism of Thought and Ideas on World-Order in the Middle Ages (12th–13th C.)), *Nauchnyi istoricheskii zhurnal* 1/2, 2: 10–28.

1915, *Osnovy srednevekovoi religioznosti v XII–XIII vekakh, preimushchestvenno v Italii (Foundations of medieval religosity in the 12th–13th centuries, especially in Italy)*, Petersburg.

Kaufmann, A., 1974, *Caesarius von Heisterbach. Ein Beitrag zur Kulturgeschichte des zwölften und dreizehnten Jahrhunderts*, 2nd edn, Leipzig.

Kazhdan, A. P., 1973, *Kniga i pisatel' v Vizantii (The Book and the Writer in Byzantium)*, Moscow.

Kelle, J., 1901, *Über Honorius Augustodunensis und das Elucidarium*, Sitzunsgber. der kais. Akad. d. Wiss., phil.–hist. Cl., 143, 13, Vienna.

Keller, H., 1968, '"Adelsheiliger" und Pauper Christi in Ekkeberts *Vita sancti Haimeradi*': pp. 307–24 in *Adel und Kirche. Festschrift für Gerd Tellenbach*, Freiburg–Basle–Vienna.

Kieckhefer, R., 1976, *European Witch Trials: Their Foundations in Popular and Learned Culture 1300–1500*, Berkeley–Los Angeles.

Klapper, J., 1914, (ed.), *Erzählungen des Mittelalters*, Breslau.

Kleinschmidt, E., 1974 (ed.), *Rudolf von Schlettstadt: Historiae Memorabiles. Zur Dominikanerliteratur und Kulturgeschichte des 13. Jahrhunderts*, Cologne–Vienna.

Koch, G., 1962, *Frauenfrage und Ketzertum im Mittelalter*, Berlin.

Kottje, R., 1980, *Die Bußbücher Halitgars von Cambrai und Hrabanus Maurus. Ihre Überlieferung und ihre Quellen*, Berlin–New York.

Kretzenbacher, L. 1958, *Die Seelenwaage. Zur religiösen Idee vom Jenseitsgericht auf der Schicksalswaage in Hochreligion, Bildkunst und Volksglaube*, Klagenfurt.

1966, 'Des Teufels Sehnsucht nach der Himmelschau. Zu einem Motiv der slovenischen Legendenballade', *Zeitschrift für Balkanologie* 4: 57–66.

Labitte, Ch., 1842, 'La divine comédie avant Dante', *Revue des deux mondes* 31, 4: 704–42.

Lacroix, B., 1972, and P. Boglioni (eds), *Les religions populaires: Colloque international 1970*, Quebec.

Lammers, W., 1982, 'Gottschalks Wanderung im Jenseits. Zur Volksfrömmigkeit im 12. Jh. nördlich der Elbe': pp. 139–62 in *Siztungsber. der Wiss. Ges. an der Johann Wolfgang Goethe-Universität*, Frankfurt/M., 19/2, Wiesbaden.

Laux, J., 1935, 'Two Early Medieval Heretics: An Episode in the Life of St Boniface', *Catholic Historical Review* 21: 190–5.

Le Diable, 1979, *Le Diable au moyen âge (Doctrines. Problèmes moraux. Représentations)*, Senefiance, 6, Aix-en-Provence.

Le Goff, J., 1965, *La Civilisation de l'Occident médiéval*, Paris.

1974, 'Les Mentalités, une histoire ambiguë': pp. 76–94 in *Faire de l'histoire*, vol. III: *Nouveaux objets*, ed. J. Le Goff and P. Nova, Paris.

1977, *Pour un autre moyen âge, Paris;* trans. as *Time, Work and Culture in the Middle Ages*, Chicago–London, 1986.

1981, *La Naissance du Purgatoire*, Paris.

Le Roy Ladurie, E., 1978, *Montaillou: The Promised Land of Error*, trans. B. Bray, London.

Lea, H. C., 1896, *A History of Auricular Confession and Indulgences in the Latin Church*, vol. I, London.

Leclercq, J., 1961, and F. Venderbrouke and L. Boouyer, *La Spiritualité du moyen âge*, Paris.

Lecouteux, C., 1981, 'Introduction à l'étude du merveilleux médiéval', *Etudes germaniques* 36: 2763–90.

Lefèvre, Y., 1954, *L'Elucidarium et les lucidaires: Contribution par l'histoire d'un texte, à l'histoire des croyances religieuses en France au moyen âge*, Paris.

Lehmann, P., 1963, *Die Parodie im Mittelalter*, Stuttgart.

Leroi-Gourhan, A., 1964, *Les Religions de la préhistoire*, Paris.

Levi, C., 1947, *Christ Stopped at Eboli*, trans. F. Frenaye, New York.

Levinton, G., 1975, 'Zamechaniia k probleme "literatura i fol'klor"', ('Remarks on the "literature and folklore" problem'), *Riiklitu Ulikooli toimetisted / Uchenye zapiski Tartuskogo gos. universiteta / Acta et Communicationes Universitatis Tartuensis... [Trudy po znakovym sistemam]7: 76–87.*

Levison, W., 1921, 'Die Politik in den Jenseitsvisionen des frühen Mittelalters', in *Festgabe Fr. von Betzold*, Bonn–Leipzig; repr. in Levison 1948, pp. 229–46.

   1948, *Ausgewählte Aufsätze*, Düsseldorf.

Liebermann, F., 1960, *Die Gesetze der Angelsachsen, rpt*, Aaalen.

Likhachev, D. S., 1967, *Poetika drevnerusskoi literatury (Poetics of Old Russian Literature)*, Leningrad.

   1973, *Razvitie russkoi literatury X–XVII vekov. Epokhi i stili (Development of Russian Literature 10th–17th C.: Epochs and Styles)*, Leningrad.

Linsenmayer, A., 1886 (ed.), *Geschichte der Predigt in Deutschland von Karl dem Großen bis zum Ausgang des vierzehnten Jahrhunderts*, Munich.

Little, L. K., 1979, 'La morphologie des malédictions monastiques', *Annales E.S.C.* 34: 43–60.

Loomis, C. G., 1948, *White Magic: An Introduction to the Folklore of Christian Legend*, Cambridge, Mass.

Losev, A. F., 1978, *Estetika Vozrozhdeniia (The Aesthetics of Renaissance)*, Moscow.

Lotman, Iu. M., 1964, *Lektsii po struktural'noi poetike, vyp. 1 (Lectures on Structural Poetics, pt 1)*, Riiklitu Ulikooli toimetisted / Uchenye zapiski Tartuskogo gos. universiteta / Acta et Communicationes Universitatis Tartuensis, 160, Tartu.

Lotman, Iu. M., and Uspenskii, B. A., 1973, 'Mif–imia–kul'tura' ('Myth, name, culture'), *Riiklitu Ulikooli toimetisted / Uchenye zapiski Tartuskogo gos. universiteta / Acta et Communicationes Universitatis Tartuensis [Trudy po znakovym sistemam]* 6: 282–303.

Lotman, Iu. M., Uspenskii, B. A., 1977, 'Novye aspekty izucheniia kul'tury Drevnei Rusi' ['New Aspects for the study of the culture of Old Russia'], *Voprosy literatury* 3: 148–66.

Macfarlane, A., 1970, *Witchcraft in Tudor and Stuart England: A Regional and Comparative Study*, New York.

McNeill, J. T., and Gamer, H., 1938, *Medieval Handbooks of Penance*, New York

Mâle, E., 1924, *L'Art religieuse du XIIe siècle en France*, 2nd edn, Paris.

   1958, *L'Art religieuse du XIIIe siècle en France*, Paris.

Mandrou, R., 1964, *De la Culture populaire aux 17e et 18e siècles: La bibliothèque bleue de Troyes*, Paris.

Manselli, R., 1975, *La Religion populaire au moyen âge: Problèmes de méthode et d'histoire*, Québec–Paris.

Marwick, M., 1975 (ed.), *Witchcraft and Sorcery: Selected Readings*, Harmondsworth.

Meletinskii, E. M., 1976, *Poetika mifa (The Poetics of Myth)*, Moscow.

Mercier, V., 1962, *The Irish Comic Tradition*, Oxford.

Meyer, A., 1936, 'Religiöse Pseudo-epigraphie als ethisch–psychologisches Problem', *Zeitschrift für neutestamentliche Wissenschaft* 35.

Mikhailov, A. D., 1976, *Frantsuzskii rytsarskii roman i voprosy tipologii zhanra v srednevekovoi literature (The French Chivalric Novel and Problems of Typology of Genre in Medieval Literature)*, Moscow.

Mikoletzky, H. L., 1949, 'Sinn und Art der Heiligung im frühen Mittelalter', *Mitteilungen des Instituts für österreichische Geschichtsforschung* 57: 83–122.

Mohrmann, Ch., 1955, *Latin vulgaire, latin des Chrétiens, latin médiéval*, Paris.

Morris, C. A., 1972, 'A Critique of Popular Religion: Guibert of Nogent on the Relics of the Saints': pp. 55–60 in *Popular Belief and Practice*, ed. G. J. Cuming and D. Baker, Studies in Church History, 8, Guildford.

Morris, R., 1896 (ed.), *Old English Homilies. First Series*, Early English Text Society, OS, London.

Moser, H., 1961, 'Maibaum und Maienbrauch', *Bayerisches Jahrbuch für Volkskunde*, 115–59.

Muchembled, R., 1978, *Culture populaire et culture des élites dans la France moderne (XVe–XVIIIe siècles)*, Paris.

1979, 'The Witches of the Cambrésis World in the Sixteenth and Seventeenth Centuries': pp. 221–76 in *Religion and the People*, ed. J. Obelkevich, Chapel Hill.

1979a, *La Sorcière au village (XVe–XVIIIe siècle)*, Paris.

Mühlmann, W., 1968, *Messianismes révolutionnaires du tiers monde*, Paris.

Munthe, A., 1929, *The Story of San Michele*, New York.

Naess, H. E., *Trolldomsprosessen i Norge på 1500–1600-tallet*, Oslo.

Nessel'shtrauss, Ts. G., 1964, *Iskusstvo Zapadnoi Evropy v srednie veka (Art of Western Europe in the Middle Ages)*, Leningrad–Moscow.

Neugass, F., 1927, 'Teufel, Tiere und Dämonen im mittelalterlichen Chorgestühl', *Kunst und Künstler* 25, 11: 415–25.

Neveux, H., 1979, 'Les Lendemains de la mort dans les croyances occidentales (vers 1250–vers 1300), *Annales E.S.C.* 34: 245–63.

Noonan, J. T., 1966, *Contraception: A History of its Treatment by the Catholic Theologians and Canonists*, Cambridge, Mass.

Oakley, Th. P., 1923, *English Penitenial Discipline and Anglo-Saxon Law in their Joint Influence*, New York.

1940, 'The Penitentials as Sources for Medieval History', *Speculum* 15: 210–23.

Oexle, O. G., 1983, 'Die Gegenwart der Toten': pp. 19–77 in *Death in the Middle Ages*, ed. H. Braet and W. Verbecke, Leuven.

Owst, G. R., 1961, *Literature and Pulpit in Medieval England*, Oxford.

1965, *Preaching in Medieval England*, Oxford.

Ozanam, A. F., 1873, *Oeuvres complètes*, t. IX, Paris.

Patch, H. R., 1950, *The Other World according to Descriptions in Medieval Literature*, Cambridge, Mass.

Payne, J. F., 1904, *English Medicine in Anglo-Saxon Times*, London.

Peters, E., 1915, *Quellen und Charakter der Paradiesvorstellungen in der deutschen Dichtung vom 9. bis 12. Jahrhundert*, Breslau.

Piekarczyk, St., 1968, *Barbarzyńcy i chrzescijansktwo (Barbarians and Christianity)*, Warsaw.

     1971, 'Vera i sud'by. Gruppa, individ, etalony povedeniia (Nekotorye vyvody na istochnikov epokhi vikingov)' ('Faith and Destiny: Group and Individual Standards of Behaviour. (Some Inferences from Sources of the Viking Age)'), *Srednie veka* 34: 96–116.

Pinskii, L. E., 1961, *Realizm epokhi Vozrezhdeniia (Realism of the Age of the Renaissance)*, Moscow.

Poliakova, S. V., 1972, *Vizantiiskie legendy (Byzantine Legends)*, Leningrad.

Ponomarev, A., 1886, *Sobesedovaniia sv. Grigoriia Velikogo o zagrobnoi zhizni v ikh tserkovnom istoriko-literaturnom znachenii (The Dialogues of St Gregory the Great on the Afterlife and their Meaning for Ecclesiastical Literary History)*, St Petersburg.

Prinz, F., 1965, *Frühes Mönchtum im Frankenreich*, Munich–Vienna.

Propp, V. Ia., 1976, *Fol'klor i deistvitel'nost'. Izbrannye stat'y (Folklore and Reality: Selected Articles)*, Moscow.

Randall, L. M., 1957, 'Exempla as a Source of Gothic Marginal Illumination', *The Art Bulletin* 39: 97–107.

Rapp, F., 1971, *L'Eglise et la vie religieuse en Occident à la fin du moyen âge*, Paris.

Riché, P., 1962, *Education et culture dans l'Occident barbare, VIe–VIIIe siècles*, Paris.

Richter, M., 1976, 'Kommunikationsprobleme im lateinischen Mittelalter', *Historische Zeitschrift* 222:43–80.

Rosenfeld, H., 1969, 'Fastnacht und Karneval. Name, Geschichte, Wirklichkeit', *Archiv für Kulturgeschichte* 51: 175–81.

Roskoff, G., 1869, *Geschichte des Teufels*, 2 vols., Leipzig.

Rothkrug, L., 1979, 'Popular Religion and Holy Shrines: Their Influence on the Origins of the German Reformation and their Role in German Cultural Development': pp. 20–86 in *Religion and the People, 800–1700*, ed. J. Obelkevich, Chapel Hill.

     1980, 'Religious Practices and Collective Perceptions: Hidden Homologies in the Renaissance and Reformation', *Historical Reflections / Réflexions historiques* 7, 1: 1–286.

Rüegg, A., 1945, *Jenseitsvorstellungen von Dante und die übrigen literarischen Voraussetzungen der 'Divina commedia'. Ein quellenkritischer Kommentar*, 2 vols., Cologne.

Russell, J. B., 1964, 'Saint Boniface and the Eccentrics', *Church History* 33.

     1965, *Dissent and Reform in the Early Middle Ages*, Berkeley–Los Angeles.

Saenger, P., 1982, 'Silent Reading: Its Impact on Late Medieval Script and Society', *Viator* 13: 367–414.

Saintyves, P., 1907, *Les Saints successeurs des dieux. Essai de mythologie chrétienne*, Paris.

Sanford, E. M., 1948, 'Honorius, Presbyter and Scholasticus', *Speculum* 23: 397–425.

Sauer, J., 1902, *Symbolik des Kirchengebäudes und seiner Ausstattung in der Auffassung des Mittelalters mit Berücksichtigung von Honorius Augustodunensis, Sicardus und Durandus*, Freiburg/B.

Schieffer, Th., 1954, *Winfrid–Bonifatius und die christliche Grundlegung Europas*, Freiburg/B.

Schmitt, J.-C., 1976, '"Religion populaire" et culture folklorique', *Annales E.S.C.* 31: 141–53.

Schmitt, J.-C., 1979, *Le Saint lévrier. Guinefort, guérisseur d'enfants depuis le XIIIe siècle*, Paris; trans. M. Thom as *The Holy Greyhound: Guinefort, Healer of Children since the Thirteenth Century*, Cambridge, 1983.

Schorbach, K., 1896, *Entstehung, Überlieferung und Quellen des deutschen Volksbuches Lucidarius*, Strasbourg.

Schreiner, K., 1966, '"Discrimen veri ac falsi." Ansätze und Formen der Kritik in der Heiligen- und Reliquienverehrung des Mittelalters', *Archiv für Kulturgeschichte* 48: 1–53.

Schreiner, K., 1966a, 'Zum Wahrheitsverständnis im Heiligen- und Reliquienwesen des Mittelalters', *Saeculum* 17: 131–69.

See, K. von, 1971, *Germanische Heldensage. Stoffe, Probleme, Methoden. Eine Einführung*, Frankfurt/M.

Shejnman, M. M., 1977, *Vera v d'iavola i istoriia religii (Belief in the Devil and History of Religion)*, Moscow.

Shepelevich, L., 1892, *Apokrificheskoe 'Videnie sv. Pavla' (The Apocryphal 'Vision of St Paul')*, pt II, Kharkov.

Sidorova, N. A., 1953, 'Narodnie ereticheskie dvizheniia vo Frantsii v XI i XII vekakh [Popular heretical movements in France in the 11th–12th C.]', *Srednie veka* 4: 74–102.

Silverstein, Th., 1935 (ed.), *Visio sancti Pauli*, London.

Silvestre, H., 1960, 'Le Problème des faux au moyen âge', *Le Moyen Age* 66: 351–70.

Soriano, M., 1968, *Les Contes de Perrault: Culture savante et traditions populaires*, Paris.

Souriau, A. M., 1897, *La Préface de Cromwell*, Paris.

Spilling, H., 1975, *Die Visio Tnugdali*, Munich.

Spörl, J., 1935, 'Gregor der Große und die Antike': pp. 198–253 in *Christliche Verwirklichung. Romano Guardini zum 50ten Geburtstag*, Rothenfels/M.

Sprandel, R., 1972, *Mentalitäten und Systeme. Zugänge zur mittelalterlichen Geschichte*, Stuttgart.

Steinen, W. von der, 1967, *Menschen im Mittelalter*, Berne–Leipzig.

Stock, B., 1983, *The Implications of Literacy: Written Language and Models of Interpretation in the Eleventh and Twelfth Centuries*, Princeton.

Strunk, G., 1970, *Kunst und Glaube in der lateinischen Heiligenlegende. Zu ihrem Selbstverständnis in den Prologen*, Medium Aevum: Philologische Studien, 12, Munich.

Suits, H., 1911, *Jenseitsmotive im deutschen Volksmärchen*, Leipzig.

Sumption, J., 1976, *Pilgrimage: An Image of Mediaeval Religion*, Totowa, N.J.

Tenenti, A., 1952, *La Vie et la mort à travers l'art du XVe siècle*, Paris.

Thomas, K., 1971, *Religion and the Decline of Magic*, London.

Thorndike, L., 1923–58, *A History of Magic and Experimental Science during the First Thirteen Centuries of our Era*, 8 vols., New York.

Tokarev, S. A., 1959, *Sushchnost i proiskhozhdenie magii (Issledovaniia i materialy po voprosam pervobytnykh religioznykh verovanii) (Essence and Origin of Magic: Studies and Materials to the Problem of Primitive Religious Beliefs)*, Trudy Inst. etnografii im. N. N. Miklukho-Maklaia, n.s., 51, Moscow.

Töpfer, B., 1957, *Volk und Kirche zur Zeit der beginnenden Gottesfriedensbewegung in Frankreich*, Berlin.

Toussaert, J., 1960, *Le Sentiment religieux en Flandre à la fin du moyen âge*, Paris.

Tubach, F. C., 1969, *Index Exemplorum: A Handbook of Medieval Religious Tales*, FF Communications, 204, Helsinki.

Turner, V. & E., 1978, *Image and Pilgrimage in Christian Culture: Anthropological Perspectives*, New York.

Ullmann, W., 1963, 'The Bible and the Principles of Government in the Middle Ages': pp. 187–227 in *La Bibbia nell'alto medioevo*, Settimana di studi, 10, Spoleto.

Vagner, G. K., 1974, *Problema zhanrov v drevnerusskom iskusstve (Problems of Genre in Old Russian Art)*, Moscow.

Vauchez, A., 1973, 'Eglise et vie religieuse au moyen âge: Renouveau des méthodes et de problématique d'après trois ouvrages récents', *Annales E.S.C.* 28: 1042–50.

  1975, *La Spiritualité du moyen âge occidental. VIIIe–XIIe siècles*, Paris.

  1981, *La Sainteté en Occident aux dernières siècles du moyen âge d'après les procès de canonisations et les documents hagiographiques*, Rome.

Veit, W., 'Toposforschung. Ein Forschungsbericht', *Deutsche Vierteljahrsschrift für Literaturwissenschaft und Geistesgeschichte* 37: 120–63.

Veselovskii, A. N., 1866, 'Dante i simvolichesakaia poezija katolichestva' (Dante and Catholic Symbolic Poetry), *Vestnik Evropy* 1, 4: 152–209.

Villeneuve, R., 1957, *Le Diable dans l'art: Essai d'iconographie comparée à propos des rapports entre l'art et le Satanisme,* Paris.

Vogel, C., 1974, 'Practiques superstitieuses au début du XIe siècle d'après le Corrector sive medicus de Burchard, évêque de Worms (965–1025)': pp. 751–61 in *Mélanges E. R. Labande*, Poitiers.

Vovelle, G. and M., 1970, *Vision de la mort et de l'au-delà en Provence d'après les autels des âmes du purgatoire, XVe–XVIIIe siècles*, Paris.

Vovelle, M., 1974, *Mourir autrefois. Attitudes collectives devant la mort aux XVIIe et XVIIIe siècles*, Paris.

  1976, 'Les attitudes devant le mort: Problèmes de méthode, approches et lectures différentes', *Annales E.S.C.* 31: 120–32.

  1978, *Piété baroque et déchristianisation en Provence au XVIIIe siècle*, Paris.

  1979, 'Y a-t-il un inconscient collectif?', *La pensée* 205: 125–36.

1980, *De la cave au grenier: Un itineraire en Provence au XVIIIe siècle. De l'histoire sociale à l'histoire des mentalités*, Quebec.

1982, 'Encore la mort: Un peu plus qu'une mode?', *Annales E.S.C.* 37: 276–87.

1983, *Le Mort et l'Occident de 1300 à nos jours*, Paris.

Wachtel, N., 1974, 'L'Acculturation': pp. 124–46 in *Faire de l'histoire, 1: Nouveaux problèmes*, ed. J. Le Goff and P. Nora, Paris

Walter, E. H., 1966, 'Hagiographisches in Gregors Frankengeschichte', *Archiv für Kulturgeschichte* 48: 291–310.

Waschnitius, V., 1913, *Perht, Holda und verwandte Gestalten. Ein Beitrag zur deutschen Religionsgeschichte*, Siztungsber. d. kais. Akad. d. Wiss., phil.–hist. Cl., 174, 2, Vienna.

Weber, G. W., 1969, *'Wyrd'. Studien zum Schicksalsbegriff der altenglischen und altnordischen Literatur*, Bad Homburg.

Weinand, H. G., 1958, *Tränen. Untersuchungen über das Weinen in der deutschen Sprache und Literatur des Mittelalters*, Bonn.

Welter, J.-Th., 1927, *L'Exemplum dans la littérature religieuse et didactique du moyen âge*, Paris–Toulouse.

Wright, T., 1844, *St Patrick's Purgatory: An Essay on the Legends of Purgatory, Hell and Paradise, current during the Middle Ages*, London.

Young, K., 1936, 'Instructions for Parish Priests', *Speculum* 11: 224–31.

Zender, M., 1959, *Räume und Schichten mittelalterlicher Heiligenverehrung in ihrer Bedeutung für die Volkskunde. Die Heiligen des mittleren Maaslandes und der Rheinlande in Kulturgeschichte und Kulturverbreitung*, Düsseldorf.

INDEX

Modern authors are italicized. *Abbreviations:* Abp = archbishop;
 Bp = bishop

Abelard, Peter, 2
Adam, P., 103
Adelbert ('heretic'), 65–71, 73
Agobard, Bp of Lyons, 43
Alban, Abp of Mainz, 69
Alberich of Monte Cassino, 134
Albero, Abp of Trier, 5
Alcuin, 7, 50, 72
Amand, Abbot of Elnon, 58, 72
Ambrose, Bp of Milan, 160
Ansellus Scholasticus, 129
Anselm, Abp of Canterbury, 2, 32, 214,
 266–7
Anskar, Abp of Bremen, 130
Ariès, Ph., 120, 122, 139, 145–6, 149–51
Aristotle, 182
Attila, 7
Auerbach, E., 14, 17, 189
Augustine, Abp of Canterbury, 53
Augustine, Bp of Hippo, 7, 154, 160, 171,
 175
Averintsev, S. S., xvii

Bakhtin, M. M., viii–x, 35, 99–100, 176–
 80, 182, 185, 193, 208
Bede, 12–13, 20, 25, 34, 53–4, 116–20, 128,
 139, 160
Benedict of Nursia, 92
Benedict, R., 102
Berdjaev, N., 170
Bergson, H., 79
Bloch, M., vii, 215
Boethius, 13, 182
Boniface, Abp of Mainz, 65, 67, 69, 71,
 121, 128, 141, 144
Brendan the Navigator, 131, 133
Bromyard, John, 218
Burchard, Bp of Worms, 25, 27, 29, 36,
 81–9, 92–4, 98

Caesarius, Bp of Arles, 8–9, 12–14, 16–17,
 19, 36, 72, 185
Caesarius of Heisterbach, 7–10, 12, 21–4,
 42, 138, 185–9, 191–4, 196–8, 200–3, 205

Calvin, Jean, 55, 171
Carozzi, C., 174
Cassian, John, 30
Cassiodorus, 13
Charibert, King of the Franks, 49
Charlemagne, 67, 122–3
Chartier, R., 139
Chaunu, P., 120, 122
Childebert, King of the Franks, 48
Chilperich, King of the Franks, 40, 60
Chrétien de Troyes, 8
Cicero, 110
Claudius of Turin, 43
Clement ('heretic'), 66–7, 70–1
Clovis, King of the Franks, 51–2
Cumin, St, 44
Curtius, E. R., 13, 181–2

Dagobert I, King of the Franks, 130
Dante Alighieri, viii, 20, 109–11, 132, 134,
 141, 143–4
Delehaye, H., 20, 50
Delumeau, J., 219–20
Desiderius, Bp of Vienne, 13
Desiderius ('false prophet'), 60, 69
Dinzelbacher, P., 146–9
Donne, John, 211
Duby, G., vii, ix, xviii, 76

Egbert, Bp of York, 25
Engels, F., 6
Engussa (count in Ireland), 44
Erikson, C., 79
Ernulf, Bp of Rochester, 211
Ethelbert, King of the Anglo-Saxons, 53

Ferté, J., 219
Fortunatus, St, 189
Frejdenberg, O. M., 183, 193
Friard, anchorite, 58
Fridolinus, St, 49

Gall, St, 58
Gamalbert, St, 57

273